Politics in Sierra Leone 1947–67

CARTWRIGHT, John R. Politics in Sierra Leone, 1947–67. Toronto,
33 E. Tupper St., Buffalo, N.Y. 14203, 1970. 296p map tab
bibl 71-18592. 15.00. ISBN 0-8020-1687-1

CHOICE SEPT. '71
Political Science

Anyone with an interest in contemporary African politics and political modernization can benefit from this excellent study of Sierra Leone.
The major thesis is that Sierra Leone, unlike many other similar states,
was able to maintain peaceful political competition because of a ruling
oligarchy which included both the professional leaders and the chiefs,
a loose party structure which resulted in a community of interest based
on parliamentary rather than party membership, and the existence
of groups beyond the control of the oligarchy such as the Creoles.
The argument is thoroughly defended in a highly readable style which
balances detail and generalization. Considerably superior to Collier's
Sierra Leone (CHOICE, Dec. 1970). Recommended for both experts
and novices. Index.

JOHN R. CARTWRIGHT studied at Queen's
University and the University of Toronto.
From 1963 to 1966 he lectured in politics
at Fourah Bay College, the University
College of Sierra Leone, and travelled the
length and breadth of the country. During his stay he observed at first hand the
change in leadership following the death
of the first Prime Minister, Sir Milton
Margai, and much of the short but stormy
career of the second Prime Minister, Sir
Albert Margai. Since 1969 he has been
Associate Professor of Political Science
at the University of Western Ontario.

Politics in
Sierra Leone 1947-67

JOHN R. CARTWRIGHT

University of Toronto Press

©University of Toronto Press 1970

Printed in Canada by

University of Toronto Press

Toronto and Buffalo

ISBN 0-8020-1687-1

To

the men and women

of Sierra Leone who have

struggled to make their country

a better place for

all its people

Acknowledgments

This study began in 1963 when I took up an appointment as a Lecturer in Politics at Fourah Bay College, the University College of Sierra Leone. During my three years' stay there, I was able to travel widely in Sierra Leone, visiting many political activists in all corners of the country, and to learn a great deal from my students about the politics of the country.

Any study such as this must depend upon the co-operation of many leading figures in the political life of the country, most of whom have better uses for their time than answering the questions – some naïve, some pointed or insensitive – of a young lecturer from abroad. Despite the numerous demands on them, however, the Ministers, members of Parliament, government officials, chiefs, local party leaders, and others whom I approached almost invariably were willing to "talk politics" freely and frankly. It is somewhat unfair to single out a few individuals for special mention, since I owe almost equal debts of gratitude to so many; however, for their outstanding help, I would like to thank Mr Banja Tejan-Sie, then Speaker of the House of Representatives (now Chief Justice and Acting Governor-General); Mr S. V. Wright, then Clerk of the House; Mr James Davies, then Assistant Clerk of the House (now Clerk); Mr H. E. B. John of the Diamond Corporation, formerly General Secretary of the SLPP; Mr C. A. Kamara-Taylor, General Secretary of the APC; and Mr Prince Williams, MP for Bo Town. In citing these individuals by name, I would stress that I am also grateful to many others, particularly among the Ministers and MPs, who also gave generously of their time and information. I can only hope that this study may help some of them gain fresh insights into their political systems, as a "small-small" recompense for their generosity.

I am grateful also to my academic colleagues for their frequent help. Foremost among these is Professor R. Cranford Pratt of the University of Toronto, who supervised this work in its earlier form as a doctoral thesis, and never failed to provide a thorough and detailed critique of my various drafts, despite the handicap of being located several thousand miles away during most of the time I was writing it. My other major academic debt is to Professor Robert S. Jordan of George Washington University, who as Visiting Professor and Chairman of the Political Science Department at Fourah Bay in 1965–66, encouraged and guided me until I left Sierra Leone.

Other academic colleagues who deserve particular thanks include Laurens van der Laan of Fourah Bay College, for commenting on several chapters, and providing considerable background information; Fred M. Hayward of the University of Wisconsin, for commenting on the first draft of my thesis, and for giving me access to documents and transcripts of interviews he had conducted; Richard Simpson of the University of Illinois for commenting on my manuscript and offering several helpful methodological suggestions; Leo Spitzer of Dartmouth College for his wealth of information about the role of the Creoles in politics; Henry Gaffney of Columbia University, for the use of a number of transcripts of interviews he had conducted; Ken Rothman of the University of Chicago, Fred Barnard of the University of Saskatchewan, and Jonathan Hyde and Newman Smart of Fourah Bay College for a variety of helpful comments; and Michael Rebell, formerly a Research Assistant at Fourah Bay, for checking a number of points. I am also grateful to the Geography Department of Fourah Bay for providing considerable background information and a number of maps. I must of course issue the usual exoneration of any of these colleagues for such errors of fact or poor judgment as have persisted despite their best efforts.

I should also like to thank Fourah Bay College for providing me with travel grants to facilitate my research up-country; the University of Saskatchewan, Saskatoon, for money to obtain additional documentary material after I left Sierra Leone; and the Social Science Research Council of Canada, for providing a grant-in-aid of publication of this work through funds provided by the Canada Council. None of these bodies bears any responsibility for the findings contained herein.

Finally, a special word of praise for my wife, both for her willingness to adjust to the novel surroundings of West Africa, and her ability to keep the domestic front serene while I laboured over what must to her have seemed the never-ending task of completing a manuscript.

University of Western Ontario   JOHN CARTWRIGHT

Contents

Politics in Sierra Leone 1947–67

Introduction

To govern any of the "new nations" of Africa and Asia that emerged from colonial rule after World War II proved a difficult task; to govern in a manner responsive to popular aspirations, well-nigh impossible. The unrelenting pressure of growing populations, and the discouraging pace of both industrialization and the social adjustments necessary to bring it about, came into ever sharper conflict with the "revolution of rising expectations" for economic and social improvements in the way of life. In these non-affluent societies, the struggle for political power as the most effective means to command economic and social resources often took on a rather desperate quality, with the penalties for losing as severe as the rewards for winning were high.

In the new states of Africa, the struggle for power took on an added sharpness because of the deep-rooted mutual suspicions between different peoples who had found themselves thrown arbitrarily together under colonial rule. Conflicts over who should enjoy the largest share of the meagre spoils available for sharing frequently became conflicts between "in" and "out" tribal groups, and were sharpened further by the fact that no one tribe was strong enough to establish its unquestioned predominance. At the same time, the "new men of power" to whom the colonial rulers had handed over the reins of government found that their desire for rapid social change was not fully shared by most of their people. The new elites' position as rulers was decidedly unstable; the political institutions which they found themselves operating had barely begun to sink roots in the African soil. In such a situation, it was hardly surprising to find that the rulers of most African states responded to any challenge to their precarious control with authoritarian measures, inaugurating cycles of repression and conflict which generally culminated in military *coups d'état*.

One new state, however, resisted this trend to authoritarian rule within a one-party or no-party system. Up to 1967 the little coastal state of Sierra Leone maintained a political system marked by vigorous competition be-tween parties, and by numerous opportunities for the expression of diverse and discordant views, despite the fact that the pressures working against "open" politics were no less severe than those found in neighbouring states. It was a relatively poor state,[1] it had as many potentially conflicting tribes as any other state its size, and its people were undergoing the same strains of economic and social change as other African states. Yet, the governing party of Sierra Leone, the Sierra Leone Peoples Party (SLPP), continued to permit successive opposition parties to organize and compete with it at elections, and ultimately in the 1967 general election Sierra Leone passed the critical test of a competitive political system when the opposition party, the All Peoples Congress (APC), defeated the SLPP and was called upon to form a government. This was the first time an opposition party in an independent tropical African state had come to power through the ballot box. Although the vision of a peaceful transfer of power was rudely shattered by a military coup minutes after the new Prime Minister was sworn in, Sierra Leone had already demonstrated in striking fashion how firmly a competitive pattern of politics had been established, and just over a year later, an uprising of the enlisted men of the armed forces against their officers restored the lawfully elected government, setting Sierra Leone once again, albeit somewhat less certainly than before, on the path of peaceful competition under constitu-tional rules.

The object of this study, then, is to explain what features in Sierra Leone's political system were particularly important in enabling it to maintain this pattern of political competition. While this is not an explicitly comparative study, it may help to shed some light on why other African states underwent a rather different course of political evolution. Specifically, it may help evaluate the importance of four features: the conditions under which a pluralist system[2] permitting open political competition can survive in a state struggling with the problems of rapid social change; the composition of the "political class" as a factor affecting the type of political system; the nature of party organization as a factor affecting pluralism; and the ability of a political system to cope with different types of demands from within the society. These questions will be considered in the body of the text. What I

1 / According to the rankings provided by Karl Deutsch in *Nationalism and Social Communication*, 2nd ed. (Cambridge, Mass.: MIT Press, 1966), pp. 265–70, Sierra Leone had a lower gross domestic product per capita than any other coastal state ex-cept Cameroon. See below, p. 269 for further data.

2 / By "pluralism" I mean simply the existence of any differentiated groups in the social structure which have sufficient autonomy to make their own demands on the political system. It thus includes demands based on locality, provided that these demands are made on the national political system.

consider to be the most important features of the Sierra Leone political system are sketched out below.

Peaceful political competition, and more generally the high degree of pluralism which marked the Sierra Leone political system, owed their existence to three interrelated factors: the nature of the dominant oligarchy, the form of political organization which this oligarchy used to maintain its position, and the pressures from outside the oligarchy in support of a pluralist system. While no one of these was by itself a sufficient condition for the maintenance of political competition, and while over a longer period of time even the three together might not have sufficed, during the period under study their conjunction provided the necessary conditions in which pluralism could be maintained.

The dominant group in Sierra Leone politics from the start of decolonization in 1947 to the military coup of 1967 was the "traditio-modern"[3] elite based on the ruling families of the provinces.[4] This elite included both the traditional rulers of the Protectorate chiefdoms, the Paramount Chiefs, and also Western-educated business and professional men, most of whom were related to the chiefs. This elite had first gained its dominant position by default in 1951, when most Creole political leaders went into an embittered political isolation rather than countenance sharing power with the Protectorate people. Although there were some strains between the educated Protectorate men and the chiefs, the two groups soon worked out a satisfactory division of authority, the Western-educated men holding the national government posts and exercising surveillance over the chiefs, while the chiefs ensured that SLPP-inclined candidates were elected to the national legislature, curtailed opposition party attempts to win support in their area, and ran the local government machinery. There was no deep gulf between these two groups in the extent to which they accepted changes in their society; the Western-educated men were tempered in their search for "modernization" by their links with the traditional structure, while most chiefs were ready to

3 / The term coined by Martin Kilson, in *Politics in a West African State* (Cambridge, Mass.: Harvard University Press, 1966), p. 65. Kilson uses the term primarily to describe the Paramount Chiefs, who had modified their traditional roles to take advantage of various aspects of the "modern" economy. However, it applies equally well to the Western-educated professional and business men, who retained many traditional attitudes.

4 / Sierra Leone was divided into two parts: the Colony (renamed the "Western Area" after independence, and still later the "Western Province"), a small peninsula around the capital, Freetown, and the Protectorate (later "the Provinces"). The Colony's predominant group was the Creoles, descendants of black settlers and liberated slaves from Britain, America, and other parts of Africa; the Protectorate's indigenous people were variously referred to as "up-country people," "countrymen," or "provincials."

accept cash crops, education, and other aspects of "modernization" both for themselves and for their people.

These features of the provincial elite supported pluralism in several ways. Because the attitudes of the chiefs and the Western-educated men were not far apart, the latter were not inclined to view the chiefs as an obstacle to progress to be removed at the first opportunity, by authoritarian measures if necessary. The chiefs, it should be added, had managed under colonial rule to avoid the invidious situation of being forced to work for the government against their people, and thus retained widespread respect which could be used to provide support for national leaders among the rural populace. The chiefs' legitimacy contributed significantly to the legitimacy of the national leadership of the SLPP. Furthermore, since they enjoyed high status in the "traditional" as well as in the "modern" sector of society, the SLPP leaders seemed to have relatively few doubts about their own "right to rule"; they could afford to be more tolerant of opposition groups than leaders whose status derived solely from their command of majority support at the ballot box.

The second factor in maintaining political competition was the looseness of the governing party's organization. The provincial elite's vehicle for organizing the electorate to maintain itself in power, the Sierra Leone Peoples Party, was an aggregation of local notables, each dependent primarily upon his own efforts and the efforts of the traditional chiefly structure for his election. From its inception the SLPP relied on the chiefs to organize the voters for its candidates, and never developed an autonomous organization. This made it very difficult for the national leaders to exercise control over the SLPP members of Parliament, since the parliamentarians would resist national control as contrary to their own interests, and there was no extra-parliamentary structure in the party to act as a counterweight to them. While the SLPP parliamentarians tried to curb competition within their own constituencies, they saw themselves as having a community of interest with other members of Parliament, regardless of party, to a much greater extent than would have been conceivable if they had been members of a strongly centralized party. The lack of an SLPP organization thus encouraged tolerance of opposition parties at the parliamentary level, and also prevented party leaders from gathering sufficient power into their own hands to curtail competition at the national level.

The third factor in protecting pluralism was the existence of many areas and groups beyond the control of the dominant oligarchy. The weakness of the SLPP as an organization and its lack of any reforming ideology helped to ensure that many "political" areas remained relatively autonomous. These areas provided bases for groups outside the oligarchy to press the cause of continued political competition. Foremost among such groups were the Creoles, who, although they had lost control of the elective political posts, retained strongholds in the civil service and judiciary, as well as in the teaching profession. At the grass-roots level also pressure existed to preserve political competition, although the reasons stemmed from self-interest rather than from abstract commitments. Many ordinary farmers, particularly in the north, were becoming aware of a conflict of interest between themselves and their chiefs, and perceived that the existence of an opposition party critical of the chiefs gave them some hope of improving their situation. These pressures from outside the oligarchy were to prove crucial in the fight over the one-party state in 1965–66.

Even these three features of the Sierra Leone political system might not have sufficed to preserve political competition if the competition itself had generated or supported conflicts which could destroy the political system. Two conflicts which had the potential to bring about this disruption arose in Sierra Leone during the period under study.

One of these, the "class" conflict, drew its greatest strength from the impact of the money economy upon the "traditional" sector of society. During the 1950s ordinary farmers could see the chiefs and their supporters using their positions to obtain the major share of the new goods and services which were becoming available, and the farmers' discontent erupted in violent protests. But until 1960 no political party was able to provide this class with a political outlet. Even after 1960, the party which did stress a "class" appeal, the All Peoples Congress, gradually muted this appeal in favour of a demand for regional justice. Whether a class conflict was beyond the power of the SLPP leaders to contain is problematical. Certainly their dependence on the chiefs made their position difficult, since the chiefs were the principal targets of popular discontent, but by 1967 this discontent had not reached a level where the chiefs and the SLPP might both be swept away.

In any case the class conflict was heavily overshadowed by successive "tribal" or regional conflicts. The first of these, between the Creoles and all the peoples of the Protectorate, was too one-sided to persist; once the Protectorate's numbers had prevailed, the Creoles had little choice but to come to terms or retire from politics. But a second conflict gradually arose as it became apparent that, within the SLPP, the Mende tribe was maintaining a predominant position. This predominance had developed initially as a reflection of the relative educational opportunities in different parts of the Protectorate. However, as the northern tribes gradually became aware of their position, unrest over alleged "Mende domination" developed. The first Prime Minister, Sir Milton Margai (a Mende) was able by a careful distribution of appointments and patronage to keep this nascent tribal rift from growing too deep. But when Sir Milton died and was succeeded by his brother Albert in 1964, the discontent of the Temnes and other northern tribes mounted rapidly and Sir Albert Margai was unable to contain it.

Again, it is doubtful whether the conflict between the Mendes and the northern tribes necessarily posed a real threat to the continuation of the political system. Regional demands could be met by a redistribution of resources within the existing framework, and by a reconciliation of the dissident groups. Even though they had not been reconciled by 1967, the APC still showed a commitment to the existing constitutional order in that they were prepared to seek political power through the mechanism provided by that order. This behaviour, and the willingness of the SLPP to allow the APC to make this attempt, showed quite clearly that the regional conflict was still being waged within the bounds of ordered competition. In short, up to 1967 the Sierra Leone political system showed it could handle the major social conflicts within the country.

In summary, this study will examine how the provincial elite came to power, the means it used to maintain itself, and the challenges with which it had to contend. Since political change in Sierra Leone was an evolutionary process, it is presented in chronological form, focusing on certain key turning points. Part I considers those features of the pre-colonial and colonial periods which set constraints on the operation of the system after 1947. Part II considers one key turning point, the adoption in 1951 of a constitution that enabled the Protectorate elite to entrench itself. A second turning point was the growth of opposition in the Protectorate to the social and political system upheld by the elite. Part III considers the growth of this opposition and its failure to find an outlet in the existing opposition parties, while Part IV examines the extent to which it was incorporated into the APC. Part V considers the effect of a change of leadership on the position of the ruling group, and the factors leading up to the military usurpation of power.

PART ONE

The background to decolonization

1

The constraints of tradition and history

No "new nation" builds its political institutions on virgin ground. Sierra Leone's political system took shape under a set of historical constraints that made the creation of a unified polity a peculiarly difficult task. Three major features in its history all worked to curtail the extent to which its people would develop a national identity. Its division into a number of tribal groups, each in turn divided among numerous chieftaincies, and most important of all, the isolation of the westernized black settlers known as Creoles meant that there was no common tradition or unifying myths to ease the task of creating a nation. The relatively limited extent to which social change occurred in the Protectorate and the selective nature of the mobilization process ensured that traditional institutions were not severely disrupted. Both the fragmentation of its societies and the slow rate of social change contributed to the third feature, the weakness of the political movements that arose.

The small circle of territory proclaimed by the British as the Sierra Leone Protectorate in 1896 was largely out of the mainstream of pre-colonial African history. A coastal possession tucked between Guinea and Liberia, it was untouched by any of the great Saharan empires and was on no major trade route from the interior to the coast.[1]

The heavy rain forest which extended across the southern half of the territory precluded all but foot travel, thus imposing a considerable obstacle to the establishment of large-scale political units. Neither the forest areas nor

1 / Some trade did flow through the territory, but the volume was small compared to that of, say, the Niger Delta, Yorubaland, or the Gold Coast. For details on the Sierra Leone trade routes, see P. K. Mitchell, "Early Trade Routes of the Sierra Leone Protectorate," *Sierra Leone Studies* (N.S.), 16 (June 1962), pp. 204–17.

ADAPTED FROM: J. I. Clarke, *et al. Sierra Leone in Maps*

the drier rocky hills of the north readily yielded a living much above subsistence. This 200-mile-wide territory was crosscut by no less than nine
major river systems; but none originated far beyond Sierra Leone's borders,
and all were limited as trade routes by their numerous swift and rocky
stretches and by the tremendous fluctuations in volume between their flood
peaks in the rainy season and their low point in May at the end of the six
months' dry season.

The heterogeneity of Sierra Leone's tribal groups, and the pattern of their
entry into the country, further encouraged fragmentation. The two largest

tribes in the country, the Mendes of the south and the Temnes of the north central area, each numbered more than 600,000 by 1963,[2] but the next largest tribes, the Limbas and the Konos, comprised only 180,000 and 100,000 members respectively. The remaining quarter of Sierra Leone's two million people was divided among no less than twelve other indigenous tribes (see Table 1:1). It is likely that all these tribes, with the possible exception of the Limbas and the Sherbros along the coast, entered Sierra Leone within the past 600 years, that is to say after about 1350–1400 A.D.[3] In most cases this migration seems to have taken place for the purpose of escaping the pressure of more powerful neighbours, and largely through the initiative of individual warriors or other leaders who established their own chiefdoms.[4] In view of the short time-span, the shifting populations, and the means by which chiefdoms were established, it is not surprising that no large-scale political units were created. Little claims some Mende warrior-chiefs "were successful and powerful enough to overawe territories far beyond their local area," but the example he cited appeared to have covered no more than 200 square miles.[5] Vernon Dorjahn notes that at one time the whole of Temne country, about 5,000 square miles, was under no more than four chiefdoms, but this consolidation did not last long.[6] Most chiefdoms comprised only a few thousand members and were constantly breaking apart and recombining as a result of family rivalries and success or defeat in wars.

Some sense of a common tribal identity was secured within the various tribes by the social and religious institutions known as the secret societies. The principal Mende organization, the Poro Society, embraced all adult males in Mendeland; Little noted that it "seems to have been the indirect means by which uniformity both in government and social custom was made possible among the congeries of widely scattered and relatively independent communities."[7] But this uniformity of structure did not imply any limiting of the autonomy of the different chiefdoms; each would go its own way, and warfare between different chiefdoms of the same tribe was common.

2 / Data on tribes is taken from *1963 Population Census of Sierra Leone*, Vol. II (Freetown: Central Statistics Office, 1967), p. 13.

3 / For differing accounts of when the various tribes arrived in Sierra Leone, see Merran McCulloch, *Peoples of Sierra Leone Protectorate* (London: International African Institute, 1950) and A. P. Kup, "An Account of the Tribal Distribution of Sierra Leone," *Man*, August 1960, pp. 116–19.

4 / See Kenneth Little, *The Mende of Sierra Leone* (London: Routledge, 1967), pp. 29–30, for a description of the process by which new chiefdoms were created in Mendeland.

5 / Kenneth Little, "Mende Political Institutions in Transition," *Africa*, XVII, 1 (January 1947), p. 12.

6 / Vernon R. Dorjahn, "The Changing Political System of the Temne," *Africa*, XXX, 2 (April 1960), p. 111.

7 / Little, "Mende Political Institutions," p. 12.

TABLE 1:1

The peoples of Sierra Leone: population, location, and affinities

Tribe	Population	% of total pop.	Location	Remarks
MENDE LANGUAGE GROUP				
Mende	672,831	30.9	Throughout Southern and Eastern provinces	Largest tribe; have assimilated most neighbours
Loko	64,459	3.0	Mostly Bombali District	Related to Mendes linguistically; heavily influenced culturally by Temnes
Kono	104,573	4.8	Kono District	
Vai	5,786	0.3	S.E. Pujehun	Offshoot of Kono: now largely assimilated by Mendes
Gallinas	2,200	0.1	Pujehun coast	Part of Vai
Susu	67,288	3.1	Northern border of country	Most of tribe in Guinea
Yalunka	15,005	0.7	Northern Koinadugu	Related to Susus
Koranko	80,732	3.7	Koinadugu	
Mandingo	51,024	2.3	Scattered over whole country: 11,787 in Kono	Spread as religious teachers, traders, warriors
"MEL" LANGUAGE GROUP				
Temne	648,931	29.8	Southwestern half of Northern Prov.; Freetown	Widely dispersed throughout South, esp. in diamond areas
Sherbro (Bullom)	74,674	3.4	Most of coast: esp. Bonthe, Moyamba	Northern Bulloms absorbed by Temnes
Krim	8,733	0.4	Coastal Pujehun and Bonthe	Sherbro; being absorbed by Mendes
Kissi	48,954	2.2	Eastern border (Kailahun, Kono)	Bulk of tribe in Liberia: being slowly absorbed by Mendes
Gola	4,854	0.2	Eastern border (Pujehun)	Bulk of tribe in Liberia: largely absorbed by Mendes
OTHER "CLASS" LANGUAGES				
Limba	183,496	8.4	Bombali, Kambia and Koinadugu north of Temnes	
Fula	66,824	3.1	About half in Bombali, Koinadugu; rest scattered throughout country	Part of Fulani, extending from Senegal to Nigeria; no historic chiefdoms of their own in Sierra Leone
Kroo	4,793	0.2	Freetown	Seamen from Liberia
Creole	41,783	1.9	Western Area	Freed slaves and other settlers

Notes: Most of data derived from McCulloch, *Peoples of Sierra Leone Protectorate*. Population figures from *1963 Census*. I am also indebted to Dr David Dalby for his comments on language classification.

All the features of Sierra Leone enumerated so far – its peopling by a diversity of tribes, its division into numerous quarrelling chiefdoms, and its physical obstacles to large-scale political units – could be found in several other West African territories. What set Sierra Leone apart from all other West African colonies was the establishment of a body of settlers committed to an essentially European way of life. While the majority of these "settlers," who became known as the Creoles, were Africans liberated from the slaving ships within a few months of their capture, the groups which set the dominant tone of the Colony were Negro immigrants from the New World who had been well grounded in Western ways. Their very westernization, however, tended to set them apart from the indigenous tribesmen; their relations with the "up-country" people[8] were always ambivalent and eventually led to the deepest of all rifts within the Sierra Leone polity.

The colonization of Sierra Leone by these settlers began in 1787 when some 300 "Black Poor" from London were landed at the coastal watering place called Freetown.[9] The fledgling colony was strengthened in the next few years by two further groups of Negroes whose links with their African past had been largely severed, some 1,100 refugees from the American revolutionary war who came from Nova Scotia in 1792, and 550 Maroons from Jamaica who arrived in 1800. After the abolition of slavery throughout the British Empire in 1807, the 2,000 settlers were joined by thousands of Liberated Africans, captives released from the slave ships captured by the British Navy. By the 1850s the population of the Colony had risen to more than 45,000, thanks largely to this influx. The Liberated Africans were officially encouraged to copy the ways of the earlier settlers. This they did so well that by the 1870s the two groups were almost fused into one, and had acquired the name "Creoles."

Another influx was less successfully accommodated. The tribal people from up-country Sierra Leone, attracted to the glitter of city life and the relative security of the Colony, began to move into Freetown in increasing numbers. By the 1880s widespread fears were being expressed among the Creoles about the deleterious moral effects of these "aborigines," and even about the threats they posed to the security of the Colony.[10] Creole hostility toward the aborigines was not of the same order as that of the white settlers in central or southern Africa or in the southern United States; there was little concern to establish an unbridgeable gulf. Numerous Creoles were in

8 / "Up-country" is a term generally applied to the Protectorate or Provinces.
9 / The standard work on the Colony is Christopher Fyfe's *A History of Sierra Leone* (London: Oxford University Press, 1962). Arthur T. Porter's *Creoledom* (London: Oxford University Press, 1963) provides a good historical analysis of the rise and fall of Creole society.
10 / See Fyfe, *History of Sierra Leone*, pp. 555–56; also his *Sierra Leone Inheritance* (London: Oxford University Press, 1964), pp. 233–35.

fact the offspring of settler – up-country liaisons; others were the children of up-country people who had sent them to Freetown to be brought up by Creoles so that they might acquire a Western education. To some extent also the Creoles responded to the growing racism of British officials by support- ing their "brother Africans" against the seeming European tendency to treat Africans as inferiors.[11] At the same time the Creoles, at least those in the higher social strata, felt that their Western education and habits pro- vided them with a badge of superiority over the "aborigines." This attitude was reinforced by their status as British subjects.

There is still considerable debate over how far the Creoles as a cultural group were Western and how far African in their habits, and more generally over the question, in view of their ability to assimilate persons of up-country origin, of what constitutes a Creole. For our purposes, however, it is suffi- cient to note that all Creoles, even the Aku from the Yoruba tribe who kept their Muslim faith, used as their medium of communication the language known as Krio, which was derived largely from English; that most were involved in the cash economy; and that among the dominant class literacy in English, Christianity, and a marked attachment to English social values and to England as a spiritual home could be considered as characteristic. They were, in short, sufficiently "westernized" to be set sharply apart from the people of the interior, and to act as spearheads of the Western cultural advance.

That this was how they were seen by up-country people was tragically shown two years after the British proclaimed the Sierra Leone Protectorate. Fears among the people of the Protectorate that the Europeans were plan- ning to take away their land, and that the "black Europeans" were aiding them in this enterprise, erupted in the Hut Tax War of 1898. Nearly a thou- sand Creoles serving up-country as missionaries and traders were killed, along with a handful of white missionaries. This slaughter, carried out chiefly by Mendes, deepened Creole fears of the "aborigines," and reinforced their growing estrangement from the tribal societies of Sierra Leone.

At the same time as their links with the up-country people were being severed, the Creoles found their relations with the British colonial authorities deteriorating. Whether justifiably or not, they had until the 1890s tended to see themselves as partners with the British in bringing Western civilization and Christianity to the heathen of Africa. Educated Creoles were allowed to hold high administrative and judicial posts in the Colony; Europeans and Creoles lived side by side in downtown Freetown and mingled socially. But about the time the Protectorate was declared in 1896, a change in relation- ships was taking place. The Creoles found themselves excluded from any

11 / See Leo Spitzer, "Sierra Leone Creole Intellectual Reactions to Westerniza- tion" (unpublished doctoral dissertation, University of Wisconsin, 1969) for illus- trations of this point.

part in the governing of the Protectorate.[12] Within the Colony, Creoles could see vacancies caused by Creole deaths and retirements being filled with Europeans; the number of senior civil service posts grew from 40 to 92 between 1892 and 1912, but the number of Creole office-holders dropped from 18 to 15.[13] In 1902 the West African Medical Service was created, and an inferior classification of Native Medical Officer was provided for the several Creole doctors in government service.[14] In 1905 the Hill Station reservation, for Europeans only, was established to allow British administrators and businessmen to live away from the malarial lowlands of Freetown. While this segregation was ostensibly based on science rather than prejudice, Creoles saw it as a further manifestation of British racism.[15] As a final blow, it was at this time that Lebanese traders began to move into Sierra Leone, as into other parts of West Africa, and soon their capacity for mutual assistance and their fierce competitiveness drove the Creoles out of much of the small store-keeping and trading functions which had provided the economic basis for their professional activities in law and medicine.[16] Meanwhile, the railway allowed the well-financed European firms to enter directly into up-country trade, offering credit and cutting prices in ways the Creoles could not match.[17]

Increasingly despised by the British as a shabby caricature of Western culture, squeezed out of their commercial niche by the impact of the big European firms and the Lebanese, yet with too strong a sense of their own superiority to join forces with the tribal people of the Protectorate, the Creoles began to show that marked lack of self-assurance and self-esteem which became so obvious to observers in later years.[18] They did, however, retain a commanding lead over the up-country people in education, a lead which was to help ensure their survival in later years. But they could no longer look forward to unquestioned leadership of the whole of West Africa, or even the whole of Sierra Leone.

12 / Porter, *Creoledom,* p. 61. See also J. D. Hargreaves, *A Life of Sir Samuel Lewis* (London: Oxford University Press, 1958), pp. 79–97.

13 / Fyfe, *History of Sierra Leone,* p. 615. For a different interpretation of the Creoles' decline, see P. E. H. Hair's review of Fyfe, in *Sierra Leone Studies,* 17 (June 1963), 291–92.

14 / Dr M. C. F. Easmon, "Sierra Leone Doctors," *Sierra Leone Studies,* 1956, pp. 85–86. Also Fyfe, *History,* pp. 614–15.

15 / Leo Spitzer, "The Mosquito and Segregation in Sierra Leone," *Canadian Journal of African Studies,* II, 1 (Spring 1968), pp. 58-60.

16 / For Sierra Leone, see Fyfe, *History,* pp. 613–14; for a more general commentary, see R. B. Winder, "The Lebanese in West Africa," *Comparative Studies in Society and History,* IV (1961) pp. 298–307.

17 / Fyfe, *ibid.*

18 / For example, see Graham Greene, *Journey Without Maps* (London: Heinemann, 1936), pp. 33–37; Roy Lewis, *Sierra Leone: A Modern Portrait* (London: HMSO, 1954), pp. 31–40.

THE EFFECTS OF COLONIAL RULE:
THE CREATION OF A "MODERN" SECTOR

When the British Crown took over the governing of the Colony from the Sierra Leone Company in 1808, it exercised its rule through a Governor and his Council, the latter holding office at the Governor's pleasure. In 1863 this Council was divided into Executive and Legislative councils, with the latter including for the first time an "unofficial" Creole representative of the business community. However, the principle of election for this representative was not conceded; he held office at the Queen's pleasure.[19] When the hinterland was made a Protectorate in 1896, the British provided considerably less provision for hearing the wishes of the inhabitants. The Governor of the Colony was also Governor of the Protectorate, but his authority up-country was exercised through the strictly executive channel of the Colonial Secretary and the District Commissioners. It was at this time also that the unofficials on the Colony's Legislative Council began to lose the limited degree of influence they possessed over the British colonial officials. Fyfe comments that by 1911 "government had ceased to pay much attention to Creole members' speeches ... almost all vestige of real partnership faded away."[20] In its formal procedures the period from 1900 to 1924 marked the peak of autocratic colonial rule.

In 1924, two changes were made which were intended to foster the integration of Colony and Protectorate and to introduce a slight measure of representativeness into the government of Sierra Leone. One British order-in-council extended the jurisdiction of the Executive and Legislative Councils of the Colony to the Protectorate, while another order-in-council made provision for three of the Colony's unofficial members of the Legislative Council to be elected, and for three unofficials from the Protectorate to be included for the first time. This still left an official majority of eleven members plus the Governor against ten unofficial members, two of whom were nominated Europeans and two others were nominated Africans from the Colony, in addition to the six already referred to. Even the elected Colony members could hardly be expected to speak for the mass of the people, since the franchise requirements excluded all but the best educated and wealthiest five per cent of the population.[21] The Protectorate representatives were all Para-

19 / The first representative, John Ezzidio, a Liberated African, was elected at a meeting of European and Creole merchants, but the Governor sanctioned his appointment only on the explicit condition that he not be controllable by the merchants. See Fyfe, *History*, pp. 319–20.

20 / *History of Sierra Leone*, p. 617.

21 / The franchise was restricted to literate males owning property rated at £10 or with an income of £100 per annum. Kilson, in *Political Change in a West African State*, p. 125, notes that in Freetown 1,016 persons were registered out of a total adult population of 25,000.

mount Chiefs because, according to the Governor, "under the tribal system no others would have adequate title to speak with authority."[22] The Western elite of the Colony and the traditional elite of the Protectorate were thus brought together for the first time, although effective control of the Protectorate still lay with a separate Provincial Administration.

But while the formal political structure, even after the modifications of 1924, offered little scope for African political participation of any kind, economic and social changes were already underway which would generate significant pressure for more change. The changes that took place – a growth in wage employment and in cash crop farming, the spread of Western education, and the growth of towns and communications – all intertwined, but for our purposes it will be best to examine them under two headings: those changes that took men completely out of traditional society and into a "modern" world, and those that took place within the existing framework of traditional relationships.

The Colony, as I have suggested earlier, had from its founding been basically a Western-type society, with a fully developed cash economy, widespread schooling, and a system of social stratification which placed heavy emphasis on (primarily economic) achievements.[23] Its population was thus "socially mobilized" into a distinctive Creole society rather than into a "modern" society which spanned all the Colony and Protectorate. The interplay of modern and traditional attitudes which contributed so much to the distinctive features of the Sierra Leone political system was not a significant feature within Creole society simply because traditional attitudes did not play a major role. The Creoles' position as "modernizers" was significant within the total Sierra Leone polity; but within their own group they were much less subject to a clash of values. This discussion of economic and social change will therefore focus largely upon the Protectorate, considering the Colony only insofar as its lead in modernization was politically noteworthy.

The declaration of a British Protectorate, limited as was the extent of British political penetration that it implied, did serve to put a halt to the wars which had raged over choice trading sites in the previous two decades, and to provide the political stability necessary for widespread economic changes. Whether as its main rationale or an incidental by-product, the colonial administration's imposition of a "Hut Tax" of five shillings on all households

22 / Address by His Excellency the Governor to the Legislative Council, November 25, 1924. Quoted in Fyfe, *Sierra Leone Inheritance*, p. 321.

23 / This is not to deny that the dominant groups, at first the settlers in opposition to the Liberated Africans, and later the Creoles against the tribal people, made considerable efforts to maintain an ascriptive basis for their superiority; but the barriers they erected were penetrated by upwardly mobile members of the lower strata with at least as much ease as, say, the English upper class was being penetrated at the same time, rather than providing an almost impermeable wall comparable to the caste system in rural India, for example.

in the Protectorate drove many Africans into the cash economy as either cash-crop farmers or wage labourers. However, the Colonial Office's insistence that Sierra Leone, like other colonies, pay its way, curtailed any further economic development. The major development project of the Sierra Leone government was a 2½-foot-gauge railway built between 1895 and 1908 to open up the southern and eastern parts of the country.[24] Its narrow gauge and winding track, an economy measure in its construction, contributed to the high operating costs which left it with a chronic deficit.[25] After 1920 a number of feeder roads were built to generate more traffic for the railway, but it was not until World War II that a road was completed between Freetown and the provinces. Other services also were scantily provided for. Education was for the most part left to missionaries and religious bodies; only three of the twelve secondary schools in the country in 1939 were directly operated by the government, although the others received some government assistance.[26] The government had begun to train Africans for agricultural extension work before World War I, but their number remained limited. By 1950 the total Senior Service establishment in agriculture was only 24, of whom 15 were field officers.

If economic development was to be left to private entrepreneurs, as the colonial administration intended,[27] these investors needed to perceive profitable opportunities. Sierra Leone, by comparison with other territories, did not offer much prospect to private investors. The colonial administration was unenthusiastic about allowing commercial firms to establish plantations and none were ever successfully formed.[28] No indigenous entrepreneurial class developed comparable to the Ashanti cocoa farmers or the Yoruba businessmen. Palm kernels, the principal agricultural export, had reached a level of 60,000 tons a year before the Depression, and a value of about a million and a half pounds,[29] which indicated that a large amount of cash was flowing into the hands of Protectorate farmers. But until after World War II, production of palm oil and kernels was seldom undertaken on a plantation

24 / A spur line was later built to the centre of the Northern Province.

25 / Since 1927, revenue had exceeded expenditure in only four years, and the annual deficit in the 1960s was approximately £500,000. In 1968 the military regime finally took the decision to phase it out.

26 / In 1940 the total government grants to *all* assisted schools in the Colony and Protectorate (exclusive of teachers' salaries) came to £8,879. *Financial Report for the Year 1940*.

27 / For example, when asked in the Protectorate Assembly to establish canning factories, a government spokesman replied that this was a job for private enterprise. *Proceedings of the Fifth Meeting*, (1948), pp. 23, 32.

28 / See Buell, *The Native Problem*, Vol. 1, pp. 869–71.

29 / The *Sierra Leone Blue Book* for 1920 showed total agricultural exports of £2,247,743, or about 26 shillings per capita. In 1930, exports had fallen by more than half, to just over one million pounds, or about 12 shillings per capita.

basis; for most farmers it remained a small-scale subsidiary operation. The same was true of such other agricultural crops as cocoa, coffee, and ginger. The impact of cash crops was thus widely diffused but rather limited in its impact on individual farmers.

Although oil palms grow well in most of Sierra Leone except the far north, the fact that transportation was more readily available in the Southern and Eastern Provinces encouraged cash crop farming in these areas more than in the north. The political cry of "northern backwardness" had its roots largely in this discrepancy of opportunities for cash-crop farming.

The most important source of wealth for Sierra Leone was the alluvial diamond deposits discovered in 1930 by the government geologist. Three years later the Sierra Leone Trust Limited was given an exclusive mining and prospecting lease covering the whole of Sierra Leone for 99 years, even though its operations were concentrated in Kono. In return it was to pay taxes on its profits at a rate of 27 per cent (later raised to 45 per cent).[30] Diamonds quickly became the mainstay of the economy of Sierra Leone; by 1938 they had become the largest single export item by value, representing some 37 per cent of the total exports of £2.3 million.[31] However, the diamond mining industry did not act as a major force for modernization until the 1950s. It directly employed less than 2,000 Africans before the outbreak of World War II, and although it assimilated these thoroughly into the modern industrial world by building up a virtual "career service" in mining, the impact of such a small group was inevitably limited. More effective in drawing men into the money economy was the more dispersed system of illicit mining and diamond smuggling which had been going on at least since the start of the war.[32] Illicit mining, however, did not develop to significant proportions until the early 1950s; before that time the number of illicit diggers probably numbered in the hundreds rather than the thousands. Once again, the mobilizing effect was limited.

The other major economic development under the colonial regime was the opening of a large iron mine in the Port Loko District in 1933. By 1938 this mine employed 4,000 men,[33] drawn mainly from the neighbouring areas of the Northern Province and, like the Yengema diamond miners, tending to settle into a permanent pattern of urban wage employment. Again, while this operation became important as a source of export earnings (28 per cent of

30 / Laws of Sierra Leone, 1946, Schedule to Cap. 63, Sections 2(1) and 4(1). The company also paid a rent of £7,000 per year into a Mining Benefits Trust Fund and nominal ground rents to the chiefdoms in which its operations were located.

31 / Sierra Leone Blue Book, 1938. By 1960 they accounted for more than 60 per cent of Sierra Leone's total exports, or some £15 million a year.

32 / Graham Greene's The Heart of the Matter, set in wartime Freetown, suggested that diamond smuggling was already a well-established business.

33 / Annual Report of the Provincial Administration, 1939, p. 16.

total exports in 1938), its influence was not widely dispersed. Finally, we may note the development of numerous small-scale gold mining operations in the Tonkolili District between 1935 and 1939, which employed an average of 6,000 miners a year in this period. Unlike the diamond and iron mining operations, this activity petered out at the beginning of World War II and was never revived on a significant scale.

Economic activity, then, did not bring about any intensive mobilization of a large number of Sierra Leoneans. Those who were torn from their traditional moorings by entering full-time wage employment in mining or other industries were relatively few in number. Many more individuals entered the money economy through cash-crop farming, but this limited and marginal participation was unlikely to have the same up-rooting effect as the total immersion of wage employment.

In addition to the relatively small numbers of men involved in wage occupations in the Protectorate, we may also note the relative lateness of their involvement. Mining industries in the Gold Coast had employed 17,000 Africans in 1911, a full quarter of a century before opportunities on a comparable scale were open to Sierra Leoneans.[34] In Nigeria the tin mines at Jos were employing 22,000 men and the coal fields at Enugu 8,000 a decade before mining started in Sierra Leone.[35] This longer time span meant, of course, that there would be more turnover of labour, and consequently more opportunities for new values to be disseminated among the workers' home villages. In the French territories also, the forced labour of the 1920s again produced a greater up-rooting of the adult male population than in Sierra Leone.

Wage labour, or complete dependence on cash-crop farming, was not the only force which could detach a man completely from his traditional society. Both Western education and urbanization could have the same effect. But in these areas also the Sierra Leone Protectorate tended to lag behind most other coastal territories. The *1931 Census* showed a total of 17,606 children in school, or about one per cent of the total population, a figure comparable to Nigeria's and just half the proportion of the Gold Coast.[36] Of these, 9,349 were enrolled in the Colony, and it is almost certain that the great majority of them were Creoles; the proportion of Protectorate children in school, therefore, was of the order of one-half of one per cent, a proportion well

34 / Buell, *The Native Problem*, Vol. I, pp. 824–25. Buell notes, however, that the number employed in mining had dropped to 13,000 by 1924.

35 / *Ibid.*, pp. 763–64.

36 / Lord Hailey, *An African Survey*, 1st ed. (London: Oxford University Press, 1938) pp. 180, 1309 gives figures for West African territories in the mid-1930s. At this time Sierra Leone still had about one per cent of her population enrolled in all schools, though it is possible that the Nigerian and Gold Coast figures may have been lower at the earlier date.

below both the larger British colonies and Senegal, roughly comparable to the Ivory Coast and Dahomey, and above only Guinea.[37] While the rankings of the states given here suggest how misguided it would be to postulate a correlation between proportion of school attenders and subsequent radical change in society, or worse still, a causal relationship, even so we could suggest that Sierra Leone did not have quite such a substantial pool of potential critics of traditional systems as did several other territories.

Urbanization was also limited. The *1931 Census* showed no town in the Protectorate larger than 2,500 inhabitants, and nearly all the larger centres were basically extended agricultural villages or petty marketing and administrative centres. In the 1930s and 1940s a number of new urban areas sprang up as a result of mining operations and the growth of trade. Yengema in the Kono District was the centre of diamond mining, Lunsar and Pepel in Port Loko were the service centre and shipping port for the iron mines, and Bo and Makeni became key trade and administrative centres. But none of these towns provided a seed-bed for nationalism or exposure to ideas from outside Sierra Leone on a par with Dakar or Lagos. They were too isolated by their inland location and poor travel facilities, and too small to create a substantial wage-earning class.[38] Finally, they remained subject to the jurisdiction of the Paramount Chiefs and their advisers, which meant that "strangers" from outside the chiefdom would be largely excluded from town affairs. This feature also allowed the chiefs to use their coercive powers to inhibit the growth of any movement directed against their position.

Freetown, the only urban area of any significance in Sierra Leone, grew steadily, thanks to streams of immigrants from the Protectorate, but slowly compared with many other African cities. From 1931 to 1951 its population rose from 55,000 to 75,000, but in the same period the population of Lagos doubled, that of Dakar increased five times, and that of Leopoldville eight times.[39] Since it was only in Freetown that individuals were likely to find the opportunities to escape confining traditions and to enjoy the self-

37 / *Ibid.* for over-all population figures and school enrolments for French West Africa. Buell, *The Native Problem*, Vol. II, p. 209, provides a breakdown for the mid-1920s of expenditure per 100 inhabitants among the different territories, which shows Senegal receiving three times the average amount, Dahomey and the Ivory Coast about the average, and Guinea two-thirds of the average. I am assuming a rough correlation between expenditure and number of pupils enrolled, and also a fairly constant division of expenditure among the different territories.

38 / As an indication of their short-comings as urban sources of exposure to outside ideas, the first newspaper outside Freetown, the Bo *Observer*, was founded only in 1949. It may be suggested, however, that the small size of these towns facilitated contact among the educated men who were stationed in them, thus encouraging the development of a self-conscious elite.

39 / Figures for other countries are taken from Thomas Hodgkin, *Nationalism in Colonial Africa* (London: Muller, 1956), p. 67.

directed life which was the hallmark of urban areas elsewhere,[40] there was somewhat less of a drive to enjoy these new opportunities in Sierra Leone than was the case elsewhere in West Africa in the 1930s and 1940s.

So far, we have been discussing social mobilization, or the lack of it, in the Protectorate. Since the gap between Creoles and tribal people was to become the most significant political feature of the decolonization period, it is worth summarizing here the extent of their divergences. We have already seen that the Colony had more children in school than the entire Protectorate in 1931, and that the great majority of these probably were Creole. The *1931 Census* also noted that 57.5 per cent of the Creoles were literate, as against 8.5 per cent of the "natives" (Protectorate tribes) who lived in the Colony.[41] Almost everyone in the Colony, and certainly all Creoles, could be considered as part of the wage economy, whereas only 2.8 per cent of the population of the Protectorate were engaged in occupations other than agriculture.[42] Most Creoles either lived in Freetown or within a day's travel of it; most up-country people lived several days' travel from even the little trading towns of the Protectorate.

Although the educational gap was narrowed over the next two decades, Creoles were still heavily overrepresented among the school-going population. In 1948 the Colony still provided more than 45 per cent of the total primary school enrolment, and nearly all the secondary school enrolment (Table 1:2). The limited educational opportunities for Protectorate youth were also shown by the fact that while there had been a number of Creole lawyers since the turn of the century, and at least 70 Creole doctors by 1950, the first 3 lawyers of Protectorate origin were called to the Bar in 1948, 1949, and 1950, while the first 4 doctors took their degrees in 1927, 1934, 1943, and 1952.[43] This Creole lead persisted for several more years: in a Government list of overseas scholarship-holders taking university or technical training between 1951 and 1956, there were 97 persons from the Colony, almost all Creoles, and only 39 from the Protectorate.[44]

40 / The town of Bonthe was also part of the Colony government, but again was hardly large enough to provide such an outlet, and was already beginning to stagnate.

41 / The rate of literacy among Protectorate people living in the Colony was still ten times the rate among those up-country. In absolute numbers, about a quarter of all literate persons from Protectorate tribes were living in the Colony.

42 / Many farmers in the Protectorate were, of course, selling part of their crops for cash. But as we have noted, this was largely marginal to their subsistence farming operations. Of the Protectorate persons in non-agricultural occupations, a substantial number of the village blacksmiths, carpenters, and fishermen probably were not involved in the money economy to any significant extent.

43 / Data on doctors are from Dr M. C. F. Easmon, "Sierra Leone Doctors," *Sierra Leone Studies*, June 1956, pp. 81–96.

44 / Cited in Sierra Leone, *Legislative Council Debates*, VIII, Session 1955–56 (September 27, 1956), pp. 12–14.

TABLE 1:2
Number of children enrolled in schools by
province (1938 and 1948)

	1938	1948
PRIMARY		
Colony	10,282	12,311
Southern and Eastern provinces[a]	8,628	11,446
Northern Province	1,988	3,291
TOTAL	20,898	27,048
SECONDARY		
Colony	565[b]	1,714[c]
Southern and Eastern provinces	—	186
Northern Province	—	—
TOTAL	565	1,900

a/These two provinces were combined as one
during the 1930s.
b/Includes 20 at Albert Academy, who were mostly
from the Protectorate, plus a few more Protectorate boys at Prince of Wales, the Government
school, and elsewhere, for a total of at most 40
Protectorate boys.
c/Includes 149 from the Protectorate, for a total of
335 Protectorate boys in all secondary schools.
Source: Sierra Leone Blue Book, 1938, pp. Q1–5;
*Annual Report of the Education Department for
the year 1948.*

Other aspects of this gap were reduced. Protectorate towns after World
War II did begin to develop to the point where they could provide an urban
environment where sizable numbers of the Western-educated men could
meet; their numbers, however, still lagged far behind those in Freetown.[45]
The mining developments in the north and in Kono provided opportunities
for permanent wage employment in areas where Creoles did not form a
superior stratum. By 1948 there were more persons employed in wage labour
in the Protectorate than in Freetown.[46]

Another tribal disparity, even though less striking, became politically significant. This was the difference in both rates and type of development
between the northern and southern parts of the country, between Temnes
and Mendes. Until the opening of the Marampa iron mine and the discovery

45 / For a discussion of the interaction among members of the Protectorate's Western elite in an urban setting, see Kenneth Little, "Structural Change in the Sierra Leone
Protectorate," *Africa*, xxv (July 1955), pp. 217–33.

46 / *Annual Report of the Department of Labour,* 1949, p. 6.

of gold in the 1930s, the bulk of the economic activity had been concentrated in the southern areas. Most palm and other agricultural products came from Mendeland, a tendency encouraged by the railways and the presence of several river ports. Most trading towns, in consequence, developed in the southern provinces; 44 of the 65 towns with a population of more than 1,000 were in the south and east in 1931, with 27 in the two major palm-producing districts of Kenema and Kailahun.[47] Economic change came to the north in the very different form of a gold rush and the permanent wage employment offered by the iron mines, both forms of involvement in the wage economy which were far more likely than agricultural cash crops to undermine traditional forms of authority.

Educational opportunities also were unequal between north and south. As Table 1:2 shows,[48] the number of children enrolled in schools in the south was more than four times greater than that in the north in 1938, and more than three times greater in 1948. Much of this disparity can be explained by the fact that the Christian missionaries concentrated their efforts in the south; the predominantly Muslim north held less promise. It may be that the Mendes have been somewhat more receptive to Western education. A study of the Western Rural Area, where Mendes and Temnes had roughly equal access to schools, showed some 40 per cent of school-age Mende children attending school in 1947 against only 12 per cent of Temne children.[49] The result of this inequality could be seen from the fact that the first lawyers and the first doctors from the Protectorate were Mende.[50] Furthermore, insofar as Western-educated men took over the reins of government when decolonialization began, the chances were high that Mendes would predominate among the Protectorate contingent.

THE MODERNIZATION OF CHIEFTAINCY

Discussion so far has focused upon the aggregate numbers of persons in Sierra Leone's population who came to be predominantly involved in that sector of society we have called "modern." But to limit ourselves to this sector would be to miss much that is significant about Sierra Leone. We also

47 / Calculated from *1931 Census*.

48 / Above, p. 25.

49 / E. M. Richardson and G. R. Collins, *Economic and Social Survey of the Rural Areas of the Colony of Sierra Leone* (London: The Colonial Office, n.d. [1952], mimeo), p. 441. Richardson and Collins noted that nearly all school-age Creole children went to school, though they also observed that Creoles tended to be concentrated in the areas where schools were most readily accessible.

50 / The first three lawyers were Albert Margai (Mende), Arthur Massally (Mende), and I. B. Taylor-Kamara (Temne). The first five doctors were Milton Margai, James Massally (the older brothers of the first two lawyers), John Karefa-Smart (Temne), Hadj Conteh (Temne), and I. B. Amara (Mende).

need to consider closely the "traditional" or "residual" sector, both because of the ways in which persons were drawn from it into the modern sector, and because of the ways in which it was itself affected by colonial rule.

The same lack of financial support from Britain that had restricted direct government support for economic development forced the colonial administration after 1896 to create a political structure that was basically one of "Indirect Rule." The British assumed from the outset that the only feasible method of governing the Protectorate was through the existing chiefly structure,[51] and sought only to exercise light supervision over the behaviour of the traditional rulers. Beyond requiring the chiefs to collect the five shilling "Hut Tax," taking jurisdiction over major crimes, and trying (rather ineffectively) to curtail the activities of the secret societies where these interfered with trade or were repugnant to European morality, the District Commissioners and Assistant Commissioners played what they regarded as a loose supervisory role over native affairs. They were too few in number to do much more; by 1936 the total establishment of District Commissioners and Assistant District Commissioners numbered only 22, or about one for every 60,000 inhabitants.[52] But even this supervision was sufficient to alter significantly the relationships between the chiefs and their people.

The pre-colonial political system of the major tribes of Sierra Leone was built around the traditional ruler known under British rule as the Paramount Chief. The chief was chosen from a restricted group, the "ruling families" of the chiefdom, whose claim to rule had originally been established by the fact that they were descended from the first settler in the area, or from a warrior who had conquered it. One important difference may be noted here between the Mende and the Temne chief. The Mende chief was a secular leader; he was the principal warrior, the judge of disputes, and an administrator, but he possessed no strong religious mystique. The Temne chief, by contrast, was invested with a "chief's holiness" at his consecration, a quality which set him apart from ordinary men by making him the embodiment of the entire community and linking him to the ancestors in the Futa Jallon.[53] Because of this sacred quality, the Temne chief was less likely than the Mende chief

---

51 / See the *Report by Her Majesty's Commissioner ... on the Subject of the Insurrection in the Sierra Leone Protectorate, 1898* (London: HMSO, 1899), pp. 77–79.

52 / Figures from *Annual Report of the Provincial Administration, 1936*, pp. 9, 18. This ratio of administrators to population was roughly a third of the ratio for French territories, where the traditional rulers were much more closely controlled by and subordinated to the administration; for example, Guinea had one French administrator per 24,050 inhabitants, Senegal one per 19,292 and the Ivory Coast one per 18,134. Buell, *The Native Problem in Africa*, I, p. 985. The ratio was comparable, however, to that of Southern Nigeria, with its one administrator per 70,000 inhabitants. *Ibid.*, p. 648.

53 / A. B. Ture, "Notes on Customs and Ceremonies Attending the Selection and Crowning of a Bombali Temne Chief," *Sierra Leone Studies*, (o.s.) XXII (September 1939), p. 95.

to be attacked on the pragmatic grounds that he failed to provide good leadership. This same quality, however, may have made his people less dependent on him for the solution to everyday problems, since they tended to regard these as outside his scope of duties.[54]

The chief did not rule alone in any traditional system. He was surrounded by a number of advisers, the most important of whom was known as the "Chiefdom Speaker," who acted as the principal intermediary between the chief and his people; persons having disputes and complaints would go first to the speaker.[55] Other key figures were the section chiefs, the heads of territorial units of the chiefdom, and in Temne country the "war chiefs," who provided the chief with men, money, and supplies in his frequent conflicts with his neighbours.

These "big men" of the chiefdom had a number of direct sanctions they could use to prevent a chief from acting autocratically. The Temne chief held office for life, but his subchiefs were empowered to kill him if he fell ill – a sanction that was used with great alacrity against a chief who ruled badly.[56] The Mende chief could be deposed for misrule by the Poro society, acting through its higher officials. Whereas the chief was a member and patron of the society, these officials were not necessarily members of the ruling family, although they were generally men of high standing.[57]

There were other curbs on the chief. The persistence of conflicts between chiefdoms rendered Temne chiefs dependent on their "war chiefs" for support; and in Mende country chiefs were constantly rising and falling as a result of their success or failure in war.[58] More generally, the chief had to obey the traditional rules in order to retain the support of his people. As the "father of his people," he was expected to feed needy members of the chiefdom, care for women abandoned by their husbands, and provide other welfare services out of the tribute provided by his subjects. Failure to fulfil these obligations would destroy a chief's reputation among his people, a loss not to be borne lightly in a small society.[59] If all else failed, the people of a chiefdom might leave their chief and seek the protection of another.

These restraints probably were sufficient to deter a chief from the exclusive pursuit of his personal interests at the expense of his people. However, the ordinary farmers and slaves did not have a direct voice in the governing of the chiefdom, and it was conceivable that the chiefdom and Poro officials

54 / Michael Banton, *West African City* (London: Oxford University Press, 1957), p. 195.
55 / Little, "Mende Political Institutions," p. 10.
56 / Dorjahn, "Changing Political System of the Temne," p. 114.
57 / Little, "Mende Political Institutions," p. 13.
58 / Little, *The Mende of Sierra Leone*, pp. 29–31.
59 / See Ruth Finnegan, *Survey of the Limba People of Northern Sierra Leone* (London: HMSO, 1965), pp. 40–41.

would condone their exploitation provided the officials received a share. On the other hand, these "big men" would be the persons responsible for collecting the various tributes of food and labour from the people, and would have to bear the odium of too heavy extractions. As a result they might tend towards acting as spokesmen for the people. It is probable, on balance, that the chief was restrained from any serious abuses against either his ordinary subjects or those immediately around him.

Although British overrule imposed a few further restraints on the chief, its principal effect was to weaken or remove existing checks on him. The abolition of slave dealing, by cutting out one source of wealth, curtailed his ability to bind followers to him.[60] The removal of all major criminal matters, and all matters involving Creoles or Europeans, from his judicial ambit,[61] took away much of what had been considered his most important power. Policing duties were carried out by a Court Messenger force directly under the District Commissioner. In all these ways the chief's position was weakened, and at the same time the traditional checks on him were cut away. The end of tribal warfare destroyed one means by which chiefs were often overthrown. If a section of a chiefdom became disaffected with the chief's rule, they could no longer simply break away and form their own chiefdom. That the colonial administration was not particularly sympathetic to attempted secessions was indicated by the comment of one important administrator: "In general, government has preserved chiefdoms as they were in 1896, often with some difficulty, as the tendency of Sierra Leone chiefdoms in times of stress is to break up into original units [sections]."[62]

More direct checks also withered. Since any murder was now a capital crime, the Temne subchiefs and secret societies did not dare assassinate even the most tyrannical chief.[63] In Mende country, the government's attempts to discourage the Poro Society meant that the society could no longer openly depose a chief, although it continued to exercise considerable influence behind the scenes.[64] While the District Commissioner's role was conceived in part as the protector of the people against abuses by their chiefs, in practice this restraint was not effective. While grievances might exist, ordinary farmers needed to be severely provoked before complaining to a District Commission about their chief's behaviour; apart from the respect adhering to the chief's office, he possessed a wide range of sanctions for use against "trouble-makers," from control over land allocation to heavy fines for the

60 / Little, "Mende Political Institutions," p. 13.
61 / The Protectorate Native Laws Ordinance, *Laws of Sierra Leone, 1925*, Cap. 169.
62 / J. S. Fenton, *Outline of Sierra Leone Native Law* (Freetown: Government Printer, 1933), p. 3.
63 / Dorjahn, "Changing Political System of the Temne," pp. 138–39.
64 / Little, *The Mende of Sierra Leone*, pp. 184–85.

violation of supposed customs. Even when subjects did complain, their complaints were not always heeded. Although the administration had recognized almost from the inception of the Hut Tax that abuses were occurring, they were reluctant to act against any chief (from 1935 to 1939 not a single chief was deposed).[65] The administration seemed more ready to banish persons who openly agitated against their chief than to act against the chief himself. To cite an example, the Report for 1935 noted that "five ringleaders of opposition" to one chief were banished.[66]

The curtailment of these checks from below, and the limited nature of the supervision from above, left the chiefs free to gain considerable personal economic advantages. The fact that they were the officially designated tax collectors for the colonial administration[67] not only acquainted them with the money economy, but helped to create the impression that any monetary demands they made would be backed by the colonial overlords. Starting modestly, with a corrugated iron roof here and a cement block house there, many chiefs gradually stepped up their exactions to finance motorcars and lorries, business enterprises, education for their children, and other items for their personal consumption. In 1937, when the chiefs' exactions were still moderate, the colonial government tried to clarify and systematize the rather nebulous form of chiefdom government by establishing Native Administrations (or "Tribal Authorities" as they were termed in the Sierra Leone ordinances) in the existing chiefdoms. Following the pattern already established in almost all other British West African territories, these Tribal Authorities consisted of the Paramount Chief and other members chosen "according to native law and custom";[68] in practice this meant that the chief could control the appointment and removal of members. The ordinance governing the Tribal Authorities' taxing power laid down that no person, including the Paramount Chief, was to receive any "tax, tribute, customary levy or labour" apart from a limited range specified in the Ordinance.[69] The hitherto unregulated tributes collected by the chief along with the Hut Tax were supposed to be replaced by a chiefdom tax (set at four shillings) to be paid into a Chiefdom Treasury and thus properly accounted for.

This ideal, however, was not realized. It would appear that the four shil-

65 / See the *Annual Report of the Provincial Administration*, 1935 to 1939. One chief was suspended in 1936, and one would have been deposed for his part in a fetish murder in 1938, had he not died before action could be taken.

66 / *Ibid.*, 1935, p. 10.

67 / And very efficient ones; encouraged by a five per cent rebate on taxes collected, they achieved a near perfect record.

68 / The Tribal Authorities Ordinance, 1937, Section 2. Technically, Tribal Authorities had to be approved by the Governor, but this was in practice a formality since their numbers ran into the thousands.

69 / The Chiefdom Tax Ordinance, 1937, Section 2 (3).

ling tax was simply collected on top of other exactions. After 1945, when the movement to bring chiefdoms under Tribal Authorities finally began to gather speed, the level of the chiefs' additional (and now illegal) levies increased considerably. A decade later, when the movement towards rule by Sierra Leoneans had led to a further slackening of the already light curbs on the chiefs' behaviour, their abuses reached the point where the Temne people finally exploded into widespread anti-chief rioting. Indeed, for several years before this explosion, many chiefs had been "modernizing" traditional relationships in ways that accrued to their personal benefit.[70]

Traditionally, for example, chiefs had been able to call upon free chiefdom labour to construct a (non-permanent) mud-block compound during their reign, and to use chiefdom labour to work their farms.[71] But after 1945 the chiefs began to call on free labour to construct cement-block houses which formed a permanent asset, and to use free labour to work large scale commercial rice farms, even in competition with other less privileged cash-crop farmers.[72] The profits from these operations seem to have gone to the chiefs' personal use.

Taxes collected for the Native Administrations also found their way regularly into the chief's personal coffers. Licences and fees were freely imposed on such objects and activities as canoes, fish-traps, sewing-machines, and palm wine tapping.[73] Very often this revenue was not accounted for in the chiefdom estimates: in one case the Cox Commission found that "Some hundreds of canoes and boats were licenced on a scale to bring in well over £1,000; the estimates provided for a revenue of £40; the estimate was reached with surprising precision; the Chief in fact paid in to revenue what was estimated and happily retained the rest."[74] After hearing evidence on the exactions of various chiefs, the Cox Commission concluded: "We believe that no chiefdom is free from the taint of unlawful levies of tribute."[75] The levies themselves were only a part of the burden imposed on the taxpayers. Both chiefs and tax assessors would demand a "Hammock fee" and "shake-hands" when visiting each village. These fees were based on traditional custom

---

70 / Most of the changes in the chiefs' position discussed below are covered in the *Report of the Commission of Inquiry into Disturbances in the Provinces* (November 1955 to March 1956) (London: Crown Agents for Overseas Government and Administration on behalf of the Government of Sierra Leone, 1956), hereafter referred to as the *Cox Report*. Cf. Kilson, *Political Change in a West African State*, pp. 53–59.

71 / The latter was justified on the grounds that a chief should be fed by his people, and also that he had to feed visitors to the chiefdom. See Dorjahn, "Changing Political System of the Temne," pp. 117, 131.

72 / See *Cox Report*, pp. 159, 161.

73 / *Ibid.*, pp. 141–3.

74 / *Ibid.*, p. 141.

75 / *Ibid.*, p. 155.

whereby the villagers would welcome their chief when he stopped in their village to see them during a journey by hammock, and would traditionally take the form of rice, chickens, and other farm produce. However, by the 1950s, chiefs were generally travelling by car, and stopping only for a few minutes in each village. Meanwhile, the "shake-hands" had turned into a cash payment (although rice, palm oil, and fowls were still collected as well), and was paid not only to the chief, but to anyone who could say he was on the chief's business. The Cox Commission noted that the cash "shake-hands" ranged from 2s.6d. a village to 20s. and that

the food supplied was ... in such a quantity that it could not be consumed and so was taken away. So great was the accumulation of rice, oils and chicken that the assessors used to send quantities back to their headquarters; in fact at Rosint in Buya Romendi Chiefdom it was stated by one of the assessors that such a large quantity of fowls were sent to the Paramount Chief that he was able to carry on a flourishing trade in that commodity.[76]

The Paramount Chiefs were thus in the forefront of the "modernization" of the traditional societies. Their strategic location as tax collectors, coupled with their still strong appeal as the "fathers of their people," enabled them to tap a substantial share of the cash which flowed in an increasing stream into the Protectorate.

The most important advantage of this system to the chiefs was that it permitted them to provide their children with a Western education, which opened up to them many of the key posts in the modern structure of government as the British departed. The fees for primary schools in 1938 were six-pence a month, and for secondary schools from £4 to £12 a year. The ordinary farmer, who already had to dig deeply for some nine shillings or more in taxes, found the additional four or five shillings per child in school fees, plus books and uniforms, a considerable burden; as for secondary education, it was beyond the reach of anyone outside well-paid wage employment or a strategic location in the traditional sector. The result was that most of the children who received secondary schooling in the 1930s and 1940s were either the second generation in the modern economy, or the sons and relatives of chiefs.

This tendency, we may add, was supported by the British. The first Protectorate school, Bo School, from its founding in 1905 until 1941, admitted only the sons and nominees of Paramount Chiefs. This school played a role in the moulding of a Protectorate elite analogous to that of the Ecole William Ponty in French West Africa, or perhaps, in view of the ascriptive criteria used to determine entry, to that of Eton and Harrow in England. A majority

76 / Ibid., pp. 121–22. Cf. the complaints made during the riots by a "strike" leader, in Daily Mail, December 3, 1955.

of the persons from the Protectorate who later became politically prominent attended it, and a number taught there. Its graduates were knit together both by their common status and by the group known as the Old Bo Boys Association. This cohesion developed despite an official British policy of encouraging tribal identification by teaching "Mende pupils ... to ... prefer Mende land to any other country, so with Temnes and all the various tribes ..."[77] Boys from the different tribes shared a common interest in chieftaincy, and in a mild way, a desire to see Sierra Leone ruled by Africans. The new generation of literate chiefs who during the 1930s and 1940s gradually took office all across the country had in many cases been together at Bo School, and were able to establish closer trans-tribal links as a result.[78]

Although the behaviour of many chiefs eventually aroused resentment, particularly in Temne country where the backwardness of the people and their own power enabled them to squeeze more advantages from their position, the colonial relationship was not as destructive of chieftaincy in Sierra Leone as it was elsewhere. Unlike the administrators in French territories, the British generally took care to preserve a facade of autonomy for the chiefs. Furthermore, the real burdens imposed on Sierra Leone chiefs by the colonial administration were relatively light. The incidence of direct tax in the 1920s, according to Buell, was only half that of the French territories,[79] and while this takes no account of the illegal impositions later added by the chiefs, there is no reason to suppose that these were notably worse in Sierra Leone than elsewhere. There was none of the hated forced labour which the French and Belgians compelled their chiefs to recruit.[80] The chiefs were not so closely identified with the colonial regime as to be rendered impotent in the politics of an independence movement.

In summary, the movement from a multitude of small-scale, parochial societies to a territory-wide pattern of interactions took place in Sierra Leone in ways that accentuated cultural and social differences. The Creole community had formed a "modern" society in terms of its economic structure, communications patterns, and political participation[81] since at least the turn

77 / Quoted from the Prospectus for Bo School, 1905, in Fyfe, *Sierra Leone Inheritance*, p. 306.

78 / No less than 9 out of the 12 Paramount Chief members in each of the 1957 and 1962 legislatures had attended Bo School.

79 / *The Native Problem in Africa*, I, p. 944. The rate of taxation was approximately that of Nigeria and the Belgian Congo.

80 / For a summary of the forms of labour required in French territories, see Buell, *The Native Problem*, I, pp. 1037–44. For some of the political repercussions see Jean Surêt-Canale, "La Fin de la Chefferie en Guinée," *Journal of African History*, VII, 3 (1966), pp. 461 ff., and Aristide Zolberg, *One-Party Government in the Ivory Coast* (Princeton: Princeton University Press, 1964), esp. pp. 55–57.

81 / Within the limits allowed by colonial control.

of the century. Within the Protectorate the Mendes were drawn into modern society to a greater extent and in a greater variety of ways than the Temnes, through the spread of cash-crop agriculture, education, and transportation. At the same time, their exposure to modernizing influences did not completely break down the traditional social structure. The Temnes, by contrast, did not have the same access to markets for cash crops or to education, but they did have greater opportunities to plunge completely into wage employment at the iron mine, or to go gold mining in the 1930s, and to emigrate to Freetown. Although the Temnes as a whole were less mobilized, for those who were the break with traditional society was more complete. Finally, the individuals from the Protectorate who received Western education, and thus were able to form a Western-type class of professional and managerial persons, were drawn largely from the traditional ruling class. This produced a continuity between the traditional elite of the Protectorate and the potential new rulers of a modern polity. At the same time, while the chiefs' success in staying in the forefront of change in the traditional sector helped prevent their obsolescence, the manner in which they changed their role built up serious tensions between them and their people.

2
African political responses to colonialism

The introduction of Protectorate representatives and elected Colony members to the Legislative Council in 1924 did not greatly widen the opportunities for African political participation. While the three Paramount Chiefs probably were as well qualified to speak for Protectorate opinion as any alternative representatives, they were open to pressure from the provincial administration, and tended to be rather reticent about speaking their minds. The Colony elected representatives, thanks to the restrictive franchise, were inevitably Creoles, who tended to concentrate their attention on matters of concern to the Colony, rather than on trying to expand their outlook to embrace the Protectorate. This tendency to focus on the concerns of their own constituencies was not unique to the Creole legislators of Sierra Leone; their counterparts from Lagos in the Nigerian Legislative Council also devoted most of their attention to local affairs. But the Nigerians, and even more the elected members in the Gold Coast, did show concern for the needs of all Nigerians and all Gold Coasters, and stressed their fundamental common identity; the Colony representatives in Sierra Leone were much more reluctant to do this.[1]

The colonial administration meanwhile did little to promote the unification of Colony and Protectorate below the level of the Legislative Council. A major source of Creole antipathy towards the Protectorate was the fact that while "natives" in the Colony enjoyed the same rights under British law as did Creoles, Creoles living up-country could be arbitrarily treated by the

1 / For Nigeria, see James Coleman's remarks about Herbert Macauley's Democratic Party, in *Nigeria: Background to Nationalism* (Berkeley and Los Angeles: University of California Press, 1958), pp. 199–200; for the Gold Coast, see David Kimble, *A Political History of the Gold Coast 1850–1928* (Oxford: The Clarendon Press, 1963), pp. 528–36. Kimble makes the point that this concern extended only to Ashanti; the Northern Territories remained an alien land.

chiefs under "native law and custom."[2] They also felt aggrieved by the land laws of the two areas, which permitted "natives" to buy land in the Colony, but forbade Creoles (or anyone else) to own land outright in the Protectorate. On the Protectorate side, there was already some antagonism among the better educated men towards Creole pretensions of superiority as well as anger over the much more limited opportunities for education in the Protectorate.

There was an almost total lack of explicitly political activity beyond the confines of the Creole elite until the late 1930s. A Freetown branch of the National Congress of British West Africa had been formed before the 1924 reforms, but it was the preserve of a few influential Creoles and became moribund within a few years.[3] Below the level of the elite, there were sporadic anti-chief and anti-administration uprisings, notably the Haidara Rebellion of 1929.[4] None of these, however, gave birth to any sustained political movement, or even provided a myth for subsequent popular political activity.

The one significant burst of political activity involving both Colony and Protectorate came in 1938 with the return of I. T. A. Wallace-Johnson, a Creole journalist, union organizer, and agitator. Wallace-Johnson, who had studied in Moscow in the early 1930s and later worked with Nnamdi Azikiwe editing the anti-colonial *African Morning Post* in Accra, soon founded the West African Youth League (Sierra Leone Branch) as a vehicle for any and all popular discontents. The grievances raised in Youth League meetings, ranging from the failure of the Freetown Council to provide adequate water supplies to labour troubles and "exploitation" by the British colonialists, were more likely to strike a response among the mass of poorer urban wage labourers than among either the Creole elite or the Paramount Chiefs. The statement of one contemporary observer that "Its ventilation of constitutional or labour grievances has begun to bridge the old deep cleavage between the Creoles and the peoples of the Protectorate"[5] was not too far off the mark, at least in respect to the persons in the lower levels of the wage economy. Its claim a year after its founding to 25,000 members in the Colony and 17,000 in the Protectorate[6] was undoubtedly an exaggeration, but it did attract con-

2 / See Kilson, *Political Change in a West African State*, p. 135, for an illustration of this problem.

3 / See Edward W. Blyden III, *Sierra Leone: The Pattern of Constitutional Change, 1924–1951* (unpublished PHD thesis, Harvard University, 1959), pp. 91–97.

4 / See Kilson, *Political Change in a West African State*, pp. 110–23, for a description of this rebellion and for an argument that these uprisings were, in fact, a central feature of political change in Sierra Leone.

5 / W. M. MacMillan, in C. K. Meek *et al., Europe and West Africa: Some Problems and Adjustments* (London: Oxford University Press, 1940), p. 76.

6 / *Sierra Leone Weekly News*, September 15, 1939.

siderable support from younger men, both school boys and wage earners, up-country as well as around Freetown. But its radical appeals (and Wallace-Johnson's Marxist orientation) turned the conservative Creole elite as well as the colonial administration against it. The Creole elite subjected Wallace-Johnson to a number of libel actions, and in 1940 he was interned for the duration of the war along with all but one of the Youth League executive. This was enough to break the Youth League organization, since it had not developed a cadre of secondary leaders. Although it was revived after the war, it did not regain its mass following. One reason for its failure to make a more lasting impact on Sierra Leone was Wallace-Johnson's own leadership. An outstanding agitator, he was, nevertheless, unable to work with others well enough to build up a solid organizational foundation.[7] Even the most brilliant organizer would have had difficulties creating a radical mass movement in Sierra Leone: most Creoles, unlike Wallace-Johnson, were not prepared to look beyond their own society to an alliance with the Protectorate. Within the Protectorate, there were not enough people in urban areas, in wage employment, and with sufficient education to break away from traditional orientations, and those who were mobilized tended to be the individuals with the strongest motives for protecting traditional societies.

Meanwhile two Protectorate groups, the Paramount Chiefs and the educated men, were beginning to organize their own quasi-political activity. Dr Milton Margai, the grandson of a Mende warrior chief and the son of a wealthy merchant, was acting as unofficial adviser to many chiefs in their dealings with the government. Partly at his instigation, the chiefs in 1940 began a series of annual meetings known as the Chiefs' Conferences. These conferences seem to have been conducted with no British officials present; when the government proposed in 1945 to replace them with the more formally constituted District Council meetings, chaired by District Commissioners as Presidents, one chief protested that this was a retrograde step in that the presence of the DC would prevent the chiefs from speaking as freely as they had in the conferences.[8] Through these conferences, the chiefs were given the opportunity to develop a common political approach and a forum through which to make their voices heard by the administration.

The educated Protectorate men had their own means of contact. Most of them were in government service as teachers, clerks, doctors, or in other occupations which brought them together in the main provincial towns where

7 / After the 1951 constitution was introduced, Wallace-Johnson made the rounds of the opposition parties, quitting or being expelled from the National Council, the United Progressive Party, the Peoples National Party (with which he was only in alliance), and the All Peoples Congress. At the time of his death in 1965, he had rejoined the APC, but was engaged in attacking its leader.

8 / *Legislative Council Debates*, 1945–46 (November 30, 1945), p. 158.

they could develop political plans for the future. In 1929 several of them, including Dr Margai and A. J. Momoh, a civil servant whose fight for equal pay for Africans had won him widespread respect among Creoles as well as countrymen,[9] came together with a number of educated Paramount Chiefs to form the Protectorate Educational Progressive Union. PEPU's purpose was to provide scholarships for Protectorate boys, in order to offset the Protectorate's educational backwardness vis-à-vis the Colony. After lapsing in the 1930s, it was revived in 1946, when one of its first acts was to send to England a young dispenser, Albert Margai, the younger brother of Dr Margai. PEPU's active members at this time included both educated chiefs and non-chiefs: Chiefs Gulama and Caulker of Moyamba and Koker of Bo were involved, along with Dr Margai, A. J. Momoh, and Amadu Wurie, a teacher and son of a chief.

The educated men soon formed a further group, the Sierra Leone Organization Society (SOS). Its purpose was ostensibly educational, but its leaders tended to view education as a process of developing popular political awareness of what they regarded as an unsatisfactory constitutional position. Its founders were Dr John Karefa-Smart, and a number of teachers including Doyle Sumner, R. B. Kowa, and Frank Anthony;[10] it was encouraged by Chief Gulama, though no other chiefs played an active role in it. However, nearly all its leading members were from ruling families; most knew each other and the leading Paramount Chiefs through their work as teachers or civil servants in different parts of the country; and most had attended Bo School or Albert Academy along with the chiefs. They formed, in short, part of the same "traditio-modern" elite as the chiefs.[11]

Even before the SOS was formed, the colonial government had anticipated demands for greater representation in the Protectorate by establishing in 1945 two levels of consultative bodies under the overall authority of the Legislative Council. The lower level was the system of District Councils, whose purpose was "to advise and to make recommendations" to the government, although they were also empowered to modify "native customary law" within their districts.[12] They were to comprise two representatives from each

9 / This was shown in 1948 when he won election to the Freetown City Council at a time when Creole-countryman tensions were rising rapidly.

10 / Those named seem to have been most important in the formation of the SOS, according to all the individuals I interviewed, and also according to Fred M. Hayward, who also interviewed a number of persons on this topic in 1965–66.

11 / It may be significant that like the first "nationalists" in Northern Nigeria, but unlike those in Southern Nigeria and the Gold Coast, the SOS leaders were predominantly teachers and other salaried government employees rather than self-employed professionals or businessmen. This left them relatively vulnerable to pressure from the government.

12 / Laws of Sierra Leone, 1946, Chapter 185, Sections 5(5) and 5(7).

chiefdom in the district, one to be the Paramount Chief and the other "a member of the chiefdom appointed by the Tribal Authority."[13] This meant that the Councils were to be basically meetings of chiefs, since the chiefs could almost always use their influence over their tribal authorities to ensure that the other chiefdom representative was satisfactory to them.

The higher level of consultative body was the Protectorate Assembly, whose sole purpose also was to advise the government.[14] The Protectorate Assembly consisted of 10 official members, 6 nominated unofficial members of whom 4 had to be Africans, and 2 members elected from the ranks of each of the 13 District Councils, for a total membership of 42.[15] Since the Protectorate Assembly was only an advisory body, the granting of a large unofficial majority did not signify any transfer of power from British hands, but it did suggest that African opinion might be listened to more closely in the future. Given the composition of the District Councils, it was quite clear what shades of African opinion would be represented in the Protectorate Assembly: in the first four sessions of the Protectorate Assembly, every one of the elected members was a Paramount Chief, and until the last meeting of the Assembly in 1955, the proportion of non-chiefs never rose above a quarter of the total elective membership.[16]

The creation of these advisory bodies by the colonial government could be considered in part an anticipation of demands from the articulate sections of Sierra Leone for greater participation in the political process, but it would be very misleading to suggest that internal pressures were the main or even a major factor in starting Sierra Leone on the road to self-government. The level of indigenous political activity in Sierra Leone in 1946 was considerably below that attained in Nigeria or the Gold Coast, and even in these territories much of the impetus for the initial changes came from the colonial overlords. The examples of Burma, Ceylon, and India may have encouraged African nationalists to press their demands more forcefully, but a more significant factor was the change in attitude of the British government itself. The motivations behind the British government's decision to move the colonies towards "responsible self-government"[17] may be debatable, but there can be little doubt that majority opinion in Britain accepted this goal both on logical and practical grounds.

13 / *Ibid.*, Section 5(2).

14 / *Ibid.*, Section 7(6). The Protectorate Assembly thus resembled the Gold Coast Colony's Provincial Councils rather than a legislative chamber. Cf. Martin Wight, *The Gold Coast Legislative Council* (London: Faber & Faber, 1947), pp. 45–51.

15 / *Laws of Sierra Leone, 1946*, Chapter 185, Section 7(2).

16 / Compiled from membership as listed in Protectorate Assembly. *Proceedings ... of the [first to twelfth] Meetings.*

17 / See the statement by the Colonial Secretary, July 9, 1946. Great Britain. *5 Parliamentary Debates* (Commons), Vol. 425, col. 240.

The application of this new British policy to Sierra Leone did not stop with the setting up of the Protectorate Assembly and District Councils. It was also considered desirable to establish an unofficial (African) majority in the Legislative Council as the first step in making government more representative. However, the 1946 constitutions in both the Gold Coast and Nigeria suggested that the British would put most of their faith in the "representativeness" of traditional authorities rather than in the direct election of legislators. Under both the Burns Constitution in the Gold Coast and the Richards Constitution in Nigeria a majority of the unofficial African members were chosen ultimately from a base of native administrations, which like those in Sierra Leone were not themselves directly elected by the people. Only a minority of the unofficial members (5 out of 18 in the Gold Coast, and 4 out of 28 in Nigeria) were directly elected from constituencies.[18]

It was hard to see any effective pressure being exerted on the British in Sierra Leone to divert them from a similar course. The educated Protectorate men were too closely linked with the chiefs and too vulnerable to government pressure to mount a mass movement which could challenge the chiefs, even if there had been sufficient popular discontent to make this feasible. The lack of discontent also probably precluded any effective radical mass movement led by trade unionists, petty traders, or others from the lower strata of the modern sector. The Creole elite might join forces with the educated Protectorate men, but to do so they would have had to break through the self-imposed barriers of decades of separation.

18 / For details regarding the 1946 (Richards) Constitution in Nigeria, see Joan Wheare, *The Nigerian Legislative Council* (London: Faber & Faber, 1950), pp. 170–75, and also the Nigerian (Legislative Council) Order-in-Council, 1946, in *ibid.*, pp. 212–47. See also Kalu Ezera, *Constitutional Developments in Nigeria* (Cambridge: Cambridge University Press, 1960), pp. 66–75. For the 1946 (Burns) Constitution in the Gold Coast, see Martin Wight, *The Gold Coast Legislative Council* (London: Faber & Faber, 1947), pp. 203–206, and also the Gold Coast and Ashanti (Legislative Council) Order-in-Council, 1946, in *ibid.*, pp. 239–67. See also F. M. Bourret, *The Gold Coast* (London: Oxford University Press, 1952), pp. 191–93, and David Apter, *Ghana in Transition* (New York: Atheneum, 1963), pp. 141–43.

PART TWO

The 1951 constitution: the SLPP is formed

3
Constitutional crisis, 1947–50

As long as all Africans were confined to minor advisory roles in the government of Sierra Leone, it did not matter much that the Creoles had more representation in the Legislative Council than the Protectorate people, or that the Protectorate's representatives were all chiefs. But once it became clear that more power was to be handed over to Africans, the question of which Sierra Leoneans would take places on the decision-making bodies aroused considerable concern. The struggle over the form of constitutional advancement which raged from 1947 to 1951 brought out sharply the conflicts and affinities between different elements in the Sierra Leone political system.

On October 13, 1947, following some preliminary discussion with members of the Legislative Council, the Protectorate Assembly and the public, Governor Sir Hubert Stevenson submitted to the British Secretary of State for the Colonies his proposals for the constitutional advancement of Sierra Leone.[1] His proposals contained two key points. The first, already accepted for Nigeria and the Gold Coast, was that the Legislative Council should have an unofficial and African majority. The other was an attempt to resolve the crucial problem of the cleavage between the Colony and Protectorate by providing that the Protectorate should have a majority of the Legislative Council members elected by African bodies, but less than a majority of the total Legislative Council membership. He proposed a total membership in the Council of twenty-three: seven officials, two unofficial members nominated by the Governor to represent business interests, four directly elected from Colony seats on the existing franchise, and ten elected by the Protectorate Assembly from among its own members.[2] The Protectorate Assembly's

1 / See Sierra Leone, *Proposals for the Reconstruction of the Legislative Council in Sierra Leone,* Sessional Paper No. 2 of 1948 (Freetown: Government Printer, 1948), p. 1.
2 / *Ibid.,* pp. 1–2.

representatives were to comprise nine chosen from among the elected District Council members, and one from among the African nominated members.[3] This meant that nine Protectorate Assembly representatives would be chosen by a four-tier process of indirect election, from Tribal Authority to District Council to Protectorate Assembly to Legislative Council, with the lowest tier under the control of the chiefs rather than effectively controlled by a popular electorate.

This proposed division of representation between Colony and Protectorate could be taken as an attempt to foster unity between the two parts of Sierra Leone. If the unofficial members of the Legislative Council were to exercise the power of a majority, it would be necessary for the representatives of Colony and Protectorate to work together. It was possible, however, to view the proposals in a more sinister light by considering the method of choosing the Protectorate representatives. This method would make it almost certain that the Protectorate representatives in the Legislative Council would be Paramount Chiefs, and it was widely felt that the chiefs were too firmly under the thumb of the government officials to act in a truly independent manner. There would, in effect, still be an official majority, composed of the government officials and chiefs. This argument was to figure prominently in the attacks made on the proposals.

One further proposal of less intrinsic importance brought out more emphatically a difference of opinion between the chiefs on the one side and the educated Protectorate men and the Creoles on the other. This was the proposal that for at least the first three years members of the Legislative Council need not be literate in English. Stevenson's concern was ostensibly that the Protectorate leaders most capable of developing widespread interest in the new Council would be illiterates,[4] though he may also have held the common colonial administrator's bias against "unrepresentative" educated Africans. His willingness to remove the existing barrier to illiterates in the Legislative Council was of benefit primarily to the chiefs, the majority of whom were still illiterate.

It was not surprising that of the three articulate sections of Sierra Leone society, the Paramount Chiefs were the ones most firmly in favour of the Stevenson proposals. Through the District Councils and the Protectorate Assembly, they endorsed nearly all the Stevenson proposals, with the one major change that each district should elect a representative of its own, rather than having nine elected for all the Protectorate by the Assembly. In proposing this change, they were clearly going contrary to official wishes; the Acting Governor had announced at the beginning of the meeting, "I am glad to see that nearly all the District Councils have agreed there should be nine

3 / Ibid.
4 / Ibid., p. 4.

members elected from the District Council members on the Protectorate Assembly. ... I have observed a suggestion that each District Council should elect a member direct to the Legislative Council. That would be a considerable change from the original proposals."[5] Five Paramount Chiefs promptly stated that their districts had all favoured one representative per district, with one adding, "From what I know, it is the wish of every district to be represented."[6] Nearly all the chiefs who spoke stressed the desirability of this more locally oriented system of representation. Only the literate and sophisticated Chief Kai-Samba of Kenema took the view that "every member will talk in the interests of the Protectorate."[7] Apart from this change, most chiefs found their interests satisfactorily served by the Stevenson proposals as they stood.

The younger educated Protectorate men who formed the sos were less pleased, mainly because the Stevenson proposals excluded them from any chance of election to the legislature. In a memorandum submitted to the Colonial Secretary of Sierra Leone in October, 1947, the sos strongly protested against the monopoly of power given to the chiefs in the Protectorate under the Stevenson proposals.[8] It argued that "the common people ... who are taxpayers ... are entitled to even more representation ... than the natural rulers of the country" and claimed that under the system of election through District Councils and the Protectorate Assembly they would not get it, since these bodies "are merely composed of the natural rulers and the tribal authorities and therefore are not democratic institutions from which an electoral body can be formed for the peoples of the Protectorate." Giving the District Councils sole power to select representatives would deny the franchise to "the literate class of Protectorate peoples ... who are not, *because of domicile* [italics mine] directly connected with tribal institutions." To avert this domination, the sos asked that the Government "widen the franchise by giving the masses of the people from the Protectorate, and especially the literate class, the freedom to elect their representatives outside of the Protectorate Assembly."[9]

While the sos demanded that ordinary taxpayers should have "even more" representation than the chiefs, it did not reject the chiefs' claim to speak for their people. All the sos argued was that "the literate class" also could speak for the masses. While it appeared to be arguing for direct election on a taxpayer franchise, its concern centred chiefly around the fact that

5 / Protectorate Assembly. *Proceedings of the Third Meeting* (May 19, 1948), p. 3.
6 / *Ibid.*, pp. 9–11.
7 / *Ibid.*, p. 10.
8 / "Memorandum of the Sierra Leone Organization Society," September 29, 1947. Quoted in *Sierra Leone Weekly News,* October 18, 1947.
9 / *Ibid.*

educated men would be excluded from participation because their occupations took them out of their home chiefdoms. If they worked in the larger
Protectorate towns, their position as "strangers" would effectively preclude
them from participation in the Tribal Authority, while if they worked in
Freetown, their votes would be swamped by those of the Creoles. Their best
hope for election was to stand from their home chiefdoms, but if they were
not domiciled there they were unlikely to be members of the Tribal Authority.
The sos showed some interest in the broader principle that everyone (or at
least every taxpayer) ought to have a vote, but its stress on "the literate
class" suggests that their own position was uppermost in the minds of the
educated men.

The differences between the educated men and the chiefs, then, were not
great; the educated men were quite willing to share power with the chiefs,
and objected only to the chiefs' prospective monopoly of office. For their
part, a number of better educated and more articulate chiefs were willing
to share power with the educated men. Thus in April 1948 the Moyamba
District Council, one of whose most influential members was Chief Gulama,
forwarded a petition asking that all Protectorate members of the Legislative
Council should be literate, and that a "native" of a chiefdom be so defined
as to include a taxpayer not domiciled in it.[10] Both these changes would
help the educated men win places among the Protectorate representatives.
At the end of 1948 Chief Bai Koblo went further by suggesting to the
Legislative Council: "We do not desire to limit elections to this council only
to Chiefs. In fact some of us are beginning to feel that as time goes on
it might even be desirable that Paramount Chiefs should retire altogether
from sitting in this council, so that their status as independent rulers shall
not be jeopardized ..."[11] Earlier, Bai Koblo and the two other Paramount
Chief members of the Legislative Council had supported the sos viewpoint,
opposing that of the chiefs in the Protectorate Assembly, when they agreed
that literacy was a desirable requirement for members of the Legislative
Council.[12] There were clearly differences of opinion over whether the Protectorate should be represented by the chiefs or the educated men, but these
differences were as evident within the ranks of the chiefs themselves as
between the two groups.

However, the chiefs who advocated sharing power were definitely a
minority. The Governor in 1948 and the Chief Commissioner for the Pro-

10 / *Sierra Leone Weekly News,* May 1, 1948. I am indebted to Leo Spitzer for
calling my attention to this item.

11 / Sierra Leone. *Legislative Council Debates,* Session 1948/49, No. 1 (December
21, 1948), p. 71.

12 / Sierra Leone. *Report of the Select Committee to Consider Proposals for a
Reconstituted Legislative Council in Sierra Leone.* Sessional Paper No. 7 of 1948
(Freetown: Government Printer, 1948), p. 2.

tectorate in 1949 both urged the chiefs to elect more educated non-chiefs to the Protectorate Assembly,[13] while Dr Margai cautioned them in 1950 that "It is a very good idea to give power to people before they start to fight for it. This idea has long been pursued in different parts of the country, and has eventually ended in a split between chiefs and non-chiefs."[14] While the chiefs approved Dr Margai's motion that "one at least of the District Councils' representatives to the Protectorate Assembly should be a non-chief,"[15] they were reluctant to act on it. In the following three years, only six of the twelve District Councils sent even one non-chief to the Assembly.

The third articulate element in Sierra Leone at the time, the Creoles, at first appeared ready to make common cause with the educated Protectorate men. The *Sierra Leone Weekly News,* the leading voice of moderate Creole opinion, agreed initially with Governor Stevenson that the Protectorate should have more members than the Colony.[16] Its main criticism was similar to that of the sos, namely that the chiefs were not a suitable voice of the people: "Even granting the dubious claim that the chiefs reflect the popular will, it would not reflect their unfettered will. ... The new Legislative Council would amount to a conclave of feudal lords diluted by the elected Municipal and Rural members and the official membership."[17] Its remedy to this danger was also similar to that proposed by the sos; it advocated direct election of members from the Protectorate, with a literacy requirement for candidates.

When the Stevenson proposals came before the Legislative Council, following their examination by the District Councils and the Protectorate Assembly, they were sent to a Select Committee consisting of the Attorney-General and all unofficial members of the Council plus a number of co-opted extraordinary members,[18] and the Chief Commissioner for the Protectorate.[19] The presence of this official led to the first sign of coming tensions. The three extraordinary members nominated by various Colony political organizations all resigned, claiming that with the Chief Commissioner present, the Para-

13 / See Protectorate Assembly: *Proceedings of the Third Meeting* (May 19, 1948), p. 3, and *Proceedings of the Fifth Meeting* (May 3, 1949), p. 2.

14 / *Proceedings of the Seventh Meeting* (October 3, 1950), p. 88.

15 / *Ibid.*

16 / "Critique of the Governor's Constitutional Proposals," *Sierra Leone Weekly News,* September 13, 1947. I am indebted to Leo Spitzer for bringing this article to my attention.

17 / *Ibid.*

18 / The extraordinary members were three Creoles, Dr R. S. Easmon, A. H. C. Bartlett, a lawyer, and N. A. Cox-George, a lecturer at Fourah Bay College, all put up by a combined meeting of Freetown ratepayers and other associations, and four Paramount Chiefs. The committee thus contained seven Creoles, seven chiefs, and two expatriate unofficials.

19 / *Report of the Select Committee,* Sessional Paper No. 7, pp. 1–2.

mount Chiefs would not be free to speak their minds.[20] The Creole members of the Legislative Council, elected as well as nominated, were more willing to co-operate with the rest of the Select Committee. They agreed to the Protectorate Assembly's request for fourteen members, adding only that they thought the Colony's representation should be increased from four to seven.[21] The chiefs on the committee also took a conciliatory stand, with only one objecting to this increase in Colony representation.[22] Both chiefs and Creoles agreed that literacy was a desirable qualification but that the subject was too delicate for them to make a blanket recommendation.[23] They accepted all the remaining points in the sessional paper, and made the additional recommendation that "consideration should be given to the election by unofficial members of the Legislative Council of four of their number for appointment to Executive Council."[24] The fact that the Creole members proposed this granting of executive power to unofficial members suggests that they did not yet see themselves as a permanent minority in opposition.

The Report of the Select Committee was unanimously approved by the unofficial members of the Legislative Council[25] and a dispatch to this effect was sent by the Governor on June 22, 1948, to the Secretary of State for the Colonies.[26] The Governor recommended acceptance of the changes in representation to seven elected members for the Colony and, for the Protectorate, thirteen elected by District Councils plus one elected by the Protectorate Assembly from among its nominated members. Since the Protectorate Assembly had approved Stevenson's waiving of a literacy requirement whereas the Legislative Council members had opposed it, the Governor recommended leaving it to the discretion of the District Councils.[27] The Secretary of State accepted all of the Governor's recommendations.

20 / Ibid., p. 2. This may genuinely have led them to resign; Laminah Sankoh, a Creole whose sympathy with Protectorate aspirations was indisputable, supported their resignation (Letter to Daily Mail, June 11, 1948). On the other hand, many Creoles were turning against the whole prospect of a Protectorate majority, whether of chiefs or educated men; see below, pp. 49–50.

21 / Report of the Select Committee, p. 2. The Protectorate at that time had 13 districts, with the additional member to come from among the nominated members of the Protectorate Assembly.

22 / Ibid. In the Protectorate Assembly debate, the chiefs had voted down a proposal to increase Colony representation from four to five seats by a vote of 22–5, with two of the five votes in favour being Creole.

23 / Ibid.

24 / Ibid., p. 3.

25 / Legislative Council Debates, Twenty-fourth Session, No. III (June 4, 1948), p. 43.

26 / Sierra Leone. Reconstitution of the Legislative Council in Sierra Leone, Sessional Paper No. 8, of 1948 (Freetown: Government Printer, 1948).

27 / Ibid., p. 7.

This was not the end of the matter, however. The sos sent a memorandum of protest to the British Secretary of State for the Colonies, in which it reiterated its earlier demands for a more democratic form of election to the Legislative Council and criticized the government for the fact that it "has never nominated 'the Progressive and younger element' outside the chiefs' class" to the Council, and in particular had failed to include any non-chief on the Select Committee to consider constitutional changes.[28]

A far stronger outcry was being raised by Creoles outside the legislature. The conciliatory attitude taken by the Creole members of the Legislative Council gave way to arguments resembling those used by the white settlers of Kenya and the Rhodesias. The *Weekly News* stressed Creole fears of being swamped by the "aborigines": "What are the Creoles to the indigenous peoples of the Protectorate? Strangers! They see the Creole in the same light as they see the white man. ... We are not indigenous to Sierra Leone. To add to this is the fact of our own Western culture. ... This council would lead to a lowering of our citizenship. And this is what staggers us and causes us anxiety for dear old England."[29] About the same time, a lecturer in economics at Fourah Bay College, in a pamphlet titled "Crucifixion of Sierra Leone?," proposed restricting the franchise for the new Council to literates, and allocating the seats between Colony and Protectorate in proportion to their number of literate inhabitants, a procedure which would give the Colony a majority.[30] In September 1948 a number of Creole organizations petitioned the British Secretary of State for the Colonies to save them from the prospect of any form of rule by the people of the Protectorate.[31] Not all Creoles had yet reached this point; the doyen of Creole political leaders, Dr Herbert Bankole-Bright, chose this time to announce that his new National Democratic Party would campaign in both the Colony villages and the Protectorate in anticipation of a forthcoming election under the new constitution.[32] He apparently did not follow this up with any pleas for reconciliation between Creoles and countrymen. In the absence of a forceful argument for moderation on the part of any respected Creole leader, Creole opinion rapidly hardened to the point where no compromise would be possible.

On December 21, 1948, the leader of the Creoles in the Legislative Council, Otto During, moved that, in the light of the widespread opposition to the proposed constitutional changes, their implementation be deferred

28 / "Memorandum to the Secretary of State for the Colonies on the New Constitution (Sessional Paper No. 8)" (typescript, n.d.).

29 / *Sierra Leone Weekly News,* August 14, 1948.

30 / N. A. Cox–George, *Crucifixion of Sierra Leone?* (Freetown: New Era Press, n.d. [1948]), p. 15.

31 / See Kilson, *Political Change,* p. 167, for excerpts from the petition.

32 / Advertisement in *Sierra Leone Weekly News,* November 20, 1948.

until they had been reconsidered.[33] Chief Bai Koblo bitterly attacked the motion and, after reminding the Council that the Chiefs of the Protectorate had given shelter to the Colony, suggested that if the Colony and Protectorate were separated, the Protectorate people might reclaim the land they had ceded to the British Crown.[34] The only official intervention in this clash between Colony and Protectorate representatives came when the Acting Colonial Secretary cited an earlier pronouncement of the Governor that "the most important thing about a constitution is not the precise detail of its form, but the spirit in which it is made to work", and added, "The Government does not propose to intervene in this matter."[35] This reference to the "spirit" of a constitution strongly suggested that the main desire of the British was to get complete agreement between the different sections. If the Creoles agreed unanimously that the constitutional proposals needed reconsideration, then the British were prepared to accede to this wish and try to work out a more acceptable compromise. With the officials abstaining, and the unofficial membership consisting of five Creoles, two expatriates, and only three Paramount Chiefs, the motion was passed without a recorded vote.[36]

A few months later, the new Governor, Sir George Beresford-Stooke, attempted to set up a committee representative of all sections of opinion in the country to reconsider the constitution. However, by this time a number of Colony organizations had reached the point of demanding that the Colony be given equal representation with the Protectorate. The Protectorate's spokesmen flatly refused to consider this, with the result that the Governor found it impossible even to get agreement on the composition of a committee.[37] He then appealed to the members of the Legislative Council to take "a last opportunity ... to come together and reach agreement," brandishing the threat that if they failed to do so, he would have no alternative but to implement the proposals as agreed on in 1948.[38]

This pronouncement was no threat to the chiefs, who now had only to sit tight in order to win the most powerful position under the new constitutional order. It served, however, to put considerable pressure on both the educated Protectorate men and the Creoles to compromise with the chiefs in the hope of winning minor concessions.

Another possible combination, the educated men of the Protectorate and

33 / *Legislative Council Debates,* Twenty-fifth Session, No. 1 (December 21, 1948), p. 66.

34 / *Ibid.,* p. 68–69.

35 / *Ibid.,* p. 73.

36 / *Ibid.,* p. 74.

37 / Statement by His Excellency the Governor, *Legislative Council Debates,* Twenty-sixth Session, No. II (April 18, 1950), p. 3.

38 / *Ibid.,* p. 4.

the more radical Creoles, had already been scuttled. In 1949 some former Protectorate members of the Youth League approached Wallace-Johnson to head a national party.[39] Whether such a party could have won much support in either the Colony or the Protectorate is very doubtful; Creole opinion by this time was highly inflamed against any dealings with the Protectorate, and there was little evidence to suggest that a party without support from the chiefs could have made headway in the Protectorate, even if there had been an electoral system in which the ordinary people could participate. But Wallace-Johnson refused to take the position, and a few months later cast in his lot with the diehard Creole resistance movement.[40] At the same time his newspaper made a considerable contribution toward the exacerbation of Creole-Protectorate relations. In January 1950 Albert Margai announced his intention of standing against Otto During in an impending Freetown by-election to the Legislative Council. Although Wallace-Johnson was certainly closer in his general outlook to Margai than to the conservative During, his newspaper strongly attacked Margai, charging that "If there is anyone anxious to widen the gap between the Colony and the Protectorate for his own personal ends it is this young man."[41] and later calling him a "cradle baby" who was not intelligent or experienced enough to represent Freetown.[42] Years later, a number of up-country men still referred to this episode as one of the best illustrations of Creole animosity towards up-country Africans. It marked the death of any possible co-operation between the two westernized elites.

With the rift between Colony and Protectorate apparently irreconcilable, the Governor recommended in May 1950 that the 1948 proposals of the Select Committee be implemented.[43] He did propose two changes to meet

39 / Interviews with A. B. Cotay, October 5, 1965, and Doyle Sumner, October 13, 1965.

40 / Some Protectorate leaders have suggested this showed a basic "Creole" bias in Wallace-Johnson's outlook; others have attributed his unwillingness to head a national party to his inability to get along with the other persons who would have been involved, notably Laminah Sankoh. My own opinion is that he was basically "Creole" at heart. Talking to me in 1965 about the SLPP government's policies, he complained that scholarships were being given to "Kamanda and Santigie [a Temne name] but not to anybody from here [Freetown]." In view of his published charges that the government was favouring Mendes at the expense of Temnes, I found it interesting that he would suggest privately that Temnes as well as Mendes were getting all the opportunities, and only Creoles were being turned down.

41 / *African Standard,* January 20, 1950. The articles in question, it should be added, were not written by Wallace-Johnson himself, but by Bamikole Sawyerr.

42 / *Ibid.,* January 27, 1950.

43 / Sierra Leone. *Reconstitution of the Legislative Council of Sierra Leone, 1950.* Sessional Paper No. 2 of 1950 (Freetown: Government Printer, 1950), pp. 1–2.

the criticisms of the educated Protectorate men: that literacy should be a requirement for membership in the new Council,[44] and that more openings for the educated men be provided on the District Councils by having the Tribal Authorities appoint one extra member for every 1,000 taxpayers above the first 2,000 and giving the District Councils themselves the power to add an additional three members.[45] These changes were only token concessions; they clearly did not reduce the power of the chiefs to ensure that these new members were acceptable to them.[46] The Colonial Office agreed to these proposals and suggested bringing the new constitution into force early in 1951.[47]

The Creole-Protectorate split was by now forcing together the two articulate Protectorate groups on the one side, and a very disparate collection of Creole organizations on the other. The sos appeared to abandon its overt opposition to the chiefs when its Freetown branch passed a resolution in July 1950 demanding that the Stevenson constitution be implemented. After observing that any agreement between the Colony and Protectorate was "most unlikely" because each wanted majority rule, the resolution asked "that the British government be called upon forthwith to implement the said Stevenson proposals ... so as to enable the people of the Protectorate to have a say in the management of their affairs and thus end the shameful and undemocratic policy of taxation without representation."[48] At the same time the various Creole leaders were coming together; Wallace-Johnson, who a year previously had dismissed Bankole-Bright as a man whose "political day is past and over,"[49] now joined with his former antagonist to "advocate one common cause, i.e. the Progressive advancement of the peoples of Sierra Leone as a whole."[50] In August 1950, representatives of all Colony political groups except Sankoh's Peoples Party united to form the National Council of the Colony of Sierra Leone (NC),[51] with Bankole-Bright as its acknowl-

44 / Ibid.

45 / These provisions were embodied in the District Council Ordinance, 1950, No. 17 of 1950.

46 / See Kilson, "Grass-Roots Politics in Africa: Local Government in Sierra Leone," Political Studies, XII, 1 (February 1964), p. 51.

47 / Reconstitution, 1950, p. 4.

48 /Sierra Leone Weekly News, July 22, 1950. I am indebted to Leo Spitzer for calling my attention to this item.

49 / African Standard, August 5, 1949.

50 / Ibid., July 14, 1950.

51 / Ibid., August 25, 1950. The groups which met to form the National Council were reported by the Standard to be: "The Sierra Leone Democracy Party" [National Democratic Party?], the West African Youth League, Sierra Leone Section, the Sierra Leone Socialist Party, the Sierra Leone Political Group, the Rural Areas Council, "the Fourah Bay and Foulah Town communities" and the African unofficial Colony members of the Executive and Legislative Councils.

edged leader. How inflamed Creole opinion had become was shown a few days later, when a letter by Bankole-Bright appeared in the *Weekly News*:

The Protectorate ... came into being after the butchering and massacre of some of our Fathers and Grandfathers ... and their blood streamed in the streets of Mendi Land because they were described as Black English Men showing the White English Men the country. Yes, their blood streamed with the blood of English men and after only fifty years of this treacherous and villainous act Loyal Sierra Leone is asked by the British Government to vacate her seats in their British Legislature (this is what it tantamounts to) for the descendants of the murderers of our ancestors.[52]

The Protectorate leaders were not slow to respond to this attitude in kind. The most widely accepted leader of the Protectorate by this time was the 55-year-old Dr Margai, who had just retired from 22 years of government medical service throughout the Protectorate. Because he was the oldest among the emerging political group in the Protectorate, and because of his wide and varied range of supporters, it was not surprising that "the Doctor" should be considered as the leading spokesman for the Protectorate. It is possible that Dr Margai was more antagonistic towards the Creoles than most other Protectorate leaders; although he had a number of Creole friends, he had perhaps not forgotten his first experiences when he returned from England as a qualified medical doctor in 1927, and was laughed at by Creoles as "the Mende doctor." In any case, when he moved in the Protectorate Assembly on September 29, 1950, that the Government be asked to implement the revised Stevenson proposals as early as possible, there was a somewhat bitter tone to his remarks:

Sierra Leone, which has been the foremost of all the West African colonies, is still saddled with an archaic constitution with official majority. The reason for this backwardness is evidently due to the fact that our forefathers, I very much regret to say, had given shelter to a handful of foreigners, who have no will to co-operate with us and imagine themselves to be our superiors because they are apeing the Western mode of living and have never breathed the true spirit of independence. ... They can never bring themselves to wipe off the superiority complex, and they imagine themselves more like Europeans than like Africans, which is indeed a very sad state of affairs; and moreover, they have never impressed us as being sincere in their actions toward us. ...

Furthermore their arguments have been so unreasonable that to think of opening up the question will only prolong our agony and unhappiness for want of proper representation. Over and above all this, feelings have run so high on both sides that no useful purpose will be served by sitting with them in a committee

---

52 / *Sierra Leone Weekly News*, August 26, 1950. I am indebted to Leo Spitzer for calling my attention to this item.

just now. After we shall have calmed down we shall all be in a better frame of mind to remodel what we have accepted.

. . .

If the 30,000 non-natives of the Colony should attempt a boycott of the proposed election for the new Legislative Council I make no hesitation to assure the government that all of the seats on the Colony side would be occupied by our countrymen. We mean to push ahead, and we are in no way prepared to allow a handful of foreigners to impede our progress.[53]

Most other speakers echoed the same feelings, even if in milder terms. Chief Bai Koblo, seconding the motion, observed that "we in the Protectorate ... must discard all differences for the common good."[54] Chief Gulama, noting that the Creoles came from African stock, said they had come to "consider that they are better and in a better position than us."[55] Albert Margai exclaimed that, if the Creoles boycotted the election, it would serve to bring in responsible representatives from the Colony with whom the Protectorate could deal.[56] Relations between the Protectorate and the Creoles seemed to have deteriorated to the point where compromise was impossible, and the two main interests in the Protectorate, the chiefs and the educated men, were being brought closer together in their common antagonism to Creole extremists. The National Council merely carried the split to its logical conclusion when they petitioned the King in Council a few days later to either annex the Protectorate and declare all its inhabitants British subjects (which they knew full well the British government would not do) or to separate the Colony and Protectorate and grant each its own legislature with full powers, and move the Colony people towards full self-government.[57]

53 / Protectorate Assembly. *Proceedings of the Seventh Meeting* (September 26, 1950), pp. 28–31.

54 / *Ibid.* (September 27, 1950), p. 32.

55 / *Ibid.*, p. 33.

56 / *Ibid.*, p. 38.

57 / The petition appears to have been published for the first time in the *Sierra Leone Weekly News*, February 17, 1951.

4

The 1951 elections: the SLPP takes shape

The new Sierra Leone constitution brought in by the British in 1951 offered a substantial share in policy-making to Africans. Twenty-one of the Legislative Council's thirty seats were to be filled by Sierra Leoneans, seven from the Colony by direct election, one from each of the twelve District Councils, and two from the Protectorate Assembly.[1] More important, "at least four" unofficials drawn from the Legislative Council would be brought into the Executive Council. However, the deep rift between Creoles and countrymen made it doubtful that either group would be able to win a majority in the legislature by itself. It was quite likely that the British would have a considerable say over who was finally chosen to enter the Executive Council.

The electorates which needed to be organized by any group hoping to win this share of power were both small and restricted. The two seats filled by the Protectorate Assembly and the twelve filled by District Councils[2] were all dominated by chiefs. The Colony electorate consisted of some 5,000 relatively well-to-do literate males out of a total population of 123,000,[3] a substantial majority of whom would be Creoles. To win seats, therefore, would not require a massive party organization to contact voters, but it would require, in the Protectorate, a means of appealing to the chiefs and, in the Colony, an appeal that would win some Creole support.

In mid-1951, a number of the leading Protectorate political figures decided to dissolve the SOS and create a political party, the Sierra Leone Peoples Party (SLPP). Among the Protectorate men, there was little doubt that Dr

1 / Two more seats were to be held by nominated unofficial members, but these were to represent European business interests. Only seven were held by officials.

2 / Karene District had been abolished in 1950, and the Protectorate Assembly was empowered to elect a second member to the Legislative Council.

3 / The number of eligible voters is estimated from data for five of the seven seats contained in the *Sierra Leone Weekly News* of November 17 and November 24, 1951.

Margai should lead the new party. He was the oldest among the educated men, and age produced deference. Equally important, as the principal adviser to the chiefs, and a man of highly conservative inclinations, he was most acceptable to the leaders who still held the confidence of the bulk of the Protectorate population, and who more immediately controlled the election of all representatives from the Protectorate.

The other leading figures in the formation of the SLPP were drawn chiefly from the SOS. Albert Margai, Siaka Stevens, Frank Anthony, A. B. Cotay, and several others had been active in that organization. A. J. Momoh had been a founder of PEPU. Kande Bureh, a former teacher who had built himself a powerful political machine as Temne tribal headman in Freetown,[4] contributed an element of strength there.[5] The chiefs for the most part remained in the background, only Chief Gulama playing any active role in forming the SLPP. A few Creoles also helped in its creation. Laminah Sankoh,[6] who had long supported the cause of the Protectorate people and recently formed the Peoples Party, brought in his small group of followers. One of these, H. E. B. John, a secondary school teacher, became general secretary for the Colony and later for all the country, while M. S. Mustapha, an Aku (Muslim) Creole, later became party treasurer.

These men, and nearly all the others prominently associated with the SLPP, were overwhelmingly from the Protectorate's bourgeoisie, and in most cases, from its second generation. Siaka Stevens, whose father had been a soldier in the West African Frontier Force, and who himself had made his mark as a trade union leader, was one of the very few persons in the party who could be considered a self-made man. Much more typical was the Margai family background of a wealthy merchant father. Furthermore, many SLPP leaders enjoyed close links with traditional ruling families; the Margais, the Massallys, Doyle Sumner, and Kande Bureh, for example, were all descendants of Paramount Chiefs. The SLPP's leadership, then, was predominantly composed of the "haves" of both traditional and modern sectors of Sierra Leone.

This situation was accentuated in the Protectorate by the SLPP's method of recruiting local support. Dr Margai's wide range of acquaintances enabled him to go to leading men in most towns of the Protectorate and enlist them as the local leaders of the SLPP. But beyond enlisting a few "big men" in each locality as its representatives, the SLPP undertook little political activity in the Protectorate. It made no effort to enrol a mass membership, or

4 / See Banton, *West African City*, pp. 176–77.

5 / Though only a few tribal people had the vote in 1951.

6 / Born E. N. Jones, and later ordained a minister. Legend has it that he took the tribal name "Laminah Sankoh" as a gesture of solidarity with the Protectorate people. The reason he himself gave for the name change was more prosaic: as a writer in the 1930s he found that he had to take a more African name than Jones to be accepted as a genuine African by editors. See *Vanguard*, July 31, 1951.

to stir up popular participation by rallies or other activities. In Freetown, it was slightly more active, holding regular public meetings in the last half of 1951, but even there it made no real effort to develop a body of committed supporters.

Within the SLPP, the educated men still seemed to be interested in supplanting the chiefs at the national level. Since the chiefs controlled the elections to the national legislature, this was a delicate operation. A few weeks before the elections, the general secretary for the Protectorate asked that "something be put in about Paramount Chiefs [in the SLPP manifesto] as we need their support if the Party is to have *non-chiefs elected in all the Districts*" [italics mine].[7] The manifesto was accordingly amended to include two promises close to the hearts of the chiefs, that their "inadequate" salaries would be reviewed, and that "at all enquiries affecting Paramount Chiefs a Supreme Court Judge [rather than an administrative official] must preside."[8]

However, these promises were not enough to induce the chiefs to elect all the candidates favoured by the SLPP leaders. Paramount Chiefs took eight of the twelve seats filled by District Councils, defeating three persons backed by the SLPP. The SLPP casualties included A. J. Momoh in Bo and Arthur Massally, a lawyer, in Pujehun. Dr Margai was returned unopposed from Bonthe, and two other SLPP leaders, Rev. Dr W. H. Fitzjohn of Moyamba, a Fourah Bay College lecturer, and Rev. Paul Dunbar of Kono, also won seats, as did a fourth non-chief in Koinadugu. Dr Margai's influence was further demonstrated by the election of Albert Margai and Siaka Stevens as the representatives from the Protectorate Assembly. However, the fact that the Protectorate representatives included eight chiefs as against only six non-chiefs suggested that the SLPP leaders would have to work closely with the natural rulers.

Some SLPP officers suspected that the British administration was working against the educated men. H. E. B. John had earlier referred to "a very strong rumor ... that political officers are trying to influence the Protectorate electorate so as to prevent the return of many highly educated Protectorate citizens who are non-chiefs."[9] A. B. Cotay also claimed before the election that "officialdom is trying to influence the chiefs against us,"[10] and A. J. Momoh later claimed that British officials had told the Bo district chiefs that he was hostile to them.[11] While such suspicions were understandable in

7 / Letter from A. B. Cotay to H. E. B. John, October 13, 1951.

8 / *The SLPP Road*, Statement of Policy Issued by the Executive of the Sierra Leone Peoples Party (typescript). I am grateful to H. E. B. John for making available to me the various drafts of this manifesto, as well as considerable correspondence pertaining to this period.

9 / Letter from H. E. B. John to the Editor, *Observer*, n.d. [about September, 1951].

10 / Letter from A. B. Cotay to H. E. B. John, October 13, 1951.

11 / Interview with A. J. Momoh, October 25, 1965.

the light of the electoral system arranged by the British, a much simpler explanation of the chiefs' election victories is that they were in a much stronger position than their commoner rivals and saw no reason why they should defer to them.

The colony presented an even less satisfactory picture for the SLPP leaders. They were not able to contest two Rural Area seats,[12] and of the five remaining Colony seats they were able to win only two on election day.[13] M. S. Mustapha, with his strong Aku Creole base and probably also with the support of the enfranchised countrymen in his constituency, won decisively in Freetown East, polling nearly double the number of votes for the runner-up. A. G. Randle, the only nominee in the remote Sherbro Urban District, which had been largely assimilated into the surrounding Bonthe District, declared for the SLPP shortly after being returned unopposed. But the other three SLPP candidates in the Colony, including Laminah Sankoh and H. E. B. John, were all defeated, each receiving only about two-thirds the number of votes won by their National Council opponents. Although the Colony electorate was clearly not unanimously hostile to the SLPP, the National Council had won five Colony seats against only two for the SLPP. In the Protectorate also the SLPP had only three avowed members elected from the District Councils, and as many defeated. However, the National Council was in a still worse position; it had not even tried to win support outside the Colony.

There seems to have been some uncertainty even in the minds of the SLPP leaders as to just how the chiefs would align themselves when the Legislative Council met. In a letter written a week before the Council was to meet, the SLPP general secretary for the Colony area referred to a garden party planned by the National Council to welcome the chiefs to Freetown, and remarked: "I sincerely wish that if they are invited that none of them will attend. These National Council men ... are now ... going all out to bolster their precarious position by attempting to infiltrate into our ranks and to find fodder for their cheap propaganda campaign."[14] While the chiefs were in "our ranks," it did appear possible that they might be won away. This fear may not have been too serious; in another letter the same day to Dr Margai the general secretary emphasized the strength of the party's position, asserting that the party was "in the majority" and would be able to get its way with the Governor if it was prepared to "stand firm."[15] This letter reported the result of a meeting held that morning between the Governor and four

12 / They withdrew their candidate from Wilberforce and York district, claiming the villagers would not give him a hearing. See *Vanguard*, November 15, 1951.

13 / For full results, see *Sierra Leone Weekly News*, November 17 and November 24, 1951.

14 / Letter from H. E. B. John to A. B. Cotay, November 22, 1951.

15 / Letter from H. E. B. John to Dr M. A. S. Margai, November 22, 1951.

SLPP representatives, Laminah Sankoh, Siaka Stevens, M. S. Mustapha, and H. E. B. John. The delegation made it clear that they were not prepared to accede to the Governor's wish for a coalition between themselves and the National Council:

> We emphasized that we were in the majority in the Legislative Council and therefore we were entitled to claim full unofficial representation in the Executive Council. ... We made it clear to the Governor that we were not mindful whether he gave all the Executive Council seats to the representatives of the National Council, but we were not prepared to join with them in a coalition. ...
>
> The Governor fully sympathised with our point of view. ... He thought, however, that the larger interests of the country demanded the co-operation of the two groups in the Executive Council and even suggested that it be tried for six months. We were stout in our opposition to this, and so stuck to our original position. He finally stated that he would propose certain names to the unofficial members of the Legislative Council next week for acceptance as the unofficial side of the Executive Council.
>
> ...
>
> I could sense at the interview that the strength of our case and our present position is fully appreciated by the Administration. We must, therefore, stand firm and hold together; victory complete and indivisible will be ours.[16]

The Governor, Sir George Beresford-Stooke, seems to have persisted in his hope of a coalition up to the actual meeting of the Legislative Council. Opening the new Council on November 28, he observed that henceforth the Executive Council would make policy, and the unofficial members of this council would therefore have to be persons who enjoyed the confidence of a majority of the elected members of the Legislative Council. He then went on:

> Where there is a well developed "party system" it is the practice for His Majesty the King or his representative to send for the leader of the party which commands a majority and invite him to form a Government. Here in Sierra Leone today I am not sure that the party system is yet quite sufficiently developed for me to introduce a procedure modelled *mutatis mutandis* on that which I have described.
>
> I propose therefore on this occasion to consult unofficial members at a private and informal meeting in the choice of those who are to be invited to join the Government.[17]

The "private meeting" was duly held the following day. While no official record of the proceedings was ever published, there was a fair degree of agreement in later discussions among the participants about what happened.[18] Everyone agreed that a split soon appeared between the National Council

16 / *Ibid.*
17 / *Legislative Council Debates,* Session 1951/52 (November 28, 1951), pp. 8–9.
18 / *Ibid.* (January 31, 1952), pp. 263–85.

members on the one side and the SLPP on the other, although there was some disagreement as to what brought this out into the open. The National Council members claimed that Dr Margai rejected the idea of a further meeting between the unofficial members on the grounds that "we have had four years of this," which led Dr Bankole-Bright to observe, "We are like two hills that cannot meet."[19] The SLPP account was that Bankole-Bright made his "two hills" remark before Dr Margai rejected a further meeting.[20] In any case, once it became apparent that there was no hope of compromise, the Governor called for a division, in which all but one of the members from the Protectorate voted to support the SLPP.[21] Such an outcome was hardly surprising. The National Council's attitudes towards Protectorate people assured its rejection by the chiefs. Dr Margai at least was an acceptable leader, even though some of his lieutenants might want to undercut the chiefs' position.

As leader of the majority party[22] Dr Margai was able to determine the selection of the unofficial members of the Executive Council, the embryonic ministers.[23] He chose a group judiciously balanced by region and tribe, but almost completely excluding the chiefs. The five men whose choice he approved were his brother Albert; Siaka Stevens, a northerner and the country's leading trade unionist; Chief Bai Farima Tass, a leading northern chief; A. G. Randle, who although half Mende, was from a Colony seat; and M. S. Mustapha, who had a strong following in Freetown, particularly among his fellow Muslims.[24] A willingness to conciliate Colony opinion was suggested

19 / *Ibid.*, pp. 276–77.

20 / *Ibid.*, p. 285.

21 / See Dennis Austin, "People and Constitution in Sierra Leone: The SLPP Comes to Power," *West Africa*, No. 1858 (October 4, 1952), p. 917. Essentially the same account is given by Laminah Sankoh in *The Two Ps, or Politics for the People* (Freetown, n.d.), pp. 16–17, although Sankoh further claims that two days earlier, *before* the Legislative Council opened, the same members had signed declarations that they belonged to the SLPP, and these declarations were sent to the Governor (p. 13). If true, this might raise some question concerning the propriety of the Governor's action in trying to bring about a coalition. However, I have found no other reference to these declarations.

22 / Or as Dr Margai himself termed it, "the group I was dealing with – call it a party, a small community, or merely a number of people." *Legislative Council Debates*, 1951/52 (January 31, 1952), p. 271. Certainly the SLPP fell far short of being a party in the sense of an organized body.

23 / His control was still negative; as he described the process, the Governor "suggested names and I approved or disapproved of them." *Ibid.*

24 / In 1953 they were sworn in as Ministers and allocated responsibility for specific departments. Dr Margai became Chief Minister and took responsibility for Health, Agriculture and Forests; Mustapha, Works and Transport; Randle, Trade and Commerce; Stevens, Lands, Mines and Labour (which covered all diamond arrangements); Albert Margai, Local Government (entailing control over chiefs), Education

by Dr Margai's rationale for bringing in Mustapha and Randle: "We would have made a vital mistake if we had decided to rest just on our majority and select only Protectorate people. But we decided as the position was almost two to one, that we were to appoint the executive in the same proportion, and therefore asked that the only two Colony members who were on our side should be brought in."[25] This statement also underlined the somewhat marginal position of Creoles in the SLPP; they were clearly not considered essential to "our majority."

In view of the importance of the chiefs in bringing the SLPP to power, it may be asked why only one chief became a member of the Executive Council. One reason was that, as local rulers, chiefs could not afford to spend the time in Freetown that an Executive Council position would entail.[26] Furthermore, a number of chiefs had doubts about the wisdom of being too closely involved in central government administration which could compromise their position as local leaders.[27] While this feeling never was strong enough to lead them to demand a legislative chamber of their own, it did restrain them from demanding a larger share of executive positions.[28] Finally, many of the chiefs were only interested in central government insofar as it affected their local interests. All they needed to do was maintain a watching brief.

Overshadowed by the Creole-countryman split was a feature of the SLPP that was to loom increasingly large within the decade: the heavy representation of Mendes in its leadership. Besides Dr Margai, other leading members of the SLPP in 1951 included his brother Albert, Chief Julius Gulama, A. J. Momoh, Arthur Massally, and William Fitzjohn who, while not "tribalist," nevertheless were all Mendes.[29] The only northerners on the inner circle of the SLPP were Kande Bureh, whose base was in Freetown, Stevens, and Alex Cotay. In view of the casual and personal nature of SLPP's organization and

and Social Welfare. Chief Bai Farima Tass became a Minister without portfolio. Defence, external affairs and finance remained in the hands of the Governor and the Financial Secretary, and the Colonial Secretary, the Attorney-General and the Chief Commissioner for the Protectorate continued as members of the Executive Council.

25 / *Ibid.*

26 / From the time Ministers were first created in 1953, Paramount Chiefs holding ministerial rank always were Ministers without Portfolio. Although they would frequently assume departmental responsibilities on an acting basis, they did on the whole spend less time in Freetown than other Ministers.

27 / As illustrated by Chief Bai Koblo's remarks, above, p. 46.

28 / Though the then pro-Creole *Daily Mail* claimed several chiefs were in fact dissatisfied with the Executive Council appointments, saying that two places should have gone to chiefs. December 5, 1951.

29 / Fitzjohn actually was half-Creole. One might also add to this list Frank Anthony and Doyle Sumner, who were Sherbro but were often identified with the Mendes.

the scarcity of northerners who could join the small educated elite of the Protectorate, this Mende predominance was probably unavoidable. Further-more, in the earlier years it does not seem to have produced any tribal or regional favouritism; all the Protectorate men were too unified in their antagonism to the Creoles to be greatly concerned about tribal differences. Nevertheless, as time went on and continued Mende predominance seemed less inevitable, northern suspicions were destined to grow.

Throughout this initial phase of the transfer of power, one element was strikingly absent from the Sierra Leone scene. In the Gold Coast the 1946 (Burns) Constitution's provisions for a chief-dominated legislature were ren-dered obsolete and replaced by 1951. No small part of the pressure for constitutional change came from the middle strata of Gold Coast society, the wage workers and primary school leavers in the towns and the cocoa farmers in the countryside, whose demands were taken up by the United Gold Coast Convention and later the Convention Peoples Party.[30] In Nigeria much the same process took place, with the National Council of Nigeria and the Cameroons, the Zikists, and other groups with strong popular support in the larger urban areas demonstrating clearly to the British administration that a more representative form of government was needed.[31] But in Sierra Leone none of the participants in the constitutional struggle made any attempt to arouse mass support. Even if some leaders had tried this as a means of forcing the hand of the British, it is doubtful that they would have met the same response as in the two better developed colonies. There was some agita-tion against particular chiefs,[32] but it would have taken an exceptionally astute organizer to translate these localized discontents into a militant nationalist movement. The urban workers were divided along Creole-countryman lines and, in any case, showed few signs of concern about the political arrange-ments being negotiated between the British and the contending African elites.[33]

For their part, the SLPP leaders showed no desire to draw the masses into politics. All of them came from the bourgeois sector of Sierra Leone society,

30 / See Dennis Austin, *Politics in Ghana, 1946–60* (London: Oxford University Press, 1964), pp. 49–152.

31 / See Coleman, *Nigeria,* pp. 271–318.

32 / See below, pp. 75 ff.

33 / Kilson's hypothesis that mass pressure on the colonial system creates a situation of instability in which the African elite(s) gain the chance to play a mediating role seems to me to be less applicable to Sierra Leone than to other West African states (see *Political Change,* pp. 105–23). There was not enough mass involvement in politics to create any threat to stability, nor is there any evidence to suggest that the British administrators feared such instability would develop if they did not institute constitu-tional reforms in the colony. They seem to have been motivated much more by two external factors: the British government's policy of decolonization, and the examples of the Gold Coast and Nigeria.

and all had close ties with the traditional rulers. It was hardly surprising that they showed no inclination to effect a radical transformation of Sierra Leone society, but were content to work out a transfer of control of the existing political institutions from the British to themselves. How little interest the SLPP leaders had in developing a mass political base, and how difficult they found it to handle mass demands, was to be shown clearly in their first decade in office.

PART THREE

The entrenching of the oligarchy

5

The turbulent years: social mobilization and political protest

If an observer were to look solely at the constitutional evolution of Sierra Leone in the decade after 1951, he would have the impression that the territory proceeded smoothly to its independence in 1961. The legal transfer of power from the British to Sierra Leoneans took place in a series of orderly and limited steps. In 1954 the government accepted an independent commission's recommendation that there should be a two-stage movement towards universal adult suffrage. In 1956 the legislature's membership was enlarged and provision was made for the separate election of Paramount Chief members and ordinary members, the latter by direct popular voting. In 1958 all British officials except the Governor left the Executive Council, with the Governor retaining control over defence and foreign affairs only, while the African Ministers functioned virtually as a Cabinet. Finally, in 1960 an all-party conference reached agreement with the British on an independence constitution for Sierra Leone, and this constitution was put into effect on April 27, 1961.

But this surface appearance of orderly constitutional progress was misleading. While the first of these constitutional changes were taking place, major upheavals occurred in the diamond-digging areas of Kono and in much of the Northern Province. The first of these upheavals, the diamond rush, created a substantial body of men who had been torn from their habits of traditional obedience, while the second, the Northern tax riots of 1955–56, showed the existence of a widespread and profound discontent with local political structures. Together they indicated a considerable potential for a political movement directed against the existing social order.

Meanwhile the SLPP was becoming firmly entrenched as the spokesman for that same social order. While the balance of power between the chiefs and the Western-educated men shifted markedly toward the latter, neither group showed much awareness or understanding of the mass rumblings.

However, they did show considerable skill in accommodating a variety of regional and local demands that could be met within the existing social order, and in absorbing the leaders of opposition parties.

The most striking feature of this period is the failure of opposition parties to capitalize on the discontents that had already surfaced. Part of this failure may be attributed to the SLPP's techniques for containing opposition political activity. But much more significant was the nature of the opposition parties themselves. Neither in the composition of their leadership nor in their attitudes were the two major opposition parties of this period notably more radical than the SLPP. In the course of challenging the SLPP, the opposition parties drew into their second-level ranks a number of young men who were later to lead more radical movements, but their leaders were as "bourgeois" as those of the SLPP, and almost as unlikely to demand a major restructuring of society. We could say of this period that the battles between the SLPP and the opposition parties were mainly over place and position, while the more broadly based opposition to the SLPP's rule found no constitutional outlet.

THE DIAMOND RUSH

The diamond rush to the Kono, Kenema, and Bo districts in the mid-1950s was the greatest single force for social mobilization in Sierra Leone during the decade. Its political repercussions, while less immediately visible than those of other events, were far reaching. Most immediately, it preoccupied the fledgling SLPP Ministers and the British officials to the exclusion of nearly all other problems. It led directly to the formation of the first radical class-oriented opposition party in Sierra Leone, the Kono-based Sierra Leone Progressive Independence Movement (SLPIM). Less directly, it helped stimulate discontent in the whole Northern Province, contributing in the first instance to the 1955–56 riots, and later to the formation of a class-conscious political party, the All Peoples Congress. More generally, it introduced and diffused new values and new attitudes towards traditional authority through much of the country.

The diamond rush got underway in 1952, and exploded to crisis proportions in 1954. Van der Laan[1] has provided estimates of the number of persons involved in the rush which give a graphic idea of its scale (Table 5: 1). Some idea of the impact of this rush on the process of social mobilization in Sierra Leone can be gained by noting that the total number of persons

1 / Laurens van der Laan, *The Sierra Leone Diamonds* (London: Oxford University Press, 1965). While primarily an economic study, this book contains numerous observations on the social implications of the rush. I have relied to a great extent on this study and Mr van der Laan's personal comments and suggestions in preparing this section.

calculated by the Labour Department as being engaged in wage employment in this period was between 75,000 and 80,000;[2] in other words, as many men left the land in a three-year period to search for diamonds as had left it over half a century to seek wage employment. The rush was so great that the Director of Agriculture attributed a marked drop in rice production in 1955 to the fact that there were not enough people left to work the land.[3]

TABLE 5:1

Estimated number of
diamond diggers, 1952–58

1952	5,000
1953	5,000
1954	30,000
1955	40,000
1956	50,000–75,000
1957	50,000–70,000
1958	25,000

Source: H. L. van der Laan,
The Sierra Leone Diamonds,
p. 65.

The way in which men were involved in diamond mining was of even more significance socially than the numbers involved. Like men drawn into any mining or industrial operation, they found themselves "strangers" in their place of work, thrown together with men from many other places and tribes, and thus largely freed from the restraints on behaviour of traditional authority. But unlike men entering a highly organized industrial operation, they were not subjected to any industrial discipline which could serve as a substitute for traditional controls. The result was that the diamond mining areas for several years verged on anarchy, with armed bands of as many as 400 to 500 men raiding the SLST and licensed miners' areas, and on occasion doing battle with the police.[4] A further feature of some importance was that diamond digging tended to be a seasonal operation because of the flooding produced by the rains, and thus the persons engaged in it returned to their home areas each year, possibly with their new attitudes towards law and order. The impact of the diamond rush was thus diffused much more rapidly than that of a large-scale mining operation, where men would be more likely

2 / This figure is from Annual Report of the Labour Department, 1957, p. 3. It excludes all the diamond miners except those employed by SLST.

3 / Sierra Leone. 1955 Report of the Department of Agriculture (Freetown: Government Printer, 1957), p. 1.

4 / See, for example, Daily Mail, October 18, 1958. Similar clashes had been going on since 1955.

to stay for two or three years before returning home.[5] Diamond mining, then, not only maximized the juxtaposition of old and new values, but ensured that the new values acquired possessed a very high disruptive potential.

In view of these potentially disruptive effects, it is significant that the largest contingents of miners seemed to come from the Northern Province. While there is no direct evidence of the tribal origins of the miners during the height of the rush,[6] in 1963 there were some 36,000 Temnes and Limbas in the principal diamond-mining chiefdoms.[7] The total of licenced miners at this time was 45,000,[8] though of course not all the Temnes and Limbas were engaged directly in mining. In the Kono District diamond-mining chiefdoms, where Mendes also were "strangers," the Temnes and Limbas outnumbered the Mendes by a 2:1 ratio.[9] Other northern tribes, notably the Mandingos, also provided substantial numbers of participants in the diamond industry, both in digging and trading.

Even if we were to assume that the number of Northerners engaged in diamond mining in the 1950s was substantially less than the number present in the diamond areas in 1963, we could still say that some 20,000 men, or one out of every ten adult males in the Northern Province, had gone diamond hunting at some time. If, as is more likely, the numbers were at least as great during the 1950s as in 1963, then about one out of every five men from the Northern Province had taken part.[10] This massive and abrupt immersion in a social milieu free from traditional restraints undoubtedly contributed

5 / By contrast, many of the workers in the iron mine at Marampa lived in Lunsar for 10–30 years. The same stability among mine workers for a large corporation is suggested by Epstein's study of a Copperbelt town. See A. L. Epstein, *Politics in an Urban African Community* (Manchester: Manchester University Press, 1958), p. 12.

6 / The only evidence regarding origins is the fact that some 45,000 non-Sierra Leoneans were expelled in 1956. Assuming that most of these foreigners were miners, this would mean that there were probably some 25,000–30,000 Sierra Leonean miners of all tribes present.

7 / Calculated from *1963 Census of Sierra Leone*, Vol. II, Table 3.

8 / Personal communication from Ken Swindell, formerly of the Geography Department, Fourah Bay College.

9 / This apparently low proportion of Mendes could be misleading, since the heaviest concentrations of miners were in Mende chiefdoms in Kenema. While Northerners mining in these chiefdoms stand out as "strangers," it is not possible to determine how many Mendes were engaged in mining in Mende chiefdoms. Mendes may well have stayed in their own chiefdoms to dig, while the Temnes, who had no diamonds at home, had to scatter to all the diamondiferous chiefdoms. On the other hand, Mendes mining in their home area, while freed from dependence on their chief for land, would still remain more closely bound by the web of traditional obligations.

10 / This makes no allowance for the possibility of turnover among the diggers. Judging by the frequency with which I encountered individuals who had gone digging for "a year or two," turnover may have been fairly high, and consequently an even larger proportion of the adult male population involved.

significantly to the willingness of Temnes to challenge the authority of their chiefs from 1955 onward.

The SLPP Ministers had been overseeing their departments for little over a year, and had already negotiated one new agreement with the Sierra Leone Selection Trust[11] when the rush to the diamond districts made it apparent that maintaining the SLST's legal monopoly of diamond digging was no longer feasible, even if the SLPP Ministers had found it politically expedient. The government began fresh negotiations with SLST in 1954, with the goal of introducing "licensed mining of diamonds on a scale which shall allow substantial participation by the people of this country."[12] Under an agreement reached in September 1955, SLST surrendered its rights to all but 450 square miles (containing the most promising reserves) in the Kono and Kenema districts, in return for compensation of £1,570,000.[13] The rest of the country was opened to licensed Sierra Leonean miners. By March 1956 some 1,500 licences had been issued, which would indicate that up to 30,000 of the former illicit diggers were now under licence.[14] In the same year some 45,000 African foreigners were expelled from the diamond areas.

However, smuggling of diamonds still remained a major problem, since under the 1955 agreement the Diamond Corporation, an agent for de Beers' Central Selling Organization, was the sole legal purchaser for the African miners' output. The Diamond Corporation's margin of profit plus an export duty collected by the Sierra Leone government encouraged the growth of a lively smugglers' market in Monrovia, which offered better prices. The magnitude of this smuggling is hard to determine, but it was certainly substantial; the value of diamonds smuggled out of the country (and therefore producing very little benefit for Sierra Leone) probably exceeded legal exports by a factor of one-and-a-half or two (see Table 5: 2). This smuggling was only halted by a joint project of the government and the Diamond Corporation, a Government Diamond Office which shaved its margin of profit and the government's export duty in order to offer dealers prices competitive with those in Monrovia. Although both illicit mining and smuggling continued to make difficulties for the government, their scale was at last reduced to manageable proportions.

A feature of the diamond crisis which was to lead to considerable discontent, particularly in Kono, was the method of licensing Sierra Leoneans to

11 / This agreement, reached at the end of 1953, raised the rate of tax from 45 to 60 per cent of profits, and added other benefits for the government, in return for a promise of increased protection for SLST against illicit digging and selling of diamonds. See *Legislative Council Debates,* Session 1953–54, Vol. I (December 17, 1953), pp. 155–7.

12 / Statement of government policy in *Daily Mail,* April 29, 1955.

13 / For details of the Agreement, see *Legislative Council Debates,* Session 1954–55, Vol. IV (September 30, 1955), pp. 49–57.

14 / Each licensee was permitted to employ up to 20 men.

dig for diamonds. While the Mines Department issued the licences, the Chief and Tribal Authorities of the chiefdom concerned had to give their approval, and a number turned this into a very lucrative business for themselves. Though theoretically a farmer who was dispossessed from his land when it was leased to a digger was supposed to get a share of the proceeds, in practice most of the money went to the chief and his associates. Since the chiefs who benefited from this SLPP-supported arrangement showed their gratitude by siding with the SLPP, it is not surprising that many of their people developed both a strongly anti-chief class consciousness and a close identification with a party staunchly opposed to the SLPP.

TABLE 5:2

Legal and illegal exports of diamonds
from Sierra Leone, 1957–60

	Value of exports (£'000)	
Year	Legal	Illegal
1957	6,425	9,500–15,000
1958	7,184	11,000–15,000
1959	6,808	8,500–15,000
1960	16,474	Very low

Sources: W. E. Minchinton, "The Sierra Leone Diamond Rush," *Sierra Leone Studies*, January 1966, p. 82. The low estimates of smuggling are contained in the Governor's 1960 address to the House of Representatives, *Sessional Paper* No. 1 of 1960, p. 9.

This party, the Kono Progressive Movement (later the Sierra Leone Progressive Independence Movement), grew out of essentially regional dissatisfaction with the 1955 diamond agreement. Most Kono leaders felt their undeveloped district should have had a larger share of the benefits of the diamond mining,[15] and the District Council went so far as to vote to reject the agreement. The Chairman of the District Council, T. S. Mbriwa, a prominent druggist, member of a ruling family, and political rival of Paul Dunbar, then formed the KPM on the program of using Kono's wealth to develop Kono. The behaviour of the chiefs in the diamond areas attracted to the KPM most of the young men and the more discontented of the ordinary

15 / Even the SLPP leader in Kono, Rev. Paul Dunbar, remained conspicuously silent when all other members of the Legislative Council were congratulating the government on the agreement. See *Legislative Council Debates*, Session 1954–55, Vol. IV, pp. 49–69, 77–146.

farmers, and helped give it a distinctive "class" attitude which co-existed with its regional particularism throughout the 1950s.

THE FREETOWN RIOTS: URBAN ANTI-ELITISM?

Just when the SLPP Ministers and their British officials were engaged in negotiations with the SLST over diamond mining, further trouble was building up in Freetown. In February 1955, the usually tranquil capital was torn by two days of rioting and looting, following a strike of two major trade unions. The strike itself was sparked by a rapid increase in the cost of living in late 1954, probably due in large measure to the diamond rush[16] and consequent demands by leading unions for wage increases. After protracted negotiations between the unions and a group of European firms, a deadlock was reached and the unions went on strike February 9, 1954.[17]

Two days after the strike started, mobs of up to 1,000 people surged through the east and central areas of Freetown (the areas most congested by recent immigrants from the Protectorate), stoning police, looting some Syrian shops, and attacking individuals wearing collars and ties.[18] At the same time mobs attacked the homes of three Ministers, Siaka Stevens, M. S. Mustapha, and Albert Margai. In Mustapha's house "nearly every pane of glass was destroyed," his furniture smashed and his personal effects and £300 in cash stolen. A crowd also entered Stevens' house, destroying much of his furniture and personal effects.[19] While such attacks might seem like simple vandalism, the purpose behind them may have been more involved; a similar destruction of chiefs' property in the northern riots was a form of reprisal for the chiefs' exploitation of their people. In the case of the three Ministers, an indication of the motive behind the attacks appeared a year later in the Legislative Council. Demanding an inquiry into the personal finances of Ministers, I. T. A. Wallace-Johnson said there were rumours that one Minister, since entering the Executive Council, had built houses worth £9,000 and had £5,000 cash in various banks; another Minister owned £6,000 worth of buildings, a transport company and 100 acres of land

16 / See van der Laan, *The Sierra Leone Diamonds*, p. 171. For an official account of the events leading up to and during the strike, see the *Report of the Commission of Inquiry into the Strike and Riots in Freetown, Sierra Leone*, during February 1955 (Freetown: Government Printer, 1955). Hereafter referred to as *Shaw Report*.

17 / The leader of one of the two unions involved, Marcus Grant of the Artisans and Allied Workers, had announced there would be a "General Strike." However, it was by no means clear whether this was intended to mean anything more than a strike by all members of the two unions involved. See *Shaw Report*, pp. 12–13.

18 / For a comment on this last feature, see *West Africa*, No. 1998 (June 11, 1955), pp. 529–30.

19 / *Daily Mail*, February 15, 1955.

in a rural area village; a third Minister was supposed to be able to sign cheques up to £30,000 "without the slightest doubt of the cheque being dishonoured by the bank."[20] The three Ministers appear to have been Stevens, Albert Margai, and Mustapha, respectively; it is worth noting that it was the houses of these three which were attacked, since rumours about ill-gotten wealth, whether true or not, would certainly be widely circulated around Freetown.

The extent to which the outbreak of violence took the Sierra Leoneans as well as the British officials unawares[21] was indicative of the lack of contact between the SLPP leaders and the urban working class. Dr Margai's already distrustful attitude towards "Freetown people" was undoubtedly strengthened by this episode; from that time on he appeared to regard the unions in particular as a permanent opposition.[22] His attitude during the strike was unyielding; when it was suggested to him on the second day of rioting that the first step should be to approach Marcus Grant to call off the strike, he refused to have anything to do with Grant.[23] His posture was shared by other SLPP leaders. Mustapha joined him in refusing to deal with Grant[24] and the party newspaper ascribed the riots to the "unemployed or the very dregs of the working class."[25] The SLPP leaders' position suggested they were not much concerned with the problems of men who had left the traditional

20 / *Legislative Council Debates*, Session 1955–56, Vol. VIII (November 5, 1956), pp. 520–1. Both Margai and Stevens, replying to Wallace-Johnson, stressed that he was merely repeating rumours; Margai further commented that it was "repulsive" that a person's financial position should be inquired into because he was a Minister. Mustapha said that the claim that a businessman could sign cheques for £30,000 was something Wallace-Johnson should be proud of, since it was evidence that Africans were gaining economic control of the country. *Ibid.*, pp. 522–23, 531.

21 / The total lack of anticipation on the part of British officials and Sierra Leonean Ministers that there might be trouble suggests a considerable degree of ineptitude. The Governor had left for a tour of the Provinces just before the strike was called, and was clearly not aware of the explosive situation in Freetown; he did not return when the strike was called, but only when the riots erupted. The police had taken only "routine precautionary moves" against the possibility of trouble *(Shaw Report,* p. 12).

22 / For example, in 1963, after the unions had attempted to call a general strike to protest the government's failure to take any action on a commission of inquiry which showed serious shortcomings in government accounts, Sir Milton suggested on his return from a trip abroad that the unions had been careful to call the strike in his absence: "They know how we dealt with them in 1955. We would have taken the same strong action." *Daily Mail,* September 23, 1963. A similar attitude was expressed elsewhere in the party. Before the 1960 constitutional conference, the *Vanguard* criticized the opposition parties for failing to include a trade unionist in their delegations. "Labour organizations as such have never been identified with the SLPP ... [but] with the opposition parties." January 27, 1960.

23 / See testimony of Ernest Beoku-Betts, the Vice-President of the Legislative Council, before the Shaw Commission. *Daily Mail,* April 26, 1955.

24 / Ibid.

25 / *Vanguard,* February 18, 1955.

framework of authority. Here was one element of the population which would have to look elsewhere for a means of making its demands heard.

UPHEAVAL IN THE COUNTRYSIDE: THE 1955–56 TAX RIOTS

While the SLPP leaders' failure to anticipate the Freetown riots was serious enough, an infinitely more dangerous situation for them erupted a few months later in the Northern Province. The SLPP had come to power through the backing of the Paramount Chiefs and continued to rely on the chiefs as its point of contact with the rural population. Now a widespread rebellion was to reveal that in the North at least, the chiefs had so far lost the confidence of their people that it was questionable whether they could continue to control their societies.

Anti-chief riots were not unheard of in Sierra Leone; there had been sporadic uprisings, for example, in the Bo, Kenema, Kailahun, and Pujehun districts between 1948 and 1951, largely as a protest against excessive and irregular levies by chiefs.[26] Three Paramount Chiefs were subsequently deposed; it is significant that all the depositions occurred before the introduction of SLPP members onto the Executive Council. Equally significant is the fact that all the major riots occurred in the south. Until the 1955 explosion, northern chiefs had apparently retained a much stronger hold on their subjects than had the Mende chiefs in the south.

Several factors contributed to the Temne chiefs' continued ability to hold the obedience of their subjects. We have already noted the paucity of cash crops in the north, the lack of schools, and the relative scarcity of towns. Until the 1950s there had been few opportunities for wage labour, apart from migration to Freetown; the Marampa iron mines and the Tonkolili gold fields did not employ sizable numbers of men. Until the 1950s, fewer men in the north had been drawn out of the habit of obedience to their natural rulers than in the south.

Two other features of northern society reinforced obedience. Islam, with its strong tradition of obedience to existing powers, was considerably more widespread in the north than in Mende country. The second feature peculiar to the Temnes was the fact that their chief, unlike those of the Mendes, Limbas and other tribes, was a semi-sacred figure with strong religious as well as secular attributes;[27] whereas chieftaincy among the Mendes was essentially based on instrumental values, among the Temnes it was consum-

26 / See the *Report on the Sierra Leone Protectorate for the Years 1949 and 1950* (Freetown: Government Printer, 1952), pp. 4–5, and *ibid.*, 1951, pp. 2–3. The most serious of these riots involved some 5,000 individuals protesting against the chief of the Luawa Chiefdom, Kailahun District. Some 15 years later his successor, from a different ruling house, was driven from office by a similar popular uprising.

27 / See Banton, *West African City*, p. 195.

matory.[28] The Mende chief simply could not demand of his people the degree of blind obedience demanded and obtained by the Temne chief.[29] But this ability to demand almost unlimited obedience contributed to the Temne chiefs' downfall; when they altered their own roles, they undermined their hold.[30]

At the same time as the chiefs were changing the rules to benefit themselves, the people of the Northern Province were coming increasingly into contact with modernizing influences. The road network, with its influx of lorry drivers, was less developed than in the South, but it was spreading; towns, while less numerous, were increasing in number;[31] and schooling, while open to fewer children than in the south, was growing at a rapid rate.[32] Finally, the fact that the diamond rush had begun just a year before the riots erupted must not be overlooked. While this is conjectural, it would be surprising if the return home of the first diamond miners had not stimulated questioning of the need to obey the chiefs' every whim.

The process of mobilization could work two ways on the ordinary villager. Up to a point, it provided a safety valve; the spread of the road network and opportunities for wage-earning in the towns or diamond-digging in Kono allowed men who felt frustrated by traditional constraints to leave the chiefdoms. But the roads brought lorry-drivers and traders to the villagers; the establishment of schools brought teachers indoctrinated in Western ways of thought. The stay-at-home villager thus was exposed to new voices questioning the right of the chiefs to rule in the old way, and at the same time he could see the chiefs changing their behaviour to take advantage of the money economy.

We have already considered the long-term changes in the behaviour of

28 / See David Apter, *The Politics of Modernization* (Chicago: University of Chicago Press, 1965), pp. 84 ff.

29 / This was illustrated during the 1955–56 riots by two meetings in Mende chiefdoms at which the chiefs agreed to drop their demands for tax increases, with almost no attempt to seek compensating adjustments. See *Daily Mail*, December 14 and 15, 1955. Temne chiefs took the attitude that their people should obey their wishes without question.

30 / Cf. Apter, *Politics of Modernization*, pp. 102–103.

31 / Most of the annual reports for this period do not provide a breakdown between provinces, and after about 1952, some also stopped providing a breakdown between the Protectorate as a whole and the Colony. However, from the time of the *1931 Census* to the *1963 Census*, we can note that the number of towns in the Northern Province of 1,000 or more people rose from 21 (out of 65 in the whole Protectorate) to 55 (out of 156 for all the Province).

32 / Primary school enrolment in the Northern Province rose between 1948 and 1963 from 3,291 to 27,000 pupils. *The Development Programme in Education for Sierra Leone* (Freetown: Government Printer, 1964), p. 6. The five Mende districts, with 11 per cent more population, had 60 per cent more children in school.

the chiefs which took place as the money economy gradually spread across Sierra Leone: the levying of irregular taxes to provide personal possessions for the chiefs; the constant demands from Native Administration officials for "dashes" (bribes) and "shake-hands"; the use of forced (free) labour for the chiefs' personal benefit; and the use of the local courts to enforce these extortions.[33] It remains to consider certain more immediate changes that brought simmering discontents to a head.

Concurrently with the assumption of responsibilities by African Ministers in the central government, Tribal Authorities were encouraged to take on more responsibility at the local level. As part of this encouragement, the District Commissioners terminated their customary habit of being present when the village headmen paid their taxes to the Native Administration. The Cox Commission noted: "as the several Native Administrations gained strength and endeavoured to stand on their own feet, many requested the District Commissioner not to attend on such occasions, and he, anxious to encourage them, agreed. ... This, in the light of later events, was a mistake, the taxpayers not being at all satisfied that the full amount of money paid in by the several collectors was properly accounted for."[34]

A further diminution of the District Commissioner's authority came in 1954 when the government passed an ordinance permitting unofficial members to replace the DCs as heads of District Councils.[35] Within a year all districts but Koinadugu had installed unofficial presidents. In doing so, some of them managed to create the impression that the new District Council Presidents were taking over the functions of the District Commissioners; it was reported that the people of Port Loko were told that Paramount Chief Bai Koblo was being "installed ... as their first African District Officer."[36] The Cox Commission found that many people believed that because the District Commissioner was no longer President of District Council, "the Paramount Chief is now bigger than the D.C."[37]

At the same time the District Commissioners found themselves more cut off from contact with the people. In 1954, with the introduction of the Sierra Leone Police Force into the Protectorate, the Court Messengers were disbanded. These men, besides acting as the DC's police force, had served as an intelligence service, apprising him of all events of interest. Their abolition cut the DC off from much information about the growth of unrest.[38]

The Sierra Leonean Ministers and the British officials, however, increasingly gave the impression that they were backing the chiefs against their

33 / See above, pp. 30–32.
34 / *Cox Report*, p. 117.
35 / District Council (Amendment) Ordinance, No. 9 of 1954.
36 / *Daily Mail*, August 10, 1955.
37 / *Cox Report*, p. 219.   38 / *Ibid.*, p. 220.

people. The Cox Commission reported that many persons felt "the D.C. sends us back to the Paramount Chief," and that "the present District Commissioners are backing the chiefs rather than the poor people."[39] At the same time Dr Margai asserted in the Protectorate Assembly that "our chiefs must be protected" against intrigues and attacks by their people, and criticized "lack of confidence" charges against chiefs as a "myth" stirred up by people out to "ruin the Protectorate."[40] His words were supported by actions; there was the conspicuous reliance by Ministers on the chiefs and Tribal Authorities as their point of contact with the people, and the fact that no chief had been deposed since the SLPP came into office.[41]

A final legal straw was piled on the taxpayers in 1955 when the District Councils were given the power to levy a rate, called a "precept," on their chiefdoms.[42] This precept added to the head tax[43] of about ten shillings an additional charge ranging from nine to sixteen shillings in 1955, and due to increase by an average of just under five shillings more in 1956.[44] Although this meant that legal local taxes had just about tripled in three years, the government seemed oblivious to the rising discontent with the taxes, levies, and extortion in local government. A few weeks before the first riots took place, a line story in the *Daily Mail* warned that an increase in the local tax was inevitable for the coming year. It continued: "A spokesman of the Ministry of Local Government yesterday denied allegations of excessive taxation in the Protectorate of Sierra Leone. He said that the Minister of Local Government, Mr. Albert Margai, was conscious that there was a limit to the size of local taxes, and would not impose heavy taxes which would bring hardships to the people".[45]

The match was applied to this powderkeg by the member of the Legislative Council for Port Loko, Paramount Chief Alikali Modu III. With the consent of his Tribal Authority, he proposed in November 1955 to levy an

39 / *Ibid.*, pp. 218, 222.

40 / See Protectorate Assembly. *Proceedings of the Eleventh Meeting* (October 28, 1954), pp. 13–14.

41 / See *Cox Report*, p. 250. It should be added that for the period 1945–56 there had been a total of only eight depositions, two of them from the north. The colonial regime does not seem to have been much more harsh on chiefs than the SLPP. Also, the lack of northern depositions suggests there were fewer complaints reaching the ears of the government from that area than from the south.

42 / The Local Tax Ordinance, 1954, Section 20. Up to this time the Councils had been financed principally by central government grants.

43 / Until 1954 still called a "House Tax," although in practice levied on all adult males. The change in terminology in the 1954 Ordinance apparently led many people to think that a new tax was being imposed. In fact, the number of taxpayers did jump sharply under the new Ordinance. See *Cox Report*, p. 112.

44 / *Ibid.*, p. 255.

45 / *Daily Mail*, October 21, 1955.

extra five shillings on all taxpayers in his chiefdom to build himself a new house. When a group of men in Port Loko town protested to the District Commissioner,[46] the chief at first said he would only give up the special levy if his people would provide free labour in lieu of payment.[47] By the time the DC had persuaded him to withdraw the five-shilling levy unconditionally, a crowd of 8,000 people were also complaining about extortion by the chiefdom assessment committee, lack of consultation by the Tribal Authorities, and the fact that the total chiefdom taxes were too high.[48] No compromise could be reached and tension rose, with demonstrations against the chief.

Other disturbances followed quickly. The chief of Buya Romende Chiefdom, Port Loko District, was driven from his house and his chiefdom remained unruly until he went into voluntary exile two weeks later.[49] Crowds in Marampa-Masimera Chiefdom burned the house of a section chief;[50] in Makari-Gbanti Chiefdom, Bombali District, a meeting erupted into a riot in which eight buildings belonging to Tribal Authorities were burned.[51] Trouble flared up in the more western parts of Port Loko and Kambia Districts a few weeks later; in Kambia town and neighbouring villages, most of the property belonging to the Minister without Portfolio, Paramount Chief Bai Farima Tass II, was destroyed,[52] while in Samu Chiefdom, Kambia District, 28 houses belonging to Tribal Authorities and property belonging to Paramount Chief Yumkella were destroyed.[53] That the "riots" were not just an orgy of destruction was suggested by the fact that the riot leaders in one instance returned goods taken from a Lebanese shop, and in another helped a Lebanese load a launch with his goods before burning his shop, which was owned by Chief Yumkella.[54] When they encountered the police, the Kambia rioters stressed that they were not out to fight the police, but only to kill their Paramount Chiefs and burn their property.[55] It was clear in all parts of the country where riots occurred that they represented an expression of popular feeling towards the chiefs; as the Commission suggested, the situation was one "better described as civil war than as a disturbance."[56]

By the time the riots finally died down in mid-March of 1956, property had been destroyed and chiefs and Tribal Authorities attacked in nearly every chiefdom in the Port Loko and Kambia Districts, and in several chiefdoms in the Bombali, Tonkolili, and Moyamba Districts. At least 23 men had been killed as a result of police actions, and three policemen had been kidnapped and were believed murdered.[57] Property damage estimated

46 / See *Daily Mail*, November 19, 1955, and *Cox Report*, p. 19.
47 / *Cox Report*, p. 20.
48 / *Ibid.*, p. 23.
49 / *Ibid.*, p. 28–29.
50 / *Ibid.*, pp. 30–31.
51 / *Ibid.*, pp. 33–34.
52 / *Ibid.*, p. 57.
53 / *Ibid.*, p. 63.
54 / *Ibid.*
55 / *Ibid.*, pp. 57, 59–60.
56 / *Ibid.*, p. 82.
57 / *Ibid.*, p. 85.

at £750,000 by the Commission of Inquiry had been done in the affected areas;[58] nearly all of the buildings and supplies destroyed belonged to the chiefs and tribal authorities. Much of the destruction seemed to be aimed at destroying wealth which the people regarded as having been taken from them illegitimately; in one chiefdom, the corrugated iron roofing of a chief's house was systematically rendered useless by holes punched through every sheet with a spike.

The government's handling of the northern riots showed graphically the limitations imposed on the SLPP leaders both by their own preconceptions and by their key supporters. In partial mitigation it may be noted that for much of the year before the riots broke out, the two most capable Ministers, Siaka Stevens and Albert Margai, as well as the Chief Commissioner for the Protectorate, had all been preoccupied with negotiating a new mining agreement with Sierra Leone Selection Trust and trying to cope with the diamond rush. It may also be noted that the Sierra Leoneans' responsibilities were considerably less than those of their British officials. Even so, the actions and attitudes of the SLPP leaders did not indicate much comprehension of the nature of northern discontent.

When the disturbances first occurred, the government's immediate reaction was to send out Paramount Chiefs on a tour of the troubled districts to explain the government's intention of holding District Council precepts to their 1955 level.[59] A month later, nearly all the Ministers were busily touring the provinces,[60] but they still seemed oblivious to the meaning of the riots; it was announced that on his tour Albert Margai would "have talks with *Tribal Authorities*" [italics mine].[61] It was not until March 1956 that any direct contact with the "strikers" took place on an extensive basis, and then through a conciliation committee of Kande Bureh and A. B. Magba-Kamara, two prominent northern members of the SLPP.

Given the sources of their information, it was hardly surprising to find the government attributing troubles along the railway line to hooligans who were not residents but had come in to stir up dissatisfaction against the chiefs and Tribal Authorities.[62] Another possibility, that the whole situation arose from plots by opposition parties, was suggested by the SLPP's provincial newspaper at the end of December:

The trouble now is in the Provinces where the younger vigorous peasant class are agitating for lower rates of taxation which seem more or less rather unreasonable and fantastic. It seems to a large extent that the same unseen forces which were responsible for the February situation are now again at work in the game of

58 / *Ibid.*, p. 15.
60 / *Daily Mail*, December 29, 1955.
62 / *Ibid.*, December 9, 1955.

59 / *Ibid.*, pp. 87–98.
61 / *Ibid.*, January 27, 1956.

power politics. This journal will not agree with backdoor methods. If people have anything to offer, let them come out with it boldly and courageously, instead of playing up to the emotions of ignorant people.[63]

In a statement on January 26, 1956, Dr Margai finally appeared to recognize the gravity of the situation. After saying it was desirable that District Councils and Tribal Authorities should be more representative, he noted that the Provincial Administration had revealed "many complaints not connected with tax, and a full enquiry into underlying causes would be necessary. Government has decided that such an enquiry should be held as soon as possible and that the terms of reference should also include the use of force during the disturbances. The commissioners will be appointed and the inquiries pursued and concluded as speedily as possible."[64]

A commission under the chairmanship of Sir Herbert Cox, QC, a former Chief Justice of both Northern Rhodesia and Tanganyika, was formed two months later,[65] and after holding hearings in all the riot areas, issued a damning indictment of the behaviour of the chiefs and of the laxity of administrative control over them. Citing instance after instance of greed, extortion, and corruption on the part of the chiefs and of all the persons involved in native administrations, it commented that it had found "a degree of demoralization among the people in their customary institutions ... which has shocked us,"[66] and termed the clashes of the people against their chiefs "a civil war rather than a disturbance."[67] However, it could see no alternative to the chiefdom as the local unit of administration. The District Councils had failed utterly to be either representative or effective.[68] The chiefdom was a "natural" unit which commanded the loyalty of its inhabitants; most witnesses made it clear that they still had great respect for the office of chief,

63 / *Observer* (Bo), December 31, 1955.

64 / *Ibid.*, January 27, 1956.

65 / Its other members were A. T. A. Beckley, a retired Creole civil servant who had been a strong supporter of the SLPP and also a member of the Keith-Lucas Commission; A. J. Loveridge, an English Colonial Office administrator from the Gold Coast; and Mr. Justice S. P. J. Q. Thomas, a Nigerian judge, who had to retire from the commission proceedings because of ill health and took no part in the final report.

66 / *Cox Report*, p. 9.

67 / *Ibid.*, p. 82.

68 / *Ibid.*, pp. 205–206, 212–16. While I am inclined to agree with Kilson's contrary judgment that the "District Councils represent a more modern (rational) system of local government than Native Administrations" and therefore ought to supplant them as the basic unit of local government (*Political Change*, pp. 212 ff.), I am a bit dubious of his argument that the main difficulties besetting the District Councils could be attributed to the predominance of the Native Administrations. It would appear to me that on the basis of their performance the District Councils' members were even more likely than chiefdom councillors to serve their personal interests, although they were less prone to act in the interests of a ruling group of a particular chiefdom.

if not for its holder, and that what they objected to was the illegal extra taxes, licence fees, and fines which the money economy had made it possible for the chiefs to extort from them.[69] To meet these objections, the Commissioners proposed replacing the Tribal Authorities by smaller, more representative bodies,[70] and by improving central government supervision of the local authorities.[71]

Whether these reforms would have been effective if they had been tried is questionable; there probably were not enough men available in Sierra Leone who were honest, prepared to serve in the chiefdoms, and capable of carrying out the administrative tasks required. In any case, it is hard to see what use such reforms would have been. With an average population of about 13,000–14,000, and an average annual revenue of just over £3,200[72] out of which came not only the chief's salary but also those of the Speaker, Court President, chiefdom clerk, and other officials, the chiefdoms clearly could not hope to finance many of the development projects such as wells and feeder roads which were being increasingly demanded. To work through the chiefdoms would be to maintain a politics of the *status quo,* with financial limitations curtailing the possibilities of change through local government units.

In any case, the government showed little willingness to accept the findings of the Cox Report. Its own analysis[73] dismissed Cox's "oversimplification" that local maladministration was to blame, and instead attributed the uprising to "the unsettlement following upon the war, the decline of moral standards in general, the undermining of respect for law and order following on widespread discoveries of diamonds and the economic consequences."[74] In the South, people began to "detest and resent as extortion and oppression practices which they had previously accepted," and as a result a number of chiefs were deposed, and some effort was made to "democratize" the Tribal Authorities.[75] In Temne country, by contrast, the people were so loyal to their chiefs that they were unwilling to report abuses to the administrative officers. It was the diamond boom and increasing communication between North and South that spurred the northerners to act and changed their attitude "from one of consent or tolerance to one of bitter resentment."[76]

69 / *Cox Report,* pp. 150–51.
70 / *Ibid.,* pp. 174–86.
71 / *Ibid.,* pp. 225–26.
72 / Kilson, *Political Change,* p. 215, cites a total revenue of £626,097 for 141 Native Administrations in 1956, of which £165,972 went to District Council precepts. This figure, of course, does not include illegally collected sums, but these were clearly not available for general revenue.
73 / Sierra Leone. *Statement of the Sierra Leone Government on the Report of the Commission of Inquiry into Disturbances in the Protectorate* (Freetown: Government Printer, 1956).
74 / *Ibid.,* p. 6.
75 / *Ibid.*
76 / *Ibid.,* p. 2.

While there was some truth in the government's suggestion that education, better communications, and economic changes had made men more conscious of the oppressiveness of practices they had previously tolerated, the implication that the chiefs' behaviour was not undesirable *per se* was a bit hard to swallow. The government did take steps to remedy the worst abuses; it prohibited a large number of types of fees and licences, forbade any forced labour, and promised to institute inquiries into the conduct of chiefs, sub-chiefs, or headmen whose conduct might have contributed to the uprisings.[77] The conduct of fifteen chiefs and eight other chiefdom officials was investigated in 1956 by three special British commissioners, including two former Chief Justices of other colonies.[78] They found the conduct of eleven chiefs to have been "subversive of good government"; the government accepted their findings and deposed four of the chiefs, required five more, including the Minister without Portfolio and another member of the Legislative Council, to resign, and suspended the other two.[79] However, it may be noted that within four years three of the nine chiefs deposed or forced to resign, as well as the two who had been suspended, were reinstated in office.

Even these actions went much further than the SLPP's supporters would have liked. In the debates on both an opposition motion of censure on the government's handling of the uprisings, and a bill to abolish forced labour, almost all SLPP members who spoke claimed that the chiefs were being made scapegoats. In the debate on the forced labour bill, Chief Koker claimed "this abolition of forced labour under native law and custom ... is mainly made to usurp the right of chieftaincy ... one side cannot all the time be sacrificing for the sake of development."[80] In the debate on the Cox Report, Chief Gamanga claimed that the "shake-hands" termed by the Commission a form of extortion was a universal African form of hospitality, that the report was one-sided in blaming the chiefs because the opposition parties had played a part in stirring things up, and that bringing in "young men" rather than tribal elders was wrong.[81] Chief Dura, who also asserted that "the chiefs are made the scapegoats," levelled a serious charge against the British officials:

Who was responsible for this breakdown? ... I suggest, sir, that it was primarily the District Commissioners with the blessings of the Provincial Commissioners. While I have no cause to quarrel about some of these recommendations, I would

77 / Sir David Edwards of Uganda and Sir Harold Willan of Malaya and Basutoland.

78 / Sierra Leone. *Reports of the Commissioners of Enquiry into the Conduct of Certain Chiefs and the Government Statement Thereon* (Freetown: Government Printer, n.d.) and *Further Reports of the Commissioners of Enquiry*, etc. (Freetown: Government Printer, n.d.)

79 / *Ibid.*

80 / *Legislative Council Debates*, 1955/56, VIII (October 16, 1956), pp. 338–9.

81 / *Ibid.* (October 23, 1956), pp. 420–22.

suggest that in view of the attitude of some District Commissioners and the atmosphere of intrigue that exists in some chiefdoms, Government must consider appointing more and more African District Commissioners and sending the other District Commissioners to work in the central offices in Freetown.[82]

The same charge that the officials were responsible for stirring up trouble was made by Dr Fitzjohn[83] and Chief Koker.[84] Other members, particularly Albert Margai, stressed that the opposition parties were responsible for fostering the trouble.[85] There was very little willingness on the government side to concede that the chiefs' own actions were largely to blame for the uprising. Dr Margai appeared to be taken aback by the refusal of the chiefs to acknowledge their own failings:

I have often spoken in this House that if we have to move toward progress we must move hand in hand with our chiefs, and I feel a little bit hurt when some of them get up and say they have a doubt in their minds. I think they are doubting the one who is their greatest friend. I do not ask that they should go on pressing their subjects but that they should continue ruling their people. ... My conscience would not allow me to uphold a chief who goes on oppressing his people. But a chief who has not done any wrong, I am always here to uphold him.[86]

Besides protesting in the Legislative Council, the chiefs tried to organize politically. It was first rumoured that they would form a new political party in the North;[87] later they formed a pressure group known as the Sierra Leone National Association whose aims included the preservation of "the sovereign rights" of Paramount Chiefs "as provided by International Law, and as to the treaties and agreements made between various Kings and the late Queen Victoria."[88] All the officials of the association were members of the Legislative Council. It is possible that this display by the chiefs of their willingness to come together to defend their privileges may have had some effect in influencing the government to override the recommendation of the Cox Commission that no special compensation be paid for losses suffered by the victims of the rioters;[89] the government ultimately paid substantial sums in compensation to a number of chiefs.[90]

82 / *Ibid.*, pp. 433–34.
83 / *Ibid.* (October 22, 1956), p. 407.
84 / *Ibid.* (October 23, 1956), p. 417. Another founder of the SLPP told me that British officials had fomented the riots as revenge against the chiefs for the latter's role in starting the SLPP.
85 / *Ibid.* (October 24, 1956), p. 451. Siaka Stevens also implied that the opposition parties had played a role in stirring up trouble. *Ibid.* (October 23, 1956), p. 426.
86 / *Ibid.* (October 25, 1956), p. 480.
87 / *Daily Mail*, October 2, 1956.
88 / *Ibid.*, December 5, 1956.
89 / *Cox Report*, pp. 14–15.
90 / The Riot Damages (Provinces) Commission recommended a total of £394,360

Against this strong pressure from the strategically located indigenous elite, the main counter-pressure seems to have come from the British Colonial Office. In September 1956 a vigorous young Governor, Maurice Dorman, replaced the ailing Sir Robert Hall. One of his first acts was to tour the riot areas, emphasizing that the government was determined to stop the "big men" abusing their power and that it was going to use the District Commissioners as its channel for hearing complaints.[91] One high SLPP official, who blames the riots on "the feudalistic tendencies of the chiefs," claims Dr Margai was told that before there could be any further constitutional advances he had to show he had the confidence of the country by damping down the riots and winning the forthcoming District Council elections. A further indication that it was British pressure that forced the government to go as far as it did in implementing the Cox recommendations appeared in Dr Margai's defence of a bill to abolish the right of the chiefs to claim forced labour: "... we should be very careful to consider the international complement of the whole thing. We are rapidly advancing towards self-government and it is a thing which we should by all means try to eradicate in our midst. ... [At the International Labour Organization there was] some embarrassment to the Home Government that a certain amount of it still exists in a Colony governed by the British Crown. ... But at the same time we *do not expect to really abolish communal labour* [italics mine]."[92] He then went on to suggest that Tribal Authorities could describe what they meant by "communal labour" and that this could be permitted by the Governor in Council. His whole attitude seemed to be that abolishing this privilege of the chiefs was a distasteful necessity. The same attitude was apparent in his remarks the following week when he wound up the debate on an opposition motion of censure over the Cox Report: "The impression has been given that chiefs have been very much dissatisfied, or are made scapegoats. We have to understand that if we are running the country as a Government there are certain recommendations which would be doing more harm to the country by not implementing them and that is one ... if we have a Commission which comes all out and says that an inquiry should be held in a certain number of chiefdoms, we shall be doing more harm to ourselves as a country and to even chiefs, if we say no."[93]

The outcome of this conflict between the chiefs and British officialdom

in compensation, and the Government apparently accepted this. See the Commission's *Final Report* (mimeo. Freetown, 1960), p. 1528. Chief Yumkella was awarded £32,290 (p. 240).

91 / See *Legislative Council Debates*, Session 1955/56, VIII (September 27, 1956), p. 3; also *Daily Mail*, September 22, 1956.

92 / *Debates*, 1955/56, VII (October 16, 1956), p. 349.

93 / *Ibid.* (October 25, 1956), p. 477.

was largely a victory for the chiefs. Beyond the immediate actions of banning a number of fees and licences, prohibiting all forced labour, and instituting inquiries into the conduct of specific chiefs, the government did little to change local government. A reform of the District Councils planned before the riots, direct election of non-chief members, was implemented, but such a reform was fully in the interest of the educated non-chief members of the SLPP, and in any case the chiefs still held between a quarter and a third of all the seats in each District Council. The Tribal Authorities remained almost unchanged; while a small Chiefdom Committee came into greater use, this body was just as much under the control of the chief as was the Tribal Authority itself. Central supervision of the two levels of local government was not noticeably strengthened.

The SLPP leaders' actions in dealing with the northern tax riots indicated a potentially dangerous inability on their part to handle demands of this nature. While the rioters' demands were essentially "reactionary" in that they apparently wanted a return to British supervision,[94] many of them could probably have been swung behind a party proposing radical changes. It was certainly clear that the current behaviour of the chiefs could not continue indefinitely without drastic repercussions. Yet the SLPP leaders appeared to be incapable of imposing the necessary restrictions on the chiefs' behaviour. To determine how far the SLPP was indeed bound to the chiefs, we shall now turn to a consideration of the governing group's organization and attitudes.

94 / *Cox Report,* p. 17. Ten years later, a highly respected opposition leader asserted to me that people up-country were again telling him that they would rather have the British back than continue under the rule of their chiefs.

6

The SLPP: the hegemony of an elite

We have seen that the SLPP were able to assume office mainly because the Paramount Chief members of the Legislative Council were prepared to support the leadership of Dr Margai rather than that of the Creoles. The SLPP leaders had had little scope for displaying organizational talents in the 1951 elections. Since the electorates consisted of either a few hundred well-to-do voters or a conclave of the Paramount Chiefs of a district, the personal following of a candidate was almost bound to carry more weight than his party affiliation. What remained to be seen was whether the SLPP leaders had the ability or the inclination to change this situation and build an organization which would be able to appeal directly to an enlarged electorate, and to stimulate the development of a national consciousness.

It quickly became apparent that the SLPP leaders were doing little in the way of party-building. Writing in 1952, Dennis Austin observed: "The party is ... weak in branch organization. Although the National Executive claims a total paid up membership of between 7,000 and 10,000, it is doubtful whether it can reckon on more than half-a-dozen local branches."[1] Three months later, announcing the opening of the party's headquarters, the party paper noted that "the *clerk in charge* is Mr. F. A. Sesay [italics mine]."[2] Three years later the *Daily Mail* lamented in an editorial: "Interest in things political in this country is almost nil ... Once a political party has been formed for one reason or the other, usually to afford a handful of people a chance to run for immediately pending elections, and that object has been achieved, then there is very little heard of and from that party until election time comes around again ..."[3] How true this was for the SLPP was shown

1 / "People and Constitution in Sierra Leone: The Danger of Easy Success," *West Africa*, No. 1859 (October 11, 1952).

2 / *Observer*, January 24, 1953. It should be added that the party did have a General Secretary at this time, but he held another full-time job as a teacher.

3 / "Almost Dead," *Daily Mail*, January 13, 1956.

by attendance at its 1956 national convention, the first it had held since 1953.[4] A total of only 70 delegates attended; Paramount Chiefs Alikali Modu III and Bai Farima Tass II apparently represented the entire Northern Province.[5] In view of the fact that both of these chiefs were shortly to be deposed for their contributions in bringing about the recent riots, it might be suggested that in the North at least, the SLPP was not entirely representative of popular opinion.

The SLPP's lack of any meaningful organization can be attributed at least in part to Dr Margai's personal preference for working through the traditional institutions. Finding no pleasure in appealing to a mass audience, he tried as far as possible to utilize small meetings with the chiefs, Tribal Authorities, and other notables; the following description of a trip around the Protectorate was typical: "Dr. Margai has been addressing District Councils to explain the present set-up of the Government. He discusses with members of District Councils and prominent men and women some of the country's problems."[6] Some of his Ministers sought their information from the same restricted circle; a report of a trip by the Minister without Portfolio to "look into local needs" mentioned several consultations with members of the Legislative Council and other prominent local leaders, but no meetings with the common people.[7]

This failure of the SLPP leaders to build an alternative channel of contact with the people forced them into a symbiotic relationship with the chiefs. While the SLPP leaders negotiated with the British new constitutional arrangements which protected the interests of the chiefs as a class but at the same time retained for themselves the ability to impose sanctions on any individual chief, the chiefs ensured that their people supported the SLPP. Despite the apparent breakdown in the north of the chiefs' hold on their people during the 1955–56 riots, they generally managed to keep up their end of the arrangement. Their continued hold was suggested by the SLPP rally in the Southern Province (one of the few signs of local party activity in these years) at which a meeting of 1,000 people elected their Paramount Chief president of the local SLPP branch and their Chiefdom Speaker, Treasurer.[8] It was further suggested by the comment attributed to a Kambia District villager who, speaking of the candidates in the forthcoming election, remarked: "We are looking to the chief to whomever he will direct us."[9]

4 / *Daily Mail*, November 23, 1955. The party had held a rally in the Protectorate in 1954, organized by local branches and attended by Ministers, but had held only executive meetings in 1955.

5 / *Ibid.*, March 26, 1956.

6 / *Observer*, February 7, 1953.

7 / *Ibid.*, March 28, 1953.

8 / *Daily Mail*, August 29, 1956.

9 / Quoted in D. J. R. Scott, "The Sierra Leone Election of May 1957," in W. J. M.

Even among urban and literate groups the chiefs retained high prestige which probably could be translated to some degree into political influence. Little noted that in Bo Town in the early 1950s the Paramount Chief was still accorded some deference by the educated elite,[10] while Gamble found in a survey of the Temne town of Lunsar in 1959 that "Paramount Chief" was among the most highly rated occupations, above such "modern" positions as diamond-dealer, magistrate, and education officer.[11]

The close identification of the chiefs with the governing party undoubtedly had advantages for all concerned. The chiefs' participation in the modern political procedures of elections helped make these new procedures comprehensible and legitimate for the bulk of the electorate. With its legitimacy in the eyes of the masses thus underpinned by the chiefs, the SLPP government could afford to devote less energy to ensuring its own acceptance than was the case with governments less securely rooted in tradition. In the short term at least, it also appeared to benefit the SLPP leaders by sparing them the difficulty of building an autonomous party structure to organize the mass of the people. The chiefs, for their part, could rest assured that their interests would be safeguarded by an SLPP government.

From the point of view of developing an effective political party, however, the SLPP's reliance on the chiefs was little short of disastrous. Since the members of the Legislative Council had won their seats not through any party support but through their personal efforts, it was not surprising to find them showing practically no interest in preserving a united party front or in establishing a strong party organization which might be turned against them. Dr Fitzjohn, for example, felt it necessary to deny in 1952 "that I happen to be an internal opposition member of the government," and then proceeded to attack the government's policies on the cost of living and on education.[12] The party press frequently complained bitterly about the lack of interest in party affairs shown by the members of the legislature:

There are three or four SLPP elected members in the Legislative Council who jumped into the bandwagon for the sweets of office, but who are not supporting the party financially and are doing very little to strengthen it in their chiefdoms. ... It is time the National Executive of the Party takes disciplinary action against these men by asking them to resign if they cannot fulfil their financial obligations to the party. They should be made to realize that the Party's programmes are

Mackenzie and Kenneth Robinson, *Five Elections in Tropical Africa* (Oxford: Clarendon Press, 1960), p. 173.

10 / Kenneth Little, "Structural Change in the Sierra Leone Protectorate," *Africa*, xxv (July 1955), p. 225.

11 / David P. Gamble, "Occupational Prestige in an Urban Community (Lunsar) in Sierra Leone," *Sierra Leone Studies* (N.S.), 19 (July 1966), p. 105.

12 / Legislative Council Debates, Session 1951–52 (January 28, 1952), p. 145.

being held back for lack of money. These men would be receiving about £ 600 of taxpayers money this year; they should keep faith with the Party that makes it possible for them to receive this allowance.[13]

A few months later, the newspaper became more specific, attacking one member for failing to appear at a party committee meeting in Bo,[14] and charging that another member had never called a meeting in his constituency to tell the people what their representatives were doing.[15] The backbenchers defended themselves by claiming that they were kept in the dark by the Ministers; the one who had been accused of failing to call meetings said the Ministers "sometimes took major decisions without consulting backbenchers or the Executive of the Party."[16] A party executive meeting in September 1953 complained that the Ministers had not carried out the statement of policy of the executive, and that only one Minister, Albert Margai, had revealed the policy of his Ministry to the public.[17]

However, none of these complaints produced any effective action. There is no evidence that any member of the Legislature was ever disciplined for failing to inform his constituency about party policies, except by the electorate at the next election. Nor is there any evidence that any of the Ministers improved their relations with the backbenchers. The one step taken was to co-opt three members of the SLPP executive who were not in Parliament into the Parliamentary caucus, so that "there should be some links between those in power and those out of power," in the words of one of those co-opted. This was not a victory for the non-parliamentarians since they were heavily outnumbered in the caucus; it was simply a recognition of the fact that the caucus was a more important decision-making body than the SLPP executive.

Since the lack of an extra-parliamentary party structure gave the chiefs an important role in the SLPP, we should consider the extent to which the chiefs acted as a single group, and the conditions under which they appeared to get their way. We have already noted one situation, the aftermath of the 1955–56 northern riots, where the chiefs were generally united in opposition to proposals for change, and to a very large extent succeeded in preventing those proposals being implemented.[18] We can now consider another rather different situation in which the chiefs appeared divided in their views.

It will be recalled that most of the educated Protectorate men, speaking through the SOS, did not regard the Tribal Authorities as a suitable elec-

13 / "Discipline in the SLPP" (editorial), *Observer*, January 3, 1953.
14 / *Ibid.*, March 28, 1953.
15 / *Ibid.*, May 2, 1953.
16 / *Ibid.*, September 5, 1953.
17 / *Ibid.*
18 / See above, pp. 83–84.

torate for the Legislative Council or favour the continued dominance of the chiefs in the legislature. What they wanted was a system of direct elections on a broad franchise which would enable them to appeal directly to the people and thus reduce their dependence on the chiefs. However, lacking a party organization, they would still need the good will of the chiefs even if the franchise were widened. They could not therefore afford to impose a wider franchise if the chiefs were unwilling to accept it.

To resolve this dilemma, in June 1954 the government set up an independent Commission for Electoral Reform under the chairmanship of Bryan Keith-Lucas of Nuffield College, Oxford. The Leader of the Opposition, Dr Bankole-Bright, and A. T. A. Beckley, an slpp supporter, represented the Creole community; Y. D. Sesay, the vice-principal of Bo School, and Banja Tejan-Sie, a lawyer, both represented the younger educated Protectorate men, while the chiefs were represented by Paramount Chief Kai-Samba, one of the most capable and progressive of their number.[19]

During the five weeks of hearings held by the Commission throughout Sierra Leone, it became clear that there was no coherently organized body of opposition to the principle of extending the franchise. The younger educated Protectorate men, not surprisingly, all favoured the extension; their attitude was well summed up by M. J. Kamanda-Bongay of Bo (later a Minister), who commented that it was astonishing that in 1954 the question of whether universal adult suffrage should be introduced should be the subject of a commission of enquiry.[20] More interesting, because less predictable, were the views of the Paramount Chiefs who testified. There were a few who opposed the principle of popular elections, for example, the one illiterate chief from Kailahun who objected to a taxpayer franchise because it would mean all men were equal.[21] But the majority of chiefs who testified favoured either a universal or a taxpayer franchise; of the seventeen chiefs who appeared to testify personally before the commission, five favoured a universal franchise, six a taxpayer franchise, and only six the existing system, with two of these adding that they thought a broader franchise could be introduced in about 15 years' time.[22] To some extent these attitudes towards the franchise appeared to depend on whether the chiefs concerned were literate; all those favouring the universal franchise were literate, three of the six favouring a taxpayer franchise were literate, while four of the six favouring the existing system were illiterate. A slight tendency towards a similar division along literate/illiterate lines appeared in the attitudes of the District

19 / See *Report of the Electoral Reform Commission* (Freetown: Government Printer, 1954), p. 1. Hereafter referred to as *Keith-Lucas Commission*.
20 / Keith Lucas Commission. *Transcript of Evidence* (typescript), August 4, 1954.
21 / *Ibid.*, August 11, 1954.
22 / Compiled from *ibid.*

Councils, which were still dominated by the chiefs. As suggested by Table 6:1, those districts with the largest proportion of literate Paramount Chiefs tended to be the ones in favour of widening the franchise, although the relationship is by no means clear cut.

TABLE 6:1

Relationship between percentage of literate Paramount Chiefs in districts and stand of District Councils on question of widening franchise

District	Literate chiefs (%)	Attitude of District Council			
		Universal franchise	Taxpayer franchise	Existing system	No opinion
Bo	55		×		
Moyamba	50				×
Pujehun	50	×			
Kenema	50			×	
Kailahun	47		×		
Bonthe	44		×		
Kambia	42	×			
Kono	31			×	
Bombali	30			×	
Tonkolili	27		×		
Port Loko	16		×		
Koinadugu	9			×	

Sources: Data on literacy of chiefs from Protectorate Handbook, 1954; on attitudes of District Councils, from Keith-Lucas Commission, Transcript of Evidence (typescript), passim.

The pattern of testimony before the Keith-Lucas Commission showed that "the chiefs" did not form a monolithic bloc. The literate chiefs appeared to feel, as did the educated non-chiefs, that all men should have a voice in government, and perhaps they also considered that the long-term interests of chieftaincy were best safeguarded by a withdrawal from political leader-ship.[23] The non-literates, for their part, may have been less willing to recog-nize that changes were taking place in their relations with their people. In view of this apparent division along literate/illiterate lines, it is significant that 60 per cent of the chiefs who testified were literate, whereas only 38 per cent of all the Protectorate chiefs were literate at that time. It is quite likely that the demand for extending the franchise appeared to the Commission to be more widely supported than was in fact the case.

The Commission recommended a two-stage progression towards universal franchise, the first stage to be in time for the election due in 1956. This stage provided for a taxpayer (or in effect a universal male) franchise in the Pro-

23 / Cf. Bai Koblo's views expressed in 1948; above, p. 46.

tectorate, and an income (or in effect a universal) franchise in the Colony.[24] The second stage, to be introduced in time for the second general election, was to be the universal franchise. The commission also recommended that Paramount Chiefs be given separate representation in the legislature. The old system of contesting against non-chiefs both lowered the status of the chiefs and placed the non-chief at a great disadvantage.[25] It also recommended that the non-chief members from each chiefdom on the District Council be elected directly rather than appointed by their Tribal Authority.[26] The government accepted all these proposals, and ultimately brought them into force in time for the 1956 District Council and 1957 general elections.

The question of how much representation the chiefs should retain in the national legislature was outside the ambit of the Keith-Lucas inquiry. This question, however, needed to be settled before a further election, since to implement the Keith-Lucas proposals would eliminate the representation of chiefs in the existing Legislative Council. The other major forum for the chiefs, the Protectorate Assembly, was abolished in 1955 on the grounds that its functions had been superseded by the Legislative Council. It was necessary, therefore, to introduce further constitutional changes to safeguard the chiefs, even apart from the desirability of further steps towards self-government.

Dr Margai had first called for proposals on the next stage of constitutional advance in December 1954,[27] but the Freetown riots delayed the submission and publication of proposals until October 1955.[28] The SLPP National Executive, on which the younger educated men predominated over the chiefs, proposed a unicameral 52-seat legislature, with one of the three seats from each district to be reserved for a Paramount Chief.[29] The SLPP's most radical

24 / The Protectorate franchise was to include women who paid tax, were literate, or owned property – a small minority. The Colony franchise was to include all men and women of 21 or over who either occupied premises rated at £2 annually or had a yearly income of £60, and who had resided in the area for the previous six months. The literacy requirement for Colony voters was to be dropped. While in 1954 there may have been some grounds for the Creole belief that the income requirement would exclude a large number of tribal residents of Freetown, by the time the election was held in 1957 nearly every resident could plausibly claim to meet this standard. See *Keith-Lucas Report*, pp. 5, 7, and Scott, "The Sierra Leone General Election of May 1957," pp. 182–83.

25 / *Keith-Lucas Commission*, pp. 14–15. This view was shared by most of the chiefs who testified before the Commission, as well as by practically all non-chiefs.

26 / *Ibid.*, p. 10.

27 / *Legislative Council Debates*, Session 1954–55. Vol. I (December 22, 1954), p. 413.

28 / Sierra Leone, *Collected Statements of Constitutional Proposals, September 1955* (Freetown: Government Printer, 1955).

29 / *Collected Statements*, p. 7. Besides the 36 seats thus allocated to the Protectorate, three additional seats were to be given to the three main Protectorate urban areas, and the remaining 13 seats were for the Colony.

proposal was that all officials other than the Governor should be removed from the Executive Council, and the Prime Minister should advise the Governor on the allocation of other portfolios. However, the Governor's powers to reserve legislation for the approval of the British government and his control over defence and external affairs were to be retained.[30]

The District Councils, in which the chiefs were preponderant, all agreed with the SLPP that Paramount Chiefs belonged in a single legislative chamber, and that each district should have one chief among its representatives. However, nearly all of them emphatically opposed direct election of chiefs, preferring the District Councils or the chiefs themselves as an electoral college.[31]

The diehard Creoles of the National Council continued to maintain that the basic feature of Sierra Leone was its division into the two irreconcilable communities, the Settlers of the Colony and the peoples of the Protectorate, and proposed an equal division of seats between these units, with officials holding the balance.[32] A less uncompromising stance was taken by a new Creole-led political party, the United Sierra Leone Progressive Party (UPP), which advocated only 14 seats for the Colony in a 43-seat Assembly, but at the same time proposed restricting the number of Paramount Chiefs in this House to 7, with the remaining chiefs joining other notables in a second chamber called the Council of State with limited powers.[33] On one point, however, the National Council and UPP were agreed – neither wanted to remove the official members from the Executive Council.

The northern riots prevented early discussion of these proposals and it was not until March 1956 that Dr Margai tried to convene an all-party conference to work out some agreement on the requests to be made to the British government. When this attempt failed because of the opposition parties' refusal to accept a government majority at the conference,[34] Dr Margai tried to call a "non-party" conference, but the opposition spurned this also on the grounds that too many participants were SLPP "members and associates."[35] Finally the government brought together those invitees to the non-party conference who were willing to come, while the opposition parties held their own rump conference.

The conference approved the key proposals put forward by the SLPP and District Councils that there should be a unicameral legislature with three members, including one Paramount Chief, from each district, and that the

30 / Ibid.
31 / Ibid., pp. 17–31, 57–60.
32 / Ibid., pp. 1–2.
33 / Ibid., pp. 46–47.
34 / Daily Mail, April 2, 1956.
35 / Ibid., May 5, 1956, and June 22, 1956.

chiefs should be elected by the District Councils rather than directly by the people.[36] It agreed, however, to leave the question of changing the Executive Council for the new post-election legislature to decide.[37]

This cautious approach in the matter of the Executive Council was perhaps due to the SLPP leaders' awareness that the British Colonial Office was not impressed by the SLPP's support in the aftermath of the Freetown and Northern Province riots. Dr Margai indicated this in his explanation of why he had tried to call an all-party conference: "So widely representative a body would show that degree of public opinion which [the Secretary of State for the Colonies] had indicated as a prerequisite for his consideration."[38]

Despite this warning, the British evidently did not consider the lack of support from the opposition parties as a sufficient reason for refusing the SLPP government's 1956 requests for changes. The unicameral legislature outlined in the Sierra Leone (House of Representatives) Order-in-Council, 1956, consisted of 57 members, including 4 officials and 2 nominated members.[39] The 51 elected members comprised 12 Paramount Chiefs, one elected by each District Council, 14 ordinary members from the Colony, and 2 ordinary members from each district plus one from Bo Town. In accordance with the Keith-Lucas Commission's recommendation, all ordinary members were to be elected from single-member constituencies, except for those from Freetown and the Sherbro Urban District, who were elected from two-member constituencies.

These changes, while they represented some diminution of the chiefs' powers from their existing role in the Legislative Council, ensured their strong position. While they were reduced to holding only 23 per cent of the elective seats in the new legislature, the seats were guaranteed, and such a block of votes was substantial in view of the weakness of the parties in the legislature. Less directly, the "decision" to use single-member constituencies also aided the chiefs. The single-member constituency made it easier than did larger units of representation for a candidate to make his appeal in local and personal terms. If the units of representation had been larger (say, province-wide multi-member constituencies), it would have been necessary for would-be legislators to organize support on a wider basis, a task for which

36 / For this point, see *Daily Mail*, May 26, 1956.

37 / Sierra Leone. *The Government's Proposals for Constitutional Change*, Sessional Paper No. 2 of 1956 (Freetown: Government Printer, 1956).

38 / Sierra Leone, *The Government's Proposals for Constitutional Change (Historical Background)*, Sessional Paper No. 1 of 1956 (Freetown: Government Printer, 1956), p. 9. Cf. the remark of an SLPP leader that the British government wanted Dr Margai to show he had control before they would grant him further constitutional advance. Above, p. 85.

39 / The four officials disappeared when the Executive Council was changed in 1958, and the two nominated members at independence in 1961.

the chiefs' essentially local interests and influence left them ill-suited. With single-member constituencies, on the other hand, a single chief could hope to sway a sizable portion of the electorate and consequently his favour would be more eagerly sought by aspiring candidates. The single-member constituency, in short, reinforced the tendency within the SLPP for members to seek election on their personal merits, and to rely heavily on the support of the chiefs in doing so.

The greatest gainers in the 1956 constitutional reforms, however, were the Western-educated men of the Protectorate. With direct competition between them and the chiefs eliminated, they were almost guaranteed 25 of the 51 elective seats, unless some mass movement suddenly arose. Beyond this, they could expect to predominate in the enlarged Cabinet, particularly if many Creoles remained in opposition. However, whether they could use their numerical superiority remained to be seen; even more than the chiefs, they were divided along lines of temperament, age, social status, personal relations with Dr Margai and his associates, and occasionally tribe.

The 1957 general elections confirmed both the ascendancy of the SLPP over other parties, and of the Protectorate-educated men within the SLPP. The party won the elections largely by default. Only two other parties, the UPP and the Kono Progressive Movement, contested seats outside the Colony. The UPP, hoping to capitalize on the discontents revealed in the northern riots, ran 6 candidates up-country, as well as 12 in the Colony, but won only 5 seats, of which 3 were in the Colony.[40] The Kono Progressive Movement was the only other party to score any success; it won one of the two Kono seats. Official SLPP candidates won 25 of the 39 popularly elected seats, including 9 in the Colony; the remaining 8 ordinary members were all Independents who, for the most part, had considered themselves just as loyal to the SLPP as the official party candidates, and who all declared for it immediately after the election. The 11 Paramount Chiefs[41] elected by the District Councils also supported the SLPP, bringing its total membership to 44 out of the 50 elected members of the House of Representatives.

40 / There were only two Colony seats where a candidate of any party other than the SLPP or UPP managed to come as high as second place. The other parties which contested some seats were the National Council, the Labour Party (formed by a leader of the Freetown strike in 1955), and the Sierra Leone Independence Movement (SLIM), a nationalistic movement formed by Edward Blyden III, a former extramural lecturer at Fourah Bay College. For a full account of the election, see Scott, "The Sierra Leone General Election."

41 / After a number of depositions of chiefs in the wake of the 1956 riots, Tonkolili District had no literate chief who was able to stand for election, the sitting member being too ill. Tonkolili remained without a Paramount Chief representative until 1960, when Chief Bai Bairoh II was re-elected to office, and subsequently to the House of Representatives.

The backgrounds of SLPP Protectorate ordinary members elected in 1957 showed two features clearly: their prominence in the "modern" sector, and their links with the traditional elite. No less than 19 of the 25 had come from professional or subprofessional occupations in which at least secondary schooling was required.[42] Only two came from wage-earning backgrounds, and one of these, Siaka Stevens, had achieved eminence before entering politics. In most cases, these men were the second generation in relatively high-status occupations; at least 10 of the 25 had fathers who had been in business, professional, or white-collar occupations, and a further 6 were the sons of Paramount Chiefs. The continuity between the traditional and modern elites of the Protectorate was further shown by the fact that besides the 6 who were children of chiefs, an additional 10 of the 25 (or a total of 64 per cent) were members of ruling families.

In view of the way the election had been fought, it was quite apparent that only its self-discipline as an elite could hold the SLPP parliamentary group together; the external discipline of party certainly would not do it. Despite the efforts of a "reconciliation committee" sent around the Provinces to prevent election contests between party members,[43] a total of 43 candidates ran as Independents, and at least 35 of these were SLPP supporters.[44] The fact that only 8 of them won election was a tribute, not to the SLPP's strength as an organized party, but to its ability to select that man among the would-be candidates in each constituency who seemed most popular, and to bestow the SLPP symbol on him.[45] Throughout the Protectorate, party organization was notably absent during the election. Party candidates as well as independents had to finance their own campaigns, and based their claims for election chiefly on the grounds that they could increase water supplies, roads, and other amenities for their constituency better than their rivals.[46]

42 / I have considered as "professional" such occupations as teacher, surveyor, and druggist, as well as those requiring a higher level of training such as lawyer and doctor. Under "subprofessional" I have included government clerks and others who attained a measurable level of training. Persons engaged in trade have been excluded on the grounds that the level of their training was not readily measurable, unless they held a position of responsibility in a European firm.

In these calculations I have included three persons of Protectorate origin who were elected from Colony seats: Kande Bureh in Freetown, and the two members for Sherbro Urban District.

43 / *Daily Mail*, March 12, 1957.

44 / The only Independents who were definitely not SLPP were the two in Kono. We can probably also exclude two of the three who ran in the Rural Area, and possibly some of the five in Sherbro Urban District, though two of these joined the SLPP on winning the election. The only two Freetown Independents claimed to be SLPP members, and two up-country Independents designated themselves "Independent SLPP."

45 / Scott, "The Sierra Leone Election," p. 231.

46 / *Ibid.*, pp. 214, 223–25.

These rivalries within the loose structure of the party polarized within a few days of the election into a contest for the leadership. Since 1951, there had been rumblings from the younger men that Dr Margai was too cautious and too pro-British, and that his brother Albert should replace him. "Freetown Correspondent" had commented in 1952 that Dr Margai "lacks the energy and experience to lead his party through the trying months and years ahead. The SLPP now needs a more active leader and the obvious man is Mr. Albert Margai ..."[47] In 1956 the Bo branch of the SLPP openly proposed that Dr Margai should be replaced as leader;[48] in the compromise eventually reached, Dr Margai was unanimously re-affirmed as parliamentary leader, but Albert won election to the new post of Party Chairman.[49] It was not hard to see why Albert Margai appealed to the younger men; on "nationalist" issues he was often openly impatient with his brother's restraint, as when he asserted in 1953 that Sierra Leone ought to seek self-government "NOW," and that the powers over the chiefs vested in the [British] Chief Commissioner for the Protectorate ought to be handed over immediately to a Sierra Leonean Minister of Local Government.[50]

A few days after the 1957 election, a number of younger men who were dissatisfied with Dr Margai's leadership arranged for Albert Margai to contest the post of parliamentary leader at the parliamentary caucus, May 19. Albert won by 22 votes to 21, but a few hours later announced he was stepping down out of respect for his older brother.[51] However, he thought he had secured the concessions of a voice in the selection of the Cabinet and the right to be consulted in all matters of policy.[52] After several days of negotiations, the doctor acceded to nearly all his brother's demands, offering Albert the post of Internal Affairs,[53] and proffering ministerial posts to both Siaka Stevens and Dr Fitzjohn, two of Albert's closest supporters.[54] However, Albert announced that he "now found it difficult to accept any offer of compromise ... which fell short of Dr. Margai relinquishing the leadership of the Parliamentary Committee of the SLPP."[55]

This failure to achieve a compromise did not lead immediately to Albert Margai's secession from the party. On July 4, 1957, a conciliation committee

47 / West Africa, No. 1860 (October 18, 1952), p. 976.

48 / Daily Mail, March 26, 1956.

49 / Ibid., March 27.

50 / Observer, April 11, 1953. It will be recalled that the Minister overseeing Local Government at that time was Albert Margai.

51 / See Vanguard, May 21, 1957. Albert's original action in trying to take away the leadership from his elder brother, was, of course, profoundly shocking to many Sierra Leoneans.

52 / See Albert Margai's speech reported in Daily Mail, May 27, 1957, and the account of the meeting and subsequent events in Vanguard, May 21.

53 / A vital post, since it controlled all the chiefs. Albert had held this post under the title of Local Government since 1953.

54 / Daily Mail, May 28, 1957.   55 / Ibid., May 29, 1957.

announced that it had succeeded in getting both brothers to agree to its recommendations that "Dr. Margai retains the Leadership of the Party ... Albert Margai remains the Deputy Leader of the Party and ... should enjoy full ministerial status as soon as practically possible so as to enable him to exercise effectively the dignity and functions of his office."[56] Despite this promise, the weeks and months went by and Albert remained a backbencher. Stevens, at whose expense the truce between the Margais appeared to have been arranged, announced his resignation from the SLPP;[57] a few weeks later he lost his seat as the result of an election petition. Meanwhile, Dr Margai undertook to cut away his brother's base of support within the party by appointing two of Albert's supporters to ministerial secretaryships, another as government whip and yet another as Deputy Speaker.[58] After his Minister of Health, Rev. Paul Dunbar, had been unseated on an election petition, he kept this portfolio invitingly open until May 1958. The appointments, and the prospect of further ones, provided a considerable incentive for members to remain loyal to the chief minister.

Hopes that the rift between the Margai brothers might yet be resolved were raised by the fact that Albert Margai, although still a backbencher, attended the constitutional talks in London in December 1957. The purpose of these talks was to arrange for the reconstitution of the Executive Council to remove all official members except the Governor;[59] this meant that a Sierra Leonean would be able to take over the position of Minister of Finance, and it was rumoured that the man to fill the post would be Albert Margai.[60] But when the appointments to the new Executive Council were announced on August 14, 1958, M. S. Mustapha was given the Finance portfolio, and Albert Margai was excluded.[61]

On September 2, 1958, Albert Margai and three other members of the SLPP parliamentary group announced that they were resigning and founding a new party, the Peoples National Party.[62] The breakaway group was no-

56 / *Daily Mail*, July 5, 1957. The conciliation committee was headed by a Paramount Chief, and included "school teachers, ministers of religion, Paramount Chiefs [and] Chiefdom Speakers." *Ibid.*, July 2.

57 / *Ibid.*, July 11, 1957.

58 / Kallon and Kamanda-Bongay were appointed ministerial secretaries, S. T. Navo was made party whip, and A. J. Massally was elected Deputy Speaker by the House. R. G. O. King, who by some accounts was also a sympathizer of Albert Margai's, also was given a ministerial secretaryship.

59 / See Sierra Leone. *The Government's Proposals for Further Constitutional Change*, Sessional Paper No. 1 of 1958 (Freetown: Government Printer, 1958).

60 / *Daily Mail*, December 9, 1957.

61 / *Ibid.*, August 15, 1958.

62 / *Ibid.*, September 3, 1958. The other three MP's were S. T. Navo, A. J. Massally, and H. I. Kamara. Maigore Kallon resigned his post as Parliamentary Secretary and joined the PNP a few weeks later. Siaka Stevens was also a major force behind the creation of the new party.

where near as sizable as might have been expected from the leadership vote a year earlier; Dr Margai's skilful appointments had seen to that. But it did mean that the more "modernizing" elements in the Protectorate were no longer all concentrated in the SLPP, while the more traditionally inclined were still concentrated there behind Dr Margai. The balance which had been so heavily tilted by the 1956 constitutional changes and the 1957 election now swung back somewhat towards those who favoured protecting the chiefs' central political role.

While the breakaway of the PNP group ensured that the leadership of the SLPP would remain in Dr Margai's hands, and thus that the chiefs' interests would be heeded, the chiefs after 1958 would have to depend on the good will of an all-African Cabinet for their survival. The power to depose a chief had already in 1954 been vested in the Governor-in-Council, or in effect in the hands of Dr Margai, tempered by the continued presence of British officials in the Council. When these officials were withdrawn in 1958, the power of Dr Margai (or any other Prime Minister) to deal with chiefs as he saw fit was left almost unchecked.

More generally, one could say that the 1958 change of the Executive Council into a Cabinet significantly reduced the influence of British officials on Dr Margai and his colleagues. Instead of being able to present their views directly to the whole Cabinet, senior British officials now had to convince their own African Ministers, who in turn had to convince their African colleagues. The Governor, facing an all-African Cabinet alone, was clearly in a weaker position than when he was supported by four other officials. This applied to even as strong-minded an individual as Maurice Dorman.

The British role in government had not, of course, become negligible. As late as 1957, an expatriate Director of Education apparently concealed from his Minister, Albert Margai, the politically explosive fact that a number of expatriates had started a school which did not admit Sierra Leoneans.[63] Even after African ministers took control of all departments, their senior advisers were still British; for example, the Secretary to the Prime Minister was an expatriate until 1962 and the Secretary to the Cabinet until 1961.

The lack of visible friction between the Sierra Leoneans and British over the pace of withdrawal must in large measure be attributed to the desire of Dr Margai (who in January 1959 became Sir Milton Margai) to seek agreement with the British, rather than to provoke conflict. For example, he assured the 1958 SLPP conference that "We have won confidence at the Colonial Office so much that we shall always be granted our wants."[64] His willingness to retain expatriate civil servants to the end of their term rather

63 / See *Daily Mail*, January 12, 1957. When he learned of this, the Minister ordered the school closed.
64 / *Vanguard*, December 9, 1958.

than to ease them out as soon as qualified Africans became available,[65] suggested the same attitude towards the British. He was also apparently willing to take the advice of his British advisers against the rest of his Ministers; for example, one former Minister alleged that Sierra Leone's failure to hold a census until 1963 was due to the advice of the Chief Commissioner for the Protectorate, who had persuaded Dr Margai not to hold it.

Two further features of the SLPP after the 1957 election need to be noted. The first was the fact that the Cabinet and the parliamentary party became the central organs of the SLPP. Until 1957, the fact that a number of its active founders had been unable to win seats in the legislature created some pressure to ensure that persons outside Parliament were included in the SLPP's decision-making processes. But, as a result of the 1957 elections, most of these leading activists won seats in Parliament; those who did not tended to concentrate thereafter on strictly local politics. The parliamentarians, and even more the Cabinet, had certain organizational advantages over outsiders. They lived in the same location (at least for part of the year), met frequently, and had a common interest in preserving their positions. Since members of Parliament had won elections without any assistance from a party organization, they had little incentive to develop party machinery; in fact, it was safer for them to rely on personal contacts which they could control than to encourage the creation of a local party branch which might fall under the control of rivals. But as the group which was in closest contact with the central government, they were the persons primarily responsible for disseminating information about government policies among the people of their constituencies. In most cases they would do this through the chiefs, whose influence had been largely responsible for getting them elected; and whether they worked through the chiefs or built up a personal machine, they would concentrate their attention on local issues, rather than on trying to develop any sense of national interest or a national identity among their people.

The other feature of the SLPP after 1957 was the increased strength of the Mende contingent in Parliament. The 44 SLPP supporters elected in 1957 included 19 Mendes, or 43 per cent of the total group. Even after the PNP defections had removed four Mendes from the SLPP caucus, they still comprised 39 per cent of the total SLPP parliamentary strength. While a better balance was maintained in the Cabinet, which after 1958 comprised four Mendes, four Temnes, and four others, such a large block of Mendes in the Parliamentary caucus could have given grounds for concern to the Temnes,

65 / See *Daily Mail*, February 13, 1959. However, about the same time he told a meeting of students that if he had his way, "I would push all Europeans out of Sierra Leone today," and that it was only because the country needed them that he took this conciliatory attitude. *Ibid.*, February 11.

who themselves comprised only 22 per cent of the parliamentary caucus at the end of 1958. It should be stressed that this Mende predominance was not the result of any deliberate plot; it arose primarily because the Mende-dominated districts were smaller than those in the north. But the fact of substantial Mende over-representation was none the less real, whatever its origins, and was to give increased grounds for discontent in the years ahead.

The inclinations of the SLPP leaders in the 1950s should now be apparent. Although themselves members of a bourgeoisie, their familial links with the traditional rulers and their dependence on the chiefs for election to the legislature predisposed them towards a very considerable sympathy for the wishes of the chiefs. Their willingness to allow local institutions to go on much as before even after the 1955–56 riots suggested how far they were committed to preserving the powers and privileges of the chiefs. They were clearly far less sensitive to the demands of the chiefs' subjects, and also to the demands of the lower classes in urban areas, as was evidenced by their reactions to the Freetown riots of 1955. Towards expatriates both in government and in private industry, their attitude was respectful; they did not try to rush "Africanization" of the civil service, or try to impose a high degree of control over the operations of the diamond mines, or for that matter, over any foreign enterprises. They managed to include representatives of all major Protectorate tribes in their ranks, and by 1958 were beginning to reconcile the Creoles as well, with the result that regional demands at least could be worked out within the party's ranks by bargaining. Their major blind spot was their insensitivity to the "class" demands of lower status city and country dwellers, which had been expressed so violently in 1955 and 1956. This was one type of demand which the SLPP leaders' own attitudes and their base of support made them incapable of handling.

7
The game of opposition

The uprisings in both urban and rural areas of Sierra Leone, and the SLPP government's reluctance to deal with their root causes, indicated bright prospects for an opposition party that could transform this discontent into political support. But although two parties tried to challenge the SLPP nationally during the 1950s, neither of them succeeded in making significant inroads on its base. Some part of their failure can be attributed to the techniques of suppression developed by the SLPP during this period, but far more important as a cause of their failure were the constraints imposed by their own leadership.

THE RISE AND FALL OF THE UPP

It was obvious to all but the most diehard Creoles after 1951 that the National Council's ultra-Creole appeal would doom it to permanent minority status. With the impending spread of the franchise, any party wishing to compete with the SLPP would have to appeal to a substantial part of the Protectorate peoples as well as to Creoles.

Just before the Keith-Lucas Commission began its hearings in 1954, a brilliant Creole lawyer, Cyril Rogers-Wright, announced the formation of the United Sierra Leone Progressive Party, whose aim was to remove the barriers between Colony and Protectorate.[1] It immediately drew into its ranks I. T. A. Wallace-Johnson, who had sat as an Independent since quitting the National Council in 1952.[2] Most of its other activists, however, were

1 / *Daily Mail*, July 14, 1954.
2 / Wallace-Johnson stayed with the UPP until just after the 1957 election, when he was expelled for unstated reasons. See *Daily Mail*, May 29, 1957. The most likely reason for his expulsion was that since Rogers-Wright had failed to win a seat, Wallace-Johnson might be able to usurp the position of leader. Cf. Scott, "The Sierra Leone Election," p. 185.

persons who had not participated previously in the Colony-Protectorate feud. In its testimony before the Keith-Lucas Commission and in its constitutional proposals of 1955, the UPP seemed to see itself as competing with the SLPP for the votes of the ordinary people of the Protectorate. It strongly supported the universal franchise, and proposed a new legislature with an increased majority for the Protectorate, but with most of the chiefs shunted aside into a second chamber.[3] Its goal seemed to be an alliance between the more moderate Creoles and the commoners from up-country who were restive under the chiefs. This goal was not entirely unrealistic, as the 1955–56 riots showed, but to achieve it would require a considerable grass-roots effort to awaken people to the possibility of voting against their chiefs, and also a careful playing down of any "Creole" pretensions to superiority.

Its first two years did not give the UPP much time to spend on organizational activities: Rogers-Wright and his associates were kept busy, first before the Keith-Lucas Commission, then in the aftermath of the Freetown riots,[4] next preparing its constitutional proposals, and finally in trying to take advantage of the promising situation created by the northern tax riots. It made some effort to reach the "grass-roots" by the use of touring teams of speakers. One observer stated in 1956 that the only evidence of political activity in towns up-country was that "members of the UPP came here the other day and spoke," but he added that the party had made no effort to establish branches after the teams of speakers had left.[5] Travelling UPP agitators played a small part in the northern riots. Wallace-Johnson, accompanied by two Protectorate members of the party, was reported as telling anti-tax demonstrators in Port Loko that they should work with their chiefs and take complaints to the District Commissioners.[6] Two other members of the UPP took a different approach. Mahmoud Ahmed, a district organizer, was alleged to have advised a crowd attacking Chief Modu's house,[7] while A. B. Kamara apparently encouraged the strikers in two other Port Loko chiefdoms.[8] Rogers-Wright later appeared as counsel for the people of the chiefdoms in several of the inquiries into the behaviour of certain chiefs.[9]

3 / Sierra Leone, *Collected Statements of Constitutional Proposals*, pp. 46-47.

4 / Where Rogers-Wright played an active and inflammatory role as counsel for the unions before the Shaw Commission; the *Daily Mail* reported that he twice accused white military officers of having shot down unarmed and peaceful civilians, despite evidence from witnesses that the men shot were actually leaders of large and threatening mobs. See *Daily Mail*, April 1 and 2, 1955.

5 / A. K. Turay, "Are Your Party Branches Active?," *Daily Mail*, February 16, 1956.

6 / *Ibid.*, January 9, 1956.

7 / *Ibid.*, April 13, 1956.

8 / *Cox Report*, pp. 54, 147.

9 / See *Daily Mail*, October 23, 1956. These appearances were a major factor in his by-election victory in the Port Loko East constituency. He was later disbarred for the second time in his career as a result of one of these appearances, when the *Vanguard*

While all of these activities would gain sympathy for the UPP up-country, it needed to establish a closer identification with these people than was possible through fleeting visits by teams of speakers. Without a local organization to maintain the initial goodwill its stands would bring it, the UPP could not hope to win many elections. It was seriously handicapped in its efforts to attract up-country organizers by its "Creole" identity and leadership. At its first convention, held in April 1956, it elected three up-country men as vice-presidents, but its other officers were all Creole.[10] The up-country men did not stay long in the UPP. In August 1956 the National Propaganda Secretary, M. A. Tarasid, resigned and joined the SLPP, charging that the executive had discarded him in favour of a "Colony born" man.[11] Earlier the vice-president for the Northern Province and two other "big men" in that area alleged to be members had resigned,[12] and in 1957 the vice-president for the Eastern Province turned up as the official SLPP candidate for Kono North. Within a year of their victories in the 1957 election, the two Protectorate members of the UPP in the legislature had crossed to the SLPP; six months after crossing, Mahmoud Ahmed became a ministerial secretary. In 1956, the UPP also won over Peter Kamara, the most prominent of the northern strike leaders; this was an important factor in its winning the Port Loko West seat. But by 1959 Peter Kamara too had been persuaded to declare his support for the SLPP.

Offsetting these desertions were several election triumphs. Following the 1957 election, seven election petitions instigated by Rogers-Wright against successful SLPP candidates had succeeded in unseating the winners, and in five cases by-elections were held as a result.[13] UPP candidates won all five seats, with Rogers-Wright becoming the first Creole to win a Protectorate

reported that the courts found that he had taken money to act for a Paramount Chief, and also had taken money to act for the people of the chiefdom against the chief. See *Vanguard*, February 21, 1959.

10 / The vice-presidents were Ahmed Hassan, a Temne; Amadu Kai, a Kono; Muhammed Turay, a Mende; and I. T. A. Wallace-Johnson. Rogers-Wright was elected President; John Nelson-Williams, the young son of a prominent Creole lawyer, General Secretary; and Dora J. Wright, a Creole businesswoman, Treasurer. M. A. Tarasid (a Mende) was appointed National Propaganda Secretary, and a Temne, a Sherbro, a Kono, and a Creole were appointed as national regional secretaries. *Daily Mail*, April 24, 1956.

11 / *Ibid.*, August 1, 1956.

12 / *Ibid.*, May 24, 1956. The other two, besides Hassan, were Sanfa Adams of Magburaka and G. A. Keister of Makeni. Both became prominent in the SLPP in their respective areas. Adams received a substantial government loan to build a hotel a few weeks after declaring for the SLPP.

13 / Two of the seven MPS challenged resigned their seats before the petitions were heard. In two other cases the Supreme Court declared the runner-up elected, and in the remaining three it declared the election void.

seat, Port Loko East.[14] However, with the desertion of the two northern members to the SLPP, only Valecius Neale-Caulker, the by-election victor in Moyamba North, could speak for the Protectorate in the UPP's parliamentary group of six members. Eventually, in the final break-up of the UPP, Neale-Caulker's local branch severed all connections with the party because of what they saw as Rogers-Wright's "asserting the superiority of the Creole man over the countryman."[15]

Some of these desertions can undoubtedly be attributed to inducements offered by the SLPP leaders; the government loan to Sanfa Adams and the ministerial post for Ahmed showed their willingness to use government largesse to win over opposition members and thus weaken the opposition parties. There was also considerable justification for the contention of the up-country men who left the UPP that it was really a "Creole man's party." In 1956, when the opposition parties and the government had once again reached a stalemate over the government's proposals for further constitutional advances, the UPP leaders joined the other opposition parties[16] in a letter of protest to the British against the "higher intellectual culture" of the Colony being submerged by the "94 per cent illiteracy" of the Protectorate.[17] After the 1957 elections and by-elections had established the UPP as the main opposition party, it concentrated its attention on matters primarily of concern to Creoles. For example, one of its major attacks on the government was for failing to provide opportunities for Sierra Leoneans to purchase freehold land in the Protectorate, a goal dear to the hearts of Creoles, but strongly opposed by everyone from the Protectorate.[18] Another of its criticisms was against the participation of several SLPP leaders in a demonstration against the judiciary; from the remarks of UPP members, it was quite clear that their concern was with the anti-Creole attitude of the demonstrators rather than the threat to judges.[19] This Creole orientation provided a very effective argument for the SLPP leaders to supplement the sanctions they could bring against Protectorate "big men" who might incline toward the

14 / He had failed to win a seat in the general election. The other seats won by the UPP were Freetown Central and Freetown West, both won by Creoles, Moyamba North, and Kono South. In Kono South, A. A. Mani ran under the UPP symbol, but was really a leader of the SLPIM, and did not join the UPP parliamentary group.

15 / *Daily Mail*, February 18, 1960.

16 / The National Council and the Labour Party, both clearly identified as "Creole" in sentiment and membership.

17 / See J. D. Hargreaves, "Constitutional Reform in Sierra Leone," *West Africa*, No. 2053 (August 18, 1956), p. 611.

18 / See *House of Representative Debates*, Session 1958–59, Vol. I (August 27, 1958), pp. 153–62. Even the UPP's one Protectorate member abstained from supporting his colleagues on this motion, while all the SLPP members who frequently voted with the UPP supported the government.

19 / *Ibid.* (August 25, 1958), pp. 85–105.

UPP. With anti-Creole feelings still running high among the Protectorate elite, few notables wished to be associated with a "Creole" party.

The northern riots showed that the "big men" were not the only possible leaders of the Protectorate; a mass agitational party might break the shaky grip of the notables and direct the mass of the people into radical attitudes. But to build such a party would require both a large number of organizers and a radical leadership. Neither of these requisites was available to the UPP. Party organizers were scarce in Sierra Leone, and the UPP was further handicapped by a lack of money. Without a mass membership base, it needed donations from men of wealth, but wealthy men were likely to support the government or stay neutral, unless they had a strong commitment to the opposition party. The result was that Rogers-Wright apparently financed much of the party's activity himself.[20] The party newspaper, *Shekpendeh*, was also his personal property.[21] This centralization of control in the hands of one man left the party vulnerable to its leader's whims, and further inhibited the growth of an organization.

Even if the shortage of organizers and funds to pay them had been overcome, the UPP was not willing to offer a radical alternative to the SLPP. Although it acquired the reputation of being somewhat more radical than the SLPP, this reputation was based on such tenuous claims as its promise in the 1957 election to bring independence by 1960 (as opposed to the SLPP's "within the lifetime of the present legislature," i.e., by 1962),[22] and Rogers-Wright's objections to the continued presence of nominated members in the new House of Representatives.[23] Its claim to be more "nationalist" than the SLPP by being more concerned with breaking down the barriers between the Colony and Protectorate was doubtful in the light of its "Creole" biases discussed above.

In the absence of an effective party organization which could educate the electorate to support party candidates, the UPP, like the SLPP, found its parliamentary contingent composed of individuals who had won election by their personal efforts. It could derive some cohesion from the fact that nearly all its leading members were Creole, but this was a major handicap to its efforts to develop a base in the Protectorate. "Creole solidarity" was in any case too weak a cement to hold together in opposition men who could see little difference between their views and those of the governing party, and

20 / It was claimed at the 1958 UPP conference that he had paid the party's debts of £9,600 entirely from his own pocket. *Daily Mail*, June 13, 1958.

21 / He also had the sole power to appoint the members of the party's Central Committee. See Kilson, in Coleman and Rosberg, *Political Parties and National Integration*, p. 107.

22 / Scott, *Five Elections*, p. 219.

23 / *House of Representatives Debates*, Session 1958–59, Vol. I (August 20, 1958), p. 4.

who had little cause to hang together. In the latter half of 1959, the UPP fell apart. In August the General Secretary, John Nelson-Williams, resigned after a rebuke from the party executive.[24] More vehement charges and counter-charges began to fly between Rogers-Wright and Nelson-Williams, with each accusing the other of being about to take a post in the SLPP government.[25] The remaining UPP MPs then seceded from the party, stating that they would not recognize Rogers-Wright as leader, and eventually formed a new grouping, the Independent Progressive Party, with Neale-Caulker as Leader and Gideon Dickson-Thomas as Secretary.[26] This new party was solely a parliamentary grouping; it never made any attempt to organize support beyond the personal followings its members had built up in their own constituencies. With no strong organizational base or ideology to sustain them, its members would be inclined to seek the best terms they could from the government. They would certainly not be inclined to undertake the major organizational effort required to start a fresh challenge to the SLPP.

THE PNP: RADICALISM IN THE ELITE?

We have already noted the division within the SLPP between the more cautious and conservative chiefs and other supporters of Dr Margai and the younger, more impatient "modernizers" who clustered around his brother Albert. Albert Margai's surprise victory over his brother at the parliamentary party caucus May 19, 1957, showed the strength of the "young men" in the party.[27] Their strength, however, was not sufficient within the SLPP to ensure their dominance; pressure from the chiefs and other traditionalists induced Albert Margai to step down in return for concessions.[28]

24 / He had opposed a government motion to pay Valecius Neale-Caulker an allowance for acting as Leader of the Opposition, on the grounds that this was contrary to party policy. The UPP executive criticized him for this opposition. See *Daily Mail*, August 6, 1959.

25 / For Rogers-Wright's denial of the charge against him, see *ibid.*, August 8; for his accusation against Nelson-Williams, *ibid.*, August 11.

26 / For various stages of this secession, see *Daily Mail*, August 18, 1959; *ibid.*, August 20; *Vanguard*, September 23; *Daily Mail*, October 10; and for the formation of the IPP, *ibid.*, January 9, 1960.

27 / The split was not strictly on age lines; H. E. B. John, Mrs. Constance Cummings-John and Dr Karefa-Smart, among Dr Margai's supporters, were all relatively young, while Stevens and Y. D. Sesay, two of the foremost supporters of Albert, were older men. But on the whole, Albert's support came from the younger MPs.

28 / It is still a matter of conjecture as to why Albert backed down so quickly. The fact that he was not acceptable to many chiefs and other traditionalists in the party, and the probability that these would have broken away and perhaps formed a coalition with the UPP, thus leaving Albert's group in opposition, were likely the most important considerations. We must add to this the fact that the British administration,

When Albert Margai and his close supporters finally broke away in 1958 to form the Peoples National Party, they brought together a group which could conceivably have organized a strong popular challenge to the SLPP. The PNP leaders differed in certain ways from their SLPP counterparts.[29] They were a much younger group than the SLPP ministers of the same period, with more than half their executive's 13 members under 40, while only two of the 15 SLPP ministers were under this age, and 9 were 50 or over. This undoubtedly contributed to the more impatient temperament of the PNP leaders and to their greater appeal to the less educated young men in the towns. Furthermore the PNP leaders had experienced greater exposure to Western influences in their education and in their occupations than had the SLPP ministers. No less than 9 of the 13 PNP executive members had university degrees or equivalent training, and 10 had studied abroad, whereas only 5 persons out of 15 in the SLPP ministry had university training, and only 6 had studied abroad. Seven of the PNP executive, including 3 of the 5 parliamentarians, were lawyers, giving rise to the PNP's nickname of "the lawyers' party." While the SLPP ministry, like the PNP executive, included 9 members who could be considered in "professions," 3 of these were teachers and one a surveyor who had not gone outside of Sierra Leone and who had kept close links with traditional society. The PNP leaders had been uprooted to a considerably greater extent from traditional society.

In other ways, the PNP leaders still hewed close to the SLPP pattern. All the members of Parliament, and nearly all the non-Creole members of the executive, had connections with ruling families. The largest ethnic group in the PNP executive, as in the SLPP, was the Mendes; 6 of the 13 PNP members, like 5 of the 15 SLPP ministers, were Mende. The PNP executive also included 4 Creoles, against 3 in the SLPP ministry. It also put greater stress on the

including the Governor who would select a Prime Minister, greatly preferred Dr Margai to his brother. There was a good prospect, therefore, that while Albert might retain the leadership of the SLPP, he might find his brother still in power.

It can also be suggested that Albert was not very skilful in this struggle; if he had quickly offered some of Dr Margai's supporters ministerial posts, he might have broadened his base of support to the point where no Governor could deny him the Prime Ministership.

29 / The first PNP executive included the following members: Albert Margai (Mende, lawyer), Leader; Siaka Stevens (Limba, union organizer, ex-Minister), General Secretary; Maigore Kallon (Mende, recent graduate in business administration), Organizing Secretary; S. T. Navo (Mende, lawyer); H. I. Kamara (Temne, retired civil servant); M. S. Turay (Mende, ex-policeman); T. J. Ganda (Mende, clerk); Gershon Collier (Creole, lawyer); Berthan Macauley (Creole, lawyer); Dr Claude Nelson-Williams (Creole, doctor, brother to UPP general secretary); Abu Koroma (Kono, lawyer); Ken During (Creole, lawyer); A. J. Massally (Mende, lawyer). All members of Parliament were automatically members of the executive. Some young northerners who later became prominent in the APC joined in 1959.

need for playing down the Creole-countryman feud.[30] Its most conspicuous weakness in ethnic terms was its lack of northerners; it included only 2, against 5 in the SLPP ministry, and of these Stevens alone was of any stature.

The PNP rapidly acquired the reputation of being the more radical party, but its radicalism was hard to perceive when faced with concrete issues. On the most crucial question facing Sierra Leone politicians, their attitude towards the country's traditional rulers, the PNP leaders said little that would cause the chiefs concern. A few PNP men were anti-chief[31] but most simply wanted to pry the chiefs away from the SLPP. For example, a motion by two PNP leaders asked for a separate House of Chiefs so that "the chiefs should be free to their consciences" and not "tied down because of party ties and other threats." The aim of the motion, they asserted, was to enable the chiefs to "play a better part in the administration of their chiefdoms."[32] Similarly, the party newspaper attacked as "false and mischievous" an SLPP claim that the PNP would abolish chieftaincy and asserted:

The Peoples National Party strongly maintains that chieftaincy has and will continue to have a most important place in our national development for a very long time. To this end, the Party is determined to do everything possible and will spare no efforts in helping to enhance the prestige of that office.

The position of chiefs in our society demands that in order to enhance their dignity and respect, they should clearly stay out of politics. ...

Recent developments in some West African territories (both British and French) emphasize our contentions dramatically, and should serve as a warning to our chiefs, not to allow themselves to be misused by politicians for selfish partisan gratification.[33]

Also, when the SLPP announced that it was abolishing the post of second speaker, the PNP attacked this move as one which would have "disastrous effects ... on chieftaincy."[34] Such actions may have been simply a public pose to refute the SLPP's charges that the PNP would destroy chieftaincy.[35]

30 / See, for example, *Liberty* (the PNP paper), September 18, 1959. In part this conciliatory attitude may have resulted from the closer personal connections between the largely professional PNP leaders and the Creole professional men, though the PNP leaders also seemed more responsive to the currents of opinion flowing from other African states, which strongly condemned any appeal to tribal sentiments as dangerously divisive.

31 / One told the writer the chiefs were "a necessary evil at that time"; another said the PNP was opposed to the chiefs.

32 / *Daily Mail*, April 9, 1959.

33 / *Liberty*, August 8, 1959.

34 / Peoples National Party, "Statement on Abolition of Post of 2nd Speaker" (mimeo, n.d. [1958]).

35 / For example, one story in the SLPP party newspaper was headlined "PNP Wages War on Chiefs." The "war" consisted of a declaration by the PNP general secretary that the chiefs "should clear out of politics" by entering a separate House of Chiefs. *Vanguard*, January 20, 1960.

One could take as equally significant the fact that the PNP adopted as its party symbol the elephant, which had been used by the Parti Démocratique de Guinée. SLPP speakers in the 1959 District Council elections cited this as evidence that the PNP would treat the chiefs in Sierra Leone just as the PDG had treated them across the border.[36] But, in view of the fact that all the parliamentary members of the PNP and most of its other leaders were themselves members of ruling families, it is unlikely that they were as anti-chief as they were portrayed. What they did object to, quite understandably, was the way in which the government was able to use the chiefs for its own ends, including the suppression of the PNP. This certainly did not mean that, if the PNP came to power, it would destroy chieftaincy.

In its attitude towards the use of expatriates in government service, the PNP appeared relatively radical, but in reality it held a moderate position. It pledged itself to "Africanization in all branches of the service as soon as trained men are forthcoming ... the trained African ... must be given first preference in his own country."[37] Such a position, which implied easing expatriates out of pensionable posts before their terms expired, was in marked contrast to the Prime Minister's statement on the same question: "I would not, if I had a European at the head of the civil service, and he was doing his best for the country, replace him merely because there was a qualified Sierra Leonean. The European would serve his normal term ... and the African step in afterwards."[38] However, before concluding that the PNP would have greatly speeded up the process of Africanization of the civil service if it had been in office, we should consider the comment made by Siaka Stevens when he was on the ministerial benches and replying to opposition criticism of the continued bringing out of expatriates: "It makes very good propaganda stuff for a meeting of this kind, especially when you have the public in attendance. But if we are realistic and if we want to face facts we will have to admit that we have not got the men trained yet."[39] It is probable that in its demands for more Africanization, the PNP was indulging in "very good propaganda stuff." S. T. Navo at one time apparently charged that the SLPP was importing redundant "white men" into Sierra Leone and then promised that the PNP would end this practice and instead bring in Germans, Russians, and others.[40] The PNP appeared to be appealing simply to what it thought was a widespread dislike of the continuing influx of British personnel. It did, however, appear to recognize the need to import trained workers from somewhere. The restrained view put forward by Siaka

36 / Martin Kilson, who was in Sierra Leone shortly after the elections, has drawn attention to this charge. See Kilson, "Sierra Leone," *West Africa*, July 2, 1960, p. 745.

37 / *Daily Mail*, February 21, 1959.

38 / *Ibid.*, February 13, 1959.

39 / *Legislative Council Debates*, Session 1951/52 (January 25, 1952), p. 130.

40 / See *Vanguard*, April 25, 1959.

Stevens in 1959 probably best represented the party's stand. Stevens said that expatriates were necessary, because of the skills they possessed, but

the Sierra Leonean must be master in his own house ... we ... must be given the opportunity of deciding the number, the quality and the calibre of the people who should come to us, and what is more important, to negotiate with such outsiders on a basis of equality, the conditions under which their services would be made available to us.

Our policy therefore ... would be to invite and give every encouragement to expatriates who have a specific contribution to make ... the PNP will have no place for the know-all type of paternalistic expatriate.[41]

Houphouet-Boigny or Hastings Banda could hardly have said less. It would be very difficult to term this stand by the PNP a radical one.

The PNP's attitude towards foreign capital investment was marked by some ambiguity. At one extreme, Dr Claude Nelson-Williams suggested that "the time is not too distant when the diamond industry will be nationalized";[42] at the other, the government was attacked for having failed to encourage an "Israeli American business promoter" who wanted to start a margarine factory in Sierra Leone.[43] Stevens took the view that Sierra Leone had to obtain outside capital to finance its development, but that it should be careful.[44] The PNP did seem to be somewhat more suspicious of foreign investors than the SLPP, at least if we compare their statements with the actions of the SLPP, whose "Open Door" policy welcomed investment from any source, provided the investors obeyed the laws and tried to employ Sierra Leoneans. The SLPP also emphasized that it had no intention of nationalizing any foreign firm.[45] However, again it might be suggested that the difference between the parties was primarily due to the fact that one was in power and the other out; a few years later, after Albert Margai had become Prime Minister, he was criticized by Stevens, who was then Leader of the Opposition, for failing to impose stricter terms on foreign investment in the country. The Prime Minister replied that while he would have liked to impose stricter controls on foreign investment, Sierra Leone simply could not afford to do so, since she was only one of a number of small countries competing for capital on the world markets.[46]

Such radicalism as the PNP leaders displayed was largely symbolic. It sent a delegation to Guinea shortly after that country had voted itself into independence,[47] and other delegations to the 1958 and 1960 All-African Peoples

41 / Siaka Stevens, "The Peoples National Party and Expatriatism," *Liberty*, July 25, 1959.

42 / *Ibid.*, August 8, 1959.

43 / *Ibid.*, July 18, 1959.

44 / *Ibid.*, July 25, 1959.

45 / *Daily Mail*, March 11, 1961.

46 / *House of Representatives Debates*, 1964/65, II (September 16, 1964), cols. 53–54.

47 / *Daily Mail*, October 21, 1958. The SLPP conspicuously failed to mark this event.

Congresses at Accra and Tunis.[48] Its attacks on expatriates and on foreign investment might also be termed "symbolic radicalism," the expression of emotionally satisfying general attitudes or slogans, with care being taken not to spell out the details of these radical proposals to the extent that the impossibility of realizing them became apparent.

Although the leadership of the PNP was drawn essentially from the same social strata as that of the SLPP, and its attitudes to social change were hardly such as to threaten the existing order, the party's hints of radicalism and its need for cadres to offset the SLPP chiefs were enough to draw a new group into political participation. The younger government clerks, teachers, commercial employees, and others with primary and sometimes secondary education had hitherto had little place in politics; the SLPP's reliance on older, more established community leaders gave them no opportunity, and Dr Margai's conservatism did not appeal to them. These young men were among the first from non-chiefly families to profit from Western education; often their fathers had made enough money at petty trades to provide their children with some schooling. However, these young men's occupations were not lucrative enough or their prospects for advancement bright enough to allow them to become part of the bourgeoisie which formed the "modern" component of the SLPP. Their best hope for getting ahead lay in politics, and the PNP provided them with their first opportunity for political participation[49]

These young men were of considerable importance in the towns; their support was sufficient for the PNP to win all three seats in the Bo Town Council elections in the SLPP's Mende heartland, in May 1959.[50] But the towns by themselves could not provide electoral majorities for any party (see Table 7:1); the PNP's message had to be carried into the chiefdom villages.

Such a feat was not totally impossible. Already in West Africa two "radical" and "populist" parties, the Union Soudanaise of the French Soudan and the Parti Démocratique of neighbouring Guinea, had turned the trick against chief-oriented parties supported by their colonial governments. But two basic factors in these popular parties' success were lacking in Sierra Leone. The chiefs in all of Sierra Leone, unlike those in most parts of the Soudan and Guinea, were *traditional* rulers, not the creations of a colonial administration.[51] They retained far more residual support from their subjects, even in

48 / *Ibid.*, January 2, 1960. Albert Margai represented the PNP. The SLPP also sent a delegate, but he was merely a young propaganda secretary.

49 / Cf. David Apter's comments on the rather different "marginal" group in Ghana who provided much of the push for early post-war nationalism. *Ghana in Transition*, p. 275.

50 / *Daily Mail*, May 24, 1959.

51 / We should note in particular Ruth Morgenthau's comment that "the centre of PSP [the chiefly party's] strength was among the Bambara and the Fulani, whose official

TABLE 7:1
Proportion of population living in towns by province (1963)

| | Percentage of total population | | | |
Size of town	Whole country	Eastern Province	Southern Province	Northern Province
5000 and up	7	12	6	4
2000 and up	12	22	9	8

Source: *1963 Census*, pp. 16–38. The high proportion for the Eastern Province is misleading in that most of these individuals were "strangers" living in the diamond mining centres, and as "strangers" their influence was minimal.

the north, than was the case in the Soudan and Guinea. The other factor which was critical in carrying the US-RDA and the PDG to election victories was their intensive organization. The Union Soudanaise, working through a network of traders, had support not only in the towns, but in most villages of the countryside. The PDG similarly maintained a tight hierarchical structure which reached down to the smallest villages; in 1955, while still in opposition, it could claim 300,000 members.[52] For the PNP to claim a tenth as many members in Sierra Leone would have been to invite derision, and it did not try.[53] In 1959, according to Kilson, its organization consisted of a Freetown branch and three organizing secretaries to cover the whole country.[54]

Without a much more powerful and pervasive organization, the PNP could not hope to succeed. The SLPP could survive with a minimum of party structure because it had pre-empted the chiefly structure of authority for its own purposes. This same chiefly structure was also an effective deterrent to the growth of opposition parties. It would take a brave man in a village to risk losing a favourable allocation of farmland, suffering a boycott of his business on the chief's orders, or being constantly hauled before the Native Administration court for "disrespect to the Paramount Chief." In the south, where the chiefs were still widely respected, to make such an apparently vain sacrifice would appear foolish. In the north, where more widespread discontent

chiefs ... often had pre-European claims to rule." *Political Parties in French-Speaking West Africa*, p. 280. It is also relevant that the Fulani regions of Guinea, where the chiefs had strong traditional claims, were the last to be overwhelmed by the PDG.

52 / Morgenthau, *Political Parties*, p. 247.

53 / The PNP does not seem to have ever undertaken a serious membership drive with the aim of inducing large numbers of people to commit themselves to it. The numbers of "members" its leaders claimed were as vague as those put forward by the SLPP.

54 / Kilson, "Sierra Leone Politics: The Approach to Independence," *West Africa*, No. 2248 (July 2, 1960), p. 745.

with the chiefs offered some hope that such defiance might bring about an improvement, the PNP was under the further handicap of lacking any prominent northern leaders apart from Stevens. While few villagers were likely to be aware of "Mende domination," this was becoming a matter of concern to politically conscious northerners, who could see little reason to support one Mende-dominated party rather than another.

The major test of the PNP's support came with the 1959 District Council elections. The PNP had demanded a further general election before Independence so that "the people [could] ... decide at the polls which political party they wish to lead them to this desired haven."[55] The results of the 1959 District Council elections indicated general acquiesence in SLPP rule. Of a total of 309 seats, the PNP captured only 29, of which 13 were in Albert Margai's home district of Moyamba. Another 59 were won by Independents, some of whom were PNP sympathizers unable to show their views openly, but 219 were taken by persons claiming to be members of the SLPP.[56] The PNP made a particularly poor showing in the north, despite claims of support there, winning only 3 seats against 89 for the SLPP. At the same time the PNP made a very poor showing in the Freetown Council elections, receiving only 10 per cent of the total vote and finishing far behind the SLPP (which won two of the three seats) and the UPP in all three seats.[57] It was quite clear that the PNP had made no major breakthrough in electoral support; and with the coming of independence it could not reasonably expect an improvement in its opportunities to seek that support.

The PNP's defeat in the District Council elections and the collapse of the UPP came at a critical time. The final constitutional talks which would lay down the constitution under which Sierra Leone would become independent were scheduled for early 1960. While few people expected Sir Milton to deal more harshly with the opposition once the last remaining British restraints were lifted, it was unrealistic to expect that opposition leaders would have any greater chance of turning the SLPP out after Independence. The stage was set for a grand reconciliation.

On March 25, 1960, Sir Milton Margai announced that the opposition leaders had agreed to join a United Front government following the completion of the pending constitutional talks. This master stroke of his career effectively decapitated all organized opposition within the country, and thus ensured his own and his party's continued dominance for some time to come. In this United Front, the fact that the SLPP was bargaining from strength was plainly apparent. The initial announcement stated that the parties "have agreed in principle to form a United National Front under the leadership of

55 / *Liberty*, August 8, 1959.
56 / *Vanguard*, October 28, 1959.
57 / *Sierra Leone Gazette*, November 12, 1959, p. 859.

Sir Milton Margai, our Premier."[58] By accepting the continuation in office of the man whose leadership had been a prime target of their attacks, the opposition parties clearly indicated that they were in effect yielding and coming under the umbrella of the SLPP. Since "the details of this united front are still being worked out,"[59] the opposition parties had given away the crucial bargaining point of who was to hold the post of Prime Minister.

Few substantive issues divided the government from the opposition parties. The opposition were on record as wanting the Paramount Chiefs removed to an upper house,[60] but this could be viewed simply as a means of reducing the SLPP's majority in the legislature. In the Report of the Constitutional Conference, however, no mention was made of changing the legislature from its unicameral form which included Paramount Chief representatives, and the conference further agreed that among the constitution's "entrenched" clauses should be one guaranteeing the continuance of the office of Paramount Chief "as existing by customary law and usage."[61] The opposition were also expected to ask for a revision of land tenure laws in the Protectorate;[62] this had been a long-standing Creole grievance, and the UPP had already raised it in the legislature.[63] But again, there was no mention of any change in the land tenure laws in the Report, and the prohibition on freehold in the provinces remained. Although the PNP had been critical of Dr Margai's intention to arrange a defence agreement with Britain,[64] with the exception of Siaka Stevens, all delegates now accepted the government view that an agreement should be ratified and signed after independence.[65] The other major point of contention had been the opposition claim that there should be fresh elections before independence;[66] but again with the exception of Stevens, all the delegates now accepted the government's position that no further elections were necessary before independence. The SLPP clearly had its way in the conference, but there were no major points of principle at stake on which any party would have to make concessions.

Shortly after his return home from the conference, the Premier announced his new United Front Ministry. Three opposition leaders were included, against a total of 13 SLPP ministers.[67] Albert Margai took the portfolio of

58 / *Vanguard*, March 26, 1960.

59 / *Ibid.*

60 / *Daily Mail*, March 16, 1960.

61 / *Report of the Sierra Leone Constitutional Conference, 1960* (Freetown: Government Printer, 1960), p. 7.

62 / *Daily Mail*, March 16, 1960.

63 / See *House of Representatives Debates*, Session 1958–59, Vol. I (August 27, 1958), pp. 153–62.

64 / See PNP statement in *Daily Mail*, February 21, 1959.

65 / *Report of the Constitutional Conference*, pp. 7, 9.

66 / See, for example, *Liberty*, August 8, 1959.

67 / *Daily Mail*, June 1, 1960 gives the full list of appointments.

Natural Resources from A. J. Demby, who in turn took responsibility for Mines and Labour from John Karefa-Smart, leaving Karefa-Smart with Lands and "special responsibility" for Defence and External Affairs. Cyril Rogers-Wright was given Housing and Country Planning, which was carved out of Kande Bureh's Ministry of Works and Housing. Gideon Dickson-Thomas became the IPP representative in the Cabinet, taking Social Welfare from H. E. B. John's portfolio of Education and Welfare. Some time later, John Nelson-Williams of the IPP and S. T. Navo of the PNP were made ministerial secretaries. At the same time, M. S. Mustapha was appointed Deputy Premier.

The rather paltry allotment handed out to the opposition leaders was probably the best they could expect in view of the weakness of their position. This weakness, we have seen, was only partially due to the hold the SLPP leaders possessed through the chiefs on the electorate. To a considerably greater extent UPP and PNP weakness was due to their irrelevance to the major discontents of Sierra Leone. Neither party held any ideology which could differentiate them from the SLPP and give their activists faith during the long, painful struggle to win power on their own. This lack of any firmly held distinctive beliefs contributed to the failure of both parties to establish an organization which could offset the chiefs. The UPP was further handicapped by its "Creole" biases, while the PNP's leaders may have been inhibited from taking a "radical" stance by their social origins. Politics to the opposition parties was very little more than a game in which the "outs" tried to supplant the "ins."

AN SLPP HEGEMONY: SUMMARY AND IMPLICATIONS

Few serious differences separated the major political parties in Sierra Leone by 1960. Their divergences in policies stemmed principally from whether they were in or out of office, to a limited extent from their personalities, and scarcely at all from any comprehensive view of the world. Their divergences in social background were even slighter than their policy differences (see Tables 7:2 and 7:3). Practically all were from high-status business or professional occupations, and most, among the opposition as well as the government, enjoyed close links with the traditional elite as well. It was a UPP member, Valecius Neale-Caulker, who once told the House of Representatives: "One thing that gives me satisfaction is that 90 per cent of the members of this House are from ruling houses."[68]

This homogeneity of social background was reinforced by personal links. A large proportion of the legislature had attended the same schools. Bo School, which claimed among its Old Boys six SLPP ordinary members, nine

68 / *Parliamentary Debates*, III (mimeo), October 3, 1961, p. 77.

TABLE 7:2

The 1957 Parliament: occupations of ordinary members before election by party

Party	Professional				Business		Poli-tician	Civil servant, clerical	NA or DC	Wage worker
	Law	Doctor	Teacher	Other	Trader	Manager				
SLPP (N = 23)	1	2	6	3[a]	3	2	1	2	2	1
PNP (N = 5)	3	—	—	1[b]	—	—	—	1	—	—
SLPIM (N = 2)	—	—	—	1[c]	—	—	1	—	—	—
UPP (N = 9)	1	—	1	1[d]	1	—	4	1	—	—

Notes: "Trader" includes petty traders and cash crop farming; "Manager" includes persons owning their own large businesses, which also implies a higher degree of entrepreneurial skill.
a/Two dispensers, one surveyor. b/Economist. c/Dispenser. d/Accountant.

TABLE 7:3

The 1957 Parliament: occupations of fathers of ordinary members by party

Party	Paramount Chief	Other traditional authority	Western profession	Trader, wage worker	Farmer	Other, Unknown
SLPP (up-country) (N = 17)	6	1	2 (2)	7 (4)	—	1
SLPP (Creole) (N = 6)	—	—	2	3	—	1
PNP (N = 5)	—	2	1 (1)	2 (2)	—	—
SLPIM (N = 2)	2	—	—	—	—	—
UPP (N = 9)	—	—	3 (1)	3	2	1
TOTAL	8	3	8 (4)	15 (6)	2	3

Note: Numbers in parentheses indicate number of fathers who were also members of ruling families.

Paramount Chiefs, and two PNP members, was most significant because of its deliberate fostering of the belief that it was the training ground for an elite. Albert Academy, with five SLPP members and one each from the KPM and UPP, also was well represented, while St. Edward's and the Prince of Wales School had Old Boys in all three parties.

A further factor making for cohesion among the Protectorate representatives was that as individuals in "professional" occupations or government

service they generally knew each other before entering the House, sometimes through working together in organizations like the Amalgamated
Teachers Organization and often simply through being stationed together
in the various district and provincial capitals. Of the traders and others who
did not have these occupational links, some had developed connections
directly through political activity either in the SLPP or in District Councils.

These links did not, of course, create sufficient sympathy in the SLPP to
allow opposition parties to compete with it on completely equal terms. In the
1959 District Council elections, besides utilizing government transport and
personnel freely for its political campaigning, the SLPP put several obstacles
in the way of intending PNP candidates, including advancing the days for
nominations and changing the locations for submission of nomination papers.
They also called the chiefs and Tribal Authorities into service against the
PNP. A reasonably accurate picture of this situation is given in the PNP's
complaint to the Governor after the election:

Most of the Paramount Chiefs, Section Chiefs and Tribal Authorities played
a most significant part in the elections. They played a major role in the selection
of candidates, and brought great pressure to bear on their people to vote for the
SLPP. At least one chief refused permission for political meetings to be held in
his chiefdom and threatened to arrest anyone who convened or attended any PNP
meeting – this was only a few days before the election. ... The chief refused
permission for the use of the public NA barri on application by a member of the
Tribal Authority.[69]

"Big men" who showed too much sympathy for opposition parties were often
disciplined. The Mende Tribal Headman in Freetown, A. B. Paila, found
his appointment revoked in September 1959 as a result of his covert support
of the PNP.[70] This example was enough to warn others. A few weeks later,
the Kroo Tribal Headman, described as a "long-standing member of the
UPP," announced he was joining the SLPP because he was "very much concerned about the welfare of the Kroos in Freetown ... The UPP cannot do
anything to help the Kroos. Only the SLPP can."[71]

But as long as the legislators continued to be drawn from fairly high-status
occupations, and as long as the SLPP leaders were content merely to safeguard their personal hold on office, the struggle for political power was not
likely to take on a desperate quality. While the salaries of legislators were

69 / *Daily Mail*, November 17, 1959.

70 / Most of the leaders in the Mende community in Freetown supported Paila (*Daily
Mail*, June 18 and July 30, 1959), but the government revoked his appointment for
"defying government authority" after he had refused to attend a hearing without his
lawyers being present (*ibid.*, August 7, and September 5, 1959). The lawyers were all
PNP leaders.

71 / *Vanguard*, October 3, 1959.

TABLE 7:4
Salaries of legislators, 1957–67

Rank	Basic salary (£)	Allowances		Other perquisites	
		Entertainment (£)	Constituency (£)	Housing	Car
Chief Minister	4000	300	180	Free	Free
Ministers	3000	240	180	Free	Mileage allowance[b]
Junior Ministers	1650	60	180	Free	Mileage allowance[b]
Leader of the Opposition	1500	200	180	—	Mileage allowance[b]
Government Whip	1200	—	180	—	—
Ordinary members	920	—	180	Allowance[a]	Loan[c]

a/Members receive £2 per night when sleeping away from their houses during parliamentary sessions.
b/For all trips on official business, at one shilling a mile (later provided with free ministerial cars).
c/Loan of up to £500 at 5 per cent interest.

higher than those they could hope to obtain in alternative occupations (Table 7:4), and the perquisites and prestige considerably greater than those attaching even to the office of Paramount Chief, the gulf between the legislators and other "big men" was not so great as to be unbridgeable. In strictly monetary terms, a teacher could expect to receive £500 a year or more; a trader handling a sizable volume of business might have net earnings of £1,000 or more; and a chief could often exceed this amount, although he would be under the same pressure as an MP to distribute his wealth as benefits to his people. Equally important was the fact that many areas of life were not politicized; for example, a lawyer identified with an opposition party might not receive government business, but there were plenty of clients available who would not shun him on political grounds. In short, it would not be disastrous for a man whose background gave him some security of occupation to side with an opposition party or to cross to it in Parliament. However, it would be much more dangerous for an ordinary farmer or petty artisan or trader to undertake work for an opposition party; the sanctions that could be imposed on him by his chief could be considerably more severe than any that would be imposed on the elite individual. It would not be a great exaggeration to say that opposition politics was permissible for the elite, but largely out of bounds for the ordinary people.

Within the ranks of the parliamentarians party divisions were not deep. Whatever their party, members owed their election largely to their personal efforts; their party could hardly punish them by denying them the nomination. This situation fostered a common interest in their re-election among all MPs, an interest considerably more compelling than the claims of party loyalty. However, there was one division in the Parliament. Not only were Ministers much better paid than backbenchers, but they were in a better position to influence the direction of government patronage. With this gulf between the ministerial elect and the "have-nots," and the lack of a serious gulf between parties, it is perhaps not surprising that an informal alliance eventually crystallized into the Backbenchers Association.

This group appears to have been formed before the United Front, although the first public reference to it was made by Barthes Wilson in 1961: "A committee of all backbenchers was formed in which they listed over twenty demands which they wanted as backbenchers. I was in that committee ... at one time it was headed by Paramount Chief Yumkella and at another time by myself."[72] The Association was concerned, as Wilson's remarks made clear, with obtaining privileges for the backbenchers. Wilson made his remark during a debate over MPs' rent allowances, while at other times the backbenchers united to demand a pay increase,[73] and to bring about a change in the constituency flags they were allowed to fly on their cars. The Association continued in existence during the 1962 Parliament, even though there was a somewhat greater gap between the SLPP and the All Peoples Congress than between the SLPP and previous opposition parties. It may have become less effective after 1962; one APC member claimed that the SLPP members ignored suggestions put forward by the APC. Still, it is significant that the backbenchers did see themselves as having a common interest cutting across party lines.

Within the ranks of Parliament, the overall picture was one of happy harmony. Other influential groups were equally satisfied. The chiefs could be content with the fact that their office was entrenched in the Independence Constitution, with their representation in the central government, and with the perpetuation of their control over local affairs. The Western elite could be equally satisfied in that they dominated the Cabinet and legislature, with all the personal privileges and power entailed, and were rapidly taking over the civil service from the British.[74] One major rift, the division between Creoles and countrymen, appeared to be partially healed. Although many Creoles had simply withdrawn from politics, those who remained found themselves well treated by the SLPP. Of the five new ministerial posts granted in the

72 / *House of Representatives Debates*, Session 1961/62, II (July 31, 1961), p. 124.

73 / *Daily Mail*, April 16, 1964.

74 / By 1960, 245 out of 583 senior civil service posts were filled by Sierra Leoneans, including such top posts as Secretary for Training and Recruitment, Solicitor-General, Permanent Secretary of Lands, Mines, and Labour, and Engineer-in-Chief of the Electricity Department. The Creoles still held a long lead over up-country people; only 53 of the Sierra Leoneans appear to have been of up-country origin. Data compiled from *The Staff List*, 1960.

aftermath of the United Front, three went to Creoles. The Colony (renamed the Western Area after Independence) remained heavily over-represented in Parliament[75] and although the Creoles were no longer the dominant ethnic group in the area, they continued to receive a substantial share of the government nominations.[76] The extent to which the Creoles had been reconciled was indicated by the fact that the leader of the National Council's remnant, Columbus Thompson, agreed to join the United Front and participate in the 1960 constitutional conference.[77] Furthermore, with four-fifths of the African-held senior civil service posts in their hands, the Creoles appeared well entrenched. Too small a group to comprise an independent electoral force, the politically inclined Creoles seemed to have come to terms with the SLPP and to be prepared to make use of their special aptitudes to ensure a strong place for themselves.

But other elements in the Sierra Leone polity were not so well served by the United Front. The ordinary farmers had found no party during this period which could articulate their grievances against their chiefs, but this did not mean they lacked grievances. The less affluent members of the new urban societies had found some outlet in the PNP, and in Freetown in the UPP; it remained to be seen how strongly the leaders of these parties would speak for their interests once they had entered the government. A different type of discontent was the growing unhappiness of northerners at the apparent neglect of their region, and the suspicion that this might be a deliberate Mende design. Similar discontent, reinforced by dislike of their own chiefs' behaviour, pervaded Kono. The materials still existed for opposition movements to be built; what they had lacked up to 1960 were leaders to build them.

75 / In the 1962 redistribution, Freetown and the Rural Area each retained their six seats. Their populations entitled them to only four and two seats, respectively.

76 / In the 1962 elections, nine SLPP candidates in the Western Area were Creole, and only three were of up-country origin.

77 / See *Daily Mail*, March 3, 1960. Apart from the trip to England, Thompson's action was free from self-serving motives; since neither he nor any other NC member had a seat in the House of Representatives, they could receive no ministerial portfolio in the United Front.

It should be added that some Creoles still carried on a rearguard action, contesting the legality of the British Order-in-Council handing sovereignty to the Sierra Leone government. Their action was not disposed of by the High Court of Appeal until 1965.

Other Creoles insisted on retaining British passports rather than accept those of Sierra Leone. A few emigrated to England rather than live in an independent Sierra Leone.

PART FOUR

The growth of a new tribal polarization

8

The birth of the All Peoples Congress

The United Front appeared to be the most satisfactory arrangement obtainable for the leaders of the UPP and PNP, from both the viewpoints of personal interest and of their social groups. Creole interests could be at least as well defended inside the SLPP as from outside it, while the "young men" who headed the PNP were not strongly antipathetic to the more traditionalist elements in the SLPP. However, other elements of Sierra Leone society which had no spokesmen of their own in the political elite, notably the wage workers in towns and the ordinary farmers, were unlikely to accept the United Front with enthusiasm. At the same time, tribal and regional rifts were beginning to appear in the hitherto solid ranks of the "countrymen," with both northerners and Konos developing doubts about the behaviour of the government.

Unease among northerners, and particularly Temnes, had been growing slowly as Sierra Leoneans assumed a greater share of power in the government. Sir Milton had taken steps to allay Temne fears in 1957 by appointing Kande Bureh and I. B. Taylor-Kamara as well as his close supporter Dr Karefa-Smart to important portfolios,[1] and later added Y. D. Sesay (a Loko) and Paramount Chief Bai Koblo to the Cabinet, but in 1960 his concern for a balance seemed to lessen. The Temne leaders in the SLPP hoped in 1960 for the appointment of one of their number to the newly created post of Deputy Prime Minister "to bring peace between the two tribes,"[2] but instead the position went to Mustapha, an Aku Creole. A further blow to Temne pride came with the announcement of the new United Front Ministers; the Mendes received one additional post, the Creoles three, but the Temnes none. Two of the new appointments were carved out of Temnes' ministries, which appeared to many Temnes to be a further indication that they were

1 / Works and Housing, Trade and Industry, and Lands, Mines and Labour, respectively.

2 / See Kilson, "Sierra Leone Politics," *West Africa*, No. 2249 (July 9, 1960), p. 774.

being downgraded. At a rally for the United Front, it was reported that an SLPP speaker "told the Temnes in particular not to be annoyed over the present coalition. She said that dividing a Minister's portfolio did not affect his salary. She condemned all protests against Mr Mustapha's new appointment as Deputy Premier."[3] A correspondent in *West Africa* also noted that among the Temnes "there have been signs of hostility to the new dispensation. ... Kande Bureh, on tour of the Port Loko District was recalled by the Prime Minister, and a meeting of the Temne in the East Side was unexpectedly visited by the Premier himself."[4] One SLPP northern Minister commented that as a result of the United Front, with which he disagreed, "I became dormant." Martin Kilson's judgment that "the UNF can be viewed as a convenient arrangement for perpetuating Mende predominance in Sierra Leone politics"[5] seemed to be shared by many Temnes.

The Konos too were slighted in the United Front. Since Rev. Paul Dunbar had lost his seat in 1957, there had been no Kono in the Ministry, and when the United Front was formed, both the SLPIM representatives remained back-benchers.[6] The central government had appointed a special Development Officer for Kono in 1958 and set aside some funds, but this was not enough to convince Konos that they were getting a fair share of the wealth their diamonds were providing for the rest of the country. The United Front did not produce a local truce between the SLPP and SLPIM in Kono. Just three weeks after the United Front was announced, the SLPIM trounced the SLPP in the Kono District Council elections, winning 24 out of 30 seats.[7]

Two other sources of discontent had a class rather than a tribal basis. The northern chiefs had not learned from the 1955–56 riots; they continued to extort money and other goods, and to use the proceeds to accumulate real estate and set up private businesses. The central government had done little to stop this. It had deposed or suspended eleven chiefs whose abuses had been particularly flagrant, but two of these had already been reinstated.[8] No more effective controls had been placed on the chiefs to prevent a repetition of the same situation; in fact, since the riots the chiefs' position had been enhanced by the fact that the SLPP leaders came to rely on them to suppress political activity by the PNP and UPP. The continuing abuses by the chiefs and their identification with the SLPP provided a wide opening for a radical anti-chief party, at least in the north.

Another base for a radical movement was provided by the growing number

3 / *Daily Mail*, June 29, 1960.
4 / "Muslim Anxieties," *West Africa*, No. 2247 (June 25, 1960), p. 713.
5 / Kilson, "Sierra Leone Politics," *West Africa*, No. 2249 (July 9, 1960), p. 774.
6 / Though Mbriwa was a delegate to the Constitutional Conference.
7 / *Daily Mail*, April 13, 1960.
8 / And three more were to be reinstated within a year of the United Front.

of young men entering the lower levels of the wage economy as lorry drivers, clerks, traders, and wage workers. These young men, who congregated in the towns, had little attachment to a government which supported the seemingly irrelevant traditional institutions which they had abandoned. They were attracted to the PNP's anti-traditionalist stand and its goal of more rapid development, but were left politically homeless by the United Front. Their numbers were becoming substantial; by 1960 almost a quarter of the adult male population was engaged in non-agricultural employment.[9] The greatest number of these individuals had very limited education. Primary school enrolment had more than tripled between 1948 and 1958,[10] but less than half of those entering the first form completed primary schooling, and of those who did finish, only a third were able to enter secondary schools.[11] This produced a pool of about 6,000 boys a year during the late 1950s who either had dropped out of or finished primary school and were entering the labour market. Very few returned to their family farms. These young men were ripe for appeals to develop the country more rapidly through such "radical" means as keeping Sierra Leone's wealth in Sierra Leone by nationalizing foreign firms, and by distributing wealth more equally, at least down to the level of the wage workers. While they were not numerous enough to provide an electoral majority by themselves, they could provide the cadres of organizers needed to stir up other discontents.

A radical appeal, whether to the peasants against their chiefs, or to the urban school-leavers against the bourgeoisie, required in Sierra Leone a very different approach to politics than a tribal appeal. Tribal or regional appeals were not the road to exclusive power since no tribe or region controlled more than a third of the seats in the legislature.[12] A tribal strategy would call for electing representatives to the legislature who could bargain for improvements within the existing framework of "brokerage" politics. A radical appeal, on the other hand, could produce an electoral majority, if it

9 / The *1963 Census* showed some 600,000 males age 15 and up. The Department of Labour in the same year reported some 57,000 persons in wage employment on the basis of returns from employers of six or more persons, and exclusive of diamond tributers. These employers in the 1950s engaged somewhat over half the wage labour force. We thus obtain the following numbers of persons in wage labour outside agriculture:

Employed by larger employers (Labour Dept.)	57,000
Other wage earners (estimated)	50,000
Diamond tributers (Swindell's calculation)	43,000
	———
Total wage earners	150,000

10 / From 21,330 to 65,172. *The Development Programme in Education*, p. 4.

11 / *Ibid.*, pp. 1, 2. More than a third of the primary pupils, and a larger proportion of drop-outs, were girls.

12 / Excluding, of course, the SLPP's earlier appeal to all "countrymen."

could succeed in cutting across tribal lines. To mobilize this majority would require a resort to a more ideological form of politics, and specifically an insistence that the existing social structure be drastically altered. Tribal demands, in short, could be accommodated within the SLPP; radical demands could not.

Beyond these partially politicized segments of the population, there was widespread uneasiness at the approach of independence. This uneasiness was suggested by the type of questions asked in letters to the *Daily Mail* in December 1960:

After Independence what will be the procedure of "woman damage" in Marampa Chiefdom as the present fixed price is not less than £10 which is more or less a business enterprise.[13]

Will the members of the House of Representatives allow a reduction in their salaries so that more money may be made available for development projects?[14]

Prices have been raised on some commodities; there are higher rates and taxes; house rents are soaring. Why is it that Independence is bringing hardship upon us?[15]

Will all those who were born in Sierra Leone continue to lease land in the provinces?[16]

The problems raised by these queries – abuses of power by the chiefs, the tendency for the political elite to consider their own welfare before that of the country, the general costs of living and hardships faced by ordinary citizens, and the question of land tenure – were among the most worrisome to large parts of the population. Ordinary villagers, particularly in the north, had no reason to be enthusiastic about the attainment of full power by a government which would undoubtedly permit their chiefs to continue to control them. Many Temnes were worried about the prospect of a predominantly Mende government. The Creoles were unhappy about land tenure laws which permitted up-country people to buy large tracts of land in the Western Area, but prohibited Creoles from buying land in the provinces. Some people in the provinces feared that at independence these laws might be changed, with the result that their land could be sold to strangers. The leader of an English parliamentary delegation noted these widespread misgivings: "Many times we were asked, 'Why are you leaving us? You have been our friends and have helped us. Why do you want to go?' In one confidential meeting in the Protectorate, a small group of Africans holding responsible posts all

13 / *Daily Mail*, December 6, 1960.
14 / *Ibid.*
15 / *Ibid.*
16 / *Ibid.*

agreed that in their district opinion was four to one against independence now."[17] He added that these doubts did not seem to exist "among Ministers or to many other members of the governing groups."[18] But among the public at large, it appeared that there was a widespread feeling that Independence was something arranged to suit the convenience of the politicians, not a great event in the lives of anyone else.

Such attitudes clearly demonstrated a lack of nationalist fervour. This was further demonstrated by the government's announcement in July 1960 that it was about to launch a campaign to "explain to the people what independence means,"[19] a remark indicating how little the political parties had done up to that time to impress on the public the significance of this step.

The organization of these discontents under a single political banner could have created a formidable challenge to the SLPP. While most of the political leaders had been swallowed up in the United Front, some of the PNP men outside Parliament were not prepared to accept the new dispensation. By far the most prominent of these was Siaka Stevens, the principal victim of the constitutional conference's decision not to hold an election before independence. Stevens startled the conference by abruptly refusing to sign its report on the grounds that it committed Sierra Leone to a defence agreement with the United Kingdom and made no provision for elections before independence.[20] In taking this stand, he split with Albert Margai, who signed the report and dissociated himself from Stevens' refusal to sign. On returning to Freetown, Stevens explained the action of his erstwhile close colleague in terms tinged with bitterness: "Human nature being what it is, it would not be unnatural to expect the non-Government members of the delegation to London to watch their personal interests. I should therefore not expect a man who is being groomed by his brother for the Premiership to agree with me on such a point."[21]

Stevens was not the only PNP leader to object to the Constitutional Conference and the United Front. From Peking, where he was paying a short visit, the PNP's Organizing Secretary, M. O. Bash-Taqi, denounced the conference as "bogus" and in the interests of the "British colonialists" whom the PNP was "determined to kick out."[22] In letters of resignation from the party published some months later, both Taqi and another northerner, Prince Koh, the Deputy Secretary General, charged that the leaders had failed to consult

17 / Rt. Hon. Hilary Marquand, "The ? Over Sierra Leone," *New Commonwealth*, vol. 39 (April 1961), p. 216.

18 / *Ibid.*

19 / *Daily Mail*, July 4, 1960.

20 / See *Report of the Constitutional Conference*, and *Daily Mail*, May 19, 1960.

21 / *Daily Mail*, May 19, 1960. Albert retorted that it was "significant" that Stevens' objections began after the decision not to hold an election. *Ibid*, May 26.

22 / *Ibid.*, May 16, 1960.

the rank and file of the party on the formation of a United Front, and had allowed the PNP to be completely submerged by the SLPP.[23] Taqi and Koh, both in their early thirties and employed as clerks until they entered politics on a full-time basis, were representative of the younger radical members of the PNP. A number of other young men also left this party after the United Front was formed. However, tribal as well as radical feelings played a part here. All those who left were northerners; the Mende young men, on the other hand, seem to have accepted the United Front.

Even some northern leaders of the SLPP were disturbed enough over the tribal issue to provide surreptitious help in forming a new political party. The meeting at which it was decided to form the All Peoples Congress was held at the house of A. G. Sesay, a prominent Temne supporter of the SLPP. Kande Bureh, too, apparently played a behind-the-scenes role in arranging the founding of the APC. The new organization first took the form of the Elections Before Independence Movement (EBIM), a catch-all movement appealing to a wide range of dissidents. In two mass rallies in Freetown in July 1960 the EBIM attacked the United Front coalition as "unrepresentative" and demanded that the electorate be given a chance to make its views known before Independence.[24] This was its main political argument. The rest of its program simply tried to appeal to the most widespread current grievances. It objected to the alleged defence agreement which it accused the government of having already concluded with Britain; it charged that the government had failed to allow the "natural rulers" to discuss the future of chieftaincy by themselves; and it criticized the deportation of individuals from the Kono district.[25] After two months, the EBIM gave way to the All Peoples Congress, with Siaka Stevens being anounced as the leader of the new party.[26]

From the time of its formation, the APC was led entirely by northerners. Both Stevens and the Secretary-General of the party, C. A. Kamara-Taylor, were Limba; others who were leaders from the outset, such as M. O. Bash-Taqi, S. I. and S. A. T. Koroma, and S. A. Fofana, were Temne.[27] One

23 / For Koh's letter, see *ibid.*, November 3, 1960; for Bash-Taqi's, *ibid.*, November 21, 1960.

24 / See *Daily Mail*, July 18 and August 1, 1960, for reports of the rallies.

25 / For full texts of the resolutions passed by the two rallies, and the government's comments on them, see *ibid.*, September 8, 1960.

26 / *Ibid.*, September 13, 1960.

27 / While the composition of the APC executive was not entirely clearcut, the following were the most important among its founders: Siaka Stevens (Limba, trade unionist and politician, commoner); C. A. Kamara-Taylor (Limba, clerk and transport owner, commoner), S. A. Fofana (Temne, tailor, ruling family); S. I. Koroma (Temne, transport owner, commoner); S. A. T. Koroma (Temne, transport owner, commoner, but with mother the daughter of a chief); M. O. Bash-Taqi (Temne, politician, ruling family); Prince Koh (Limba, politician, son of chief).

leader explained this on the grounds that "you have to start from some-where – you need a base in order to get to others." But as we have seen, this northern composition of the APC leadership reflected the fact that northerners were particularly disquieted over the apparent downgrading of their tribes in favour of the Mendes. Even some chiefs were suspected of favouring the APC, although of course they could not openly support it.

In certain ways, the APC appeared to be a successor to the PNP. Stevens and two other members of the "inner circle," Bash-Taqi and Prince Koh, had been members of the PNP executive; the Koromas and Kamara-Taylor had all been members of the party, though not on the executive. Of the key members of the APC, only S. A. Fofana had not come in through the PNP; he had been active in the Youth Section of the SLPP, and when he entered the APC brought a number of other northerners with him. While a number of individuals from the UPP, both northerners and Creoles, also came over to the APC in the next two years,[28] the main source of recruits to its "activist" cadres was the PNP.

In some of its attitudes also the APC appeared as a successor to the PNP. Its suspicion of any defence agreement with Britain was similar to the general suspicion of the colonial power expressed earlier by the PNP. Its advocacy of "non-alignment" in foreign policy and of the development of the educational system "so as to make it reflect the African personality and way of life,"[29] both harked back to the Pan-African and non-aligned outlook of the PNP.

In other ways the two parties differed sharply. The key difference, of course, was that the APC was almost entirely a northern party, whereas the PNP had been predominantly southern with some Creole support. This difference was to be the most significant one in determining the party's pattern of electoral support. However, other distinctions were also important. Whereas almost all the members of the PNP executive (except the Creoles) were members of ruling families, only three out of the seven APC leaders would be eligible to stand for the position of Paramount Chief.[30] Moreover, nearly all the APC leaders' fathers worked as petty traders, shop assistants, or in minor clerical posts; while they were in the money economy, they tended to be at its lower levels. The members of the PNP executive tended to be drawn predominantly from the ranks of the professions or other occupations requiring post-secondary education; nine of the executive members had university training or its equivalent, and seven were lawyers. None of the APC leaders, by contrast, had gone beyond secondary school, and all had

28 / For example, Barthes Wilson, Mrs Stella Ralph-James (Creoles) and Mucktar Kallay (Mandingo).

29 / "1962 General Election Manifesto of All Peoples Congress" (mimeo, N.D.).

30 / One other was related to a ruling family through his mother.

earned their livings in clerical or trading occupations, mostly on a rather small scale.[31] Three could be described as full-time politicians before joining the APC.

The APC leaders also stood in marked contrast to those of the SLPP. The SLPP leaders, like those of the PNP, generally came from families with high status in either traditional society or in the money economy, and frequently in both. Half of the APC leaders were from families without standing in either traditional or modern society. The SLPP leaders, while not as well educated on the average as those of the PNP, still included a sizable proportion of university graduates in their ranks; the APC had none. The SLPP included a number of leaders who had attained a recognized standard in their chosen occupations; the APC leaders came from occupations where such standards were not required. Finally, there was a pronounced generation gap between the members of these parties. The median age of the SLPP ministry in 1960 before the United Front was 53; the median age of the APC leaders at this time was 35.

These differences suggested a number of possible features of the APC as an opposition party. The age difference suggested that the younger men had finally entered the political scene on their own, rather than as units of the existing parties. The leaders' lack of links with either the traditional or the Western elites suggested they would be freer to take a stand in radical opposition to these groups than any previous opposition party. Finally, overshadowing all other features, even though it was not played up, was the prospect of a tribal clash between a northern APC and a largely southern SLPP.

More than any previous opposition party, the APC maintained a marked ideological tone. Its leaders professed to be socialist, and its constitution laid down as a goal for Sierra Leone the establishment of "a welfare state based upon a socialist pattern of society in which all citizens, regardless of class, tribe, colour or creed, shall have equal opportunity and where there shall be no exploitation of man by man, tribe by tribe, or class by class."[32] It regarded itself as the party of the "common people" as opposed to the privileged elite, particularly the chiefs, and some of its leaders seemed to believe that the potential for a class struggle existed in Sierra Leone. But it was rather vague about how socialism would be introduced into Sierra Leone. Although it recognized that "the kind of socialism it envisages ... is based upon a high degree of industrialisation and agricultural productivity"[33] it never did spell out how this industrialization would be achieved, nor did it ever clarify the meaning of "a socialist pattern of society." At one time it proposed that

31 / S. A. Fofana owned a tailoring shop which employed several people; none of the transport owners owned more than three or four vehicles.

32 / *The Constitution of the All Peoples Congress* (Freetown, 1965), Part I, Section 3 (iii).

33 / *APC Constitution*, Part I, Section 3 (v).

foreign capital be placed under "political control,"[34] and it suggested that the Cable and Wireless Corporation, a private British firm which shared control of Sierra Leone's external telecommunications, should be nationalized,[35] but these demands seemed to be motivated more by the fact that these enterprises were foreign owned than by the fact that they were private. The APC leaders were by occupation petty bourgeoisie rather than wage-earners; apart from Stevens more than a decade earlier, none of them had close connections with wage-earners. When they insisted that political independence was meaningless without economic independence, their goal seemed to be to substitute Sierra Leonean businessmen for foreigners. Their 1962 election manifesto asserted: "The APC believes that there are many ways by which Sierra Leoneans could be encouraged to get into the trade and industry of this country. ... Certain fields of the retail trade should be left to local people. ..."[36] In a discussion with the writer, one of the allegedly most radical leaders of the APC argued against having the government raise capital and operate industries itself on the grounds that the government was bound to be inefficient since "it doesn't care about making a profit." He preferred to have ownership in the hands of individual share-holding Sierra Leoneans, and seemed unconcerned about the prospect that this would buttress inequalities within Sierra Leone. The APC leaders' attachment to "socialism" appeared to remain at the level of general inclinations; they made no attempt to work out any comprehensive exposition of what socialism would involve in an African context.[37] Their "radicalism" in the economic field was basically compounded of demands for more rapid development, suspicion of foreign private investment, and curbs on the conspicuous consumption of wealth by politicians.[38]

The APC's attitude toward chieftaincy was more genuinely radical. Some of its leaders saw the relations between chiefs and people in class terms, with the well-being of the chiefs being irreconcilably opposed to that of their people. *We Yone*, the party newspaper, frequently attacked the Tribal Authority system as "feudal."[39] The APC leaders were probably not disposed to destroy the institution of chieftaincy utterly, even if they had thought such

34 / See *We Yone*, January 16, 1965.

35 / *Daily Mail*, March 19, 1963.

36 / All Peoples Congress, *1962 General Election Manifesto*.

37 / This contrasted with the serious attempts by other African radicals to come to grips with the problem, notably Sekou Touré in *L'Expérience guinéene et l'unité Africaine* (Paris: Présence Africaine, 1959) and, on a more modest scale, Tom Mboya in the Kenya Government pamphlet, *African Socialism and its Application to Planning in Kenya* (Nairobi, 1965).

38 / The 1962 election manifesto called for curbing "unnecessary expenditure" such as "excessive numbers of Ministers" as well as promising more schools, hospitals, encouragement for agriculture and industrial development.

39 / For example, see *We Yone*, January 23, 1965, editorial "Chiefs and Politics."

a course feasible. Their concern seemed rather to be to "democratize" the system by making the chiefs accountable to their people, rather than leaving them subject to the control of a central government. Thus the 1962 APC election manifesto declared:

The APC would without hesitation revoke the law which lays down that the names of candidates who desire to stand for Chieftaincy should be vetted by the Governor-General who is advised by the Prime Minister, and should the Governor-General rule that a particular candidate is not entitled to stand, then that candidate will not stand whether the chiefdom people like that or not.

The APC objects *in toto* to this kind of arrangement which, in the view of the party, will turn Paramount Chiefs into glorified civil servants.

The APC holds the view strongly that this is unnecessary interference and that chiefdom people should be left to themselves to elect their chief.[40]

At its 1963 convention the APC stated its general policy regarding Paramount Chiefs in these terms:

The APC ... has every regard for the Natural Rulers of the country and would like to see them in a house of their own ... rather than that they should be fettered by sharing a single legislature with the rest of the country.

The APC believes that chieftaincy has a very important role to play in the future development of the country and therefore chiefs should be encouraged and given every assistance to adapt themselves to changing conditions.[41]

However, this concern for the welfare of the chiefs should be qualified by noting that the APC was subject to the same harassment as previous opposition parties by the chiefs acting for the SLPP government. If it succeeded in gaining power, the APC was committed to mobilize the population through its own organization, and was unlikely to allow the chiefs to exercise any significant independent power. One could suspect that while it might preserve the institution, an APC government would reduce chieftaincy to a largely ceremonial role. In this matter the APC could certainly be considered the most "radical" party ever to appear on the Sierra Leone political scene.

The immediate preoccupation of the APC in 1960 was to force a general election before independence while the chances of a fair contest were relatively good. The widespread popular doubts about the desirability of independence, and the lack of any strong nationalist feeling to override these doubts, encouraged them in this hope, while the widespread tribal and class discontents promised a more permanent base.

The APC's first success came quickly. On November 1, 1960, in the annual

40 / "1962 General Election Manifesto."
41 / *Daily Mail*, April 19, 1962.

Freetown city council elections, their candidates won two of the three seats by substantial margins, and missed winning the third by only 27 votes.[42] Since the leaders of the UPP, IPP, and PNP had all announced their support for the SLPP's candidates, the victory was an impressive one. Stevens immediately seized on Sir Milton's earlier argument that the SLPP's win in the District Council elections had shown their strength, and insisted that now by the same argument the electorate of the capital had shown they had no more confidence in the coalition government.[43]

As the government continued to ignore the APC's demands for an election, and April 27, 1961, the date of independence, rapidly came closer, the APC leaders turned to more violent means of persuasion. On February 19, 1961, the Prime Minister's office warned that Sir Milton was "concerned about the threats, intimidating words and malicious and false rumours which are being uttered by certain irresponsible members of the community. ... The government will no longer tolerate such behaviour. ..."[44] The very day the Prime Minister issued this warning, a severe clash took place between APC and SLPP supporters. A number of APC leaders were subsequently charged with incitement and three were eventually found guilty. At the trial of the ringleader, M. O. Bash-Taqi, a witness testified that Taqi had urged his supporters to assault Ministers, "stop traffic, sink launches, stop trains,"[45] and to break up a meeting of Mendes being held that afternoon on the grounds that "independence is a national issue and not a tribal one."[46] For his activities he received a sentence of one year in jail.[47] Some members of the SLPP prepared to counter violence with violence; the former Mende Tribal Headman, A. B. Paila, announced in April the formation of the United Front Volunteers,[48] a "civil army" of 1,300 uniformed young men. Meanwhile Stevens, Kamara-Taylor, and I. T. A. Wallace-Johnson, who had announced the merger of his Radical Democratic Party with the APC shortly after the formation of the

42 / The results of the election were as follows:

East Ward	A. B. T. Jalloh (SLPP)	976	
	S. A. Fofana (APC)	949	Turnout 10.8%
Central Ward	S. I. Koroma (APC)	1,112	
	F. L. Nicol (SLPP)	405	Turnout 9.6%
West Ward I	J. T. Kanu (APC)	643	
	I. B. Sesay (SLPP)	329	Turnout 6.1%

Daily Mail, November 2, 1960. It should be noted that all three APC candidates were Temne.

43 / *Daily Mail*, November 11, 1960.
44 / *Ibid.*, February 20, 1961.
45 / *Ibid.*, February 21, 1961.
46 / *Ibid.*, February 24, 1961.
47 / *Ibid.*, May 6, 1961. He actually served nine months.
48 / *Vanguard*, April 12, 1961.

latter,[49] were charged with the publication of a seditious pamphlet.[50] Stevens and Kamara-Taylor were eventually sentenced to six months each,[51] although Stevens was later acquitted by the Court of Appeal.[52]

Finally, on April 18, just nine days before Independence, the government proclaimed a state of emergency and detained 18 of the leaders of the APC, including Stevens, Kamara-Taylor, Bash-Taqi, Wallace-Johnson, and all the rest of the executive, on the grounds that they were planning to commit acts of sabotage just before independence.[53] Other persons in Freetown suspected of being active in the party were also detained later, bringing the total number by Independence Day to 43. In a broadcast the night the emergency was declared, the Minister of Information (Y. D. Sesay, a northerner) asserted that the APC had tried to obtain explosives, had threatened to burn down a newspaper office, and blow up private homes, and had encouraged a general strike.[54] There seems to have been some justification for these accusations; on April 21 explosions occurred at both of Freetown's power stations, and the telephone lines between Freetown and the provinces were cut,[55] while on April 23 an unsuccessful attempt was made to sabotage a major bridge in the city.[56] The government was almost certainly justified in blaming these actions on APC extremists, and though the leaders were in jail at the time and thus not directly implicated, some of their more intemperate remarks may well have encouraged their supporters to resort to violence.

When the House of Representatives debated the detentions, all members present agreed that the APC leaders had deserved to be detained.[57] Sir Milton stressed that their detention was a temporary expedient: "I do not expect that detainees will be kept longer than is really necessary; as soon as we are satisfied that the country is out of danger, we will let almost all of them out."[58] True to his word, all the detainees were released by mid-May,[59] and the emergency regulations were revoked late in August.[60] Following his release, Stevens issued a statement stressing the APC's willingness to abide by the laws:

49 / *Daily Mail*, September 28, 1960.
50 / *Ibid.*, March 28, 1961.
51 / *Ibid.*, May 24, 1961.
52 / *Ibid.*, July 24, 1961.
53 / *Ibid.*, April 19, 1961.
54 / The text of Sesay's broadcast appears in *ibid.*
55 / *Ibid.*, April 22, 1961.
56 / *Ibid.*, April 26, 1961.
57 / Wallace-Johnson, the APC's only member in Parliament, was in jail. Two UPP members expressed concern that the legislation might be used unjustly at some future date, but agreed that the APC leaders needed to be detained. See *Parliamentary Debates*, 1961, I (April 28, 1961) (mimeo.).
58 / *Ibid.*, p. 9.
59 / See *Daily Mail*, May 17, 18 and 19, 1961.
60 / *Ibid.*, August 30, 1961.

"Independence having become an accomplished fact and the Government having given the assurance of General Elections in 1962, the APC calls upon all its members to maintain the Party policy line of (a) full respect for law and order (b) constitutional and lawful procedure in all matters. The APC has never stood, and will never stand, for violence, sabotage or unconstitutional action. ..."[61]

Despite Sir Milton's demonstration of tolerance, and Stevens' assurance of good behaviour, the political system of Sierra Leone was clearly entering a more stressful period than any since 1948–51. The division that was developing now was one between the ruling coalition of traditional and Western elites, and a tribally based movement headed by men of radical inclinations. The attempts at violence before independence did not augur well for continued good relations between these divergent groupings; and now there would be no British overlord to referee their disputes.

61 / *Ibid.*, May 29, 1961.

9
The 1962 election

In the Speech from the Throne on Independence Day the government promised that "elections will be held at the appropriate time not later than next
year ... on the basis of universal adult suffrage."[1] True to his word, Sir
Milton announced on April 17, 1962, that the House of Representatives
was being dissolved, and that a general election would take place May 25,
with the election of Paramount Chief members being held May 23. Nomination day was set for May 7.[2] Nearly all political activists had been antici-
pating the election for some time; the struggle for office, both between parties
and within the SLPP, was already well under way.

In 1957, the SLPP had retained office almost by default. Then it had been
able to capitalize on its claims to be the party of all Protectorate people
against the "Creole party," the UPP, in the handful of seats where there had
been any organized opposition at all. Now Protectorate solidarity was broken
by the emergence of this new opposition basing itself on the neglected Northern Province, and led by men who had few inhibitions about stirring up anti-
chief feelings to get at the SLPP. With the twin bases of tribal and anti-chief
feelings, and a potential corps of restless young men to mobilize those feelings, the APC provided a threat of unknown magnitude. It remained to be
seen how successfully the loose, ramshackle coalition of local notables comprising the SLPP could contain this challenge.

The open nature of the SLPP was illustrated once again in the pre-election
period by its absorption of the PNP and of part of the UPP. Bringing the PNP
members back to the fold presented no difficulties after the northern members had left to join Stevens in the All Peoples Congress. Shortly before
Independence, the former Mende Tribal Headman, A. B. Paila, appealed

1 / *Daily Mail*, April 28, 1961.　　　2 / *Ibid.*, April 18, 1962.

to Albert Margai to bring the PNP back into the SLPP. He made this appeal at a meeting of the Mende community in Freetown,[3] an act which helped to demonstrate the identification between the SLPP and the Mende tribe. The PNP responded by agreeing at its national convention in April 1961 to merge with the SLPP,[4] and at the SLPP convention in January 1962 the dissolution of the Peoples National Party was announced.[5]

An attempt by Cyril Rogers-Wright in August 1961 to merge the UPP with the SLPP[6] met greater resistance. A rump of the UPP national executive dissociated itself from Rogers-Wright's action, and declared him and his followers expelled from the UPP.[7] It subsequently elected Neale-Caulker and Barthes Wilson as Leader and Deputy Leader of the UPP. Within the SLPP, Rogers-Wright's application stirred equally critical reactions. The party newspaper noted that "C. B. Rogers-Wright has done NOTHING to justify his being returned or for that matter to be granted a merger with the SLPP."[8] The merger finally did go through at the SLPP's 1962 convention, although not without considerable opposition, as indicated by the party newspaper's account: "The main point of contention [at the convention] was an item in the agenda about the merger of the UPP which some Ministers of the Government were very much against the Party's acceptance into the fold of the SLPP [sic]. ... The Prime Minister ... was able to calm the raging billows when he gave a ruling that he was prepared to accept every true Sierra Leonean into the fold of the SLPP."[9] The open nature of the SLPP could hardly be shown more clearly than by this remark of Sir Milton's. There was no question of a new member's accepting a philosophy or policy; all that was necessary was a willingness to join.

With the PNP back in the fold and Rogers-Wright merged into the SLPP, there were few opposition members left in Parliament at the beginning of 1962. One former UPP member, Kester-Campbell, had crossed to the SLPP in 1961. The two UPP men who entered the Ministry, Dickson-Thomas and Nelson-Williams, dropped their party identification, but declined to join the SLPP until after they had successfully retained their seats as Independents in the 1962 election. Four backbenchers considered themselves members of the United Front, but not of the SLPP; Caulker and Wilson retained their identity as members of the UPP,[10] while Tamba Mbriwa and Aiah Mani maintained the Sierra Leone Progressive Independence Movement in Parliament. I. T. A. Wallace-Johnson was alone among MPs in staying out of

3 / *Ibid.*, March 10, 1961.　　　　4 / *Ibid.*, April 5, 1961.
5 / *Ibid.*, January 12, 1962.　　　　6 / *Ibid.*, August 15, 1961.
7 / *Ibid.*, August 23, 1961 and *Vanguard*, September 2, 1961.
8 / *Vanguard*, August 19, 1961.
9 / *Ibid.*, January 20, 1962.
10 / Wilson stood in 1962 as one of the four candidates under the UPP symbol. Caulker planned to run as an Independent, but failed to submit his nomination in time.

the United Front; when the APC was formed in 1960, he had dropped his two-year-old alliance with the PNP and joined the new party, giving it its sole voice in the House.

The process of nominating SLPP candidates for the 1962 election brought out clearly several features of the party: the strong position of its parliamentary caucus; the lack of any central control over its local units; the importance of the Paramount Chiefs in the local party organization; and the persistence of rivalry and conflicts between leading members of the party.

The parliamentary party's strength was shown by the way in which the sitting members managed to obtain the official party symbol in their constituencies. In January 1962 the party conference had decided that rather than automatically allocate the party symbol to each sitting member, the local party committees should decide who was to receive it.[11] However, just before the House was dissolved, the parliamentary party announced that sitting members who wished the SLPP symbol would receive it automatically, without having to go through the local committee.[12] Although the SLPP constitution clearly subordinated the parliamentary party to the party conference,[13] the parliamentarians had their way. Out of the 32 ordinary members of the 1957 House who considered themselves eligible for the SLPP symbol, 30 obtained it. In the only two cases where a sitting member did not receive the party symbol, Freetown Central I and Sherbro South, there were already fairly strong local SLPP committees whose composition the MP could not control. In a number of other constituencies, there was no local committee in existence, and the MP's first task was to form one.[14] This made it quite simple for the member to form a committee which would endorse his own application for the party symbol. By the time other prospective candidates came to apply for the party nomination, it had been pre-empted by the sitting member. The fact that the MPs were the party's principal links between the centre and the constituencies made it possible for them to exercise this power.

Since the number of ordinary members' seats in the House had been increased considerably over 1957, from 39 to 62, there were still a number

11 / This was stated by the *Daily Mail*, April 21, 1962, in its story on the MPs' decision to alter the rule.

12 / *Ibid.*

13 / Clause IV, Section A (1) and (3) made it clear that the conference was supposed to be the supreme authority of the party, while Clause IV, Section D, confined the Parliamentary Council to matters coming before the legislature. It should be recalled that the MPs were not predominant in the party conference; the constitution had been altered after the PNP broke away to give the largest voice to the local authorities and chiefs, who could be counted on to support Sir Milton as Prime Minister.

14 / Most of the "big men" in every district confirmed that the MPs had taken the initiative in bringing them together to decide on the allocation of the SLPP symbol for new constituencies.

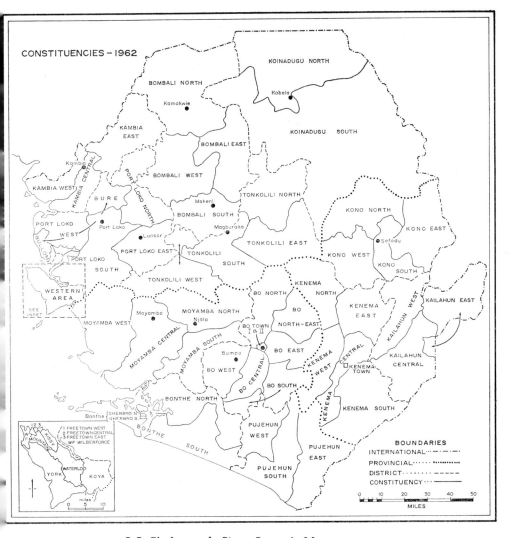

CONSTITUENCIES - 1962

KOINADUGU NORTH

BOMBALI NORTH

Kabala

Kamakwie

KAMBIA EAST

KOINADUGU SOUTH

BOMBALI EAST

Kambia

KAMBIA WEST

KAMBIA CENTRAL

BURE

PORT LOKO NORTH

BOMBALI WEST

Makeni

TONKOLILI NORTH

KONO NORTH

PORT LOKO WEST

Port Loko

BOMBALI SOUTH

Magburaka

KONO EAST

Lunsar

Sefadu

PORT LOKO SOUTH

PORT LOKO EAST

TONKOLILI SOUTH

TONKOLILI EAST

KONO WEST

KONO SOUTH

WESTERN AREA

TONKOLILI WEST

KENEMA NORTH

BO NORTH

KENEMA EAST

KAILAHUN EAST

SEE INSET

Moyamba

MOYAMBA NORTH

Njala

BO

NORTH-EAST

KENEMA WEST

KAILAHUN WEST

MOYAMBA WEST

BO TOWN I & II

KAILAHUN CENTRAL

MOYAMBA CENTRAL

MOYAMBA SOUTH

Bumpe

BO EAST

BO WEST

BO CENTRAL

KENEMA CENTRAL

KENEMA TOWN

BONTHE NORTH

BO SOUTH

KENEMA SOUTH

Bonthe

SHERBRO N.

SHERBRO S.

BONTHE

PUJEHUN WEST

BONTHE SOUTH

PUJEHUN EAST

BOUNDARIES

INTERNATIONAL

PROVINCIAL

DISTRICT

CONSTITUENCY

PUJEHUN SOUTH

1 FREETOWN WEST
2 FREETOWN CENTRAL
3 FREETOWN EAST
WF WILBERFORCE

WATERLOO

YORK   KOYA

miles
0   5   10

0   10   20   30   40   50
MILES

ADAPTED FROM: J. I. Clarke, *et al.*, *Sierra Leone in Maps*

of places where an aspiring candidate could obtain the SLPP symbol. Every district except Koinadugu received at least one additional seat, with Bo's representation rising from three to eight, and Kenema's from two to six. This meant that some individual or group would have to decide which of the persons who were planning to contest each of these new constituencies should be given the palm tree, the SLPP symbol.

Such party organizations as existed at the district or constituency level in the provinces consisted of the local members of Parliament, the more politically active Paramount Chiefs, other traditional officials such as Court Presidents and Chiefdom Speakers, and a handful of wealthy businessmen and other "notables" such as dispensers, teachers, and District Council officials. In Bo, for example, the selection committee, formed at the instigation of the Prime Minister, consisted of the three members of Parliament plus all the Paramount Chiefs in the district. In Tonkolili, it consisted of the sitting members plus a handful of businessmen and local government officials from the district capital of Magburaka. In Bombali, the Minister of Works, Y. D. Sesay, seems to have been personally responsible for allocating the party symbol to candidates. In Kenema Town, the selection was made by the section chief, the town chief, and a few co-opted "young men." In Port Loko East, the National President of the SLPP Youth Section, A. H. Kabia, had already begun campaigning as the SLPP candidate when the Central Committee in Freetown announced in May that the symbol was going to another man.[15] Paramount Chief Bai Koblo had written the committee saying Kabia could not win and naming the other candidate. In at least one case, an attempt by a candidate to bypass the local committee backfired. An ambitious young teacher in Tonkolili South decided to go directly to the Central Committee in Freetown to obtain the party symbol. This so annoyed the local selection committee that they gave the symbol to a rival candidate, a chiefdom speaker who was supposed to be weaker in popular favour than the teacher. There was one case in which the Central Committee did overrule a local selection committee's choice. The Bo district selection committee had recommended for Bo West the popular District Council Secretary R. B. Kowa, who had been a founder of the SOS and close to Dr Margai. The Central Committee, however, awarded the symbol to a man who worked in Freetown. The reason for the Central Committee's decision was that the Paramount Chief of the sole chiefdom in the constituency had written them recommending the Freetown man as the official candidate; one Central Committee member observed that "Naturally we had no alternative but to accept him."

No district or constituency committee that the writer spoke to had made any effort to persuade a suitable person to stand as a candidate; all simply looked over the men who had already announced their intention of standing for Parliament and bestowed the symbol on the one who appeared to have the best chance of winning. This rather casual approach to the selection of candidates left the party in three instances with no candidate at all. In Moyamba North, a young lawyer had built up such a powerful personal position that no one else felt it worth while running against him, and he

15 / *Daily Mail*, May 7, 1962.

simply was not interested in taking the SLPP symbol. He was returned unopposed as an Independent.[16] In Tonkolili North the three chiefdoms comprising the constituency had planned to agree upon a single candidate who would be returned unopposed and thus save election expenses. The SLPP committee in Magburaka assumed that whoever stood as the candidate would accept the symbol. However, an APC organizer turned up on nomination day just as the three chiefs were settling on their candidate, and when the candidate had been decided, offered him a choice of accepting the APC's rising sun symbol or fighting the election against an APC candidate. The candidate, aware that the APC had considerable support in his constituency, accepted the symbol. The APC's triumph, however, was short-lived, since the member crossed to the SLPP soon after the election; but during the election campaign they made great play of the fact that the government had failed to nominate candidates for all seats. In Bombali East, the APC had nominated a strong candidate, and was generally regarded as the more popular party in the area. The Minister of Works, Y. D. Sesay, offered the SLPP symbol to one man who had failed to get the APC nomination, but he turned it down, saying he thought he had a better chance as an Independent. On nomination day, however, his nomination was disqualified, and the APC candidate was returned unopposed.

In the provinces, the allocation of a party symbol was not a vitally important matter for the candidates. Those who failed to win the SLPP nomination simply stood as Independents. In Freetown, by contrast, it was felt that a considerable number of voters did vote for a party symbol rather than an individual, with the result that the struggle for the party nominations was somewhat more protracted. But even in Freetown, where the assignment of the party symbol might have a significant effect in determining the winner of the election, the local organizations had their way. One well-publicized battle, which showed both the inability of the central executive to control local party groups and also the extent of the rivalries within the SLPP, took place in the Freetown Central II constituency. The sitting member was John Nelson-Williams, who had become Minister of Information and Broadcasting in the United Front government, but had not joined the SLPP. When the time came to consider the nomination of a party candidate, the Central Ward executive, or at least part of it, refused to consider Nelson-Williams and instead chose Mrs Constance Cummings-John, a school principal who had been a staunch Creole supporter of the SLPP from its earliest days. She had also founded the Sierra Leone Women's Movement, an organization which included many influential women traders, and had been among the more

16 / However, he did follow the other Independents in declaring for the SLPP after the election.

vociferous advocates of the rights of Protectorate people, an attitude which did not endear her to her fellow Creoles. She was also suspected of having been pro-PNP, which made her somewhat suspect among the "old guard" of the SLPP. Nelson-Williams, who was only 31 years old, had been a strong critic of the SLPP from the time he first became General Secretary of the UPP up to the United Front. However, he had adapted his views readily, and had a considerable following among the younger men, tribal as well as Creole.

Following Mrs Cummings-John's nomination as the official SLPP candidate, rumours began to spread that the Prime Minister wanted Nelson-Williams elected, and some younger members of the SLPP ward executive began to work for him rather than for Mrs Cummings-John. At the end of April a rally for Nelson-Williams included among its speakers Y. D. Sesay, who was one of the Ministers closest to the Prime Minister, and A. H. Kabia.[17]

On May 1 a government spokesman announced that the wives of Ambassadors should stay with their husbands at their posts; the target of this pronouncement was clearly Mrs Cummings-John, whose husband was Ambassador to Liberia.[18] Some members of the Central Ward executive sent a petition to the Prime Minister on May 2 congratulating him on this stand and claiming that Mrs Cummings-John had not been properly selected as the official candidate; two meetings had been held, they said, but both had ended in a "fiasco" and no decision had been taken.[19] The next day Mrs Cummings-John announced that neither she nor her husband had received any letter from the government regarding the proper place for Ambassadors' wives.[20] On May 4 the Prime Minister himself announced that the Cabinet had decided on April 17 that Ambassadors' wives should accompany their husbands to their posts.[21] He had already told a delegation from the Central Ward executive that he did not favour Mrs Cummings-John as a candidate because of her support for the PNP, and that he wanted Nelson-Williams elected. As a final twist, just a few hours after the Prime Minister had made his statement regarding the place of Ambassadors' wives, an official of the SLPP introduced Mrs Cummings-John to a rally as the official candidate "in the name of the President and party."[22] Mrs Cummings-John's box bore the palm tree on election day. However, though she won the symbol, she lost the election, receiving 1,321 votes to 1,356 for Nelson-Williams.

The conflict between Nelson-Williams and Mrs Cummings-John differed from other campaigns in which different members of the SLPP backed opposing candidates only in the amount of publicity it received. These conflicts were not between the Central Committee as an organized group and the

17 / *Daily Mail*, May 1, 1962.
18 / *Ibid.*, May 3, 1962.
19 / *Ibid.*
20 / *Ibid.*, May 4, 1962.
21 / *Ibid.*, May 5, 1962.
22 / *Ibid.*, May 5, 1962.

constituency or district SLPP as a rival group; rather, they were between rival personalities at both the local and the national level.[23]

Rivalries within the party led to Independents challenging several SLPP leaders. In Freetown East II, Alhaji Gibril Sesay, a prominent Temne religious leader and a long-time member of the SLPP, stood against the Minister of Finance, M. S. Mustapha. In this he was backed by the Minister of Communications, Kande Bureh. One SLPP official claimed that on the night Bureh and Mustapha were presented as the official candidates, a van travelled through Freetown East urging people to vote for Bureh and Sesay. Later Bureh and Sesay spoke together at a meeting, with Bureh allegedly urging that Temnes should vote solidly for Temne candidates.[24] While Bureh and Sesay were making common cause against the Minister of Finance, an SLPP city councillor was running against Bureh, charging that Bureh was preaching "tribalism."[25]

The same rivalries also appeared in other constituencies. In Kailahun Central, the former private secretary of the Resident Minister, Taplimah Ngobeh, ran against Maigore Kallon, allegedly on the Resident Minister's urging. In Freetown West I, a young barrister who ran against H. E. B. John, the Minister of Education, was allegedly backed by Albert Margai. We have already noted that several Ministers and other officials of the SLPP supported John Nelson-Williams against the official SLPP candidate in Freetown Central.[26]

Even where they received no encouragement from Ministers or other leading SLPP members, scores of independent candidates ran against the SLPP's official nominees. In nearly all cases they were no more and no less sympathetic to the party than were its official candidates. Since the standard-bearers had usually been selected when they were not the sitting members, simply on the basis that they seemed the most likely persons to win in their constituencies, this was hardly surprising. Some Independents had held national office in the SLPP; thus A. H. Kabia in Port Loko East had been National President of the Youth Section, and Mana Kpaka in Pujehun East had been Assistant General Secretary of the party. But national affiliation meant little to the candidates in any case. Most contests between SLPP and

23 / The clearest example of this was Kande Bureh's support of a fellow Temne against his ministerial colleague, M. S. Mustapha, in Freetown East II. See below.

24 / *Daily Mail*, April 24, 1962. He later claimed that what he had said was "the leaders of the various tribes should be vigilant in seeking the interests of their people in the interest of the country," though he did not deny he had been speaking on the same platform as Sesay. *Ibid.*, May 1, 1962.

25 / *Ibid.*, April 25, 1962. While denying he would make use of such "dangerous propaganda," this candidate did manage to observe that he had a blood connection with the Temnes.

26 / See above, p. 144.

Independent candidates were really contests between the representatives of rival ruling families or of different chiefdoms within the same constituency.[27]

Despite its internal quarrels, the SLPP was able to put up official candidates in all but three constituencies. The opposition parties were much more sectional in their base of support. The APC managed to contest 15 of the 18 seats in the Northern Province and 11 of the 12 in the Western Area, but only 6 of the 32 in the Southern and Eastern Provinces.[28] Its tribal composition was shown even more strikingly by the fact that of its 6 candidates in the south and east, 3 were "strangers" from the Northern Province, one was a Creole, and one was half-Mandingo.

The APC professed to be a mass party, with its basic "branch" units in "all towns and villages."[29] However, in view of the handicaps facing opposition parties which tried to develop an organization reaching down to the villages, it is not surprising that most of its activities were carried on by travelling national organizers, and that most of its branches were in the larger towns, where native courts would not repress APC supporters quite so blatantly as in the smaller villages. It was not always easy for the APC to find candidates, even though there were numerous indications that its anti-chief appeal and tribal orientation would make it a formidable challenger in the north. Thus one organizer claimed that in the constituency where he finally stood himself, he had asked two other people to take the symbol, but they had both refused. A successful candidate noted that "I was the only person seeking the APC nomination," while another said that generally it was "difficult" to find candidates to run for the APC. This difficulty helped undermine the criterion of party loyalty which the APC had hoped to use in selecting its candidates. In Kambia Central its candidate was a well-known local trader who had tried for, but failed to obtain, the SLPP nomination. In Kenema Town, the APC candidate had first tried for the SLPP nomination, then taken the APC symbol because he thought he would do better with a party standing behind him than if he ran as an Independent.[30] In Tonkolili North, as we have seen, the APC simply pressured a man who had already been selected as the sole candidate into accepting its symbol. In Bombali South the APC apparently first tried to nominate a man who had been a long-time member of the SLPP, and after he had turned them down, persuaded a man who was planning to stand as an Independent to take the symbol.

27 / For example, in Kambia West a candidate from the small Binle chiefdom stood as an Independent against the official SLPP candidate from Samu. In Kailahun Central, four members of a ruling family from Bambara stood against Maigore Kallon, who was from Jawi; one explicitly stated he had stood to try to get more benefits for the chiefdom.

28 / Excluding the four SLPIM candidates in Kono.

29 / APC Constitution, II, 3 (i).

30 / He did; he won 12 per cent of the vote, against 10 per cent for the highest Independent.

The APC also professed to be educating voters to support the party rather than the individual candidate, but in practice it paid considerable attention to each candidate's local ties with his constituency. Of the 32 candidates, all but 9 were natives of the constituencies where they stood, and only 3 of these 9 did not live in their constituencies at the time of the election. The APC pattern of nominations showed that, as well as being an essentially regional party, it followed in the pattern of previous parties in two important respects. Like other parties, it accepted the need for a candidate to have local roots in his constituency, with the implication that its members of Parliament would be strongly oriented towards the local needs of their constituencies. It also was willing to accept a rather low degree of party loyalty among its candidates, with the corresponding risk that these candidates could be lured over to the government side after being elected. However, it differed considerably from all previous parties in nominating candidates from comparatively low-level occupations, and without close ties to ruling families.[31]

The SLPIM was still essentially a local protest group critical of both the central government's failure to use diamond wealth to develop Kono and of the Kono chiefs who had enriched themselves by leasing the land of Kono farmers to strangers. The leaders of the SLPIM resembled those of the SLPP in social background; their leader, Mbriwa, had been elected a Paramount Chief in 1961, and three of their four candidates in 1962 were sons of chiefs.[32] The second echelon of the SLPIM, and the greater number of its supporters, were the younger, less well-to-do men discontented with the status quo. This base of support led the leaders to take a strong stand against the privileges and powers enjoyed by the chiefs in the diamond areas.

As Sierra Leone moved into its first general election following independence, the governing party was still a loose collection of local notables, with no significant party structure distinct from the traditional organization of the chiefdoms. It exerted very little control over its supporters, with the result that these contested freely against each other for office. What gave it some unity of purpose was the common association of its members with the traditional elite.

In its role as the party representing the traditional elite, the SLPP was facing its first serious challenge from a more radical group. The APC combined an anti-chief appeal with a clear sectional base, at a time when there were both growing fears for northerners in the future scheme of things and serious criticisms of the abuses by northern chiefs. But the APC was unable to function as a thoroughgoing mass party, because the SLPP and the chiefs possessed sufficient coercive powers to prevent it developing a widespread organization. It did, however, succeed in breaking sharply with the previous pattern of drawing party candidates largely from ruling families and from

31 / See below, p. 148.
32 / The fourth was also a member of a ruling family.

TABLE 9:1

Occupations of candidates in 1962 election by party

	Professional[a]	Teacher	Business[b]	Clerical[c]	Farmer	Other[d]	Unknown
SLPP (N = 59)	15 (25%)	11 (19%)	17 (29%)	12 (20%)	1 (2%)	3 (5%)	—
APC (N = 32)	1 (3%)	4 (13%)	17 (53%)	3 (9%)	—	7 (22%)	—
Ind. (N = 117)	13 (11%)	19 (16%)	36 (31%)	26 (22%)	5 (4%)	8 (7%)	10 (9%)

a/Includes dispensers and others with only secondary education.
b/Includes petty traders (the largest component).
c/Includes both central civil servants (retired) and persons employed by NAS.
d/Mostly full-time politicians.

TABLE 9:2

Number of candidates from ruling houses, by party
(excluding Creoles)

	Yes	No	Unknown
SLPP (N = 44)	29 (66%)	12 (27%)	3 (7%)
APC (N = 25)	9 (36%)	10 (40%)	6 (24%)
Inds. (N = 102)	47 (46%)	23 (23%)	32 (31%)

Note: Most candidates who are in the "unknown" category probably did not have ruling family connections within the constituency. In this table connections through the mother's as well as the father's side have been included, since these were equally effective in enlisting support.

occupations requiring a high degree of skill. While the SLPP and Independent candidates tended to come from occupations requiring some secondary schooling, the APC candidates were more often petty traders or full-time politicians (Table 9:1). The APC candidates were also less likely to come from ruling families (Table 9:2). Both of these features suggest a somewhat lower-status group challenging the established coalition of Western and traditional elite members. This challenge was to appear during the election campaign in the Northern Province, with a fair degree of success.

THE PARTIES CAMPAIGN

An election cannot be simply a struggle for power between contending parties: if it is to provide any real indication of the feelings of the electorate, it must be fought within a framework of rules which permit the electorate to make a reasonably free choice between the contenders. Sierra Leone's general election of 1962 made history in tropical Africa in that it was the first election to be held in an independent African state in which competing parties were able to contest freely.

The allocation of seats among the different districts had been carried out by the Prime Minister and his ministerial colleagues, with the newly established Electoral Commission responsible for the delimitation of boundaries within each district.[33] The distribution between districts was basically in accordance with what were believed to be their relative populations, although the Western Area was deliberately over-represented.[34] The Electoral Commission, under an expatriate Chief Electoral Commissioner and Chief Elections Officer, carried out the actual running of the election in a generally fair manner. At any rate, there were no major complaints from the opposition about the administration of the election machinery.

Some government powers were used to curtail opposition activity in the Kono area. Before the writs for the election were issued, the Provincial Secretary of the Eastern Province had declined to prevent the chiefdom authorities in the Kono District prohibiting APC meetings.[35] A more direct blow to the opposition came just two weeks before election day, when the APC and SLPIM announced that they were forming an alliance to contest the four Kono seats.[36] The day after this news was made public, the Ministry of Internal Affairs announced that Chief Mbriwa was being suspended from office for "general misbehaviour" and "flouting the authority of the government."[37] In a further statement, the government denied that this action had been taken "for political purposes" and claimed it was because "for some time now the Paramount Chief's conduct has been below the standard expected from a person holding the office of Paramount Chief, has not been in the best interest of good government and has frequently been contrary to instructions conveyed to the Chief by officers of the Government in authority over him."[38] Since Chief Mbriwa was a figure of considerable personal prestige as well as the leader of the popular party in Kono, this action by the government made it clear that no Paramount Chief could stray beyond the limits the government saw fit to impose on him, no matter what his personal

33 / See Sierra Leone *House of Representatives Debates,* Session 1961/62, v (January 17, 1962), pp. 139–47.

34 / *Ibid.,* p. 139. There were a few other discrepancies; for example, Pujehun, with 20,000 persons on its tax roll, received three seats, while Koinadugu, with 26,000, was given only two.

35 / *Daily Mail,* April 3, 1962. See also *ibid.,* March 23.

36 / *Ibid.,* May 8, 1962.

37 / *Ibid.,* May 10.

38 / *Vanguard,* May 19, 1962.

standing. Support for local protest movements was apparently within these limits, but support for a nationally organized opposition was not.

The deposition of their leader did not immediately demoralize the SLPIM. The party continued to campaign vigorously, and on election day swept all four seats and won two-thirds of the vote. It was only after the election that the loss of their leader helped to bring about the break-up of the party.[39]

Throughout most of the country, the election was basically a series of local contests between individuals, each claiming that he could best represent local interests. In Bo, Bonthe, Moyamba, Pujehun, Kailahun, Kenema, and Koina-duga, where there was virtually no organized opposition to the SLPP,[40] this pattern of local contests was most pronounced. In Bombali, Kambia, Port Loko, and Tonkolili the rival candidates who ran as SLPP or Independent were also largely concerned with promoting the claims of their own chief-doms or ruling families, although superimposed on this was the more general conflict between the chiefs and their supporters, and the younger APC men without standing in the traditional structure. In Kono, there was almost a straight party fight between the SLPIM and the SLPP, with the former advo-cating a better deal for the Kono man and the latter trying to defend the government's diamond policies. In Freetown, where there was no traditional structure through which parties or candidates could work, and where the voters tended to support parties to a greater extent than up-country, there was more party activity than elsewhere; but here also candidates stressed what they could do for Freetown rather than for the country as a whole.

Central party organizations played a very limited role in the election. The SLPP was too riven by personal quarrels to be able to throw support behind one candidate in any constituency, even if it had had the resources. Because they were the government, the SLPP leaders were able to draw upon various businesses for financial support, but this was not used for the party as a whole. The Diamond Corporation and SLST gave £25,000 and £20,000, respectively, for the use of the party, but the Ministers retained this entirely for their own use.[41] Neither the sitting members who were backbenchers nor the official SLPP candidates in the new constituencies received any financial aid from the central office of the SLPP; they even had to pay their own deposits, as well as all their out-of-pocket expenses, which usually ran to at least £500 and more often £1,000.[42] The central organization did provide

39 / See below, pp. 171–73.

40 / There were four APC candidates in Kenema, and two in Bo Town, but these seem to have appealed chiefly to the northerners in these areas.

41 / The Minister who cited these figures claims that when the backbenchers learned of this money, they went to the Ministers to demand a share, but the latter denied there was any such money available.

42 / These are the sums mentioned to the writer by candidates for their own expendi-tures. They probably are on the conservative side.

a van for each district, but these seem to have been monopolized by the Ministers. It also sent a few canvassers to help in some areas, but these were probably not of much use, because as one backbencher who lost his bid for re-election complained, "They didn't know anybody." This lack of effective party support apparently came as a shock to some backbenchers who had failed to maintain close contact with their constituents on the assumption that the party would help them in the election.

The Prime Minister travelled around the southern part of the country shortly before the election,[43] visiting the Tribal Authorities, and in some cases urging the people to vote for the official SLPP candidate if they wanted him as Prime Minister. However, in other areas where a number of Independents were running against SLPP candidates, the Prime Minister gave his blessing to all his "children." Other Ministers for the most part campaigned in their own constituencies. In some districts, the SLPP candidates would help each other campaign, but generally each candidate fought his own battle within his constituency without outside help.

The opposition parties presented somewhat more of a united front. Only two APC members who failed to get their party's nomination stood as Independents. The APC central organization gave no more financial help to its candidates than did the SLPP, but it did send around teams of young men to canvass. Its four candidates in the Kenema District campaigned as a team in support of each other, although this may have been due simply to a desire to offset their vulnerability as "strangers" in the district. In the north, candidates tended to work more on their own, even though the leading men in the party did campaign outside their own constituencies.

The SLPIM in Kono also tended to work more as a team than did the SLPP, sending groups of canvassers around to the villages of the entire district, and having their candidates appear in support of each other. The campaign in Kono was a rough one: the SLPIM workers were constantly harassed and jailed by the chiefs and Tribal Authorities through the NA courts, while one SLPP candidate claimed his car was stoned and some of his canvassers wounded. Money flowed freely, primarily for the SLPP side; one candidate claimed to have spent £4,000 and his opponents suggested this was an underestimate. The SLPIM leaders told their followers to take the money if it was offered, but to remember their ballots were secret and to vote for the SLPIM.[44]

The Paramount Chiefs played a considerably more important role than the party organizations in the elections. Their role was supposed to have

43 / *Daily Mail*, May 14, 1962.

44 / APC candidates in the north also corrupted the morals of the voters in this way; one claims part of his campaign was financed through money given to his supporters by the SLPP candidate.

been circumscribed by law; the Electoral Provisions Act of 1962 specifically forbade them to interfere with any political meeting unless it was "likely to lead to a breach of the peace, or had ... become disorderly."[45] They were also prohibited, like everyone else, from using threats or fetishes to influence electors.[46] They were permitted to advise their subjects how to vote, but only on the voter's request.[47] However, all of these limitations on their activities applied only during the period after the official announcement of the polling date;[48] before that time, the chiefs were free to control political activity as they saw fit, subject only to the untested provisions of the Constitution guaranteeing freedom of assembly and organization.[49]

Throughout the election, many chiefs in fact played an active role. In the south, where Independents were considered to be just as loyal to the SLPP as were its official candidates, the chiefs would campaign for whichever candidate they preferred. Thus in Kenema North, a chief called his Tribal Authorities together and informed them that if anyone failed to vote for the chief's favoured candidate, an Independent, that man would lose his office.[50] In other constituencies, the chief's pressures, while more subtly applied, would make his wishes equally clear. In the north and in Kono, the chiefs played a more negative role, being primarily concerned with stopping their people from supporting the APC and SLPIM. Some relied on threats of what would happen to the area if an opposition candidate were elected, while others took the more direct approach of threatening to jail anyone who showed the APC's rising sun symbol. However, not all chiefs in the north attempted to crush the APC. At least one told his people that, while he was an SLPP supporter, he would not force anyone else to support that party. Others may have sympathized with the APC's grievances about the lack of northern representation and, while the example of Chief Mbriwa served to deter them from coming out against the government, they were not going to handicap the APC. Some chiefs were restrained in their partisanship by the fact that they were themselves trying to win election and, since some of the Tribal Authorities who formed their electorate were pro-APC, they could not afford to side too openly with the SLPP.[51]

45 / Section 85.

46 / Sections 72, 83.

47 / Section 86.

48 / Section 68 (2).

49 / *Constitution*, Sections 21, 22. The first constitutional test case of these sections arose in 1965.

50 / This was brought out in evidence during a subsequent election petition. See *Daily Mail*, October 3, 1962. However, the Court of Appeal found the judge had erred in accepting this evidence and dismissed the petition.

51 / One APC candidate said that one of the two chiefs in his constituency had been "neutral" because the chief was standing for re-election; the other, who was not standing, said he would jail anyone who showed the APC symbol.

In the absence of effective party organizations, the main responsibility for contacting the voters fell on the candidates themselves. For the SLPP and Independent candidates this normally entailed visiting each village in the constituency, paying their respects and a small "shake-hands" to the village headman or section chief, and requesting him to call the villagers together for a meeting. The candidate would then proceed to explain how, if elected, he would try to obtain better roads, a dispensary, or, if in a larger town, schools, a water supply and electricity.[52] There were variations on this pattern; in one constituency the sitting member, a lawyer, apparently confined his campaigning to those villages he could reach by car, while one of his opponents, a teacher, canvassed vigorously among all the farmers of the area. This probably was the most important factor in contributing to the lawyer's defeat, although the accusation by his opponent that he was subordinating the interest of the constituency to "national interests" also probably hurt him.

Campaigning in the "bush" was expensive. Many candidates found it necessary to buy or hire vans for transport and loudspeakers for publicizing their activities; frequently they would also hire "propaganda secretaries," young men who were supposed to go and canvass for them. Then too, there were the "shake-hands" for section chiefs, village headmen, and other more minor functionaries, each of whom could be expected to influence a number of voters if his goodwill were obtained. Since all candidates would generally try to obtain the goodwill of as many village leaders as possible in this way, probably their gifts tended to cancel each other out, and the village leaders would actually vote according to the criterion of the candidate's closeness to their particular village. Nor was it always clear that "shake-hands" to village leaders would procure the votes of the villagers. If a headman kept the money for himself (as many did) and the villagers found out about it, they might turn against the candidate.[53] Few candidates, however, were in a position to reach the voters in any other way; it would have cost them even more to build up a private political machine and, with the lack of roads, illiteracy, and other obstacles to communication, they could not hope to contact the voters directly.

The opposition parties could not work through the chiefs and their subordinates so readily. To some extent they relied on their own teams of canvassers and on using their candidates as roving teams. But they too relied largely on contacts among the leaders of non-political groups. The most

52 / Nearly all candidates, both successful and unsuccessful, whom the writer interviewed followed this pattern of campaigning.

53 / One young man who was distributing sums of £2 to £5 for a candidate in a Rural Area seat claims this happened in several instances. The same thing happened during the 1966 District Council elections in one Northern chiefdom. The section chiefs were each supposed to have been given £100 by the Prime Minister to encourage them to canvass for the SLPP. When they went to their people to canvass, the people demanded the money, and when it was not forthcoming, voted almost solidly for the APC.

important of these groups were the "Hunting Societies" of young men, found mostly in the Western Area, and usually organized on a tribal basis, though sometimes cutting across tribal lines. One APC leader claimed that if the APC could get the leader of a Hunting Society on its side, he might bring along as many as 50 followers. Also significant were the "compins" of young men formed for the purpose of providing a team of workers for hire for farm work, and widespread in the north.[54] The role of these associations as channels of communication to the electorate was suggested by the frequent references to them in election petitions after the election; several victorious candidates were accused of having corrupted the voters by giving presents of money, food, and liquor to the leaders of these societies.[55] The societies were of particular importance to the APC in the north, since it needed channels there to offset the SLPP's control of the traditional structure.

In the Western Area, and particularly in Freetown, the absence of a system of traditional authorities meant that the SLPP candidates as well as the APC had to rely on these voluntary associations. The SLPP in Freetown had its own party organization, consisting of an executive of some 80 to 100 members in each constituency. These would carry out a fairly intensive door-to-door canvass, although this was concerned primarily with extolling the virtues of the party's candidates rather than with determining the voting allegiance of the householders.[56] The party made no organized effort on election day to "get out the vote." Besides this door-to-door canvass, it relied heavily on nightly "pocket meetings," small rallies aimed at specific neighbourhoods and tribal groups.[57]

Even in Freetown, the SLPP organization was split among different candidates; in four of the six constituencies a supporter of the SLPP was running as an Independent, and drawing support from those workers in the party who preferred him to the official candidate. Personal rather than party attachments also were important to the electorate as a whole. One Minister with a strong tribal following commented: "I like to have more people running against me than one man – I have a base." That these personal attachments were important to the opposition party candidates as well as to the SLPP was demonstrated in Freetown West I. In the general election the APC candidate,

54 / For a discussion of the various types of young men's societies, see Banton, *West African City*, pp. 163–83.

55 / See, for example, *Daily Mail*, June 8, and June 18, 1962.

56 / Several party workers the writer has talked to reacted to the suggestion that canvassers should try to find out the allegiance of voters as if this were highly immoral. It is quite possible, of course, that they simply thought this was the reaction the "white man" should see.

57 / The writer observed the same procedure in the 1964 City Council election. These "pocket meetings" attracted a considerable number of the curious as well as a hard core of the party faithful.

Samura Sesay, received 1,161 votes, while Barthes Wilson, running for the UPP, received 741. Four months later, in a by-election brought about by Sesay's being unseated on petition, Wilson ran for the APC and received 1,238 votes. Sesay ran as an Independent and won 595, suggesting that his personal or tribal following had been responsible for about half the APC votes.

In those parts of the country where the SLPP was not faced with an organized opposition, the election was fought entirely on local issues. In the north and Kono, however, the divergent bases of support for the SLPP and the opposition parties led to somewhat more general issues being raised. In Kono, while the SLPIM ran candidates of as high standing as those the SLPP could put up, it drew its support mainly from the younger and less wealthy sections of the community. The grievances it championed – the loss of Kono's wealth to the outside world and the abuses of the chiefs – were ones which would appeal particularly to these strata of society. The SLPIM had always emphasized voting for the black pot symbol rather than for the individual candidate, and there was general agreement among members of both parties that most Kono voters did in fact vote on a party basis.

In the Northern Province, the two questions of the behaviour of the chiefs and of the representation of northerners in the government overshadowed all others, although both were more often presented in the more local terms of how a particular Paramount Chief was treating his subjects and whether the constituency was receiving its share of development. APC candidates for the most part have claimed they concentrated on such abuses by the chiefs as the continued use of forced labour and the levying of illegal taxes such as a tree cutting tax; one asserted that "You can win any election in the North by being anti-chief." Some SLPP leaders also have suggested that much of the success of the APC was due to its being anti-chief, although others have attributed it more vaguely to a popular feeling of discontent and a desire for change. "We were too majestical, and had the power and the rich men, while the APC had the young men," commented one SLPP secretary. Other SLPP men emphasized the status difference between the leaders of the two parties. One described the APC as made up of "discontented men who had been driven out of the diamond areas"; another termed them "young and inexperienced" with "no background"; while another more tactfully remarked that they were "not so well educated." These remarks suggest that the APC was perceived by its opponents as being a challenge to the established order. APC candidates made the same point in different terms, saying they were for "the people" as opposed to the chiefs.

The APC's northern composition was also significant. Some SLPP candidates charged that the APC "preached any amount of tribalism" and in particular used Stevens' Limba ancestry to identify itself as "the Limba man's party." But other SLPP leaders, as well as the APC, have denied that the APC preached tribalism or regionalism. Furthermore, the SLPP had its own northern leaders such as Dr Karefa-Smart, Y. D. Sesay, I. B. Taylor-Kamara, and Kande Bureh, and all of its candidates were as much "sons of the soil" as those put up by the APC. Undoubtedly many people felt that the SLPP's northern representatives had not done enough for their areas, and that they were of less importance in the SLPP than were the Mendes. But while a desire to be represented by "our own" [regional] party was undoubtedly a strong motivating force for many northern voters, still if the chiefs had retained the confidence of their people they could have kept most of them behind the SLPP. It was because the chiefs' abuses and the SLPP were inextricably intertwined that the APC was able to wage a successful campaign, overtly directed more against the chiefs than against "Mende dominance."

THE RESULTS

On the surface, the results of the 1962 election were not very satisfying for the government. The official candidates of the SLPP won less than a majority of the ordinary members' seats, and only eight more than the two allied opposition parties (Table 9:3). But the party had reserves of strength. As long as no other organized group won more seats, it would be most unlikely that the Governor-General would dismiss the Prime Minister and call on the leader of another party to form the government.[58] As long as the SLPP continued to form the government, it would retain the support of the twelve Paramount Chief members, who followed the policy of supporting whatever government was in power. This alone was enough to provide it with a majority in 1962. Furthermore, nearly all the Independents considered themselves supporters of the SLPP.

It was not surprising, therefore, to find all fourteen Independents who had won seats declaring their support for the SLPP a few days later.[59] Although

58 / The Constitution gave the Governor-General considerable discretion. Section 58 (6) (a) provided that the office of Prime Minister shall become vacant when "after any dissolution ... the person holding that office is informed by the Governor-General that the Governor-General is about to re-appoint him as Prime Minister *or to appoint another person as Prime Minister*" [italics mine]. This exercise of the Governor-General's power was limited by the provision of Section 58 (8) that "The Governor-General shall not remove the Prime Minister from office unless it appears to him that the Prime Minister no longer commands the support of a majority. ..." But a Governor-General could plausibly argue that a Prime Minister whose official party candidates won less than a majority of seats no longer had the support of a majority of members, and could call upon someone else to take the office. Once a person had been called by the Governor-General to become Prime Minister, he could use the powers of patronage in that office to create a majority for himself, and thus provide *prima facie* evidence of the rightness of the Governor-General's decision.

59 / See *Daily Mail*, May 29, 1962, and *Vanguard*, June 2, 1962.

TABLE 9:3

1962 election: seats won and votes received by party

Party	Number of candidates	Seats won	Votes received	% total vote
SLPP	59 (4 unopp.)	28 (4 unopp.)	230,118	34.7
APC	32 (2 unopp.)	16 (2 unopp.)	114,333	17.2
SLPIM	4	4	34,839	5.2
UPP	4	0	1,660	0.3
Independents	117 (1 unopp.)	14 (1 unopp.)	282,724	42.6

some had run for Parliament because they were "generally discontented with what was being done," all were by their background more predisposed to support the SLPP than the only organized alternative, the APC. Also, since nearly all the Independents could be considered as pro-SLPP, it would be fair to say that about three-quarters of the voters supported candidates who generally favoured the type of political system the government was supporting.

There were marked regional differences in the pattern of support for the parties, which showed in both the seats won and the votes cast (Tables 9:4 and 9:5). The SLPP did manage to win some seats in the north and in Freetown, even though it was less successful in these areas than the APC. The

TABLE 9:4

1962 election: seats won by party and district
(number of seats contested in parentheses)

Province	District	SLPP	APC	SLPIM	Independent
Southern	Bo (8 seats)	6 (8)	— (2)	—	2 (8)
	Bonthe (4 seats)	4 (4)	—	—	— (2)
	Moyamba (4 seats)	2 (3)	—	—	2 (3)
	Pujehun (3 seats)	1 (3)	—	—	2 (3)
Eastern	Kailahun (3 seats)	3 (3)	—	—	— (3)
	Kenema (6 seats)	2 (6)	— (4)	—	4 (6)
	Kono (4 seats)	— (4)	—	4 (4)	— (1)
Northern	Bombali (3 seats)	1 (3)	3 (4)	—	— (3)
	Kambia (3 seats)	— (3)	3 (3)	—	— (2)
	Koinadugu (2 seats)	2 (2)	—	—	— (2)
	Port Loko (5 seats)	1 (5)	3 (5)	—	1 (4)
	Tonkolili (4 seats)	1 (3)	3 (3)	—	— (1)
Western Area	Freetown (6 seats)	2 (6)	3 (6)	—	1 (4)
	Rural Area (6 seats)	3 (6)	1 (5)	—	2 (5)
TOTAL		28 (59)	16 (32)	4 (4)	14 (47)

TABLE 9:5

1962 election: percentage vote for parties by district
(number of candidates in parentheses)

District and no. seats contested	Party			
	SLPP (%)	APC (%)	SLPIM (%)	Independents (%)
Bo	50.4 (8)	1.2 (2)	—	48.4 (17)
Bonthe	43.1 (2)	—	—	56.9 (5)
Moyamba	27.2 (2)	—	—	72.7 (6)
Pujehun	33.4 (3)	—	—	66.6 (9)
Kailahun	46.1 (3)	—	—	53.9 (15)
Kenema	29.9 (6)	13.6 (4)	—	56.5 (15)
Kono	27.2 (4)	—	67.7 (4)	5.1 (1)
Bombali	30.2 (3)	38.1 (3)	—	31.7 (7)
Kambia	33.4 (3)	52.9 (3)	—	13.7 (4)
Koinadugu	40.9 (2)	—	—	59.1 (7)
Port Loko	24.6 (5)	40.8 (5)	—	34.6 (11)
Tonkolili	24.6 (2)	53.6 (2)	—	21.7 (1)
Freetown*a*	36.5 (6)	35.7 (6)	—	22.5 (5)
Rural Area	35.8 (6)	25.5 (5)	—	38.6 (13)

a/Four UPP candidates stood in Freetown, winning 5.4% of the vote.

APC probably owed several of its seats to the SLPP's weak party discipline. Of the fourteen contested seats its candidates won, the APC had a majority in only six. In the other eight, the combined vote for the official SLPP candidate and for the Independents exceeded the votes cast for the APC; and in at least six of these eight seats, the strongest Independents were SLPP supporters.[60] It does not necessarily follow that, if the SLPP had been able to prevent its supporters running as Independents, it would have won all these seats; it is possible that many electors would have supported an APC candidate on personal grounds if the pro-SLPP man they preferred was not available. But these results do suggest that the SLPP's lack of party discipline might lead to its being defeated by a less widely acceptable but better organized party.

Even where it failed to win many seats, the SLPP did not suffer an overwhelming rejection in the popular vote. In the Northern Province, its official candidates managed to win at least a quarter of the total votes in every district. Nearly all the Independents in the north, and certainly those in Tonkolili and Kambia, inclined toward the SLPP rather than the APC. Thus we can say that pro-SLPP candidates received nearly half the votes even in the two districts where the APC was strongest. The one district in which the

60 / The only two constituencies in which the Independent candidates were not definitely SLPP supporters were Bombali North and York; and in the latter, at least one had been an adherent of the SLPP for some time.

In the Koinadugu constituencies, where there were no APC candidates, some of the Independents were believed to have had APC leanings.

TABLE 9:6
Relationship between number of APC votes and number of pro-APC
northern tribes present in southern constituencies (1962)

Constituency	No. APC votes	"APC tribes"	APC vote as % of APC tribes present
Kenema North	8,381	18,991	44
Kenema Central ⎫ Kenema Town ⎬	5,371	9,603	56
Kenema East	2,951	3,836	76
Bo Town I ⎫ Bo Town II ⎬	1,001	9,250	11

SLPP was very weak was Kono, where the SLPIM candidates won more than two-thirds of the total votes. The SLPP was clearly the only party with nation-wide support, while the APC, at least in its base of support, was essentially a sectional protest movement, with limited indications that it might have some trans-tribal appeal.

The probability that the APC succeeded in attracting some southern support is suggested by Table 9:6 which shows the correlation between numbers of APC votes and number of northerners from pro-APC tribes present in the constituencies where the party ran a candidate.[61] Since an APC vote exceeding 35 per cent of the northerners present is a strong indication of non-northern support, it appears that the APC did make some headway. It should be added that the APC candidate in Kenema East was Mende.

The overall election results, however, suggested a general acquiescence in the existing system of rule, and even where there was dissent with this system, as in the north and Kono, it was largely in terms of a protest against the neglect of a particular area or tribe, or the misrule of a particular chief. The whole system remained strongly locally oriented. This was suggested

61 / The tribes whose members I have treated as predominantly APC are the Temne, Limba, Loko, Susu, and Mandingo. Other tribes which might also be considered as largely APC in inclinations, but which I have excluded, are the Yalunka, Koranko, Kono, and the Creoles; but the numbers of these groups are not large enough in any constituency to alter significantly the proportions given. I have assumed that the age distribution among the "APC tribes" in the south was the same as the national age distribution, i.e. 50 per cent of voting age. Since many northerners in the south are single adult labourers, this probably errs on the low side. I have further assumed that northerners in the south voted in the same proportions as the average turn-out in their constituencies, i.e. about 70 per cent. It does not appear that there was sufficient discrimination against northerners in either the 1962 or the 1967 elections to greatly affect this turn-out, although other factors such as their relative isolation in the community may have reduced their participation. However, if the two assumptions I have made hold, and if only northerners were to vote for the APC, we would expect the APC vote to be a maximum of about 35 per cent of the number of northerners present.

TABLE 9:7

1962 election: results in two constituencies by chiefdom

Candidate	Home chiefdom	Vote in each chiefdom by %				
		Dama	Gaura	Tunkia	Nomo	Total (%)
KENEMA SOUTH						
S. Jusu-Sheriff (Ind.)	Tunkia	19	42	35	6	31
A. M. Lansana (Ind.)	Dama	54	18	5	30	28
O. A. Njavomba (Ind.)	Tunkia	4	15	46	49	22
J. K. Taylor (SLPP)	Dama	17	4	10	7	11
B. S. Bunduka (Ind.)	Gaura	7	21	4	8	8
		Maforki	Koya			
PORT LOKO SOUTH						
S. A. T. Koroma (APC)	Maforki/Koya	29	22			25
U. H. Koroma (Ind.)	Koya	4	34			21
S. D. Koroma (SLPP)	Koya	6	27			18
A. M. Bangura (Ind.)	Maforki	36	5			18
S. H. Sesay (Ind.)	Maforki	16	4			9
S. Kanu (Ind.)	Maforki	9	8			9

by the extent to which voting for candidates in both the north and the south tended to be based on a candidate's closeness to a particular chiefdom (Table 9:7). Most candidates clearly drew their strongest support from their home chiefdoms; conversely, each chiefdom tended to favour its own candidate.

Another indication that the electorate tended to judge the performance of their individual representative rather than the performance of the party in power can be seen in the degree of success enjoyed by members of the 1957–62 Parliament in retaining their seats (Table 9:8). There is a striking contrast here between the performance of Ministers and ministerial secretaries on the one hand and SLPP backbenchers on the other; while three-quarters of the Ministers succeeded in retaining their seats, only a third of the backbenchers succeeded in doing so. The explanation for this difference is probably that the Ministers, as the politicians closest to the heart of the decision-making process, were in the best position to provide benefits for their constituencies, and thus to meet the principal criterion of a good representative. Once again, the election results suggest the essentially local nature of the election contests; if the electorate were judging the performance of the governing party as a whole, then we would expect there would be no significant difference between Ministers and backbenchers in the degree of success enjoyed in winning re-election. But when the members are judged primarily on their ability to bring benefits to the constituency, we would expect Ministers to have a substantial advantage over backbenchers, since they are in a better

TABLE 9:8
Degree of success of 1957–62 representatives in retaining their
seats in the 1962 election

| | Ordinary members | | | |
	Ministers and parliamentary secretaries	SLPP backbenchers	Others	Paramount Chiefs
Won	16 (76%)	4 (33%)	0	5 (45%)
Lost	5 (24%)	8 (67%)	2	6 (55%)

position to channel patronage to their own areas.[62] One further factor has been suggested as contributing to the Ministers' success; besides having the power of patronage, they could "make people afraid not to vote for them." Here again, this power would be exercised for personal rather than party benefit.

The new House of Representatives that emerged from the 1962 election was marked by a widening divergence between the government and opposition parties. In their tribal composition, in age, in social background, and even in schooling, the two sides were farther apart than any previous government and opposition had been.

The overall tribal composition of the 1962 House (Table 9:10) was not significantly different from that of its predecessors (Table 9:9). Northerners were slightly better represented, and the Creoles' representation dropped somewhat, in both cases because of the redistribution of seats. But the most striking feature of the new Parliament was the fact that most northerners were in opposition. This in turn meant that southerners predominated in the SLPP parliamentary party; for the first time, the southerners formed a majority of this group.

The two parties differed strikingly in age. The SLPP remained a "middle-aged" party, recruiting its members largely from among individuals who had already achieved prominence outside politics. To some extent, the much greater youth of the APC and SLPIM was due to their ability to offer a young man who had not attained high standing a "political career"; it was possible for such a man to be elected if the voters could be educated to support the party rather than an individual candidate. Probably of greater significance

62 / To argue that in an election decided essentially on a national party basis, as in Britain or Canada, the Ministers are no more likely to be re-elected than backbenchers, overlooks the possibility that Ministers may occupy a larger proportion of a party's "safe seats." The same could be true of Sierra Leone, although in view of the weakness of the parties, it is most unlikely that there is any "safe seat" for a *party* as distinct from an individual.

TABLE 9:9

Tribal affiliations by party in 1957 House of Representatives[a]

	Southern tribes			Northern tribes							
Party	Mende (30.9)	Sherbro (3.4)	Other (3.2)	Temne (29.8)	Limba (8.4)	Man-dingo (2.3)	Kor. (3.7)	Other (9.9)	Kono (4.8)	Creole (1.9)	Aku
SLPP (N = 23)	8	2	—	4	—	1	1	1[b]	—	5	1
Chiefs (N = 11)	5	1	—	2	—	—	1	1[c]	1	—	—
PNP (N = 5)	4	—	—	1	—	—	—	—	—	—	—
SLPIM (N = 2)	—	—	—	—	—	—	—	—	2	—	—
UPP (N = 9)	—	1	—	1[d]	—	—	—	1[e]	—	6	—
TOTAL (N = 50)	17 (34%)	4 (8%)	—	8 (16%)	—	1 (12%)	2 (4%)	3 (6%)	3 (6%)	11 (22%)	1 (2%)
Ministry (N = 15)a	5	2	—	3	—	—	—	2	—	2	1

Notes: Figures in parentheses below tribes represent percentage of total population, according to *1963 Census*.
a/As of December 31, 1958; includes parliamentary secretaries.
b/Loko.   c/Bullom.   d/Crossed to SLPP, February 1958.
e/Syrian (mother Temne); crossed to SLPP, February 1958.

TABLE 9:10

Tribal affiliation by party in 1962 Parliament

	Southern tribes			Northern tribes							
Party	Mende	Sherbro	Other	Temne	Limba	Man-dingo	Kor.	Other	Kono	Creole	Aku
SLPP (N = 42)	18	5	2[a]	4	—	2	1	1[b]	—	7	2
Chiefs (N = 12)	5	1	—	2	1	—	1	1[c]	1	—	—
APC (N = 20)	—	—	1[d]	8[e]	3[f]	1	1[g]	1[h]	3[i]	2[j]	—
TOTAL	23	6	3	14	4	3	3	3	4	9	2
% of House	31	8	—	19	5	4	4	—	5	— 15 —	

Notes: Affiliations are determined on basis of party to which member professed adherence at time of election. All tribal affiliations are determined according to tribe of father.
a/One Vai, one Gallinas.   b/Loko.
c/Bullom.   d/Kissi; elected SLPIM, crossed to SLPP.
e/One crossed to SLPP in 1964.   f/One crossed to SLPP.
g/Crossed to SLPP.   h/Susu.
i/Elected SLPIM, two crossed to SLPP.   /One elected at by-election.

TABLE 9:11
Age of Members of Parliament by party in 1962 Parliament
(age at time of election)

Party	60 and up	50–59	40–49	30–39	Below 30	Median age
SLPP (N = 42)	6	15	11	8	2	50
APC (N = 20)	—	1	5	12	2	36

was the fact that the APC appealed, like the PNP before it, to impatient young men rather than to their more traditionally minded elders. The "radicalism" and the youth of the APC's members were undoubtedly intertwined.

In social background, as suggested by father's occupation, the gap between the parties was not very pronounced (Table 9:12). The SLPP members were by a small margin more often from backgrounds higher in the wage economy, but the difference was not marked. The SLPP's non-Creole members had rather more links with the traditional elite, but the majority of the APC's members had similar links. In this respect the APC members were still close enough to chieftaincy that they might be expected to have some sympathy for the institution.

One interesting feature of the APC-SLPIM contingent is that the six members who were the sons of Paramount Chiefs all eventually crossed to the SLPP, but no other members did so. This may indicate that as the opposition members closest to the traditional rulers they were able to feel more at home in the SLPP. However, since the APC members who crossed did not seem to differ greatly in their general views from those who remained in opposition, it is more likely that their principal motive was a desire to attain the office of Paramount Chief themselves.[63]

In the occupational backgrounds of members before entering the legislature, the most striking difference between the parties was the relatively high level of training on the SLPP side and the dearth of professional people on the APC side (Table 9:13). Once again, this calls our attention to the gap in status between the two parties. Part of this difference may be due to the fear on the part of many individuals in better-paid occupations of associating themselves openly with an opposition party: APC supporters frequently claimed, and SLPP supporters feared, that both in Freetown and the provinces a number of prominent individuals privately sympathized with the APC but would not reveal themselves until they felt that the APC was within reach of

63 / One did in fact succeed in being elected as a Paramount Chief within two years of crossing.

TABLE 9:12

Social background (father's occupation) of ordinary members
of 1962 Parliament by party

Party	Paramount Chief	Other traditional authority	Western professional	Trader or wage worker	Farmer or other
SLPP provincials (N = 33)	10	6	3 (2)	10 (8)	4 (3)
SLPP Creoles (N = 9)	—	—	3	5	1
APC-SLPIM provincials (N = 18)	6	2	1	8 (3)	1 (1)
APC Creoles (N = 2)	—	—	2	—	—

Note: Numbers in parentheses indicate number of fathers who were also members of traditional ruling families.

power.[64] The APC did profess to be the party of the "common man" and the "workers" against the privileged classes; and the social background of its parliamentary group suggested that it was of a less privileged class than the SLPP group, although still a very privileged group in terms of wealth and education by contrast with the bulk of the population of Sierra Leone.

In their educational backgrounds also, the parties tended to diverge. The APC elected very few members with post-secondary school training, whereas a substantial proportion of the SLPP members had some kind of higher education. It is also important to note *which* secondary schools the various numbers attended, since contacts made in the secondary schools and through the Sierra Leone "Old Boys network" help to draw together an otherwise heterogeneous group of individuals.[65] The major agent of cohesion here, at least in the Provinces, was the Bo Government School, which in its policy of accepting only sons and nominees of chiefs, and its stress on education for leadership, filled a role not too different from the English public schools.

64 / For example, in 1965 there were several sharp exchanges in Parliament over whether there were APC members in the civil service, with the government suggesting that there were a number of such people and that they were being disloyal. See *Daily Mail*, December 2 and 3, 1965. One SLPP leader told the writer in respect to the 1966 District Council elections: "We don't know which big men are secretly supporting the APC [in Bo] but there definitely are some."

65 / The strength of this feeling of cohesion among at least one Old Boys group is suggested by the claim (put forward by several people) that a main cause of the protest against Albert Margai's appointment as Prime Minister was that he was not an Old Bo Boy, and that it was time a Bo School graduate became Prime Minister.

TABLE 9:13
Occupation of members of 1962 Parliament before first election by party

Party	Professions				Man-ager[a]	Trader[b]	Politi-cian	Civil servant, clerk	NA, DC[c]	Wage worker
	Law	Doctor	Teacher	Other						
SLPP (N = 42)	4	2	9	5[d]	2	8	3	4	3	2[e]
APC (N = 20)	—	—	2	4[f]	—	7	4	1	2	—

a/"Manager" includes owners of large businesses, involving higher degree of managerial skill.
b/"Trader" includes such occupations as small rice dealers, transport owners, cash crop farmers, etc.
c/Includes both traditional offices (chiefdom speaker, etc.) and paid posts (NA clerk).
d/Two dispensers, one accountant, one economist, one surveyor.
e/Includes a trade union leader who had previously been a clerk.
f/Architect, lab. technician, two accountants.

As the number of primary schools in the provinces increased, their graduates began to scatter more widely among the other new secondary schools opening up in provincial towns. The effect of this increasing diversity of opportunities for a secondary education was not reflected in the SLPP contingent, even among its younger members; the largest number of the SLPP members went to Bo School, and this group was distributed fairly evenly across all age levels. The APC group, by contrast, were from a considerably more diverse background, with a smaller proportion from the school most clearly identified with a "ruling elite." Once again, this suggests the relatively lower-status background of its representatives. However, we should once again note that anybody whose parents could afford the fees necessary to send him to secondary school was from a relatively well-to-do family, by the average standard of Sierra Leone (Table 9:14).

The rise of the All Peoples Congress as the principal challenger to the SLPP oligarchy marked two sharp shifts in the Sierra Leone political system. Most important, it showed a new regional alignment taking shape which in electoral weight presented a far more serious threat to SLPP predominance than the old Colony-Protectorate polarization. A major motivating force behind the formation of the APC had been northern uneasiness about Mende predominance in politics. The 1962 election had heightened the APC's northern (and particularly Temne and Limba) orientation by providing it with a solid bloc of northerners in Parliament, while at the same time leaving the Mendes proportionately stronger than before in the SLPP. Such a situation could in some ways be considered analogous to that which had existed after 1951, when first the National Council and then the United Progressive Party

TABLE 9:14
Secondary school attended by Members of 1962 Parliament, by party

| Party | Bo School | Freetown schools | | | | | Njala | Other | None |
		Albert	St.Ed.	POW	MBHS	SLGS			
SLPP (N = 42)	17	6	4	4	2	2	2	5	4
APC-SLPIM (N = 20)	5	3	1	3	2	2	2	3	—

Notes: Albert Academy was run by the Evangelical United Brethern; St. Edwards, Catholic; Prince of Wales, government; Methodist Boys High School, English Methodists; Sierra Leone Grammar School, Church of England; Njala (since upgraded to university status) was a teacher training college and agricultural school. Albert Academy was primarily for up-country boys; the Grammar School was largely upper-class Creole in enrolment. Some members attended more than one school.

were mainly Creole in opposition to the Protectorate-oriented SLPP. The strategy that had served Sir Milton so well with the Creoles – that of carefully conciliating their political spokesmen and then absorbing them into the governing group – might thus work on the dissident northerners. But a second aspect of the APC's emergence made this task somewhat more difficult.

The APC leaders and members of Parliament constituted a "new class" entering the political elite for the first time. Relative to the SLPP oligarchy, the APC members came from lower-status occupations, had more limited formal education, were younger, and had fewer links with ruling families. They did not articulate any coherent set of beliefs that could be called a radical ideology, but they did have rather strong feelings about the existing social structure, and in particular about the abuses they felt the chiefs were able to perpetrate against their people. Their view that they were in Parliament partly to protect their people against the chiefs, and that this was what people expected of them,[66] served to some extent to inoculate them against the ever-present temptation to move en masse to the government side. Because the SLPP was irrevocably tied to the chiefs, APC members who had won election on a platform of opposition to the chiefs' abuses[67] would have to be offered generous inducements to join the SLPP fold. The SLPP leaders, for their part, did not seem as anxious to reconcile the APC as they had earlier oppositions. While this reforming interest of the APC members was clearly subordinate to their regional concern, it was still a factor of sufficient importance to give them a longer and more successful life than any previous opposition party.

66 / One MP, whose personal commitment to any stronger ideological stand was extremely limited, explained to the author in 1965 that the reason he had resisted government blandishments to cross the carpet was that "My people wouldn't let me."
67 / Above, p. 155.

10
Sir Milton and the opposition: tolerated pluralism

The strong showing of the APC in the 1962 election did not induce Sir Milton Margai to change his political methods. Up to the time of his death on April 28, 1964, he continued to conciliate the leaders within the SLPP and the opposition parties, while allowing the chiefs to coerce opposition supporters at the local level. He made no attempt to develop mass support for the SLPP, but continued to rely on the chiefs and other "big men," while keeping the party open to anyone who wished to support it. Within two months of the election, this process of simultaneously undermining the APC's base and cajoling its leaders bore its first fruit: Prince Koh, an executive member of the APC, and Kabba Yalloh, the MP returned unopposed from Tonkolili North, both announced they were crossing to the SLPP back benches in the legislature.[1] No other opposition MPs were to follow them for another year, but their crossing showed that even in the APC personal ambitions could easily outweigh ideological solidarity.

A spectacular series of departures from the APC in October 1962 left that party tainted with suspicion of being attached to a foreign power. This incident arose out of one of the four successful election petitions that had been lodged after the general election.[2] In Freetown West I a petition unseated Samura Sesay, a Temne clerk who had been the APC candidate. To broaden its Freetown base after the general election, the APC merged with the rump of the UPP and announced shortly before the by-election that Barthes Wilson, who had contested the constituency in May as the Deputy Leader of the

1 / For Koh's crossing, see *Daily Mail,* July 13, 1962; for Yalloh's, *ibid.,* July 18.
2 / A total of 36 petitions were filed against 31 candidates, including 4 Paramount Chiefs. However, most of these petitions were dismissed for failure to comply with certain rules of procedure which had been instituted after the 1957 election and its wave of petitions.

UPP, would now be the APC candidate.[3] Sesay thereupon ran as an Independent and succeeded in retaining more than half the votes he had won as the APC candidate. Wilson, however, won the by-election, defeating the SLPP candidate by a narrow margin.

On October 20, four weeks after the by-election, Sesay announced that he was resigning from the APC because it had "no substantial political ideology" and was divided into two opposed factions of "power seekers and job hunters, and those of us who are to be considered rebels and deviationists."[4] His resignation was quickly followed by several others, most of whom cited Sesay's treatment as one reason for their departure and further charged that Stevens had "sold out" the party's principles by taking part in the Sierra Leone delegation to the United Nations General Assembly.[5] A few days later six of the ex-APC men turned up at an SLPP rally to charge that the APC had been plotting to overthrow the government before Independence, and had been receiving substantial aid from Russia, Ghana, and Guinea. The stories they told diverged considerably. One claimed that as Secretary-General of the APC branch in Conakry he had received a gift of 21 Land Rovers from Russia for use in the election, but since he was afraid to drive them across the border, he had instead taken ten men and 45,000 Guinean francs (about £30).[6] Another claimed that it was Sekou Toure who had given the APC transport for its campaign, consisting of 34 motorcycles, 38 Land Rovers and some weapons, in exchange for a promise to give Kono to Guinea if they won the election.[7] Russia's contribution, he said, was a gift of £35,000 from Khrushchev sent via London and Accra, where unfortunately Nkrumah had seized it and demanded 5 per cent commission.[8] The one charge which subsequently turned out to have some foundation was that Russia had offered a number of scholarships for Sierra Leoneans to study in Moscow and that arrangements for these students to go to Russia had been made through the

3 / See *Daily Mail*, September 3, 1962, for the announcement that Wilson would run for the APC. Speculation about this possibility had already appeared in *ibid.*, August 22.

4 / *Daily Mail*, October 20, 1962. It is interesting to note that he had not been officially expelled from the APC for running as an Independent against an official APC candidate.

5 / For the announcement that Stevens would attend the UN as a member of the Sierra Leone delegation, see *Daily Mail*, September 6, 1962. For the APC men's resignation, see *ibid.*, October 24 and October 29. A total of five men in addition to Sesay were publicly noted as having left the APC at this time. Sesay later was appointed personnel manager of the government-owned Sierra Leone Cement Works.

6 / *Daily Mail*, October 27, 1962.

7 / *Ibid.*, October 30, 1962.

8 / *Ibid.* He failed to explain whether the money had ever in fact reached Sierra Leone.

APC.[9] Albert Margai, who was present at the meeting where most of these charges were made, stated that the government would take "stringent steps to bring those responsible to justice,"[10] but no prosecutions were ever launched, although one would have thought that such charges, if true, would have been grounds for at least a charge of sedition, if not treason. However, the "exposures" did help to mark the APC as "the Russian party"; in at least one subsequent by-election SLPP workers charged that if the APC won, it would bring in Russians to take away the villagers' wives.

For the most part, the parliamentarians in opposition were treated generously by the government. They shared fully in such choice personal forms of patronage as trips abroad; Sir Milton's inclusion of Stevens in the 1962 United Nations delegation was typical.[11] They also were able to obtain personal loans from the government for building houses and obtaining farm land and rice. They were not denied all patronage for their constituencies, or favours for their constituents. While one MP claimed a Minister had refused to build a bridge between his constituency and the Minister's because the Minister "didn't want to make propaganda for the APC," others reported being able to intervene successfully on behalf of constituents in difficulties, and several pro-APC towns received water and electricity supplies.[12] They were also able to participate fully in deciding how the £3,000 annual Rural Development Grant to each district was to be allocated among the chiefdoms.[13]

In their efforts at political proselytizing, the APC members of Parliament encountered more difficulties. The Prime Minister himself seemed prepared to permit opposition MPs to campaign freely. One APC member claimed that

9 / One of these ex-APC men, subsequently asked by the writer for details about the aid that Russia had given the APC, finally claimed that when he and another APC man had gone to Conakry to arrange with the Russian Embassy there for some Sierra Leonean scholars to go to Moscow, the two of them had had their fares to and from Conakry as well as their hotel bills paid by the Russians. The Russians did in fact provide about 40 scholarships a year through the APC, although in 1966 they cut this to about 12. Mr Stevens' son, it may be noted, was among the Sierra Leoneans studying in Russia on these scholarships.

10 / *Daily Mail,* October 30, 1962.

11 / Possibly there was some mischievous calculation in Sir Milton's willingness to share such patronage; the sight of their MPs travelling abroad while the rank and file were still being intimidated by their chief was not one to encourage the ordinary villagers to work harder for the APC. Stevens came under considerable criticism for joining the UN delegation from his own radical wing.

12 / For example, Port Loko Town's water supply was extended in 1962/63, and Makeni had a new electric generator installed in 1963.

13 / This grant was generally allocated by a committee chaired by the District Officer, and comprising all MPs for the district.

when he had told Sir Milton that a chief in his constituency had threatened to arrest him for holding a meeting, Sir Milton had instructed his Permanent Secretary to send a circular to all chiefs telling them not to interfere with members of Parliament.[14] Shortly before the 1963 District Council elections, Sir Milton sent a memorandum to all Resident Ministers asking them to ensure that the chiefs would permit a fair campaign: "In order to ... permit the people freedom of thought and speech it is of vital importance that the Paramount Chiefs themselves afford all possible facilities within their means to each and every candidate, thus leaving no cause for any grievance or partiality."[15]

Sir Milton's policies, however, were not fully accepted by his followers. The Paramount Chiefs and local authorities bore the primary responsibility for curbing the APC, and sometimes exercised their powers drastically. In Samu Chiefdom, Kambia District, the young APC member of Parliament, A. B. S. Janneh, who had been unseated on an election petition in July, was sentenced in September to two years in jail by the Native Administration Court for "incitement and undermining the authority of the Paramount Chief."[16] Some 66 of his supporters were also jailed. Another MP was charged by an NA court in his constituency with "making allegations" against the Paramount Chief.[17] Most APC members of Parliament did not even bother to apply for permission to hold meetings, but simply kept in touch with their supporters by personal visits. One claimed that Stevens could not safely make speeches in the provinces for fear he would be jailed by some NA court for "undermining the authority" of a Paramount Chief. Lesser members of the APC were haled before the NA courts on a variety of charges. The most drastic suppression seemed to be in Kono, where the SLPIM members of Parliament told the Prime Minister in mid-1962 that the chiefs and Tribal Authorities had arrested some 2,000 persons suspected of being SLPIM supporters.[18]

The central government itself was sometimes willing to use the coercive powers it had inherited in order to harass or discourage opposition. In October 1962, the APC chose as a candidate in the Freetown Council elections the Bassa Tribal Headman in Freetown, J. T. Refell. On October 16, the government revoked its recognition of Refell as Tribal Headman, a post he had held since 1957.[19] On October 30 it ordered him deported to Liberia, alleging that he was a citizen of that country.[20] While citizens of Sierra Leone could not be deported, they could be banished to any part of the country

14 / I am grateful to Fred Hayward of the University of Wisconsin for this information.

15 / Memorandum from the Prime Minister to Resident Ministers, January 30, 1963.

16 / *Daily Mail*, September 12, 1962.   17 / *We Yone*, August 31, 1963.

18 / *Daily Mail*, June 4, 1962.   19 / *Daily Mail*, October 18, 1962.

20 / *Ibid.*, October 31, 1962. The Bassa tribe, like the Kroos, were originally from Liberia, but many had been settled in Freetown for several generations.

and restricted there by executive order, with no appeal to the courts.[21] In early 1963 Chief Mbriwa, the deposed SLPIM leader, was banished to Kamakwie in the Bombali District after a Commission of Inquiry had found him guilty of such offences as holding meetings in other chiefdoms without the permission of the Paramount Chiefs concerned.[22] Several prominent APC members were banished in the same period: a businessman from Magbu-raka,[23] and a whole family in Kambia district.[24] One APC member of Parliament claimed that the Resident Minister of the Northern Province used the threat of banishment to terrorize any young men who appeared to sympathize with the APC.

All these curbs helped to cut away the electoral base for the APC in the north, as well as handicapping its efforts to build a strong party organization. The District Council elections in March 1963 saw a marked falling off of the APC's share of the vote in contested seats (Table 10:1). Its candidates won more votes than the SLPP's in only one of the four districts where it had been successful a year earlier. Its activists were also being suppressed quite effectively; no less than 36 of the 73 SLPP candidates in these four districts were returned unopposed, which suggested the difficulties faced by the APC in finding candidates to run under its symbol. Siaka Stevens charged shortly before the election that the intimidation of the APC "beat all records" and that the chiefs were actively campaigning for the SLPP.[25] This almost certainly was true. The results of the election showed a fairly small drop in the popular vote for the APC, but it was enough of a decrease to suggest that local suppression and intimidation were weakening the party.

Although it seemed to be retaining its popular support more successfully than the APC, the SLPIM was the first of the opposition parties to break under government pressure. This was to be expected since the SLPIM's leaders had

21 / *Laws of Sierra Leone*, 1960, Cap. 60, Section 25 (4) provided for banishment of deposed chiefs, and Section 26 (2) for the banishment of any person whose presence was a threat to "peace, order and good government," by the Governor in Council.

22 / *Daily Mail*, May 10, 1963.

23 / *Daily Mail*, January 1, 1963.

24 / This last case arose largely out of a family feud in which the Bangura family, representing a previous ruling house, quarrelled with the Yek family, represented by the reigning Paramount Chief, Bai Sherbro Yumkella. The Bangura family aligned themselves with the APC in opposition to Chief Yumkella. A Commissioner of Inquiry had said in 1956 that "as long as ... Yolla Bangura remains in the chiefdom and continues to be dissatisfied because he is unable to obtain a position of authority in the councils of the chiefdom . . . there will always be trouble in the chiefdom." *Reports of the Commissioners of Enquiry into the Conduct of Certain Chiefs*, p. 8. Dr Margai claimed later that he had tried to bring about a reconciliation between Yolla Bangura and Chief Yumkella, but Bangura "let me down." See *House of Representatives Debates*, Session 1963/64, IV (November 22, 1963), col. 256.

25 / *Daily Mail*, February 14, 1963.

TABLE 10:1
Comparison of 1962 General Election and 1963 District Council Election
by percentage vote cast for parties in contested seats

District	SLPP		APC-SLPIM		Independents	
	1962 (%)	1963 (%)	1962 (%)	1963 (%)	1962 (%)	1963 (%)
Bombali	30	38	38	49	32	13
Kambia	33	51	53	46	14	3
Koinadugu	41	54	—	—	59	46
Port Loko	25	49	41	37	35	14
Tonkolili	25	52	54	24	22	23
Kono	27	37	68	47	5	16

Source: Sierra Leone *Gazette*, March 23, 1963.

TABLE 10:2
Central government grants to
Kono District Council (1962–64)

	MADA (£)	Roads (£)
1962	2,000	Nil
1963	6,000	Nil
1964	17,815	16,968

as their paramount goal a better deal for the Kono people, an objective which could be obtained within the existing system. The APC leaders, while they sought better representation for northerners, also sought a further goal which could only be obtained by changing the existing social structure, a more egalitarian society with no special powers for the chiefs.

Shortly after the SLPIM had won 17 seats (against 7 for the SLPP) in the Kono District Council elections, ex-chief Mbriwa was banished to Kamakwie in the Northern Province.[26] At the same time, several SLPIM councillors crossed to the SLPP. George Mani, the SLPIM's general secretary, charged that they had acted under duress: "Some SLPIM councillors have been threatened and intimidated by the authorities. ... The policy of the authorities in Kono is 'join the SLPP or no renewal of diamond licences.' "[27] The central government also joined in applying pressure to the Council. The two major grants to the district were the roads grant and the Mining Areas Development Authority grant; in 1962 and 1963 the Kono District Council received nothing in road grants and only £8,000 in its MADA grant (Table 10:2).[28] It was the opinion of most SPLIM supporters, including Council officials, that the withholding of grants was a form of political pressure.

With its leader banished, the district losing revenue from the central

26 / See above, p. 169.
27 / *Daily Mail*, June 13, 1963.
28 / Data from Accounts of Kono District Council for 1962, 1963, and 1964.

government, and its activists subject to personal harassment, the SLPIM as an organized group was ripe for absorption into the SLPP. At the end of July 1963 three of the four Kono MPs announced that they were crossing to the SLPP. Explaining their decision, the leading proponent of the merger, S. L. Matturi, made it clear that they were not changing their views on the needs of Kono, but only their tactics:

We now take a course of action which we truly believe will ease the tension in our District, and lay the way to feasible solutions of our many problems. ... Things seem to have gone from bad to worse. Development is at a standstill and relations are chilly and rigid between those in authority and the masses. It is only we who truly love and care for the welfare of our district and its people who know that the strands of the Kono problem are tangled up in that "gimmick" which we call politics in this country. ... We now wish to join forces with the Government in power and fight for the rights of the Kono people from within its ranks.[29]

Several SLPIM councillors also chose this time to cross to the SLPP, and were welcomed by the SLPP's Kono leader, Rev. Paul Dunbar, who said he hoped this merger would end the seven years of "vicious enmity" between the parties.[30] The personal enmity, however, lingered on, and Chief Mbriwa still refrained from endorsing the SLPP;[31] but now the SLPIM's demands were expressed from within the SLPP.[32] Three months after the SLPIM MPs crossed to the SLPP, S. L. Matturi became the first Kono representative in the Cabinet since 1957, being appointed to the post of Resident Minister, Eastern Province.[33]

The APC members of Parliament were more resistant to government bland-ishments and pressure. Up to Sir Milton's death, no other APC members joined the initial two carpet-crossers.[34] Several factors contributed to the APC's staying power as an opposition. Perhaps most important was their awareness that their electorates would probably turn against them if they were to join the party which backed the chiefs.[35] Then, too, "Pa" Margai

29 / *House of Representatives Debates*, Session 1963/64, III (August 1, 1963) cols. 187–88. The fourth Kono Member of Parliament, S. W. Gandi Capio, took much more of a "show me" attitude, declining to cross on the grounds that the government had not yet done anything for Kono.

30 / *Daily Mail*, July 27, 1963.

31 / He finally joined the SLPP in March 1965 just after being released from banish-ment, and was re-elected Paramount Chief two months later.

32 / The crossovers were not quite wholehearted converts to the SLPP; one continued to refer to the SLPP as "they" and none seem to have taken out party membership cards.

33 / He succeeded Taplimah Ngobeh, who had been killed in a car crash.

34 / Only one further APC member crossed to the SLPP after Sir Albert became Prime Minister, despite the latter's attempts to win over several others.

35 / They had, after all, used this line of attack effectively against the two ex-UPP men who had joined the SLPP and run for it in 1962. It is also worth noting that the three APC members who did cross all had ambitions to become Paramount Chiefs, where they would be insulated from having to win support from a mass electorate.

was the clearest symbol of the traditional oligarchy which they as "young men" without traditional status could see as the principal obstacle to their personal ambitions. Added to this was a degree of personal animosity between Stevens and Dr Margai; the events of 1957 had not quite been forgiven on either side. At the same time, the life of an opposition MP was not totally unbearable. Dr Margai was quite willing to allow the APC men to receive a share of the perquisites and patronage of office. All of these factors worked to keep them from crossing over to the government side.

Although the APC leaders were not prepared to join the SLPP, their opposition to the SLPP "system" remained moderate. Their vague populist and socialist inclinations did not provide them with any rationale for waging total war against the chiefs or the SLPP leaders, while the regional basis of their discontent fell far short of giving them grounds for demanding secession. Both their ideological and their regional demands were susceptible to bargaining within the existing political framework, even though their terms were relatively stiff. A further incentive towards maintaining this moderate stance was the APC leaders' awareness that Sir Milton Margai, despite his apparent tolerance of their conduct, was quite prepared to jail them all again if they tried to encourage any kind of violence. Sir Milton had once said he was "not prepared to let young men destroy" the system he had created,[36] and no one believed this was an idle threat. The result of their own predispositions and Sir Milton's attitude was that the APC consistently acted as a "loyal opposition" both within Parliament and outside it. Within Parliament they were not obstructive and seldom resorted to demagogic misrepresentation of issues to win popular sympathy.[37] Outside Parliament, they were generally careful not to stir the people of the north to violence against the chiefs and Tribal Authorities.[38]

Two further features of the APC had some significance in contributing to its moderate attitude. Its leader, Siaka Stevens, was not a fanatical man who would resort to any means to overthrow a government. As the General Secretary of the Mineworkers Union at the Marampa iron mines in the 1940s, and later as Minister for Mines and Labour, he had had to rely on bargaining and conciliation with opponents. When he was a nominated member of the Protectorate Assembly from 1946 onward, he had taken a strong stand in

36 / Cited in his obituary in *Daily Mail*, April 29, 1964.

37 / It should be added that their relatively unsophisticated backgrounds and lack of any members with legal training made them a considerably less effective opposition within Parliament than either the UPP or the PNP had been.

38 / Occasionally, as in the widespread disturbances in Samu Chiefdom, Kambia, in 1962, APC activists seem to have encouraged attacks on the Tribal Authorities. See *House of Representatives Debates*, 1962/63, II (November 28, 1962), col. 68. More frequently, when popular discontent against a chief flared up, the APC was ready to encourage it.

demanding more benefits for Sierra Leone from its mining agreements, but he had not launched the more demagogic and wide-ranging attacks on all aspects of colonial policy which had characterized Albert Margai.[39] He continued to take a moderate stand as Deputy Leader of the PNP.[40] Although he was a capable and witty orator, described by one scholar as comparing favourably with Azikiwe, Nkrumah, or Toure,[41] his platform style was more that of the teacher than the firebrand. Stevens was not the stuff of which revolutionaries are made.

While some of the other APC leaders were liable to be more extreme in their actions than Stevens, as had been shown at the time of independence,[42] none could be called a dedicated revolutionary. A few had been to China and Russia, but this seems to have been essentially a symbolic anti-colonialist gesture. There is no evidence to suggest that any of them had received training in methods of terrorism or ways of fomenting a revolution, or even any grounding in Marxism.

One charge sometimes made against the APC as part of more general allegations about its "revolutionary" nature was the claim that it was receiving financial support from outside powers, either African or Communist, who were interested in stirring up a "peoples' revolution." However, no convincing evidence of such support was ever produced. The allegations made by the ex-APC men in 1962 that the party had received aid from China, Guinea, and Russia were too contradictory to have the ring of truth and were never followed up. In early 1963 the Minister of Information, John Nelson-Williams, gave considerable publicity to a claim that he had a photostat of a document showing that Stevens had received the sum of 9,400 francs from Guinea.[43] Stevens later pointed out in Parliament that this money represented membership dues paid by Sierra Leoneans living in Guinea and came to about £6.10.0.[44] It can be safely assumed in Sierra Leone that the opposition party would not be able to keep secret the receipt of any substantial sum of money from abroad. If this charge that the APC received £6.10.0 from Guinea was the most serious the government could produce, it can be reasonably inferred that the APC was not receiving any help of importance from abroad.

The lack of any effective SLPP organization not only helped protect the opposition parties but also ensured a considerable amount of intra-party competition. At the time of Sir Milton Margai's death, the SLPP's local

39 / See *Proceedings of the Protectorate Assembly,* 1949–51, *passim.*

40 / For example, in "The PNP and Expatriatism," *Liberty,* July 25, 1959.

41 / Martin Kilson, "Sierra Leone," *West Africa,* No. 2248 (July 2, 1960), p. 745.

42 / Above, pp. 135 ff.

43 / The SLBS national news broadcast devoted a full five minutes of its ten-minute broadcast to announcing this charge when it was made.

44 / *Daily Mail,* April 4, 1963.

branches existed only on paper.[45] A handful of Paramount Chiefs, wealthy traders, and local government officials would come together occasionally to select official candidates for an election, but undertook no other political activity. They made no attempt to draw new recruits into the party; most of them considered anyone who voted for the party candidate (or a pro-SLPP Independent) at the last election to be a good SLPP member,[46] but would not think of expecting these voters to do more for the party. The central party organization was in no better shape. After the 1962 election the party appointed a full-time paid General Secretary.[47] He was installed in the grubby second floor of a rented building which served as party headquarters, but provided with only an intermittent supply of assistants and money. The party also closed down the official newspaper, the *Vanguard,* whose principal contributions to political education in Sierra Leone during its last years had been the persistent exposure of personal quarrels within the party.

The one enduring element within the SLPP was its parliamentary group. But this group, because of the way it came into being, could not be expected to exhibit strong party loyalty. SLPP MPs did not often reach the point of voting against the government, although this happened on occasion,[48] but they were quite uninhibited in introducing private members' motions criticizing government policies, and in raising parliamentary questions critical of the government. An examination of questions asked during three sittings of Parliament in 1962 and 1963 indicates that government backbenchers and Paramount Chief members were not noticeably less prone to ask questions which criticized the government either explicitly or implicitly than were the APC members (Table 10:3). This comparison probably underrated the extent to which government backbenchers criticized the government, since they could make their criticisms known privately through the party caucus before tabling a question in the House.

A further indicator of party loyalty is the willingness of members to contribute to party funds.[49] By this criterion, even a substantial proportion of

45 / Bo District, at the instigation of a Minister, planned a number of executive meetings and a recruiting drive in 1963, but failed to implement these plans.

46 / One MP, when asked about SLPP membership in his district, produced the population figures for the district provided by the *1963 Census.*

47 / One member of the national executive who had voted for the appointment of this individual explained, "I wouldn't say he's very good, but it's hard to get someone for the salary." For the announcement of the appointment, see *Daily Mail,* August 4, 1962.

48 / Notably on a vote of confidence over the government's handling of financial affairs, following a Commission of Enquiry into the public accounts. Three government backbenchers voted with the opposition. See *House of Representatives Debates,* 1963/64, III (August 13, 1963), cols. 590–91.

49 / These data were obtained from an undated, untitled mimeographed sheet circulated from the SLPP party office. It is partly corroborated by the Treasurer's report read

TABLE 10:3

Proportion of parliamentary questions which appear critical of
government by party affiliation and nature of question (1962–3)

	Local (%)	General (%)	Total (%)
SLPP ordinary members	31	25	27
Paramount Chiefs	37	19	25
APC members	39	37	37

TABLE 10:4

Monthly contributions to SLPP party funds by MPS
(August 1962 to April 1964)

Group	No contribution	Less than half months	More than half months	Every month
Ministers (N = 23)	2	7	8	6
Paramount Chiefs (N = 12)	6	2	3	1
Backbenchers (N = 20)	6	5	4	5
Crossovers (N = 5)	3	—	—	2

SLPP ministers could be regarded as something less than devoted adherents
of the party (Table 10: 4). There was no apparent pattern in party contributions; one Minister close to Dr Margai apparently made no contribution
during the period under review, while two backbenchers noted for their
independence both contributed regularly.

All of these features added up to a very weak party organization. Even at
the Cabinet level, the SLPP was little more than an aggregation of individuals
who had risen to prominence because of their local power base, and who
tended to consider themselves as representatives of their particular areas.
Various Ministers have noted how they felt obliged to consider the interests
of their own electorate, although one added that Sir Milton was always reminding them to keep in mind the overall interest of the country. This view
that each MP was in Parliament to get what he could for his constituents
was brought out clearly by S. L. Matturi when he promised to "fight for the
rights of the Kono people within the SLPP,"[50] and later by John Nelson-
Williams when he warned that if the people of Freetown voted against the

at Makeni. We should note that the compulsory payment of party dues noted by Kilson
(in Coleman and Rosberg, *Political Parties and National Integration,* p. 110) was no
longer in effect.

50 / Above, p. 173.

SLPP, it would be hard for their members in the government to get their share of funds.[51]

The members who won seats in the legislature did so through their personal ability to influence the electorate, and not through any help the party could give them. The fact that they were already in Parliament indicated that they did not need help from a party organization. On the contrary, if a party organization were established in an MP's constituency, it might serve to bring other persons to prominence or provide a rival with an organized body of supporters for use in the next election. It was simply not in the interest of most members of Parliament to strengthen the SLPP party structure.

The interests of most chiefs too would not be served by the development of an SLPP organization. As long as elections were fought on a personal basis, the chiefs would be in a strong position since they provided the most obvious channels through which aspiring candidates would appeal to the people. If, however, parties began to educate the electorate to vote for a party symbol, the chief could no longer mediate between the party politician and the voter. His role in influencing voters might even be taken over by a party organizer unsympathetic to chieftaincy.

To hold this aggregation together required a leader adept at reconciling diverse views rather than one who was determined to impose his own personal vision on his followers. It was not a great step from tolerating and accommodating diversities within the ruling party to tolerating slightly greater diversity outside it. The members of the governing party, for their part, realized that their bargaining strength came in part from the possibility that they might withdraw their support from the party leader. This possibility would be curtailed if opposition parties were proscribed. Then, too, the gulf between the SLPP and APC backbenchers was not so great as to preclude some community of interest between them. Often they had been to the same schools, worked together, or known each other personally, and they shared the same problems of getting what they could for their constituents and for themselves. Relations between them generally were cordial.[52] All these factors encouraged a high degree of tolerance by the SLPP leaders toward the APC.

Sir Milton's own attitudes also contributed to the tolerance of the All Peoples Congress, both directly and indirectly. His willingness to allow APC members a share of patronage and to encourage fair elections has already been noted.[53] He could be autocratic and high-handed at times; in dealing with his Cabinet, he would simply cut off Ministers who disagreed with him

51 / *Daily Mail*, October 6, 1964.

52 / For example, at tea break in the parliamentary lounge, government and opposition backbenchers would generally mingle together; it was the Ministers who most often sat at separate tables.

53 / Above, pp. 169–70.

and, if they persisted, would ask for their resignations.[54] But he would not always insist on his own way. For example, when the party's National Executive was appointing a full-time General Secretary in 1962, it turned down Sir Milton's personal choice in favour of a man put forward by his brother Albert.[55] And even when he was clamping down on the APC, as at Independence, he did not use more coercion than was absolutely necessary to maintain order. Sir Milton's willingness to conciliate a wide range of views was suggested by his defence of the large Cabinet he maintained after the 1962 elections: "I know that it is expensive to keep the present number of ministers, but it is easier to run a country with Ministers from all the provinces and from the Western Area. It would not be a good thing for fewer people to run a country."[56]

Sir Milton's lack of interest in a party organization also supported the maintenance of pluralism. With no party organization, the SLPP inevitably became a loose aggregation of local representatives, based almost entirely on the chiefs. But this provided a sufficient base for Sir Milton to achieve the modest development of, and limited control over, the country that he sought. During his final years his ill health, which kept him under sedation a good deal of the time,[57] had severely restricted his ability to direct the party, even if he had wished to make of it a more effective instrument for his rule. The limits imposed by his health were suggested by the fact that he had appointed three Resident Ministers in 1961 to perform the vital task of watching local problems such as chiefdom disputes in the three provinces to prevent their blowing up to serious proportions.

A final factor which may be noted as a protection for political competition under Sir Milton was the political culture of the elite. A belief in the desirability of free elections was the most conspicuous part of the Sierra Leonean pattern of political behaviour, but it also included such British heritages as respect for the independence of the judiciary and for the rule of laws, the legitimacy of opposition, and some regard for personal liberties. While the Creoles, with their strong British leanings, were the principal upholders of this tradition, it was also diffused among the Western elite from the provinces. For example, on his election to the position of Speaker of the House in 1962, Banja Tejan-Sie stated that "he was happy to see that democracy was fully

54 / However, one Minister added that a few minutes after uttering this threat, the doctor would laugh and all would be forgiven. The only Minister ever to resign under Sir Milton's rule was Chief Bai Farima Tass II in 1957, and this was as a result of his misrule as a Chief rather than his Ministerial conduct.

55 / SLPP Executive Committee Minutes, July 31, 1962. Sir Milton's choice was A. B. Cotay; his brother's was Julius Cole.

56 / *Daily Mail*, August 9, 1962.

57 / The writer has been told this by a medical doctor who claimed to have personally prescribed the sedation.

interpreted since there is now an Opposition which he hoped would lead to lively discussions to further the interest of the country and its people."[58] Albert Margai, also a lawyer, told the House shortly before he became Prime Minister: "When the time comes in Sierra Leone that Government lacks opposition, that will be the time that some of us will pack up our bags and baggage and quit politics. This system of government is one of the best things we have inherited from our colonial masters."[59] These professions generally were honoured in practice. The judiciary remained independent, and the civil service maintained its political neutrality. The opposition leaders, while not completely free to campaign for their party, were not under preventive detention, and had been allowed to compete fairly effectively in the last general election.

The legacy of political patterns established by Sir Milton imposed a number of restraints on any successor. The continued dependence of the SLPP on the chiefs for its local organization severely limited the range of reforms an SLPP government could institute in local government, agriculture, or any of the numerous other fields affecting the chiefs' interests. The only change of significance over the whole range of local government between 1956 and 1964 was a provision in the Local Courts Act of 1963 that local court decisions could henceforth be appealed to higher courts.[60] This change was balanced by the widening of the local courts' jurisdiction to everyone present in the chiefdom, and not just "natives."[61] The administrative arrangements of both the chiefdoms and the District Councils remained unchanged, although the former continued to spend more than half their revenue on chiefs' emoluments and other administrative costs, and the latter to be plagued by corruption.[62] If the chiefs became any more restrained in their behaviour during Sir Milton's last years, it was through fear of popular reactions, not through government pressure.

Some features of the SLPP's approach to politics laid up trouble for it over the long run. Its lack of interest in drawing the mass of the people into political participation spared its leaders some of the difficulties in satisfying unattainable popular expectations. But once an opposition party committed to widespread mobilization of the population appeared on the scene, the SLPP faced the risk that mass participation would occur in any case, aligned against the SLPP rather than under its direction. The APC's appeal to regional sentiments could be particularly disruptive if not countered carefully.

58 / *Vanguard*, July 14, 1962.   59 / *Daily Mail*, April 4, 1964.
60 / The Local Courts Act, 1963, Sections 29, 30.
61 / Section 13 (2).
62 / See Kilson, *Political Change*, pp. 198 ff., for a discussion of these two levels of government.

The SLPP leaders' attempts to end organized political opposition by absorbing the leaders of opposition parties was also a tactic of doubtful long-term utility. As long as the grievances which gave rise to opposition movements were not alleviated, swallowing up the leaders of opposition parties would simply leave the way open for more radical leaders to emerge, or would bring about spontaneous violent uprisings. The emergence of the APC after the UPP and PNP leaders entered the government had been a first step towards the "radicalization" of opposition movements. Yet with the chiefs so strongly entrenched in the SLPP, it was hard to see how anti-chief feelings in the north and Kono could possibly be assuaged.

A final problem faced by the SLPP was how to satisfy the expectations of the growing number of mobilized individuals in the field of economic development. Political bargaining over the allocation of resources inevitably led to a piecemeal process of development, with a multitude of small projects. This did avoid the risk of a spectacular waste of funds, and did serve to satisfy temporarily a wide range of demands. The weakness of the governing party also meant that the civil servants had a fairly free hand in allocating such projects as roads, water, and schools, and in formulating the development budget. But when major issues had to be resolved, the civil servants could not act on their own, and the politicians could not come to a decision. The most striking example of this tendency to drift was the government's handling of the Sierra Leone Railway, which ran an annual deficit of £500,000 (in a total government budget of £17,000,000) and from 1962 to 1964 consumed some 30 per cent of the government's £10,965,328 development expenditures.[63] Most economic and transportation advisers agreed that the railway was a costly liability which should be phased out of service. But the government, afraid of the political repercussions of throwing large numbers of railway workers out of their jobs, refused to either abandon the line or to sink into it the £30,000,000 required to modernize it.

This, then, was the legacy of Sir Milton Margai: a party system highly pluralist in nature, and highly tolerant of organized opposition, but unable to press for any radical changes in the social structure; an administration of fairly high competence and with a considerable degree of freedom from political interference; and a pattern of small incremental development projects. Whether such a system could continue to meet the aspirations of Sierra Leoneans was questionable. Many people in the towns and even in the bush were increasing their expectations to an extent that radical changes might be needed to satisfy them, but the SLPP was not a party that could readily be brought to support radical actions. A new leader would have a difficult time moving Sierra Leone along a path different from that followed by Sir Milton.

63 / Calculated from Sierra Leone, *Development Estimates, 1965–66.*

PART FIVE

The rise and fall of Albert Margai

11
1964–65: Prime Minister against party

Sir Albert Margai's career as Prime Minister falls into three stages. For over a year after he first came to power, he tried to consolidate his position as leader of the SLPP, and at the same time to curb the activities of the APC, within a competitive party framework. By late 1965 it was clear that neither Sir Albert's nor the SLPP's ascendancy were any more firmly established than when he took office. His response was an attempt to create a one-party state, which by restricting electoral competition would safeguard his position and those of his supporters. This attempt, however, foundered on the resistance of his own party, of the civil service, judiciary and other elites, and of the common people. The final phase of Sir Albert's rule was a holding operation leading up to the climactic general election of March 1967, which came to be viewed as the means by which the one-party state question would finally be settled once and for all.

When he died on April 28, 1964, Sir Milton Margai had left no clearly designated successor. Mustapha had been dropped as Deputy Prime Minister following the 1962 election,[1] and a number of Ministers had taken turns as Acting Prime Minister when Sir Milton travelled abroad. Dr Karefa-Smart had been one of these, Albert Margai had not. But Albert had been chosen as leader in 1957, and his re-entry into the government in 1960 was viewed by some observers as opening the way to his succession.[2] A few weeks before Sir Milton's death there came a very strong indication that Albert had be-

1 / The first public announcement that Mustapha had been dropped seems not to have been made until November 1963, in an answer by the Prime Minister to a question in Parliament. *House of Representatives Debates,* November 13, 1963, col. 23.

2 / For example, Martin Kilson had written in 1960 that with Albert Margai's re-entry into the government, he appeared the most likely successor to his brother as Prime Minister. *West Africa,* July 9, 1960.

come the probable successor. Until the beginning of April 1964 Mustapha had been answering the Prime Minister's questions in Parliament when the latter was away ill, but for the month of April Albert took over this task. It is possible that Sir Milton had kept the way clear for his brother to succeed by failing to designate anyone else as Deputy Prime Minister, but had felt it impolitic to name Albert because of the strong hostile reaction this would arouse in the north. This is, of course, conjecture since there is no clear evidence to show that the brothers had in fact achieved any personal reconciliation after 1960.

The night Sir Milton died, most of his Ministers met, but there was apparently no discussion of a successor. The next day, April 29, the Governor-General summoned Albert Margai to be sworn in as Prime Minister. Both the choice of Albert and the speed with which Sir Henry Lightfoot-Boston announced his decision aroused considerable suspicion that Margai had threatened to take over by force if he were not chosen legally. Although in choosing Albert, the Governor-General did appear to have reversed a decision he had made a few hours earlier to call his chief rival, Dr John Karefa-Smart, I doubt that anything so crude as the threat of a coup was used.[3] Apparently Berthan Macauley, Albert's former PNP associate and now Attorney-General, moved in on the Governor-General and by dint of continuous persuasion eventually got Sir Henry to agree to call Albert immediately. There were good grounds for this choice: Albert Margai had once been elected to head the SLPP, and neither Karefa-Smart nor any other possible leader could plausibly claim a greater following in the party.[4] Even so, the aura of a fast deal continued to hang around Albert Margai's accession to the top post.

The choice of Margai and the speed with which his appointment was announced took most political leaders by surprise. Some were not prepared to accept the Governor-General's choice immediately. On the night of April 29, within hours of the new Prime Minister's appointment, a meeting was held at the home of Y. D. Sesay. Mustapha, Karefa-Smart, and Siaka Stevens were among the 35 to 40 MPs present. Most of those at the meeting were northerners, although at least two Mende Paramount Chiefs and one Mende ordinary member attended. The meeting drew up a petition questioning the constitutionality of the Governor-General's action in appointing Margai on the grounds that he had failed to consult either Ministers or MPs. Since 14

3 / Col. David Lansana, a Mende and friend of Albert, was in charge of the army at the time, but the army probably was too mixed tribally, and for the most part too imbued with the belief that soldiers should stay out of politics, to take part in a clearly illegal action.

4 / Other possible contenders were M. S. Mustapha, neutral as between the two major tribes; Kande Bureh; Y. D. Sesay, northern and traditionalist; and possibly Salia Jusu-Sheriff, who in his urbanity and intellectualism resembled Karefa-Smart, but was a Mende with strong appeal to the younger, more radical elements in the SLPP.

of the approximately 35 signatories to this petition were APC MPs, it is not likely that the APC members would have agreed to support Karefa-Smart, much less any other SLPP leader, as Prime Minister.

The next morning the MPs went as a delegation to the Governor-General, who informed them he would have to prepare a reply and asked who was the leader of the delegation. Mustapha, the senior Minister present, said he was the leader. Then later in the day Mustapha decided to dissociate himself from the petition,[5] with the result that no one ever received a reply to it. Meanwhile, Albert Margai had learned about the meeting, and began summoning participants to pledge their loyalty to him. Four of the Ministers who had signed the petition paid a heavy price for their action; Karefa-Smart, Mustapha, Sesay, and S. L. Matturi all were excluded when Albert named his Ministry on May 1.[6] A Temne ministerial secretary, A. H. Kabia, also lost his post, but was re-appointed five months later. Mustapha, Sesay, and Matturi sent an abject letter of apology to the Prime Minister,[7] but they remained backbenchers.

The two main threats facing Albert Margai when he became Prime Minister were the danger of a radical party capitalizing on urban and rural discontent to undercut the chiefs and the SLPP, and the prospect that the political parties might polarize along Mende-Temne lines. Although these dangers were in part mutually exclusive, both were likely to grow as more individuals were drawn into political participation.

The more immediately threatening of these dangers was the split between Temnes and Mendes. The fact that a Mende was succeeding another Mende was enough in itself to rankle northerners; the purge of northern Ministers (which left only three in the Cabinet)[8] and the promotion of Mendes to key positions in the civil service further increased Temne suspicions.[9] Albert

5 / The reason he alleged for this action was that he had learned after the visit to the Governor-General that Karefa-Smart had said he would cause violence over Albert's appointment. Karefa-Smart does seem to have made some remarks which could be construed in this way.

6 / *Daily Mail*, May 2, 1964. One other northern Minister who had signed the petition, Amadu Wurie, had visited the Prime Minister on the morning of April 30 to explain that he had made a mistake in thinking that the Cabinet had to be consulted by the Governor-General, and to pledge his loyalty to Albert. He retained his portfolio, probably because Albert could not afford to remove all the northerners from the Cabinet.

7 / *Daily Mail*, May 4, 1964.

8 / Of these, Kande Bureh was based in Freetown, and Chief Yumkella had little support even in his own chiefdom. Amadu Wurie, the only Minister popularly elected from a northern constituency, was not regarded as an outstanding northern spokesman.

9 / George Panda and S. B. Daramy were already Secretary to the Prime Minister and Financial Secretary. Peter Tucker, a Sherbro, became Establishment Secretary (in charge of personnel) and John Kallon, the brother of the Minister, took charge of

tried to restore the balance by appointing Kande Bureh to the post of Deputy Prime Minister and promoting one northern backbencher to a ministerial secretaryship,[10] but these changes were not enough to outweigh the fact that the top post had gone from one Mende to another.

In order to give the north more representation in the government, Albert Margai had to get more SLPP representatives elected from that area or win over APC members. For the SLPP to be successful, it would have to break away from its dependence on the chiefs, whose actions seriously undermined it. This, however, would leave the Prime Minister with the problem of containing the APC and the chiefs were the only individuals in a position to perform this task. His problem, therefore, would be to bring about a reorganization of the SLPP's party structure, while at the same time keeping the chiefs under tight enough control to do his bidding.

THE INTRACTABLE PARTY

In his attempts to bring about a more effective party organization, the new Prime Minister met with a series of rebuffs. At first he moved cautiously. At the party's annual conference, held at Makeni just seven weeks after he took office, he accurately analyzed the root cause of the party's lack of discipline and apathy at the local level: "Some members were not quite sure what effect a well-organized party structure will have on their personal political interests, whilst others were just plainly indifferent and therefore not interested in reorganization."[11] This resistance within the party notwithstanding, he proposed a number of changes: the speedy establishment of a national headquarters building and a party press,[12] "a clear cut policy on the selection of party candidates to contest elections on our tickets,"[13] and a local party organization which could deal "swiftly and effectively" with any defiance of party discipline.[14] He also promised that "henceforth election deposits will be paid by the party for candidates adopted," a proposal which brought the loudest cheers of the day.[15]

The Prime Minister's proposals would not have entailed any great change

Training and Recruitment. These appointments were not in fact made on tribal grounds; the officers concerned were among the most senior men in the Administrative Class, and also the most capable. But however well merited their appointments, they were inevitably viewed by Temnes as part of a process of "Mendeization" of the civil service.

10 / This MP allegedly had been the first to warn the Prime Minister about the petition against him.

11 / Sierra Leone Peoples Party, *Convention 1964. Opening Annual Report by the Leader* (Freetown: Government Printer, n.d.), p. 2.

12 / *Ibid.*, p. 3.

13 / *Ibid.*, p. 6.

14 / *Ibid.*

15 / *Ibid.*, and notes by the writer.

in the relationship between local and central units, nor in the composition of the local units of the party. He even noted at one point that since intending candidates sought the support of "our natural rulers and tribal elders," the party might consider using these individuals to select official candidates.[16] The only attempt made to centralize control came in a motion put forward by the national executive after the Prime Minister's speech, which proposed that the Central Committee of the party should select candidates in consultation with the local committees, rather than ratifying the choice of the local committees. The motion was shouted down by the convention and referred for further consideration.[17]

One obstacle facing Albert Margai in his attempts to strengthen the party organization was the fact that many of the "old guard" supporters of Sir Milton had not forgiven him for breaking away to form the PNP. Although in his policy speech he asserted that "I am not leader of a group within the party, I am leader of a united party,"[18] some of his actions made it appear that a "PNP group" was gaining ascendancy within the SLPP. The appointment of Maigore Kallon to the key post of Minister of the Interior, with its control over all the Paramount Chiefs, was one indication; the increased reliance on the Attorney-General, Berthan Macauley, was another. At the Makeni convention one attempt to replace an "old guard" SLPP executive member with a PNP man was rebuffed. When the election for party treasurer was held, Mustapha was opposed by Dr Claude Nelson-Williams, who had been an executive member of the PNP. Despite a broad hint from the Prime Minister that he would like Nelson-Williams elected, a majority of the delegates voted for Mustapha in a show of hands.[19]

A chance for the new Prime Minister to test his electoral appeal came in September 1964. In addition to his tentative efforts at reorganizing the SLPP, Albert had been busily trying to project the appearance of a fresh new administration. His confidence that this appeal was succeeding now led him into an impulsive action which marked the first step in his downfall.

An APC member of the Freetown Council had earlier brought suit against the council, charging that it was improperly constituted because the SLPP majority had elected one of their members from an East Ward seat as an alderman for the West Ward.[20] The Supreme Court agreed, but left it to the

16 / *Ibid.* This in fact was the procedure followed in the 1966 District Council elections, though not for the 1967 General Election.

17 / From notes by the writer at the convention, June 20, 1964.

18 / *Report by the Leader*, p. 7.

19 / Notes by the writer, June 19, 1964.

20 / There were no SLPP councillors elected from the West Ward at that time, and rather than appoint an APC man an alderman, the SLPP had decided to ignore the act, which laid down that each alderman must be elected from among the councillors for his ward.

Council to remedy this illegality.[21] A few days later the Prime Minister took the bold step of dissolving the Council, and announced that its membership and tenure of office would be changed.[22] Instead of an election each year for a third of the membership, the entire Council would now be elected every third year. The number of nominated members was cut from 6 to 3, while the elective members were increased from 12 to 18, with the three wards being divided along the national constituency boundaries.[23] In view of the fact that only the East Ward was safe SLPP territory,[24] the government appeared to be taking a considerable risk of losing control of the Council by so sharply decreasing the number of nominated members. Its action in remodelling the Council in this way suggested a considerable degree of confidence.

In its campaign, the SLPP ignored the fact that it had been in control of the Council for the past eight years, and emphasized its new leader: "This is a new era, an era in which we are fortunate and proud to have the inspiration and leadership of Albert Margai. Even though his term in office is yet very young, he has demonstrated his capacity for hard work which is creating a quiet revolution and a new hope for all Sierra Leoneans. We therefore ask you to vote solidly for his party."[25] On the question of greatest concern in Freetown, finding enough primary school places for all children, the SLPP Manifesto noted "It is high time the City Council have a development plan for its Education responsibilities"[26] and promised to initiate one. It also noted that sanitation, roads, and street lighting all were "inadequate" and would be improved.[27] In their campaign speeches, SLPP leaders implicitly gave more recognition to the fact that the SLPP had been in control of the outgoing Council, warning that a country could not be ruled with one party in control of the central government and another in control of city council,[28] and that the council might lose its grants if it failed to support the SLPP.[29]

Despite a vigorous campaign in which the Prime Minister, most Ministers,

21 / *Daily Mail,* September 1, 1964.

22 / *Ibid.,* September 14.

23 / See *ibid.,* September 23, and the Freetown Municipality (Amendment No. 2) Act, 1964.

24 / The East Ward had always elected SLPP candidates, but the Central Ward had elected an SLPP candidate only once since 1958, and the West Ward had always elected UPP or APC candidates since that time.

25 / Sierra Leone Peoples Party. *Manifesto,* Freetown City Council General Election (mimeo., N.D.), p. 1.

26 / *Ibid.,* p. 3.

27 / *Ibid.*

28 / *Daily Mail,* October 10, 1964.

29 / *Ibid.,* October 6. John Nelson-Williams, who was reported to have made this threat, later explained that all he had meant was that if Freetown did not show confidence in the SLPP, it would be more difficult for Freetown members to justify their claims to a share of government funds. *Ibid.,* October 14.

and several other "big men" in the party took part,[30] the SLPP lost the election. The APC won eleven seats, including three of the six in the East Ward, while the SLPP won only seven, though they did make a clean sweep of West Ward I, hitherto an opposition stronghold. The APC's victory was due primarily to the government's action in changing the composition of the council. While the APC slightly improved its percentage of the popular vote, its gain was certainly not spectacular (Table 11:1). On the other hand, the results showed clearly that at least in Freetown there was no great rallying to the banner of the new Prime Minister.

TABLE 11:1

Percentage of votes, by ward for SLPP and APC in Freetown Council elections (1960–64)

	East ward		Central ward		West ward	
Election	SLPP (%)	APC (%)	SLPP (%)	APC (%)	SLPP (%)	APC (%)
October 1964	50.4	49.6	42.1	57.9	46.6	53.4
November 1963	53.1	46.9	46.2	53.8	49.6	50.4
November 1962	55.0	45.0	42.6	57.4	41.1	56.0
April 1962	67.0	32.1	43.0	43.7	40.2	53.1
November 1960	50.7	49.3	33.8	66.2	26.7	73.3

Note: Percentages do not add to 100 because of candidates from other parties and Independents.
Source: *Daily Mail*, November 2, 1960; April 17, 1962; November 2, 1962; November 2, 1963; and October 16, 1964.

The Freetown election results probably helped impel the Prime Minister to undertake a two-pronged campaign in the next few months: a drive to reorganize and strengthen the SLPP, and a strong effort to stamp out the APC at all levels of activity. He began to make frequent visits to the districts, encouraging local party organizations to broaden their base by such means as setting up youth groups as counterweights to the chiefs, and trying to reconcile disputes between the people and their chiefs in order to ensure that the people did not turn to the APC.

He also brought together a wide selection of party leaders in various "Reorganization Meetings." His intention was to create a more active party organization under more centralized control. In this latter aim, however, he was not successful. Most party members did not consider a stronger party organization in their interest in any case. Added to this was a widespread dislike of the General Secretary of the party, who was believed to be close

30 / Conspicuous among the campaigners was M. S. Mustapha, still a highly regarded figure in the party.

to the Prime Minister.[31] At the first reorganization meeting, held in Bo in January 1965, the Secretary came under severe criticism for alleged incompetence. It was largely because of dissatisfaction with his work that the meeting decided to decentralize the control of party finances by having contributors pay their monthly dues to the district organizations rather than to the central office as hitherto. All sections of the meeting also agreed that party candidates should be selected by a constituency committee rather than at any higher level.[32] All sections further agreed on the desirability of a membership drive, although the members of Parliament insisted they should be responsible for registering new party members, while the non-MPs stressed that registration "must not be the responsibility of MPs."[33] The non-MPs had a good reason for this attitude: if the MPs were to be responsible for enrolling party members, and party members selected the official SLPP candidate, the MP could pack the local committee with his own supporters.

The opposition charged that the Bo conference had also directed the Paramount Chiefs to "go all out" in encouraging their people to support the SLPP.[34] The chiefs did continue to play the most important role in the SLPP. All Paramount Chiefs in each district remained as ex-officio members of the SLPP district committees, and at the party's annual convention in Sefadu in May 1965 five of the eleven district reports on party activities were given by Paramount Chiefs.[35] Most of the reports from the districts given at the Sefadu conference concentrated on the work the chiefs had done in driving the APC out of their areas. For example, Paramount Chief Bai Kur of Tonkolili commented that in Tonkolili East "the defeated SLPP candidate is now the Paramount Chief, so there is no more stand for the APC," and that in his own constituency of Tonkolili South, now that he had become Paramount Chief, he could make sure that by the next election the APC would be unable to find a candidate.

If the Prime Minister could not force changes towards greater centralization through the existing party structure, he might be able to achieve his aim indirectly by getting his own supporters elected to Parliament. As the prospect of an election drew nearer in 1965, a large number of former PNP men began to seek the SLPP nominations in seats already held by SLPP members who were not close supporters of the Prime Minister. S. T. Navo, the Judicial Adviser to the government, was canvassing in Bo North; George Panda, the

31 / He had been proposed for the job in 1962 by Albert, and had been given it in preference to a man put forward by Sir Milton.

32 / Sierra Leone Peoples Party, *Reorganization Meeting* [mimeographed recommendations put forward by the four sections of the meeting – Paramount Chiefs, Members of Parliament, ordinary male members, and female members].

33 / Ibid.

34 / See *Salneb*, January 26, 1965, and *We Yone*, February 20, 1965.

35 / Notes by the writer, May 21, 1965.

Secretary to the Prime Minister and Head of the Civil Service, was gathering support in Kenema West,[36] while E. J. I. During, a private secretary to Sir Albert, was canvassing in the Kenema Central constituency of the Minister of Agriculture, K. I. Kai-Samba. Other PNP men who were not in the civil service were also campaigning for the SLPP nomination in other seats,[37] but it was not clear how far the Prime Minister was encouraging these attempts to undermine sitting members.

An attempt by the Prime Minister to end one of these intra-party quarrels showed clearly the extent to which the SLPP still relied on traditional authorities as intermediaries between itself and the people. By 1965 Dr Claude Nelson-Williams was once again seeking the SLPP nomination in Wilberforce against the Minister of External Affairs, Cyril Rogers-Wright. After the candidates had vied with each other for several months in attempts to win popular support,[38] the Prime Minister set up an *ad hoc* reconciliation committee headed by the Minister of Finance, R. G. O. King. The committee's objectives and procedure were set out in a letter dated April 28, 1965, and sent to all district councillors, village heads, and tribal headmen in the constituency:

A situation has arisen in the Wilberforce Rural District constituency which calls for immediate attention.

Hon. C. B. Rogers-Wright was the SLPP's official candidate in the 1962 general election. Dr. Claude Nelson-Williams, a member of the SLPP, stood against him as an independent candidate. The party does not consider that this is in the best interest of (a) the party and (b) of the members themselves.

In view of this, a Reconciliation Committee was formed by the Prime Minister to see how best the situation might be resolved. Both the gentlemen claim strong support in the constituency. In order to confirm this, it was decided that the committee should meet all concerned on village area level and test opinion. It is

36 / The Prime Minister, asked in Parliament by the MP for the constituency whether civil servants were permitted to engage in political campaigning, blandly denied that any were doing so (*Daily Mail,* December 8, 1965). On December 11, an advertisement appeared in the *Daily Mail* announcing the opening of Panda's "Unity House" in the main town in the constituency. Six months later he resigned from the civil service. Panda, incidentally, had never been a PNP man, but he was believed to be a strong supporter of Sir Albert.

37 / Including M. S. Turay in Bo North, R. E. S. Lagawo, the head of the Teachers Union, in Bo Town, and Dr Claude Nelson-Williams in Cyril Rogers-Wright's seat of Wilberforce. A particularly vicious battle was going on in Freetown Central between Mrs Constance Cummings-John and John Nelson-Williams, but this appeared to have nothing to do with the PNP-SLPP quarrel.

38 / At one point Rogers-Wright sent two Muslim leaders to Mecca on a pilgrimage (*Salneb,* February 23, 1965), while Nelson-Williams presented constituents with 200 prayer mats, and also presented the boys of some "devil societies" with cloth (*ibid.,* January 14, 1965).

proposed therefore to meet (a) all chairmen and committees of village areas (b) the chairman and members of the District Council (c) all village headmen and their committee (d) all tribal headmen and their committee, in the villages themselves.[39]

The committee did not succeed in resolving the dispute and its hearings were terminated on May 5 after a group of young men had broken up a meeting in a village favouring Nelson-Williams.[40] What is significant about this incident is the fact that the SLPP leaders still relied on soundings conducted through "big men" whose connections with the SLPP were tenuous at best instead of forming any explicitly party committees.

The distribution of power within the party did not change fundamentally during the first year of Albert Margai's leadership. The autonomy of the local committees was given formal recognition and, within the districts, the members of Parliament and the Paramount Chiefs remained the most important individuals in the party structure. Membership in the party appeared to increase spectacularly, but this was misleading. For example, the Bo branch told the Sefadu convention that it had 16,000 registered members, but then explained that the cards had been paid for by raising money from the executive members.[41] The same report noted that money for the party was being raised by a levy of £10 a month on each Paramount Chief and his executive, £20 on each Minister, and £5 on each backbench MP.[42] This concentration of party activity and finances in a few hands was typical of the districts. The SLPP was still built upon an aggregation of local notables enjoying a considerable degree of autonomy, and these for the most part opposed any change in the party structure which might weaken their position. About the only change the Prime Minister could claim was that he had stirred up the "big men" to play a more active role in the SLPP's affairs in the districts.

CIVIL SERVANTS AND CHIEFS AS POLITICAL AGENTS

If the SLPP organization proved too elusive and insubstantial for Albert Margai to grasp, there were other agencies through which he could implement changes and establish his personal control over the country. The most obvious of these was the civil service. Some former PNP executive members occupied key advisory positions in the government, notably Berthan Macauley as Attorney-General, Gershon Collier as Ambassador to the United States

39 / *Daily Mail*, May 29, 1965.
40 / For reports of the subsequent trial of 12 leaders of the group for riot and assault, see *ibid.*, May 20 to June 1, 1965. All were acquitted.
41 / Notes by the writer, May 21, 1965. Some chiefs simply handed out party membership cards to everyone in their chiefdom.
42 / *Ibid.*

and the United Nations, and S. T. Navo as Judicial Adviser on local affairs. Then, too, some of the most able young civil servants were much more sympathetic towards Albert's ideas for development than were the "old guard" of the SLPP; they could be counted on to provide sound guidance for the Prime Minister. Finally, the commanding officer of the Royal Sierra Leone Military Force, Brig. David Lansana, was supposed to be loyal to Albert, thus reducing the risk of a military overthrow.

More important than these advisers in Freetown as a means of contact with the people were the officers of the provincial administration. Albert Margai drew the District Officers and provincial secretaries deeply into political affairs. Often they mediated chiefdom disputes. In at least two districts, District Officers also helped mediate intra-party disputes within the SLPP. In Kono, the District Officer and the SLPP organizing secretary visited villages together before the Prime Minister's visit to oversee the building of triumphal arches and to encourage the villagers to give the PM a rousing reception. In Koinadugu, the DO arranged with the Paramount Chiefs for a number of cows to be given as tribute to the PM during his visit in February 1965.

If the civil servants were to be pressed into service for the leader of the SLPP, there was clearly no place for individuals who were suspected of favouring the opposition. The government's eagerness to purge suspected opponents from key positions was shown by its sacking on December 30, 1964, of the Acting Chief Electoral Commissioner, M. A. Khazali, a northerner. Khazali and the expatriate Chief Elections Officer were charged that day with conspiring to defraud the government of £104, which the Crown claimed they had pretended was paid to non-existent "intelligence staff" at a by-election.[43] They were found guilty by a Supreme Court jury, largely on the evidence of a convicted embezzler who had subsequently been employed as a clerk by the Electoral Commission,[44] but their 18-month sentences were quashed by the Court of Appeal on the grounds that there were inconsistencies in the prosecution witnesses' statements.[45] However, Khazali had been dismissed the day the charges were first laid,[46] and the vacancy from the Northern Province was filled a few weeks later by A. B. Kamara, the former UPP and SLPP member of Parliament from Port Loko West.[47] The reason for the government's haste in removing Khazali came out a few weeks later in a debate on an APC motion of non-confidence in the reconstituted Electoral Commission. The opposition charged that voter registration figures which had been compiled the year before, but never made public, showed a very

43 / See *Daily Mail*, December 31, 1964, for the charges.
44 / See *ibid.*, June 3–12, 1965, for the account of the trial.
45 / *Ibid.*, August 7, 1965.
46 / *Gazette*, January 8, 1965.
47 / *Ibid.*, March 9. A Mende took over the expatriate official's job.

large number of voters in the north, and that after Khazali had been removed, the commission had undertaken to reduce the number of registered voters in that area.[48] The government spokesmen retorted that the earlier registration figures were false, and that the commission was now busy removing these false names from the register.[49] Then the Minister of the Interior, Maigore Kallon, rose to state that he had just that morning seen the earlier voter registration figures, and asked, "Where did the Leader of the Opposition get those [registration] papers from when the Minister had not even seen them?"[50] He then went on to claim that he had letters in his possession which might be "a subject for criminal proceedings"[51] and angrily concluded: "Mr. Speaker, in view of certain things which had happened, I am very much satisfied that the Opposition was working hand in hand with the former Electoral Commissioner of Port Loko."[52] The government's haste in disposing of Khazali served as a clear warning that while political neutrality might be tolerated in the civil service, sympathy towards the opposition would not be.

However, warning the civil service against sympathizing with the APC was one thing; enlisting them actively on the side of the government was quite another matter. Many civil servants, particularly the older ones, tended to resist the Prime Minister's attempts to woo their support of his political ambitions.[53] Some of the more obviously neutral were by-passed or placed in less sensitive jobs, while men who sympathized with Albert Margai's objectives moved into some key posts in the administration. However, apart from the District Officers, whose position made it almost impossible for them to avoid being pressed into political activity, the civil service avoided any very deep commitment to the task of keeping the Prime Minister in power.

The Prime Minister also moved to bring the Paramount Chiefs more tightly under his direct personal control. For example, under the Local Courts Act, 1963, the Prime Minister acquired the power to appoint Presidents of Native Administration Courts; previously these men had been elected.[54] The new law clearly opened the way for a Prime Minister to install his personal supporters in these key positions, and there were some complaints that this had

48 / House of Representatives Debates, 1965/66, I (April 2, 1965), cols. 340–41, 350.

49 / Ibid., cols. 343–49.

50 / Ibid., col. 352.

51 / Ibid., col. 353. They never were.

52 / Ibid. Khazali, it may be added, did run for the APC in the 1966 District Council elections, and in the 1967 general election.

53 / See below, pp. 235–36.

54 / Section 4 (1). He was advised in this by a committee consisting of the Judicial Adviser, the Provincial Secretary, and the District Officer, with the Paramount Chief being consulted, but not necessarily able to influence the choice. Answer to Question by Prime Minister, House of Representatives Debates, 1965/66, II (September 22, 1965), cols. 308–99.

in fact been done.[55] However, this use of the Prime Minister's power could backfire. Many people resented the fact that a position which had formerly been elective was now filled by appointment, and the persons who had applied for but failed to get the job could blame the Prime Minister rather than the electorate.

Yet another extension of central control was the Prime Minister's announcement in January 1965 that Paramount Chiefs had the right to take part openly in politics.[56] This removed from the chiefs the one excuse they could use for not campaigning for the SLPP, the claim that they were "above politics." One northern SLPP leader said the Prime Minister's announcement was a move to "smoke out" chiefs who were secretly supporting the APC. After this announcement, any chief who did not openly work for the central government could properly be suspected of being against it, and as a result be subjected to sanctions.[57]

The Prime Minister kept a very close eye on local government affairs. Although he had officially divested himself of the Ministry of the Interior (giving it to his trusted young supporter Maigore Kallon), he insisted that all local disputes with political implications be brought directly to him for settlement. The Ministry became little more than a letter-box.

This tightening of control over the chiefs was mainly for the purpose of forcing them to put pressure on the All Peoples Congress. Most of them responded willingly. One chief in Tonkolili was alleged to have claimed he was carrying out government orders in attempting to "destroy" the APC through the local courts and the use of banishments.[58] Paramount Chief Modu in Port Loko was alleged to have replied to a government circular that "the activities of the All Peoples Congress in my Chiefdom has been very poor and all efforts to stamp it out of my Chiefdom has been very successful."[59] In Makeni, Chief Bai Sebora Kamal refused permission to the APC to open a branch office,[60] precipitating a test case on the "Bill of Rights" section of the constitution.[61] In October 1965 an APC stalwart was sentenced by a local court to six and twelve months on two charges of spreading false propaganda that if the people supported the Paramount Chiefs and the government, the time would come when "women would wear trousers and will

55 / See for example, *We Yone,* September 4, 1965.

56 / This statement was made at his monthly press conference. See *Daily Mail,* January 13, 1965.

57 / Though it should be noted that one Northern chief, Bai Kafari of Tane, was not only a brother of a leading APC member, M. O. Bash-Taqi, but was quite openly pro-APC, yet the government took no steps to remove him from office.

58 / *We Yone,* August 28, 1965.

59 / *Ibid.,* September 4, 1965.

60 / *Ibid.,* July 24, 1965.

61 / Because of delaying tactics on the part of the government, it had still not come up for hearing a year later. Eventually it was abandoned by the APC because of the cost.

have to pay local tax with men." The Court reportedly feared such claims would provoke a repetition of the 1955–56 riots.[62] In Bullom Chiefdom, Port Loko, a group of eleven men and women believed to be APC supporters, were reported to have been beaten and held captive in an underground pit for six hours on the orders of a section chief.[63]

Although he called on the chiefs to assume increased responsibility for keeping the SLPP's rivals under control, Albert was at the same time more prone than his late brother to intervene on the side of the people and against their chief in a dispute. For example, in 1965 a number of people in Koya Chiefdom, Port Loko District, complained to the Prime Minister that their chief had failed to give receipts for taxes, had levied a palm wine tapping tax, and had forced them to do communal labour on a road for which the government had supplied funds.[64] The Prime Minister made the chief abandon the illegal taxes and stop court proceedings against persons who had not paid them.[65] Compelling a chief to desist from a practice which had been illegal for nearly ten years was hardly a drastic curtailment of the rights of chieftaincy, but it *was* a step beyond what Sir Milton would have done.

In dealing with abuses by the chiefs, the Prime Minister had to follow a rather difficult path. To keep the bulk of the people, and in particular the "young men," within the SLPP, he had to hear their grievances against abuses by their chiefs; if he failed to stop the abuses, the people might go over to the APC. As he told the SLPP's 1965 convention, "When you find a chief on one [political] side and the majority of the people on the other side, you should investigate the relations between the chief and his people."[66] But the SLPP could not afford to alienate the chiefs by backing the people against them. Accordingly, the Prime Minister was careful to stress that in these disputes his aim was to bring the people and chiefs together, with concessions on both sides.[67]

In most of the north, Albert's attempts to reconcile people and chiefs met with failure, because of the way in which the chiefs were being used to suppress the APC. The APC was becoming firmly established as "the northern man's party" in opposition to "the Mende party" headed by Sir Albert. As the chiefs became identified more closely with Albert's government through the efforts to crush the APC, their already weak hold on the people was further sapped. Their methods of suppression also hurt them. In October 1965 several leaders of the SLPP youth group in Port Loko told the writer

62 / *Unity*, October 23, 1965.
63 / *We Yone*, November 20, 1965.
64 / See *Daily Mail*, January 16, 1965.
65 / *Ibid.*, May 19, 1965.
66 / From notes by the writer, May 22, 1965.
67 / *Ibid.* In one case where he finally deposed a chief (Alpha Ngobeh of Luawa) for misrule, the chief received a life pension.

that the chiefs in their area were using such drastic tactics against the APC that they were driving most of their people into that party. Similar comments were made by individuals in other northern districts. To employ the northern chiefs as their principal weapon against the APC was clearly to fight the battle with boomerangs.

TIGHTENING THE SCREWS

While the chiefs carried on most of the front-line work in rooting out the APC's local support, the Prime Minister also used some central government powers to coerce and occasionally to cajole the opposition. For his first few months in office, he refrained from any strong threats, but in a speech in Bonthe in March 1965 he reminded his audience that "I have all the power" and talked about shooting down the opposition.[68] Two weeks later in Parliament he threatened to withdraw recognition from the APC as an official opposition.[69] The threats became more real a few weeks later when he attempted to change the rules of Parliament.

On May 4, 1965, the Prime Minister introduced an amendment to the Standing Orders of the House of Representatives which appeared designed to remove four APC members as well as his chief rival in the SLPP, Dr. Karefa-Smart.[70] The amendment provided that any member who was absent for a total of 30 days during an annual session of the House without "reasonable excuse" would lose his seat. A committee chosen in proportion to the parties' representation in the House would determine the reasonableness of an excuse. In giving power to the majority party to determine whether a member should lose his seat, this rule marked a considerable change from the pre-independence rule that a member absent "from two consecutive meetings without permission obtained from *the Speaker*" [italics mine] would lose his seat.[71]

It was undoubtedly more than a coincidence that, at the time this change was introduced, four APC members of Parliament were each serving a one-year prison term for riot and assault arising out of a by-election incident a year earlier.[72] If the goal of the rule had been to improve attendance in the House, withholding members' pay would have been just as effective. When the new rule was referred to a standing committee of the House, the opposi-

68 / See *We Yone*, March 20, 1965, and M. O. Bash-Taqi's speech in *House of Representatives Debates*, 1965/66 (March 26, 1965), col. 144. The writer unfortunately missed hearing the speech on the SLBS, although it was broadcast three times.

69 / See *House of Representatives Debates*, 1965/66 (March 30, 1965), col. 260.

70 / *Ibid.*, 1965/66, I (May 4, 1965), cols. 1013–15.

71 / Sierra Leone (Constitution) Order in Council, 1958. Section 28 (3) (b).

72 / They had been sentenced to one year's imprisonment by a Magistrate's Court in July 1964. Their sentences were quashed in October by the Supreme Court but restored in March 1965 by the Court of Appeal.

tion members of the committee protested strongly that the change would "trap" their colleagues who were in jail.[73] The Leader of the House did not deny this, but simply observed (somewhat disingenuously) that the proposals "had been in existence long before these men were imprisoned."[74] He added: "We also have members on our side who have been absenting themselves from sittings of the House and this ... would also affect them. So you can see that we have not brought these amendments here for the special reason that we want to punish the Opposition."[75] His reference to "men on our side" raises the suspicion that the main intention in introducing the rule change at that time was to remove Dr Karefa-Smart, who some months earlier had accepted a post at Columbia University. It would clearly not be possible for him to attend all sessions of the House. Whether the principal target was Dr Karefa-Smart or the APC members, the effect was to reduce potential opposition to the Prime Minister.

A month later, Dr Karefa-Smart provided a spectacular epilogue to this affair by announcing that he was quitting the SLPP and joining the APC. He had good reason; the SLPP General Secretary had just warned him that anyone seen associating with him would incur the government's displeasure.[76] His departure from the SLPP gave a major boost to the tribal polarization which was already taking place.

The government also tried to make sure that little was heard about APC activities. By mid-1965 the Sierra Leone Broadcasting Service had stopped mentioning anything about the APC, after a directive had been circulated through the Ministry of Information saying that no publicity was to be given to the opposition. Sometimes this was carried to absurd lengths. On November 9, 1965, following a meeting of the Freetown Council at which Siaka Stevens had been re-elected Mayor despite an attempt by the SLPP to disrupt the meeting by force,[77] there was absolutely no mention on the national news of the afternoon's events. The first reference to the election of Stevens as Mayor came on the next night's news, when it was announced that the Minister of the Interior was taking legal action against the Freetown

73 / *House of Representatives Debates, Minutes of Standing Orders Committee,* May 4, 1965 (typescript).

74 / *Ibid.* But one Minister told the writer the rule was introduced to the Cabinet in October 1964, that is, while the APC men were first in jail.

75 / *Ibid.*

76 / See Karefa-Smart's letter of resignation from the SLPP, *We Yone,* June 16, 1965.

77 / According to *We Yone,* the Minister of Information and Broadcasting, John Nelson-Williams, and his brother, Dr Claude Nelson-Williams, had urged a large and unruly gang of SLPP supporters who had packed the meeting-hall to attack the APC councillors after Stevens had been nominated for the post of Mayor. See *We Yone,* November 10, 1965.

Corporation to have the election of Stevens as Mayor ruled null and void.[78] A later event, the Makeni Town Council elections on April 1, 1966, was fully publicized up to polling day, but the public became aware that the APC had swept all three seats only because no mention whatever of the election was made on any SLBS news broadcast after the results had become known.[79]

The *Daily Mail* also tended to become an SLPP propaganda organ after the government announced in December 1964 that it was considering buying the paper from the London *Daily Mirror* chain.[80] Though the transfer did not in fact take place until nearly a year later, its imminence showed throughout 1965. For example, the news that Dr Karefa-Smart was joining the APC was buried in a single sentence in the bottom of a story on the back page.[81] By contrast, minor functionaries in small villages who were alleged to have crossed from the APC to the SLPP were given front page coverage.[82] In fairness, the *Daily Mail* did not completely suppress all references to the opposition, or criticism of the government; for example, it continued to run the daily "Question Time in Parliament" column even after the government took over control. It was, however, careful not to print more than the odd hint that some people were opposing the one-party state.

The APC was still able to put its views across through its own newspaper, *We Yone*. But *We Yone*'s editors had a number of brushes with the libel laws, particularly after the Prime Minister undertook his drive for a one-party state. One charge which seemed to have particularly nettled the Prime Minister was an allegation made in January 1965 that he was condoning corruption in the Produce Marketing Board.[83] The editors of *We Yone* were quickly charged with sedition and defamatory libel, but a Freetown jury acquitted them.[84] This acquittal induced the government to re-institute a device originated by the colonial government to avoid the partiality of Creole

78 / From notes by the writer. The courts ultimately held that the election was in fact illegal; but whether legal or not, one would have thought it was news.

79 / The first reference to the results in any government or SLPP organ came a week later, when *Unity* charged that the APC had used intimidation to gain its victory. *Unity,* April 9, 1965.

80 / *Daily Mail,* December 16, 1964.

81 / *Daily Mail,* June 17, 1965.

82 / For example, see *Daily Mail,* March 29, April 2, May 1, May 7, May 21, 1965. Also, when an elected SLPP Freetown councillor crossed to the APC, the news was given two paragraphs on page 2 (*Daily Mail,* July 30, 1965); when he rejoined the SLPP, the news was given a three-column head on page 1 (*Daily Mail,* October 14, 1965).

83 / M. E. Yanni, "My Dialogue with the Prime Minister," *We Yone,* January 9, 1965. For details of the allegations, see below, pp. 206–207.

84 / *Daily Mail,* February 25, 1965. It should be noted that jurors had to be "literate in English" and over 30, which meant they would be largely Creole. Criminal Procedure Act, 1965, Section 151.

juries. This device was an option for the Attorney-General to apply "in the general interest of justice" for a trial by judge alone.[85] This was passed into law on October 5, 1965,[86] and was used in all subsequent trials of APC journalists.

The Prime Minister did not rely solely on threats to reduce opposition; he also tried to win over the leaders of opposition groups by personal inducements. In early 1965 he made a special trip to Kono to attempt a reconciliation between the two long-standing rivals, Rev. Paul Dunbar and ex-Paramount Chief Mbriwa. On March 8 Mbriwa announced that he was formally dissolving the Sierra Leone Progressive Independence Movement and taking out membership in the SLPP.[87] Two months later Mbriwa was re-elected to the still vacant chieftaincy from which he had been deposed three years earlier.[88]

This dissolution of the SLPIM did not end all opposition in Kono, however. In July 1965 a new party, the Democratic Peoples Congress, was formed.[89] Its aims included "radical improvement in the political, economic and social conditions of the toiling masses, whose interests appear to be woefully neglected."[90] Its leaders were all from "commoner" families and had been associated with the more radical wing of the SLPIM.[91] What seemed to have happened was that once the higher-status and more conservative leaders of the protest movement had been absorbed by the SLPP, their places were taken by more radical and lower-status individuals.

Sir Albert also tried to win over Creole opinion. Early in 1965 he was reported to have held a meeting with some prominent Creole men and women to see how Creoles could be induced to support the SLPP,[92] and in May 1965 he included in his delegation to the London Commonwealth Con-

---

85 / The Criminal Procedure Act, 1965, Section 144(2). This provision was apparently excluded from a bill prepared in 1964 but not yet presented to Parliament when the "Dialogue" verdict was given. It was essentially the same provision as had existed up to that time in the Jurors' and Assessors' Ordinance, 1905, and a 1961 amendment (Section 41A) providing for trial by judge alone, without even assessors.

86 / House of Representatives Debates, 1965/66, II (October 5, 1965), cols. 403–409. The bill had first been brought before the House on May 10 and sent to a select committee. It had then been withdrawn by the Government, May 25. On September 30, essentially the same bill was re-submitted under a Certificate of Urgency, and again sent to a select committee. Since the reports of the select committees are not made public, there was no public discussion of the bill.

87 / Daily Mail, March 9, 1965.

88 / Ibid., May 4, 1965.

89 / We Yone, July 17, 1965.

90 / Ibid.

91 / One more conservative SLPIM leader termed them "chaps who had been to China."

92 / Salneb, February 11, 1965.

ference S. H. Robbin-Coker, a former UPP stalwart and respected Creole leader. On August 19, Robbin-Coker convened a "non-political" rally of Creoles, at which he and other speakers tried to persuade the audience that all Creoles should unite and establish closer links with the Protectorate people.[93] When it became apparent that his aim was to get the Creoles to join the SLPP as a block, the younger members of the audience began to shout him down and the meeting ended in chaos. The Creole youths held another meeting three days later at which they denounced Robbin-Coker and asserted that all Creoles should work as individuals for the party of their choice.[94] It was quite obvious that few Creoles would choose to work for Sir Albert and his SLPP.

These efforts by Sir Albert to curtail the activities of organized opposition groups were one of his major preoccupations, but he was also concerned with a broader goal – to establish himself at home and abroad as an outstanding African leader. To win support at home, he tried to build himself up as the leader of all the people and as a militant nationalist. This was intended to appeal to the growing number of secondary and primary school graduates with some awareness of the world beyond Sierra Leone, who tended to be drawn to parties which espoused radical change both at home and abroad.

"ALBERT MARGAI OF AFRICA"

From the day he first took over the office of Prime Minister, Albert Margai strove to make himself the centre of public attention. A long cavalcade of police motorcycles and cars with sirens screaming accompanied him wherever he travelled,[95] and he eventually came to insist on precedence over the Governor-General in public appearances. Laudatory articles produced in the local press and by the Government Printer hailed "Albert Margai of Africa" as one of the most dynamic leaders of the new states.[96] On his first trip to the Commonwealth Prime Ministers' Conference he hired a British public relations firm to publicize his activities,[97] and on his return to Freetown, the Prime Minister's Office requested "... the public ... to line this route [from the dock to the Prime Minister's residence, about 7 miles] on that day. Commercial houses and members of the public are also asked to co-

93 / See *Daily Mail,* August 21, 1965, for a partial account of the meeting. I am also indebted to Leo Spitzer for further information about this event.

94 / *Daily Mail,* August 24, 1965.

95 / This formed a marked contrast to Sir Milton, who was only persuaded to accept an escort after being hit head-on by one of Freetown's notoriously reckless taxi-drivers.

96 / See, for example, "Albert Margai of Africa," pamphlet (Freetown: Government Information Office, n.d.), and *Daily Mail,* July 17, 1964, "Premier Opens Bold Innings of Leadership."

97 / *Newsweek,* July 20, 1964, p. 30.

operate with Government by decorating their buildings."[98] Large framed photographs of the new Prime Minister began to appear in all government offices, and the Sierra Leone Broadcasting Service managed to find some pronouncement by him for almost every night's broadcast of the national news. One aspect of this personal glorification surprised many persons who thought Albert would take a more "nationalist" line than his late brother. In the New Year's Honours List for 1965, he became Sir Albert Margai.[99]

In foreign relations, the new Prime Minister took a "radical" posture which initially won him some support from pro-APC quarters.[100] One of his first steps as Prime Minister was to seek a rapprochement with Guinea, towards which Sir Milton had been noticeably cool. At a meeting on the Guinea border with President Sekou Toure on June 14, 1964, he advocated "closer collaboration between our two countries, not only in the economical and social fields, but also in the political field."[101] In October, 1964, agreements between the two countries covering trade, transport, telecommunications, and judicial and cultural matters were signed; these had been negotiated in 1962, but never ratified under Sir Milton.[102] This new friendship with Guinea was followed by serious efforts to establish a free trade area between Sierra Leone, Guinea, Liberia, and the Ivory Coast,[103] and by a livelier interest than hitherto in the Organization of African Unity.

On the question of Rhodesia, Albert Margai took a militantly "African" stand, demanding first that Britain force the Rhodesians to accept a constitution based on the principle of "one man, one vote,"[104] and after the Smith regime declared its independence, that Britain crush the regime by force if necessary.[105] He also took a strong stand on South Africa: at his first Commonwealth Prime Ministers' Conference, he sharply criticized Britain's

98 / *Daily Mail*, August 6, 1964.

99 / *Sierra Leone Gazette*, January 1, 1965.

100 / For example, Wallace-Johnson wrote in July 1964: "There are thousands of Nkrumahs all over Africa, and we make bold to say one has recently been produced in Sierra Leone in the person of the new Prime Minister, Albert Margai" (*Salneb*, July 17, 1964). A few days later, Wallace-Johnson explained his refusal to criticize the Prime Minister during his first three months in office on the grounds that his attitudes had served to worry "foreign capitalists." *Ibid.*, July 24.

101 / *Daily Mail*, June 15, 1964.

102 / See *House of Representatives Debates*, 1964/65, III (November 19, 1964), cols. 105–6.

103 / See *Daily Mail*, August 17 and August 24, 1964, for the announcement of the talks and the results of the first meeting.

104 / See, for example, his speech to the Cairo OAU Conference in July 1964, reproduced in *Six Speeches by Sir Albert* (Freetown: Government Information Services, n.d.), p. 18.

105 / See "Commonwealth Confirmed?," *West Africa*, No. 2537 (January 15, 1966), p. 35.

failure to impose economic sanctions on South Africa in order to end apartheid.[106] He did make a further gesture toward African solidarity in 1966 by presenting Zambia with a gift of four petrol tankers to help break the Rhodesian oil blockade,[107] but for the most part, after expressing his militant views, he was willing to accept a relatively limited commitment from Britain.[108]

A further "radical" gesture by the new Prime Minister was his announcement in June 1964 that Sierra Leone would begin a policy of non-alignment between Eastern and Western blocs, and would approach the countries of Eastern Europe for economic aid.[109] At the same time he suggested that foreign private investors should be more strictly controlled.[110] These policies, however, were not pursued actively. In December 1965 Sierra Leone did sign an agreement with the Soviet Union to purchase £1,000,000 worth of agricultural machinery, to be paid for by agricultural produce,[111] but the great bulk of her trade remained with the Western countries, and all foreign technicians, teachers, and other skilled personnel still were drawn from Western Europe and North America.[112]

These gestures could be expected to appeal to the lower levels of the Sierra Leonean intelligentsia – the teachers, clerks, and others with secondary school education, who had picked up a smattering of anti-colonialist attitudes and a certain admiration for Sekou Toure, Kwame Nkrumah, Ben Bella, and sometimes the Soviet Union for their fight against colonialism. The PNP and later the APC enjoyed considerable support among this stratum largely because of their radical pretensions. At the same time, such gestures had little impact on the traditionalists, who were concerned primarily with domestic questions. Radicalism on the international scene was a cheap way to gain popularity at home, and also had the effect of making Sierra Leone's Prime Minister more visible internationally.

On the domestic scene Sir Albert had far less freedom to manoeuvre. "Radical" gestures at home would probably affect the chiefs adversely, and the Prime Minister was too dependent on the chiefs to risk seriously offending them. He was also unwilling to risk losing the benefits of foreign investment for development by imposing stringent controls on foreign investors or threatening nationalization, and so the "Open Door" policy remained.

106 / *Six Speeches by Sir Albert*, p. 10.

107 / *Daily Mail*, June 25, 1966.

108 / For example, at the Lagos conference of Commonwealth Prime Ministers in January 1966, he eventually accepted the communiqué which provided only that Britain might use force if economic sanctions failed. *West Africa*, No. 2537, p. 35.

109 / *Convention 1964 ... Report by the Leader*, pp. 14, 27.

110 / *Ibid.*, pp. 21, 26–27.

111 / *Daily Mail*, December 23, 1965.

112 / Except for one team of Chinese agricultural experts – from Taiwan.

No really radical shifts in domestic policy, in agriculture, industrial development, or in the field of local government, took place under Albert Margai's leadership.

When he first came to office, there appeared to be a possibility that the new leader might bring about social changes by aligning the radical younger men on his side as a counterweight to the chiefs. But his "radicalism" in foreign affairs was outweighed in the minds of many of these younger men by a less attractive feature of his regime. Most of the radicals held the idealistic view that political leaders should be concerned solely with the welfare of the country, and not with enriching themselves. Whether Sir Albert failed to recognize this or whether he decided a program of personal acquisition was worth the cost in loss of support from the radicals is not clear. In any case, it quickly became apparent that Sir Albert was extremely tolerant of open corruption in others, and was quite willing to use the Prime Minister's office for his personal benefit.

The most blatant case of government inaction in the face of apparent corruption involved top executives of the Produce Marketing Board. A number of PMB employees complained, first to the police, and then to the APC newspaper *We Yone*, that they had worked on the Board's time, with Board materials, constructing a number of private houses for the Board's Managing Director and Acting Manager of the Production Division.[113] The only action arising from these complaints was the firing of the employees. After trying unsuccessfully to persuade the police to take action, a senior employee of the Board, M. E. Yanni, launched a private prosecution in January 1965 against the former Minister of Trade and Industry and the Board Chairman for conspiracy to conceal a crime.[114] The Attorney-General promptly entered a *nolle prosequi,* charging that Yanni had instituted the prosecution for "political reasons" and that it would hamper the investigations which the law officers had been making "for some time" into the affairs of the Board.[115] At the same time Yanni levelled a charge of complicity in corruption against the Prime Minister himself by alleging in *We Yone* that on May 9, 1964, after he had first made his complaints to the police, the Prime Minister had summoned him to his office. After hearing the gist of Yanni's charges and what he had done, the Prime Minister told Yanni "You have done a very bad thing, to have taken the matter to the police," and three weeks later had called him back again to say: "Now when you go to Bo, don't you bother

113 / See *We Yone,* November 14, 1964, and January 2, 9, 1965.

114 / See the letter from the complainant's solicitor, in *We Yone,* January 23, 1965. The Minister, Jusu-Sheriff, had been transferred to the Health Ministry in September 1964, possibly because he was not happy about the affairs of the PMB and would have liked an investigation.

115 / See Attorney-General's statement, *Daily Mail,* January 9, 1965.

about what others are doing – you just do your own work."[116] A month after this article was published, the editor and a reporter of *We Yone* were charged with sedition and defamatory libel.[117] Although the judge in the trial told the jury the article was defamatory in that it purported to show that the Prime Minister wanted the Board's affairs covered up,[118] the jury voted 10–2 for acquittal.[119] At his next press conference, the Prime Minister denounced this verdict as "shameful"; he also insisted there was nothing to investigate in the affairs of the Board,[120] although this contradicted his Attorney-General's earlier remark that the law officers were in fact investigating. The government took no further action against the Board.

The Prime Minister was not averse to using his office for his personal benefit. For example, on one trip to the provinces, he was presented with a tribute of some 200 cows and a number of other animals at Kabala. When the opposition complained in Parliament that the government had paid just under £1,000 to have the beasts trucked down from Kabala, Sir Albert replied: "For the time being, I am Prime Minister of Sierra Leone, and if I go anywhere, whether to Timbuctu or to Russia or to Tokyo, if I am given the whole of Tokyo the Government shall be responsible for bringing my luggage home. ... No words or any name will ever change my attitude toward that."[121] He also declined to move into the official Prime Minister's residence, preferring to remain in his own private residence in a Freetown suburb. This necessitated paving a mile of road at a cost of £11,500.[122] Other works were not solely for his personal benefit. In October 1965 his home town of Gbangbatoke in south-western Moyamba District became the first to have a new airport since he had taken office. In opening the airfield, Sir Albert proclaimed his intention of constructing airstrips in all important towns, regardless of their proximity to the headquarters towns of their district.[123] It was interesting that Gbangbatoke had been singled out as the first to receive this treatment, in view of the fact that all but about 25 of the 150 miles of road to Freetown were paved, while the headquarters town of Kabala in Koinadugu District, where an airstrip was still in the planning stage, was some 230 miles from Freetown, with only 70 of those miles paved.

Government largesse was also spread in other ways. For his first Common-

116 / "My Dialogue with the Prime Minister," *We Yone,* January 9, 1965.
117 / *Ibid.,* February 13, 1965.
118 / *Daily Mail,* February 25, 1965.
119 / *Ibid.*
120 / Notes by the writer made at the time of the broadcast of the Prime Minister's press conference, March 30, 1965.
121 / *House of Representatives Debates,* 1965/66, I (March 30, 1965), cols. 265–6.
122 / See opposition criticisms made in *ibid.,* 1964/65, III (November 24, 1964), col. 226.
123 / *Daily Mail,* October 19, 1965.

wealth Prime Ministers' Conference in July 1964 the Prime Minister took a total entourage of 16 persons with him, including 3 confidential secretaries,[124] and to the 1965 Commonwealth Prime Ministers' Conference, a delegation of 32 members. This delegation cost the government £12,748 in allowances alone,[125] and the total cost including passages was approximately £20,000. Other delegations were also quite sizable; when the Minister of Trade and Industry led a group to Moscow in April 1965 for trade talks, it numbered 17, and cost Sierra Leone £5,115 in allowances.[126]

His willingness to acquiesce in other persons' corruption, and his lavish outlays of government funds on activities which, while legal, were of dubious social value, did not enhance the Prime Minister's standing with the more idealistic younger elements. But it gradually became apparent that the Prime Minister was benefiting much more directly from his high office. For example, he had developed one of the largest egg and poultry farms in Sierra Leone; in 1964 all licences to import frozen chickens were suspended.[127] The Prime Minister also had a substantial share in Sierra Leone's only fish processing company; in 1965 and 1966 most of the Ghanaian fishermen in Sierra Leone, who sold direct to petty traders, were deported.[128] In addition, he was accumulating a considerable amount of property, both at home and abroad. A summary of his known holdings published in *We Yone* in August 1966 included land worth £46,000 and buildings costing £30,000 in Sierra Leone, as well as a building in Washington worth £19,000, and one in London of unknown value.[129] The buildings in Washington and London were rented back to the Sierra Leone missions in these capitals.

The difficulty in which Sir Albert found himself a year after becoming Prime Minister was largely due to factors beyond his control, but to some extent was worsened by his own attitudes. He was limited in the degree to

124 / *Ibid.*, June 27, 1964.
125 / *House of Representatives Debates*, 1965/66, II (September 14, 1965), col. 205.
126 / *Ibid.*
127 / Information provided by manager of Patterson, Zochonis meat department.
128 / *Daily Mail*, March 21, April 14, 1966.
129 / *We Yone*, August 6, 1966. The article, by Ibrahim Taqi, concluded that since he had become Prime Minister, Sir Albert had made investments totalling not less than £156,000, while his visible earnings during the period totalled £12,500. After the military take-over, the *Forster Commission of Inquiry on the Assets of Ex-Ministers* (Freetown: Government Printer, 1968) found on the basis of Sir Albert's own testimony that his income during this period had been at least £200,000.
One interesting sidelight of *We Yone*'s exposé was the fact that it was printed on the presses of *Shekpendeh,* which was owned by the former Minister of External Affairs, Cyril Rogers-Wright. A considerable amount of detailed information about Sir Albert's holdings had come from some source in Washington, which suggested that someone in the External Affairs Ministry had been working against the Prime Minister. Rogers-Wright was dismissed from the Cabinet four days after the article appeared.

which he could implement radical changes by the nature of his own party, and tribal alignments prevented him from making an about-face and joining forces with the opposition to undercut his own traditionalists. He had gone far enough in proposing changes to antagonize many traditionalists, but his interest in self-enrichment had lost him considerable support among the more radical elements in Sierra Leone. Threatened from both front and rear, he was in no position to pursue a strong policy; he would still have to consolidate his position against the risk of electoral overthrow by the APC, and obstruction by the chiefs.

12
1965–66: towards a one-party state?

THE DRIVE THAT FAILED

Albert Margai's behaviour as Prime Minister pointed clearly towards one goal: the destruction of organized opposition parties and the imposition of a one-party state. His build-up as the great national leader, his attempts to draw everyone into the Sierra Leone Peoples Party, and his intensification of the campaign to suppress the APC all suggested that a competitive party system was not to his liking. Even his professed views underwent a shift during his first year in office. When he first became Prime Minister, he told the Bar Association he would "quit politics" if the government lacked opposition,[1] and assured Parliament that he valued highly "the supremacy of the law, the upholding of the Constitution, and the safeguarding of the rights and freedom of the individual, including freedom of speech."[2] But by January 1965 when asked about the possibility of a one-party state in Sierra Leone, he replied, "It might be."[3] Two months later, in his speech at Bonthe, he took a much more menacing line, saying that if the opposition threatened him he would shoot them down.[4] On March 30, he told the APC members of Parliament that "the tide is ebbing fast" and said it would be easy to "liquidate" them.[5] He then went on to warn:

Now coming to the one party system in this country, if my interpretation is correct the question of one party is a reality within this House. ... In past days when we speak of a two party system we had a Government and a recognized Opposi-

1 / *Daily Mail*, May 1, 1964. He also commented that "we must follow the principle of good democracy by having a two party system."

2 / *Daily Mail*, May 6, 1964.

3 / *Daily Mail*, January 13, 1965.

4 / See *We Yone*, March 20, 1965 and M. O. Bash-Taqi's speech in *House of Representatives Debates*, 1965/66, I (March 26, 1965), col. 144.

5 / *House of Representatives Debates*, 1965/66, I (March 30, 1965), col. 260.

tion. I am sure if we test the interpretation of the word "recognized" I am sure the word "recognized" would not apply to you for long. I say no more: you have drawn my attention to this question of one party. I hope sooner or later and preferably sooner rather than later, I shall ask for an interpretation of the word "recognized opposition."[6]

Shortly before this threat was uttered, a distinguished visitor had publicly advocated a one-party state for Sierra Leone. On March 23, in an address to the Sierra Leone Parliament, President Toure of Guinea had made this appeal:

... I wish Sierra Leoneans would come together to re-inforce the unity of Sierra Leone and they should do their best too for the common good. As a leader of a party and as a leader of a Government I have some experience. I know that if people are not united the leaders will be frustrated and tired; if there are two divisions the foreigners will take the opportunity to get everything. So you must unite for the progress and prosperity of your country.[7]

Two days later Prince Williams, the SLPP backbencher who had resigned the Deputy Speakership in order to protest the government's failure to act on a report condemning financial impropriety by certain Ministers, observed in the course of the Speech from the Throne debate: "Mr. Speaker, I have from time immemorial been an advocate of the two party system of government but from the performance yesterday I have come to the inevitable conclusion that the day has come when we should have one political flock and one shepherd."[8] The question of a one-party state had been thrust firmly into the centre of political debate.

Although both his threats and such actions as the sacking of a pro-APC Electoral Commissioner and the rule change in Parliament to eliminate four APC MPs all pointed towards the end of organized opposition, the Prime Minister still did not say he was seeking a one-party state. At the SLPP convention in May 1965 he asserted "the reports that we want a one-party state are false."[9] But he then went on to discuss in detail how to drive the one surviving opposition party out of existence. He told the convention he was ready to "pulverize" the APC,[10] and said the SLPP should include "every Sierra Leonean" among its members, including those who had been "misled" into supporting the APC.[11] Nearly every district report at the convention concentrated on what the SLPP leaders in the district had done to stamp out APC

6 / *Ibid.*, cols. 261–62.
7 / *Ibid.*, 1965/66, I (March 23, 1965), cols. 24–25.
8 / *Ibid.* (March 25, 1965), col. 93.
9 / From notes by the writer, May 21, 1965.
10 / Notes by the writer, May 21, 1965.
11 / Notes, May 22, 1965.

activities. While there was no open advocacy of a one-party state, few speakers appeared willing to tolerate the survival of the All Peoples Congress.

The demands for a one-party state did not seem at this time to be coming from the Prime Minister himself, but from other leading members of the party. In June the Prime Minister was quoted as saying in London that if ever there was to be a one-party state in Sierra Leone, it would come by agreement and not by compulsion.[12] Meanwhile, his Acting Prime Minister, Kande Bureh, was alleged to have told an audience in Port Loko that but for Sir Albert's leniency the government would have silenced the opposition party long ago.[13] The government had not yet officially committed itself to this policy of silencing the opposition, but a number of chiefs in the north were doing their best to stamp out the APC in their chiefdoms, apparently in obedience to government instructions.[14]

The idea of instituting a one-party state was finally broached to the SLPP caucus in October 1965. The Prime Minister was later to deny that he had initiated the discussion:

On the question of a one-party system of government, every SLPP Parliamentarian can testify to the fact that the idea was not initiated by me.

It was raised by them at a meeting, before I even got there. They discussed it and I urged them to go and think about it. When they came back, I decided to put the matter to a vote, and as a result of that put it to the entire country.

I think I should make this point very clear. I have carefully listened to the arguments for or against. I listened for a long time, and the arguments for a one-party system in my conviction were very much stronger.[15]

While this was probably an understatement of the extent to which the Prime Minister encouraged the idea, still it is apparently true that he was at first reluctant to try to bring about the one-party state, and had to be persuaded by some of his closest Cabinet associates. He did not attend the first part of a meeting of the parliamentary caucus on October 5, 1965, at which the one-party state question was discussed.[16] The advocates of the one-party system included three Ministers, Maigore Kallon, M. J. Kamanda-Bongay, and Paramount Chief Madam Ella Koblo Gulama. Its opponents included the Minister of Agriculture, K. I. Kai-Samba, two ex-Ministers, Sesay and Mustapha, and L. A. M. Brewah, who along with Kai-Samba formed part of the

12 / *Daily Mail*, June 15, 1965.

13 / *We Yone*, July 10, 1965.

14 / See below, p. 231.

15 / Quoted in *Unity*, June 25, 1966.

16 / A partial account of the meeting is in *We Yone*, October 9, 1965. This account was confirmed by two persons who were present, although one complained that it omitted the fact that the Prime Minister was not present, as well as the arguments for the one-party state and the fact that the "great majority" of the MP's favoured a one-party system.

"radical" wing of the SLPP. The meeting was unable to reach agreement on whether to support a one-party system. Shortly after the meeting, the party newspaper, *Unity*, claimed that "the SLPP has not at any time adopted or signified a desire to adopt a policy on a one-party state,"[17] and suggested that the APC was simply using this issue to distract attention from the loss of support it was suffering.

However, other actions suggested that the Prime Minister himself was leaning toward the one-party system. On October 4, President Kwame Nkrumah arrived for a one-day "brotherly and friendly visit" to Sir Albert.[18] On October 19, two full days before the OAU Heads of States and Governments meeting was to start in Accra, Sir Albert visited Ghana and stayed until October 27. He was given a very cordial welcome by the Osageyfo,[19] and while on a tour of the CPP party headquarters in Accra was quoted as having said that, like the CPP, the SLPP in Sierra Leone believed that the government was not above the party.[20] It was alleged that there might soon be another point of similarity between the government of Sir Albert and that of Nkrumah; the London *Daily Telegraph* claimed that Sir Albert "took counsel with President Nkrumah of Ghana as to how [the one-party state] will be achieved with the present judiciary firmly installed. ... President Nkrumah's advice was short as sharp: 'sack them' he said, and he would see that Sir Albert has a fine bench of judges straight out of Ghana."[21] In view of the malice and spitefulness which the *Telegraph* generally exhibited towards all African leaders and towards Nkrumah in particular, one would be inclined to discount this story. But shortly after Nkrumah's visit, an event occurred which suggested that Sir Albert was indeed concerned with the problem of opposition from the Bench. On October 30, 1965, Sir Samuel Bankole-Jones, the Chief Justice of Sierra Leone, was abruptly removed from the office of Chief Justice and "promoted" to the position of President of the Court of Appeal.[22] Several reasons lay behind this abrupt change. Sir Samuel was known as a particularly upright judge who would be unlikely to bend to government pressure. More specifically, when he had been Acting Governor-General in August and September, he had apparently embarrassed the Prime Minister by his insistence on travelling without the cavalcade of motorcycle police and wailing sirens which had become *de rigueur* for the Heads of State and Government.[23] He had also sharply rebuked the Youth

17 / *Unity*, October 16, 1965.
18 / *Daily Mail*, October 4, 1965.
19 / See *Unity*, October 23, and October 30, 1965.
20 / *Daily Mail*, October 25, 1965.
21 / *Daily Telegraph*, November 30, 1965. Quoted in *Unity*, December 4, 1965.
22 / *Daily Mail*, November 1, 1965.
23 / See *We Yone*, September 11, 1965, for praise of Sir Samuel's action, and *ibid.*, September 18, 1965, for a note that Sir Samuel had started using the escort.

Section of the SLPP when they tried to use his name as a patron of a social event, telling them his office had to be above politics.[24] This attitude could create formidable obstacles for the attempts the government was beginning to make to curb the opposition through court action.

Several weeks before Sir Samuel's "promotion," the government had launched the first of a number of prosecutions against the leading writers of *We Yone* and a lesser opposition newspaper, the Bo *Advance*.[25] The most spectacular case arose out of a story in *We Yone* September 4 alleging that the Attorney-General had received a cheque for £20,000 from the Produce Marketing Board, and the further comment: "It will be recalled that the Attorney-General cut short his overseas visit and flew from the USA to enter a *nolle prosequi* in an action instituted against three top officials of the Board, and made a statement that investigations into the SLPMB 'were current.' "[26] This insinuation that the Attorney-General had taken a bribe brought three charges of criminal libel against the editor of *We Yone*, Samuel Hollist, and its leading columnist, Ibrahim Taqi.[27] Unfortunately for the Attorney-General, evidence at the trial showed clearly that while the £20,000 had been paid by the Board for the legitimate purpose of purchasing a house owned by the Attorney-General, the house had been valued only by the Board's own untrained Building Officer, and the Board had not used a lawyer to safeguard its interest in the transaction.[28] Summarizing the case before pronouncing judgment, Mr Justice Beoku-Betts ruled that the defence had made a *prima facie* case of justification.[29] The prosecution immediately took the unusual step of entering a *nolle prosequi* at this point, but the judge refused to accept this and declared Taqi and Hollist acquitted and discharged.[30] The purpose of the *nolle prosequi* was revealed two months later, when Taqi was once again charged with defamatory libel for the same article.[31] Mr Justice Marcus-Jones quickly came to the conclusion that Taqi's plea of *autrefois acquit* should succeed and discharged him.[32]

Another charge of criminal libel had been laid against Hollist and Taqi for an article alleging that the Prime Minister, with the aid of an Afro-

24 / *We Yone*, September 11, 1965.

25 / *Daily Mail*, September 21, 1965.

26 / *We Yone*, September 4, 1965.

27 / *Daily Mail*, September 21, 1965.

28 / *We Yone*, February 5, 1966.

29 / *Ibid.*, February 15, 1966.

30 / *Daily Mail*, February 16, 1966. The Criminal Procedure Act, 1965, permitted the Crown to enter a *nolle prosequi* at any stage of proceedings, before "verdict or judgement." Section 44 (1). This had to be done either in writing or in person by the Attorney-General, a procedure which had not been followed in Taqi's case.

31 / *Daily Mail*, April 15, 1966.

32 / For the full judgment, see *ibid.*, April 25, 1966.

Lebanese diamond dealer, had offered the Secretary-General of the new Kono opposition party, the Democratic Peoples Congress, £15,000 to dissolve the party, but had been turned down.[33] Again the judge hearing the case found the article not defamatory.[34]

Hollist, however, did receive three months in jail for a story alleging that the Acting Chief Justice, Mr C. O. E. Cole had been appointed to succeed Sir Samuel Bankole-Jones "on condition that he cooperates with the ruling party."[35] Hollist based his story on a paper he took to be a Cabinet minute, but it was shown at the trial that the paper was a forgery. After serving his sentence, he resigned from the APC[36] and was given a position on the *Daily Mail*. The financial controller of *We Yone*, A. F. Thorlu-Bangura, was sentenced to a year in jail for another defamatory libel of the Prime Minister,[37] arising out of an editorial suggesting that the Prime Minister was ultimately behind the beating and imprisonment of eleven fishermen in Bullom Chiefdom.[38]

While the government was tying up the opposition in the courts, it was also taking steps to whip up popular support for the one-party state. In a speech in the Port Loko District in November, the Prime Minister made his first declaration in favour of the one-party state, saying he would probably introduce the matter into Parliament at the coming meeting.[39] A series of further meetings followed. A large Planning Committee meeting was held at Kambia on December 10, attended by 500 delegates from all parts of the country.[40] This was later referred to as "the historic Kambia meeting where the one-party issue was thrashed out."[41] The Prime Minister devoted much of his time to attacking the APC for stirring up the people against their chiefs, for using threats and intimidation to achieve its ends, and for hurting the country's image abroad by its use of smears and lies against government leaders.[42] However, he assured his audience that the APC would fail, because "I will defeat them, I will dissolve them, I will demolish them."[43]

A few days later, at Port Loko, after hearing a rally of 3,500 SLPP women advocate the creation of a one-party state and the stamping out of the APC,

33 / *We Yone*, September 4, 1965. The DPC had been formed by the younger lower-status members of the SLPIM after that party had been officially dissolved by Chief Mbriwa. See above, p. 202.

34 / *Daily Mail*, November 27, 1965.

35 / *We Yone*, November 13, 1965.

36 / *Daily Mail*, February 23, 1966.

37 / *Ibid.*, December 22, 1965.

38 / *We Yone*, November 20, 1965.

39 / *Ibid.*

40 / *Unity*, December 18, 1965.

41 / *Ibid.*, January 29, 1966.

42 / *Ibid.*, December 18, 1965 and *Daily Mail*, December 11, 1965.

43 / *Unity*, December 18, 1965.

as well as references to Sir Albert as "our natural leader," the Prime Minister said he had lost any doubts about the reasonableness of a one-party state, and would proceed relentlessly with his determination to press on with the one-party system.[44] He charged that those who opposed the one-party system were persons who did not suffer for their livelihood and did not know the degree of suffering of the people.[45]

Meanwhile, Paramount Chief Bai Bairoh of Tonkolili had laid down in Parliament a private member's motion that "To ensure the solidarity and rapid development of this country, BE IT RESOLVED that Government give serious consideration to the introduction of a unitary (one party) system of Government in this country.[46] Shortly before the motion was to be debated in Parliament, the Prime Minister held private talks with the Leader of the All Peoples Congress, in which he sought Stevens' agreement for the establishment of a committee to explore how best to set up the one-party system. Stevens was not totally opposed to the idea, but said he needed time to consult his people. He did agree to have the APC abstain on Bai Bairoh's motion.[47]

The debate on the motion that took place on December 20 and 21, 1965, was noteworthy for the conciliatory tone most government speakers expressed towards the APC in inviting them to come and join the government.[48] No government spokesman, not even the Prime Minister, spelled out clearly just what kind of one-party system was envisaged, although most seemed to be thinking in terms of a coalition similar to the United Front of 1960.[49] From the emphasis that several speakers, notably Madam Gulama and the Prime Minister himself, placed on the benefits to the APC of coming in at the planning stage, it appeared that the SLPP leaders had not yet decided what answers to give to such crucial questions as who should be admitted to membership of the single party, and whether all party members should be free to participate in the selection of representatives to the legislature.

The most striking feature of the debate was the lack of criticism by the All Peoples Congress of the principle of a one-party system. Stevens stated categorically at one point that "the APC is opposed to ANY kind of one-party system of government," but in the course of his argument and in discussions

44 / *Daily Mail*, December 18, 1965.

45 / *Ibid*.

46 / *Unity*, December 4, 1965.

47 / This was brought out in the Prime Minister's speech in Parliament on the motion December 21 and acknowledged by Stevens. *Parliamentary Debates*, December 21, 1965, cols. 38–39.

48 / See *House of Representatives Debates*, December 20 and 21, 1965.

49 / See especially Y. D. Sesay's speech, *ibid.*, December 20, cols. 51–52 and George Mani's speech, December 21, col. 27.

afterwards, it became clear that all he really objected to was the speed with which the Prime Minister was trying to rush the matter.[50] M. O. Bash-Taqi claimed the government lacked tolerance for criticism, and said that if it tried to impose a one-party state by legislation, everyone would oppose it.[51] He then added that if it were to come "by means of evolution, then it can be given thought."[52] In discussions after the debate, both he and Stevens appeared quite willing to enter a coalition with the SLPP; neither showed much concern about the effect of eliminating all organized opposition to the government.[53] At the end of the debate, the Prime Minister made a fervent appeal to Stevens to honour the agreement he had made earlier. There was a hurried consultation on the opposition bench. Then Stevens spoke: "Mr. Speaker, we on the Opposition side are abstaining."

This failure of the APC leaders to argue for the desirability of an organized opposition was no momentary aberration. Nowhere in the columns of *We Yone* up to this time had there been a rejection on principle of the one-party state; all its arguments had been concentrated on the unrepresentativeness of Sir Albert and the SLPP. Stevens himself some months earlier had said it was only the SLPP's weakness that disqualified it from seeking a one-party system.[54]

This reluctance to attack the principle of the one-party system could probably be attributed to the APC's own ideological inclination towards such a system. Its constitution stated that one of its aims was "to consolidate our Independence by maintaining the complete unity of the nation under a *unitary form of government*" [italics mine].[55] Most of its leaders seemed to think that as long as the governing party of a country was the true party of the people, it was quite justified in suppressing opposition. The charge hurled at the APC by SLPP spokesmen, that if in power it would show scant regard for opposition parties, was probably true.[56]

An ideology of this sort, if strongly held, could have been expected to sustain the APC in opposition until it was able, on behalf of the people, to sweep away the oppressor groups and take power by itself. It should not have led the leaders to seek terms with the governing party. Yet the APC leaders at this

50 / In a conversation with the writer immediately after his speech, he stressed the fact that the Prime Minister's haste was not giving him enough time to bring his followers around.

51 / *Debates*, December 20, col. 23.

52 / *Ibid*.

53 / Conversation with the writer, December 21, 1965.

54 / *House of Representatives Debates*, 1965/66 (March 29, 1965) col. 260.

55 / *Constitution of the All Peoples Congress*, Part I, 3, (i). "Unitary" in Sierra Leone generally meant "one-party."

56 / See, for example, Julius Cole, "Revelation!" *Unity*, November 6, 1965.

juncture were clearly willing to cease their opposition and come into the governing party. Such behaviour was much more consistent with their position as regional spokesmen who sought a more equitable distribution of amenities within the framework of the existing system. A further personal factor needs to be noted here. Stevens had been in opposition for eight years in 1965; none of the other APC MPs had ever been on the government side. With the prospect of enjoying some "sweets of office" if they joined the seemingly strong tide toward a one-party state, and the likelihood of finding themselves in Pademba Road jail if they stayed out, it would have taken men of strong faith in both the rightness and the eventual triumph of their cause to spurn the government's overtures. One is forced to conclude that such radical commitment to change as the APC leaders possessed was outweighed by their personal and regional interests.

Following the passage of Bai Bairoh's motion, the government embarked on an intensive campaign to demonstrate public support for the one-party system. The Minister of the Interior toured the Northern Province in January, addressing meetings of the District Councils; following his addresses, the District Councils all passed resolutions requesting the government to introduce a one-party state.[57] Resolutions also flowed in Chiefdom Councils in both the north and the south; District Officers appear to have been present at many of these meetings.[58] The Freetown City Council also sent in a resolution supporting the one-party system, after the APC councillors had resigned their seats in protest against the continued presence of nominated members.[59] Resolutions also came in from such groups as the Motor Drivers Union,[60] the Mende community of Freetown,[61] and the Kono East Constituency, which asked that the one-party state be introduced not later than April 27, 1966.[62] Some of the District Council and chiefdom resolutions were not entirely spontaneous. One APC District Councillor in Port Loko claimed that the Council skipped all the necessary rules of procedure for introducing the one-party motion, and then refused to allow his countermotion, with one

57 / See *Daily Mail*, January 10, 1965 (Koinadugu); January 14 (Tonkolili); January 18 (Port Loko). At the Bombali District Council meeting, the Provincial Secretary and District Officer were present. *Daily Mail*, January 6, 1966.

58 / The only meeting at which a newspaper report stated the District Officer was present was Makari Gbanti Chiefdom, Bombali District. *Daily Mail*, February 11, 1966. However, it was customary for District Officers to be present at most chiefdom council meetings.

59 / *Daily Mail*, March 15, 1966. With the resignation of S. I. Koroma and the defection of Hollist, they were in a minority.

60 / *Ibid.*, February 9, 1966.

61 / *Unity*, January 22, 1966.

62 / *Daily Mail*, March 9, 1966.

chief telling him that what he said didn't matter, that the council was going to pass the motion.[63] At the Bombali District Council meeting, Paramount Chief Alimamy Dura, who had been rather critical of the one-party state idea, introduced the motion; afterwards he confessed that he had done something he was very much ashamed of.[64] In Makari Gbanti Chiefdom, Bombali District, an APC member of the chiefdom council was reported to have praised the one-party system.[65] In a letter denying he had made any such remarks, he claimed that the District Officer had tried to get him to associate himself with the resolution, but that he had refused.[66] For having sent this letter, he was subsequently sentenced to six months' imprisonment by the Local Court for bringing the chiefdom councillors to ridicule and contempt,[67] but was freed on appeal to the Supreme Court.[68] Such actions by the local authorities did not help the SLPP win popular support.[69]

The APC meanwhile had overcome its initial vacillations on the one-party state question, after its leaders learned from soundings that the idea was strongly opposed by their rank and file. In January 1966 it declared:

The Executives of the APC and DPC have found that party members as well as non-Party members are totally opposed to the One-Party system of Government especially when they observe the happenings in other parts of West Africa where the system obtains.

The Parties also feel that the introduction of the One-Party system of government in the present form of the Constitution would be a violation of one of the entrenched clauses of the Constitution which guarantees the right of FREEDOM OF ASSOCIATION. The Parties feel that even if it is proposed that such an entrenched clause of the Constitution should be altered, then the electorate should be allowed to give their verdict on the proposal through the medium of the Ballot Box as laid down by the Constitution.[70]

63 / I am indebted to Fred Hayward for this information.

64 / According to two students who spoke to him immediately after the meeting. Ironically, his house was burned down a few weeks later, apparently by persons protesting against the one-party state. *Unity*, April 9, 1966.

65 / *Daily Mail*, February 11, 1966.

66 / *Ibid.*, February 19, 1966. The fact that the *Daily Mail* published this letter shows it was not completely blacking out opposition news, although at this time it was coming very close.

67 / *We Yone*, March 19, 1966.

68 / *Ibid.*, May 7, 1966.

69 / For example, this councillor had a cousin who was prominent in the SLPP, but who in May 1966 was thoroughly disaffected and seemingly on the point of moving over to the APC.

70 / Statement by the National Executive of the APC and the DPC, in *We Yone*, January 8, 1966.

This argument that the only way to settle the question of whether to establish a one-party state was to let the people decide through the ballot box remained the APC's staple one from that time onward.[71]

The public response to the Prime Minister's demands for a one-party state was less than enthusiastic. In Freetown, when the Prime Minister addressed a mass rally at the end of January, about a quarter of the crowd of 3,000 appeared strongly hostile, with another quarter indifferent.[72] One large group of hecklers was driven out of the stadium by riot police wielding clubs. The Prime Minister's speech was rather menacing in tone; while insisting that he did not intend to force a one-party state on the people,[73] he attacked the "doctors, lawyers and lecturers" who were wilfully refusing to see the blessings of such a system, and warned all Creoles: "I cannot take the bias of the Freetown people alone, but that of the whole country."[74] Opposition was not confined to Freetown. *We Yone* claimed there were demonstrations against the one-party state when the Minister of the Interior attended the District Council meeting in Tonkolili,[75] while a few weeks later the Prime Minister's car was stoned in Magburaka by schoolboys.[76] Even in the SLPP's heartland of Bo, the Prime Minister was heckled by part of a large crowd when he spoke on the one-party state.[77]

Despite considerable evidence that the idea was not receiving overwhelming support, the government continued to press ahead with demands for the one-party state. Then on February 24 came the news that the regime of Kwame Nkrumah, which Sir Albert had constantly extolled as the leading example of a stable and democratic one-party state, had been overthrown by a military coup. While this news did not lead the government to reverse its stand publicly, very little was said about a one-party state in succeeding weeks.

Nkrumah's fall also seems to have emboldened opposition within the country. On March 16 a mass meeting was convened in Freetown by A. P. Bruno-Gaston, the General Manager of the Electricity Corporation, along with

71 / For example, at a public meeting in Freetown in February the speakers simply passed over the one-party state question with the comment that the Prime Minister should hold an election on it, and then turned to the issue of corruption in government. Notes by the writer, February 20, 1966.

72 / Notes by the writer, Leo Spitzer, and Fred Hayward, January 28, 1966.

73 / It was significant that this was the first point in Sir Albert's speech referred to by both the SLBS news broadcast and by *Unity*. The latter ran as its headline "One-Party State Not By Force," *Unity*, January 29, 1966.

74 / *Daily Mail*, January 29, 1966.

75 / *We Yone*, January 15, 1966.

76 / *Think* reported the stoning in its issue of March 30, 1966; this was corroborated by observers in Magburaka.

77 / One American observer estimated there were about 500 hecklers in a total crowd of 3,000. It should be added that there were a large number of Temnes in Bo.

Bishop M. N. C. O. Scott, the (Anglican) Bishop of Sierra Leone, and Rev. S. M. Renner, a very close associate of the late Sir Milton. In his speech to the meeting, Bruno-Gaston asked that the government suspend the introduction of the one-party state until the people appeared ready for it and had been given a chance to vote on the issue. "It would appear," he declared, "that the majority of Sierra Leoneans are not yet ready for the introduction of the 'One-Party State.' "[78]

The following day, the Principal of Fourah Bay College, Dr Davidson Nicol, held a press conference at which he strongly affirmed the right of students to express their views within the College.[79] Since most of the students opposed the one-party state,[80] this was in effect support for the opposition. This was underlined by the publication the same day of a resolution by the students asking the government to "reconsider" the introduction of a one-party state, or if it still wished to introduce it, to hold a referendum.[81]

These growing signs of opposition to the one-party state seem to have induced the government to back away from the question. A news story in *Unity* on March 19 asserted that the rumours of "a plan to foist the one-party state on the people by April 27" were "unfounded," and that the introduction of a one-party state, "if at all," should be by a referendum or some other method proposed by a committee to be set up representing all interests.[82] On March 21, the Prime Minister laid before Parliament a White Paper which announced the government's decision to set up a Committee with the following terms of reference: "To collate and assess all views on the One Party System both in and out of Parliament and to make recommendations on the type of One Party System suitable for Sierra Leone and the method by which it should be introduced."[83] While it made clear by these terms of reference that it wanted some kind of one-party state, the government gave no further indication of exactly what it wanted. It did lay down that "In a One Party System one of the qualifications for election to Parliament should be membership of the Party,"[84] but did not try to suggest the

78 / For a full report of the speech, see *We Yone*, March 19, 1966. The meeting was not mentioned on the SLBS, or in the *Daily Mail*. Bruno-Gaston was sharply attacked for participating as a civil servant in politics, and the ministers for mixing religion and politics, in *Unity*, March 19, 1966, whch also suggested that they were swayed from a more neutral position by the anti-one-party state attitude of their audience.

79 / *Daily Mail*, March 18, 1966.

80 / When the issue first arose, nearly all students opposed the one-party system. But after a while it tended to become a tribal issue, with Mendes supporting and others opposing it.

81 / *Daily Mail*, March 18.

82 / *Unity*, March 19, 1966.

83 / Sierra Leone. *Government White Paper on the Proposed Introduction of a Democratic One Party System in Sierra Leone* (Freetown: Government Printer, 1966).

84 / *Ibid.*, para. 5.

degree to which party membership should be open to everyone. It further tried to allay fears about personal liberties with the rather vague statement that

Government will endeavour to ensure that no person in Sierra Leone is deprived of his fundamental rights to life, liberty, security of his person, the enjoyment of property and the protection of the law, his fundamental freedoms of conscience, of expression, and of assembly, and respect for his private and family life. Government is particularly anxious to ensure that whatever political system is adopted no person shall be deprived of his personal liberty save as may be authorized by law in any of the cases specified in the Constitution.[85]

Such vital questions as how membership in the Party would be determined, whether there would be competition between party members for election to a legislature, and how the executive could be controlled, were all left for the committee to decide. The government had not abandoned the goal of a one-party state. In spelling out the details of what it wanted, however, it had made no advance over the December proposals, while its confidence that it would attain its goal had noticeably waned.

When the groups who were to send representatives to the committee were finally announced on April 22,[86] it was apparent that the government was not weighting the committee unduly in favour of its own viewpoint. The chairman was to be the Speaker of the House of Representatives, Banja Tejan-Sie, who was certainly not an advocate of the one-party system.[87] The forty members were to include: three Ministers nominated by the government, four other SLPP parliamentarians, two APC nominees,[88] one non-Paramount Chief from each of the twelve District Councils, one member each from the Rural Area and Freetown City Councils, one Paramount Chief from each province, two representatives each from the Federation of Labour, the Teachers' Association and the universities, and one each from the Women's Federation, the Bar Association, the Medical Practitioners Association, the United Christian Council, the Catholic Church, the Muslim Congress, the Muslim community, and the Youth Council. Given the existing composition of the District Councils, and considering the position of the Paramount Chiefs, the government would be assured of a majority on the committee, but repre-

85 / *Ibid.*, para. 6.

86 / See *Daily Mail*, April 23, 1966, and *Unity*, April 23, 1966.

87 / We may recall his remarks in 1962 that he was glad that Sierra Leone had an Opposition. He also took a very scholarly approach to the question; to prepare the committee to do its work properly, he collected an assortment of learned articles which would have challenged a graduate seminar in political science, although he conceded that some members would find these readings hard going.

88 / The APC decided to boycott the committee, and launched a court action to restrain it from meeting.

sentatives of the Bar, the medical profession, and the universities would certainly be able to examine any proposals with a critical eye.

When the representatives were chosen by their groups, the extent of opposition was even more marked than expected. One of the three Ministers chosen was Kutubu Kai-Samba, the able young lawyer who had never retracted his doubts about the desirability of a one-party system.[89] The SLPP parliamentary caucus chose the three ex-Ministers, Mustapha, Sesay, and Matturi, as well as Kai-Samba's radical ally, L. A. M. Brewah. Mustapha, Sesay, and Brewah had all opposed the one-party state in October,[90] although Sesay and Brewah had supported Bai Bairoh's motion in December. The Christian Council chose Bishop Scott, who had joined in the call for a halt a few weeks earlier.[91] H. N. Georgestone, one of the Federation of Labour representatives, was a plaintiff along with some APC members in a court action to restrain the committee from ever meeting. Dr Sarif Easmon, who had been elected by the Medical Practitioners Union in preference to Dr Claude Nelson-Williams,[92] had published a number of strong attacks on the idea of the one-party state, and was also a plaintiff in the action to restrain the committee. Such a committee would not rubber-stamp any proposals the government might choose to bring before it.

Meanwhile the government had announced that District Council elections would be held on May 27.[93] Although the chiefs' harassment of the APC continued unabated, the opposition had already scored a clear triumph in the Makeni Town Council (Northern Province) elections held on April 1. Whereas in 1962 five SLPP and one APC supporter had been elected "on a non-political basis"[94] and in 1964 the SLPP had had two unopposed returns,[95] this time the APC swept all three seats by majorities of well over two to one.[96] In view of the fact that the SLPP had waged an intensive campaign, led by the General Secretary, this defeat suggested that the party might not fare well in the District Council elections.

The APC, however, faced a serious dilemma. Not contesting the elections would give an impression of weakness that would handicap it at the next

89 / It was shortly after this that he, Brewah, Jusu-Sheriff, and the Principal of Njala University Colleges, S. T. Matturi, were rumoured to be forming an alliance to fight the one-party state.

90 / See above, pp. 212–13.

91 / See above, pp. 220–21.

92 / See the letter from the Secretary of the Union in *Unity*, May 28, 1966.

93 / *Daily Mail*, May 2, 1966.

94 / *Daily Mail*, March 20, 1962.

95 / *Sierra Leone Gazette*, May 21, 1964. A third seat was taken unopposed by an Independent.

96 / The results were: Ward I – Aluseni Kamara (APC) 306, Sylvanus Koroma (Ind.) 136; Ward II – Alpha Turay (APC) 504, Boboh Paine (SLPP) 143; Ward III – Alex Koroma (APC) 278, N. Conteh (SLPP) 94. *Sierra Leone Gazette*, April 14, 1966, p. 327.

general election.[97] But if it did contest them, it would risk exposing a large number of its supporters to persecution and intimidation, with the result that they might no longer be available to support it when the real test of the general election came. Since control of a District Council could be rendered meaningless by the central government's suspension of financial grants, or even of the council, there was no victory to be gained at a District Council election except a psychological one, and the price could be very high. Such at any rate was the reasoning of most of the leaders.[98] But the younger men of the party overruled Stevens, and insisted on contesting.[99] Stevens himself left the country.

The SLPP tried first of all to gain a victory in the elections by getting its candidates returned unopposed. In the Southern and Eastern Provinces, apart from Kono, a combination of skilful selection and pressure from the Paramount Chiefs secured 172 unopposed SLPP returns out of a total of 208 seats. But in the Northern Province and Kono, despite considerable pressure from government officials and from the chiefs, the SLPP managed only 47 unopposed returns out of 165 seats.[100] The APC contested 20 of the 22 seats in Tonkolili; 16 of 20 in Kambia; 39 of 45 in Port Loko; 15 of 27 in Bombali; and even 5 of 21 in Koinadugu, where they had never run candidates before. The Democratic Peoples Congress contested 23 of the 30 Kono seats.

The campaign was marked by an intensive effort on the part of the SLPP leaders, government officials, and many Paramount Chiefs to deter people from voting for the opposition parties.[101] The effort was successful in Kono, where the SLPP candidates defeated those of the DPC in all 23 contested seats. In the north, however, it failed miserably; out of 95 contested seats, the APC won 72, attaining their highest ever percentage of votes within the boundaries of 12 of the 16 national constituencies previously contested. Such a set-back, despite their most intensive party campaign in any election, indicated a decisive rejection of the SLPP leaders in that area.

These results led the Prime Minister to back down further on his commitment to the one-party state. Even before the District Council elections, he had promised he would not introduce the one-party state unless the people gave him "a vast majority" in a referendum.[102] Shortly after the elections, in

97 / One member claimed it could successfully explain its reasons for not contesting to its supporters without their losing faith.

98 / *Unity* claimed Stevens "stood resolutely against the party's contesting the elections." *Unity*, April 23, 1966. It had earlier claimed (March 26, 1966) that the APC had decided not to contest.

99 / *Ibid.*, April 30, 1966.

100 / Calculated from *Sierra Leone Gazette*, May 26, 1966.

101 / See below, pp. 230–31.

102 / *Daily Mail*, May 12, 1966.

a speech at Bonthe, he practically disavowed responsibility for the idea, claiming it had not originated with him.[103] Again he stressed the need for a "very substantial majority" in a referendum.

The Prime Minister had not yet completely abandoned his hope of attaining a one-party state, but by now even his own party was beginning to turn against him. A scheme to by-pass the need for a general election in order to amend the entrenched clauses of the constitution by substituting a national referendum was dropped after encountering stiff opposition in the SLPP party caucus.[104] Another proposal, to make Sierra Leone into a republic, had been expected before Parliament in July, but disappeared quietly before it even reached the party caucus.[105] A more direct blow to the one-party state plan had come at the end of May, when the Acting Chief Justice, Mr C. O. E. Cole, granted an interim injunction to several APC leaders who had sought to restrain the one-party-state committee from meeting. The Prime Minister was furious with the decision, and ordered the committee to meet in defiance of the injunction.[106] Only a handful of his closest supporters were prepared to make this breach in the rule of law, and the committee finally was adjourned *sine die* while the case made its leisurely way through the courts.[107]

The development and the outcome of the one-party state issue illustrate most of the key features within the Sierra Leone political system. These features can be seen from a consideration of three questions. First, what reasons did government supporters advance for wanting a one-party state? Second, how did the government go about trying to gain support for its objective? Third, what were the sources of resistance to the one-party state drive?

103 / *Unity*, June 25, 1966. The speech was made on June 3.

104 / *We Yone*, June 18, 1966. *We Yone* stressed the fears of the Paramount Chiefs that the change could be used to destroy their entrenched rights, but other members the writer spoke to also had their doubts about the change.

105 / It eventually reappeared in January 1967, shorn of most of the features which might strengthen Sir Albert's position. Like the Nigerian Republic of 1963, it retained a parliamentary system, rather than creating an executive President. The only changes of significance were the abolition of appeals to the Judicial Committee of the Privy Council, and the vesting of the power to appoint and remove the Chief Justice (though apparently not other judges) in the hands of the President on the sole advice of the Prime Minister. See below, p. 240. Such changes would strengthen the Prime Minister's hand, but only over a long period of time.

106 / See the account of Dr Sarif Easmon in *We Yone*, July 2, 1960. No one on the government side subsequently denied this account. The main repercussion was a letter from the Attorney General, whom Easmon suggested might have given the Prime Minister his advice to defy the Court, reproaching Easmon for this suggestion, denying that he had given the committee any such advice, and by implication dissociating himself from the one-party-state idea. See *Daily Mail*, July 9, 1966, and *We Yone*, July 9, 1966.

107 / *Ibid.*, July 2.

A PARTY IN SEARCH OF SECURITY

The arguments advanced by the SLPP leaders in favour of a one-party state expressed a variety of motives. A few tried to justify the one-party state as being in the national interest by promoting development, unity against external enemies, and national integration. But more often the motives behind the desire for a one-party system were based on the desire of the SLPP leaders and the chiefs to retain their power. Much of their concern was over the threat to their position created by the APC's willingness to turn the people against their chiefs.

Of the "national interest" arguments, the one that struck the widest response was the claim that it was not a proper African attitude for an organized group to remain in permanent opposition to the government. Opposition over a specific point, or for a limited time, was legitimate, but once the issue had been settled, or some time had elapsed, those who were opposed should rejoin the governing group. This argument was put forward explicitly in a pamphlet by Dr Victor King of Njala,[108] and was implied in the frequent criticisms made of the "un-African" two-party system left by the British.[109] One corollary of this argument was that the governing group should go a long way to reconcile opposition, and certainly should not try to crush it; perhaps it was on this ground that the APC leaders, while not adamantly against any reconciliation, were reluctant to join the government on Sir Albert's terms.

A further general argument was that given Sierra Leone's condition, her leaders could not afford to spend their time fighting each other. Some leaders suggested that such political conflicts left the way open for foreign powers to intervene;[110] but more often they were regarded simply as an unprofitable waste of time when the country had need of all the energies of all its leaders in order to speed development. Although no one in the Sierra Leone government ever put forward an explanation of just how bringing all the political leaders together would produce more rapid development, it was widely assumed that this would be the case.[111]

The argument that the All Peoples Congress, by the very fact of its tribal base, was encouraging tribal polarization in the country, was valid. If the country were to divide along tribal lines, with one tribe remaining permanently in opposition, the ultimate result could be civil war. It could be argued

108 / "The Unified Party System in Emerging Africa" (pamphlet, n.d.).

109 / For example, see the remarks of Chief Yumkella, Y. D. Sesay, and D. S. Sumner in *House of Representatives Debates*, December 20, 1965.

110 / For example, D. S. Sumner, *ibid.*, and George Mani, *ibid.*, December 21.

111 / See, for example, the remarks of Chiefs Bai Bairoh and Yumkella, *ibid.*, December 20.

from this that a one-party state which brought northerners into the government would ease tribal tensions. But Sir Albert's policy of crushing the APC rather than conciliating it was not likely to make northerners support the SLPP; on the contrary, it seemed to confirm their belief that the SLPP was a Mende party out to subordinate the Temnes by destroying "their" party, the APC. A "national interest" argument would support a coalition or merger between the two parties, but not the suppression of one by the other.

Another possible "national interest" argument which was not clearly articulated by the SLPP leaders, but which seems to have been in the minds of some, was that a one-party state would provide stability by limiting popular participation in politics. The anti-chief appeals of the APC drew the common people into politics in opposition to their chiefs, and thus threatened the entire base of the established order. If the APC leaders were brought into the government, the people would not be stirred up. However, such an argument assumed that if left to themselves, the people would not rise against their chiefs. It was much more likely that if the leaders who could channel existing discontent into peaceful political channels were removed, the people would ultimately rise in a much more violent manner.

Certain other arguments were not open to the SLPP leaders. They could not, as Siaka Stevens once pointed out,[112] use the argument that the SLPP was so overwhelmingly dominant in the country that Sierra Leone had a *de facto* one-party system. Nor could they argue, as the Convention People's Party had in Ghana, that they were the only truly nationalistic party, and that the opposition was in league with imperialists and neo-colonialists. Sir Albert did charge that the APC was damaging Sierra Leone's reputation abroad,[113] but he could hardly accuse the APC of preparing to sell out the country to the British. More broadly, the SLPP could not claim any ideological justification for suppressing all organized opposition. It had certainly never pretended to rule on behalf of the masses, in the manner of the Parti Démocratique de Guinée or the Union Soudanaise. It might have tried to claim an opposite justification for suppressing opposition, namely that it alone was the expression of the "natural rulers" of Sierra Leone, the Paramount Chiefs. But this course also was closed to it, both because too many members of the Western elite within the SLPP could not accept a claim that the chiefs were the sole legitimate rulers, and because no literate outside the SLPP was likely to accept it. There was no way in which the diverse strands of the party could be woven into a single coherent ideology that could be used to justify the one-party state.

The fact that these "national interest" arguments were not often advanced, and were never developed in detail when they were advanced, suggests that

112 / *Ibid.* (March 29, 1965), cols. 201–202.
113 / *Ibid.*, December 21, 1965, col. 50.

they were not uppermost in the minds of the SLPP leaders. Concern for their class and personal interests seem to have weighed more heavily with them. One argument advanced explicitly by SLPP supporters was that the one-party state would protect the chiefs. The Minister of the Interior told the Koinadugu District Council in January 1966 that the position of chiefs would be strengthened under a one-party state.[114] Chief Yumkella alleged that a major drawback of the two-party system was that it allowed opposition members to stir up the people against their chiefs.[115] These arguments, while attractive to the chiefs, would clearly not arouse much enthusiasm among people who felt that their chiefs already had too much power over them.

One argument the Prime Minister frequently advanced in support of the one-party state was that the opposition party's charges of corruption among Ministers, in the Produce Marketing Board and elsewhere, were hurting Sierra Leone's reputation abroad and making it difficult to attract foreign investment. In a one-party state where no such charges were being made, he argued, more investment would flow in and money could be found for roads, schools, and medical treatment centres.[116]

Perhaps the Prime Minister and some of his Ministers were more anxious about the effect of such attacks on their position in Sierra Leone. In his invitation to "come and share our kingdom with us" during the debate on Bai Bairoh's motion, the Prime Minister seemed to be implying that if opposition members of Parliament would just be sensible and would come and share the spoils of office, then they might not be so ready to make charges of corruption.[117] These charges, as we have already noted, were undermining the Prime Minister's appeal among the younger radical elements,[118] and also among the urban workers. They also reinforced a more general discontent over the gap between the affluence of the SLPP leaders and the poverty of the ordinary town or village dweller, a discontent which the APC was busily exploiting in both north and south. Despite the handicaps it faced in organizing, the APC was confident it was making inroads in such southern districts as Bo, Moyamba, Kailahun, and even Pujehun,[119] and could point to the footholds it had established in the Kailahun and Bonthe by-elections as evidence. SLPP leaders did not seem disposed to deny these claims; the Sefadu conference was remarkable for the way in which even spokesmen

114 / SLBS National News Broadcast, January 28, 1966.

115 / *House of Representatives Debates*, December 20, 1965, col. 20.

116 / *Ibid.*, December 21, cols. 49–52.

117 / *Ibid.*, col. 42. This tone of "come and share the loot" was echoed in a number of speeches.

118 / See above, pp. 206 ff.

119 / It declined to expose its converts in the 1966 District Council election, except for its three candidates (all Temne) in Bo Town, and three others in Moyamba.

from the SLPP's southern strongholds talked about the APC as a possible threat.[120]

A final consideration in favour of the one-party system was that it would eliminate an organized nucleus around which the Prime Minister's personal opponents could rally. If it were not for the existence of the APC, a potential rival such as Karefa-Smart would be in a very weak position if the Prime Minister forced him out of the party. But as long as a legitimate opposition party survived, all those disaffected with the Prime Minister could rally around it, either in Parliament or in an election.

The most important motives behind the one-party state, then, were the defence of the SLPP leaders' personal position and the protection of the traditional system against what was perceived as the threat of a popular discontent. Sir Albert's desire to stop the APC's charges of corruption was motivated basically by the damage this was doing to his popular support at home. His motives in trying to suppress the APC seem to have included a wish to eliminate a rallying point for opposition to his personal rule, as well as the more general one of forestalling a radical mass challenge to both the chiefs and the SLPP.

These motives of self-preservation help to explain why the SLPP leaders never made clear what kind of one-party state they wanted. If the Prime Minister had wanted such a state for reasons of national interest, it should not have been difficult for him to commit himself publicly to a number of safeguards which many people wanted. For example, one backbencher claimed that the SLPP party caucus had insisted that any acceptable system had to provide some means by which unwanted leaders could be removed, and should provide for elections in the constituencies.[121] But this was never publicized. Sir Albert's main references to a successful one-party system were to the regime in Ghana, which was marked by much more limited opportunities for the party followers to control their leaders.[122] He also remarked in the debate on Bai Bairoh's motion that a one-party system was "one of the means that would make it possible for many Members of this House to retain their seats."[123] It would appear that the Prime Minister was not anxious to give assurances that leaders would be removable and that com-

120 / Notes by the writer, May 21–22, 1965. Most boasted they had stopped the APC from establishing a foothold; but the fact that they bothered to mention it suggested their concern.

121 / It was interesting that sitting members should want this provision for elections. Their fear probably was that if there were no elections, Sir Albert would be able to replace them with his own favourites.

122 / See, for example, Sir Albert's speech in Freetown January 28. *Daily Mail*, January 29, 1966.

123 / *House of Representatives Debates*, December 21, col. 41.

petitive elections would be held for the very good reason that he did not want these things. The effect of his refusal to spell out what he wanted was to lead everyone who was distrustful of the idea to fear the worst, including preventive detention and concentration camps.[124]

The methods used by Sir Albert in pursuing the one-party goal aroused considerable concern about the wisdom of such a system. He relied far more on threats than on persuasion to achieve his goals. But he did exercise some restraint; he did not, for example, attempt to jail all the APC leaders, or use much extra-legal violence.

The principal curbs that the central government employed against leaders of the opposition were its attempts to silence their newspapers by legal action, and its monopolization of the principal news media of Sierra Leone. It did not make any serious attempt to curb the personal freedom of the APC members of Parliament,[125] apart from the change in the rules of attendance at the House which forced out four APC members and Dr Karefa-Smart. Its main fire was concentrated on the writers of the APC newspaper, *We Yone*. Some of the prosecutions launched by the Attorney-General's department were clearly harassment, as when Ibrahim Taqi was charged for the second time with libelling the Attorney-General,[126] or in a further case when Taqi and another writer were charged with a seditious publication for demanding "redemption from 'tyranny' ... through the ballot box."[127] They were of course acquitted.[128] But they still had to spend time in court, and more important for a party with the limited resources of the APC, pay lawyers' fees, which represented a considerable drain on them.[129]

At the local level, both government officers and the chiefs were pressed into service to suppress APC activities. In the District Council elections, the Returning Officers (the District Officers, who had already been working with the local SLPP leaders) often put difficulties in the way of APC candidates. In Kambia, at least one APC candidate's nomination papers were snatched from his hands by his SLPP rival and torn to shreds while police officers stood and watched. In Kono, two DPC candidates' nomination papers found their way

124 / Both Dr Sarif Easmon and Professor Eldred Jones claimed in articles that such things were the inevitable outcome of a one-party system.

125 / In February, 1966, there were rumours of a plot to kidnap Siaka Stevens, but no attempt was ever made. One APC MP had to fight a long and costly action against a charge of defrauding a woman of some money, but this charge was instigated by a Paramount Chief.

126 / See above, p. 214.

127 / *We Yone*, December 11, 1965. This was reported as the basis of the sedition charge in *Unity*, December 18, 1965.

128 / *We Yone*, January 22, 1966.

129 / The defence of Taqi on the charge of libelling the Attorney-General cost well over £1,000 in lawyers' fees.

into the dust bin outside the Returning Officer's office, with the Returning Officer explaining after the deadline for nominations that they had decided to withdraw.[130] The Secretary-General of the DPC found his nomination voided because the Returning Officer had accepted the assurance of his SLPP opponent that one of the DPC candidate's nominators had denied nominating him.[131] *We Yone* charged that in Koinadugu, Bombali, and Tonkolili districts, the offices of the Returning Officers were filled with Paramount Chiefs and SLPP officials, who were harassing and threatening APC candidates and their supporters.[132] At the close of nominations, the Prime Minister allegedly sent out a message over the police radio congratulating all District Officers in whose districts a large number of SLPP candidates had been returned unopposed.

But the main work of suppressing APC activists fell upon the Paramount Chiefs. In the District Council elections the chiefs tried to arrange for unopposed returns of SLPP candidates, and failing that, to persuade the voters to support the SLPP. In the Southern and Eastern Provinces, by carefully selecting the most popular individuals as SLPP candidates and judiciously persuading other would-be contenders to withdraw, they achieved considerable success. But in the north and Kono, not all APC candidates could be persuaded to stand down. Some could; one teacher in Tonkolili North was persuaded to withdraw his candidacy by the assurance that, if he stood, he would be fired from his job and driven out of the chiefdom. But most of the APC candidates were obdurate, with the result that the chiefs had to urge the electorate not to vote for them. One chief in Tonkolili reportedly told his people that he could tell how everyone voted, and that if anybody voted APC, he would be driven out of the chiefdom. Several chiefs wrote in reply to APC requests that the party would not be allowed to hold meetings in their chiefdoms,[133] while others ordered APC canvassers out of their towns on pain of being jailed.[134] In Port Loko District, a man was sentenced to 12 months' imprisonment by a Local Court on the charge of "canvassing for the APC."[135] In Kabala, it was alleged that a gang of SLPP supporters, led by employees of the Government and of the Electoral Commission, smashed an APC van.[136]

130 / *Think*, May 22, 1966.
131 / *Ibid*.
132 / See *We Yone*, May 14, 1966.
133 / For example, see *We Yone*, May 14, 1966.
134 / See *Think*, June 12, 1966.
135 / *Think*, June 8, 1966. While *Unity* claimed there was exaggeration in *Think's* claim, the exaggeration seemed to be in *Think's* assertion that the Court President who passed the sentence was a "confirmed illiterate." If this was so, asked *Unity*, how could he endorse the sentence on the certificate? *Unity*, June 11, 1966.
136 / *Think*, June 12, 1966.

Some SLPP leaders directly encouraged the use of violence to intimidate opposition. The Prime Minister himself, in his major Freetown rally in January 1966, had a club-swinging squad of riot police drive a group of hecklers out of the stadium. Far more serious was the near-riot stirred up by the Nelson-Williams brothers in November 1965, when Siaka Stevens was re-elected Mayor of Freetown. Membership in the Council was deadlocked at ten each for the SLPP and APC, with the Mayor and chairmen of meetings having an original and a casting vote. By a manoeuvre of questionable legality,[137] the APC had a day earlier chosen one of their members as chairman of the meeting to elect a Mayor. But not content with contesting this action in the courts, a mass of SLPP supporters, led by John and Claude Nelson-Williams, packed the meeting-hall. The APC appealed to the police to clear the hall to prevent violence, but the police would not act. When the meeting began, the APC nominated Stevens for Mayor. Accounts then diverge. The *Daily Mail* reported that the SLPP councillors walked out of the meeting,[138] while *We Yone* claimed that as soon as the APC chairman, J. C. O. Hadson-Taylor, declared the nominations closed and Stevens elected Mayor, the Nelson-Williams brothers encouraged the crowd to attack the APC councillors.[139] In any case, before the police intervened, five APC councillors sustained injuries, one requiring hospitalization.[140] The only action to be taken against any of the participants in the fracas was a charge of malicious wounding laid against Hadson-Taylor which was later dropped.[141] Members of the APC were not the only persons to come under suspicion as potential enemies of Sir Albert. On February 8, the police searched eleven houses in Freetown and one in Port Loko, looking for ammunition, explosives, and fire arms.[142] The houses searched were mostly those of SLPP members, including M. S. Mustapha, two relatives of the Sierra Leone Ambassador to Guinea, Mahmoud Ahmed, and a relative of I. B. Taylor-Kamara, as well as Cyrus Rogers-Wright, who had earlier criticized the one-party system.[143] The search did not reveal any arms, but it may have served as a warning to potential dissidents within the party.

137 / The Council's standing orders said that a chairman for the meeting to elect a mayor was to be chosen at the start of that meeting. But if the APC had waited until that day, Stevens would no longer have been Mayor, and the two sides would have been deadlocked at 10–10. The Supreme Court later ruled that the chairman had been improperly elected, and consequently voided Stevens' election as Mayor. *Daily Mail*, January 5, 1966.

138 / *Daily Mail*, November 10, 1965.

139 / *We Yone*, November 10, 1965.

140 / *Ibid.* The writer saw two of the councillors two days later; they certainly appeared to have sustained severe beatings.

141 / See *Unity*, November 13, 1965, for the laying of the charge, and *Daily Mail*, December 14, 1965, for the announcement that it was being withdrawn by the Crown.

142 / The first public announcement appeared in *Daily Mail*, February 11, 1960.

143 / See *ibid.*, and *We Yone*, February 12, 1966, for names of those searched.

Certain groups which formed centres of opposition to the Prime Minister were also threatened. The prime target was the Creoles, who were highly critical of Sir Albert's proposed departure from British democratic traditions.[144] In his speech on Bai Bairoh's motion, the Prime Minister commented on the Creoles' "general attitude of crying the government down," which, he warned, "will only make us callous."[145] In his January speech in Freetown, he warned the "Freetown people" that their views would not be allowed to prevail over the rest of the country.[146] The party newspaper, *Unity*, tried to revive the SLPP's successful formula of the 1950s by suggesting that the Settlers (Creoles) were supporting all opposition to the one-party state because, by keeping the up-country people divided, they would be able to regain their own dominance.[147]

The higher levels of the intelligentsia, the civil service, and the judiciary, all of which were largely Creole in composition, were singled out for criticism as well. In his speech in Parliament on the one-party-state motion, the Prime Minister gave a pointed interpretation of how the "extra-judicial" power of preventive detention had come about in Ghana: "The Judiciary itself were all against the Government [*sic*] ... the Executive felt that their hands were tied and the Judiciary was fighting them."[148] In January he condemned the "doctors, lawyers and lecturers" who deliberately blinded themselves to the benefits of the one-party system.[149] A few weeks later two articles in *Unity* by the SLPP General Secretary suggested that many civil servants were disloyal to the government; he divided the civil service into four categories of pro-SLPP, pro-APC, pro-Settler, and the fence-sitters, and claimed the last three groups were all untrustworthy.[150]

For all his threats and inducements, Sir Albert was not prepared to go to any lengths to get his one-party state. He was no fanatic seeking to impose the truth on a reluctant country at any cost, but a pragmatic politician with some sense of the possible. He was not inhibited by any personal sense of restraint from taking strong actions to improve his position if he thought he could get away with them. For example, in May 1965 the attendance rule removing the APC members of Parliament had been rammed through

144 / See, for example, the radical newsheet *Think*, which in its earlier issues lauded Freetown's Creole culture as the bastion of "all that is noble and of good report in the Western and Christian way of life" (January 26, 1966). Later it referred to the judiciary of Sierra Leone as "modelled on the best and finest traditions of the English Bench" (July 17, 1966).

145 / *House of Representatives Debates*, December 21, 1965, col. 47.

146 / *Daily Mail*, January 29, 1966.

147 / For example, see cartoon in *Unity*, February 26, 1966, and accounts of Settlers' meetings in *ibid.*, April 2, 1966.

148 / *House of Representatives Debates*, December 21, 1965, cols. 45–46.

149 / *Daily Mail*, January 29, 1966.

150 / *Unity*, February 5 and February 12, 1966.

the SLPP party caucus despite what one of his supporters termed "a lot of opposition," and in October he was prepared to brave the wrath of the Bench and Bar with his unceremonious "promotion" of Sir Samuel Bankole-Jones.[151] What stopped him was the reluctance of his supporters to go to any lengths with him. When Mr Justice Cole enjoined the one-party-state committee from meeting, the Prime Minister was prepared to defy the Court, but only about three members of the committee were prepared to follow him down this pitfall-strewn path.

THE PEOPLE SAY "NO"

Why did the opposition to a one-party state in Sierra Leone succeed in frustrating the Prime Minister's plans, whereas opposition in most other African states had failed? There are four main reasons: first, the loose, unstructured nature of the governing party; second, the opposition of many members of the SLPP to any strengthening of Albert Margai's position; third, the values held by other elites outside the party system, and their positions of strength vis-à-vis the politicians; and fourth, a widespread popular feeling that the one-party state was simply a device to enrich the political elite at the expense of the ordinary people.

The SLPP, as we have noted, did not have any ideology which could have been used to justify a monopoly of power. The chiefs could conceivably claim a "right to rule" and treat the SLPP as their vehicle at the national level, but such a claim would have a hard time winning acceptance among the Western elite within the party, let alone among educated persons outside the party. Furthermore, neither the educated persons nor the chiefs formed particularly cohesive groups; each chief and each member of Parliament had to consider the interests of his own particular chiefdom or constituency. All Ministers and MPs had to weigh the prospective improvement in their chances of surviving the next election against the increased power the Prime Minister would hold over them, and how he might use this power. If a one-party state were established, a Minister whom the Prime Minister had dropped would have even less chance of working his way back into office than he did at present. The SLPP backbenchers would also suffer a loss of their bargaining power in the party caucus, and might even find themselves forbidden to stand in future elections if control over party membership were vested in the Prime Minister's hands.

More personal factors also entered the SLPP members' calculations. Many of the more traditionally minded "old guard" were unhappy about Sir Albert's attitudes and about the ascendance of the PNP. It was significant

151 / See above, pp. 213–14.

that members of the "old guard" such as Sesay and Mustapha spoke up against the one-party state in October 1965.[152] Some SLPP men outside Parliament specifically complained that persons who had remained loyal to the party from its inception were being shunted aside in favour of Sir Albert's PNP supporters. At the other extreme, some of the more radical members of the SLPP seem to have been disillusioned over Sir Albert's tolerance of corruption. Also, well-educated persons like Kai-Samba, Sheriff, and Brewah were in a better position than most members to learn about and assess the effectiveness of other one-party regimes in Africa and elsewhere.

Both the "old guard" and the radicals could also see persons closer to Sir Albert than themselves out to undermine their positions in their own constituencies. One of Sir Albert's private secretaries was running against Kai-Samba in Kenema Central, while S. T. Navo, the Judicial Advisor to the government, was trying to regain his seat from the traditionalist S. Mosere in Bo North. In all, there were at least nine seats in which sitting SLPP members were being opposed by men known to be close to Sir Albert. This was hardly likely to make these MPs more willing to support the Prime Minister. For all these reasons, then, the SLPP was by no means united behind the Prime Minister; while most could see a possibility that the one-party system might save their seats, they could also see an equal possibility that it might be the means by which Sir Albert could get rid of them.

The opposition party, on the other hand, did not take a leading role in stopping the imposition of a one-party state. We have noted that the APC was reluctant to criticize the principle of a one-party system, and that it was not until its leaders had tested popular opinion that they came out firmly against it. However, the fact that the APC remained in opposition was a critical factor in enabling resistance to succeed. If the APC leaders had accepted Sir Albert's December offer to join in a coalition or merger, other critics would have been confronted with a *fait accompli*. As it was, the APC provided a rallying point and a channel of expression for popular opposition, as well as a potential refuge for other elite groups.

Resistance to the one-party state also came from outside the party system. The judiciary and the senior civil service were quite deeply imbued with the idea that they should be "above politics," as part of a more general commitment to a pattern of democracy modelled on Britain. The judiciary in particular did not hesitate to find against the government, as was shown by Mr. Justice Cole's granting of an injunction against the one-party committee in May 1966,[153] and in their persistent unwillingness to convict APC journalists. Civil service opposition was less open, although Bruno-Gaston

152 / See above, pp. 212–13.
153 / *We Yone*, May 28, 1966.

did bring his doubts to a public forum.[154] A number of civil servants tried, however, to resist the transformation of their roles into political ones, and at times would undo the work of politicians by such means as restoring the positions of subordinates who had been posted away for political disloyalty. This resistance, which served to deny Sir Albert the organized alternative to the party machine he lacked, was recognized by the SLPP leaders; at one point the General Secretary charged that most civil servants were disloyal to the government.[155] But the resistance was widespread enough that the Prime Minister could do very little about it.

Outside the government, a number of groups showed varying degrees of concern about the Prime Minister's actions. The Bar Association protested vigorously the government's treatment of Sir Samuel Bankole-Jones,[156] while the Medical Practitioners Union showed their opposition to the idea of a one-party system by electing the most outspoken critic of the idea, Dr Sarif Easmon, as their representative on the one-party-state committee in preference to the Prime Minister's friend, Dr Claude Nelson-Williams.[157] Criticism of the one-party state also came from such groups as the students of Fourah Bay College,[158] and academics generally.[159]

Another group among whom some opposition to the Prime Minister's drive was found were the chiefs. Most chiefs probably agreed with the views of Chiefs Bai Bairoh and Yumkella that the one-party state would help them by stopping agitators from rousing the people against them.[160] But a number of chiefs were not ready to trust the leadership of a one-party state to Sir Albert Margai. Some chiefs were even prepared to allow the opposition to campaign freely in the 1966 District Council elections. For example, when the APC sent a team of canvassers to Bo, the section chiefs came running to Chief Abu Baimba to find out what to do. Chief Baimba's advice was simple: let the APC men speak, give them police protection if they needed it, and only make sure that if they told "lies" the section chiefs should tell the people the truth.[161] Chief Baimba himself did not canvass for the SLPP. This extent of non-support was probably exceptional, but there were clearly other chiefs

154 / See above, pp. 220–21.

155 / *Unity*, February 5 and 12, 1966.

156 / For a somewhat misleading account of the meeting, see *Unity*, November 6, 1965, and for a correction of this account by the Bar Association, see *We Yone*, November 27, 1965.

157 / See above, p. 223.

158 / See above, p. 221.

159 / Including some non-Creoles, such as the Principal of Njala, Dr S. T. Matturi.

160 / See *House of Representatives Debates*, December 20, 1965.

161 / Chief Baimba was of the opinion that *We Yone* was on the whole quite truthful.

who granted the APC considerable tolerance. For example, the APC had successfully opened offices in Rokupr, Kambia District, and in Magburaka, the capital of Tonkolili District.[162]

Tolerance towards the APC on the part of chiefs and lesser traditional officials was reinforced in the north by a further factor of significance. With the extended family connections that existed throughout Sierra Leone, it was inevitable that many APC supporters would be the brothers, cousins, or other close relatives of the traditional authorities or of SLPP party workers. For example, one SLPP youth in Port Loko claimed he had abstained from working in the 1962 election because his uncle was running as the APC candidate; a former SLPP member of Parliament in Bombali was thoroughly aroused against the Prime Minister because an APC cousin of his had been jailed for publicly criticizing the one-party state. Several SLPP youth leaders in Port Loko feared in October 1965 that the chiefs were already going too far in their persecution of APC members and were simply hardening their peoples' feelings in favour of the APC.

The resistance of major segments of the political elite towards the one-party state was certainly a significant factor in the Prime Minister's failure to achieve it. Probably more important than the resistance of any single elite group was the popular distrust of it at the level of the ordinary peasant or worker. A number of observers had noted widespread anger among the peasants in their areas when Local Court Presidents ceased to be elected and were instead appointed by the Prime Minister; the people realized that their power to choose these officials had been taken away from them. Several MPs and other party workers, in the SLPP as well as in the APC, remarked on popular fears that, if a one-party state were introduced, they would no longer be able to elect whom they chose as MPs. The great swing to the APC in the north in the 1966 District Council elections was to some degree attributable to the SLPP's identification with the one-party state, which could be variously identified with dominance by Mendes, by chiefs, or simply by any unpopular regime the people wished to be able to throw off. But the one-party state was also unpopular in the south. One Mende MP claimed in June 1966 that it had ceased to be a tribal question "now that the Temnes know the Mendes are also opposed to it." Many ordinary voters, and not just in the north, were fully aware that competition at election time gave them some leverage against their chiefs and, more generally, that it gave them a chance to put pressure on their representatives to provide amenities for *them* such as roads, schools, and dispensaries. If the politicians were all to combine into a single party and if there were to be no further elections,

162 / *We Yone*, July 31, 1965. It also had opened an office in Port Loko, but this was padlocked by order of the Chiefdom Council shortly after it was opened.

it would be much easier for the political elite to divide all of the sweets of office among themselves, leaving only the crumbs to the ordinary people. I think it is significant that the APC leaders were equivocal on the one-party-state question until they had had a chance to learn that there was no prospect of persuading their people that it would be desirable. When they found how unpopular the idea was, they jumped on the bandwagon; but they did not create the climate of opinion against the one-party state. It was already there. Most people had no wish to entrust unchecked power to their chiefs, as had happened before the 1955-56 riots.

We can conclude that the drive for a one-party state foundered on a combination of factors. Most important, relatively few people, either among the political elite or at the grass roots, could see much benefit in it for them-selves. SLPP members, though they might sympathize with the idea in theory, were in several cases put off the idea by the fact that it would consolidate the power of a leader whom they did not fully accept; the same was true of the chiefs. Certain elites, notably among the Creoles, found the idea unat-tractive in principle, while the ordinary people often saw it as a means by which the elite could forget their peoples' interests and fatten themselves.

Even widespread resistance would not have availed against a well-organ-ized party machine under the control of a determined leader. But the SLPP did not have a well-organized machine, and certainly not one that could be controlled by any single leader. Its members were bound together essentially as a coalition of local power brokers, and there was little leverage the leader could exert to make them respond to his wishes. If the SLPP's local leaders could see no benefits in the one-party state for themselves, they were not going to help the leader bring it about. Nor could he, in Sierra Leone, by-pass the party and work through the government machine, because the values of the top men in this system were opposed, for the most part, to the one-party idea. The existence of an organized alternative, the APC, helped strengthen these various levels of resistance, because it enabled resisters to maintain the threat that they might unite in opposition to the Prime Minister. This combination was simply too strong for the Prime Minister and his supporters, despite his rather free use of bribery and intimidation.

13

1966-67: the fall of Sir Albert Margai

Even though Sir Albert ceased to refer to the one-party state after the 1966 District Council elections, few people believed he had abandoned the goal of entrenching himself permanently in office. His actions over the next few months confirmed the suspicions of his critics, although they fell far short of a completely ruthless drive to consolidate his position and destroy all opposition.

Almost at the same time as he began backtracking on the one-party state in June 1966, Sir Albert undertook a new campaign to change Sierra Leone to a republic. Here he found himself stalled by the "constitutional strait-jacket" of the Independence constitution, which provided that Sierra Leone's monarchical form of government could only be changed by the passing of the republic bill by a two-thirds majority, then dissolving the House of Representatives and holding an election, then passing the bill again. He could not, in short, create any kind of republic, presidential or parliamentary, without holding a general election. In any case, a further entrenched clause provided that the House should stand dissolved five years after its election, which meant a general election must take place by mid-1967. The 1967 election was clearly the event which would make or break Sir Albert.

From July 1966 onward, rumours abounded about the forthcoming republic bill, which was expected to provide for a Presidential republic with a great concentration of power in the hands of the President.[1] The House was kept sitting until early August, well beyond its normal time of adjournment, in anticipation of the bill, but no bill appeared. The reason, it was alleged, was a deep split in the Cabinet over the scope of powers to be given to the President, as well as over the question of whether certain sections should be

1 / See Ibrahim Taqi in *We Yone,* July 9, 1966.

entrenched.[2] The House finally adjourned with no inkling of the kind of bill it would be asked to approve.

The draft bill finally emerged just before Christmas.[3] Falling far short of the drastic changes predicted, it retained the basic parliamentary structure, with only minor incremental changes aimed at reducing checks on the Prime Minister's power. The Governor-General became a President (the bill stipulated that the incumbent, Sir Henry Lightfoot-Boston, become the first President), who would be appointed by, and removable by, the Cabinet. This provision came under fire as taking from the President any source of power independent of the Prime Minister[4] but, while it clearly underlined his dependence on the government of the day, this was not really such a great change from the existing situation in which the Queen acted on the advice of the Sierra Leone government.[5] Appeals to the Privy Council would be abolished, and the Chief Justice, who became Head of the Judiciary, would be appointed by (and again removable by) the President acting on the advice of the Prime Minister. All other judges, however, could be removed only by a two-thirds majority of Parliament, for inability to act or for misbehaviour. A number of changes were made in the Bill of Rights, the net effect of which was to curtail the protection provided by these clauses for opponents of the government.[6] The protection of an intervening election before any amendment of the entrenched clauses, including the Bill of Rights and the position of the judiciary, was retained.

The main effect of the bill's provisions was to make overt powers which already lay covertly in the Prime Minister's hands. Some changes, notably his enhanced control over the President and the Chief Justice, did strengthen his hand, but he already possessed sweeping powers to appoint and remove individuals from office, and the Bill of Rights already contained enough qualifications to make the effectiveness of its protection extremely doubtful.[7]

2 / See R. Sarif Easmon, "Breakers Ahead," *We Yone,* July 2, 1966.

3 / *Sierra Leone Gazette,* xcvii, 100 (December 22, 1966).

4 / See, for example, Livesey Luke's criticisms, *Daily Mail,* January 13, 1967; also Memorandum from the 1963 Committee, Fourah Bay College, in *Unity,* January 19, 1967.

5 / There were, admittedly, some situations in which the far greater speed of removal possible under the republic bill would be critical; for example, if after an election the President were to decide to choose a new Prime Minister, the Cabinet could forestall him by removing him first. However, if things were to reach such a state, it was unlikely that considerations of legality would prevail in any case, as the aftermath of the 1967 election was to suggest.

6 / These proposed alternatives were criticized in detail by a meeting of the Departments of Law and Political Science at Fourah Bay College. "The Proposed Republican Constitution for Sierra Leone," January 14, 1967 (mimeo.).

7 / Most of the prohibitions on government acts in the existing constitution allowed the government to act in the interest of "public safety, public order, [or] public morality" and to act in any way that was "reasonably justifiable in a democratic society."

While the furore over the provisions of the republic bill was still going on, Sir Albert took one step intended to allay fears about his intentions. On February 8, 1967, he told the House of Representatives that his proposals for a "democratic one-party system" had been dropped, and the committee to examine them abolished.[8] Unfortunately for Sir Albert, his announcement was too late; by that time scarcely anyone believed the one-party state would be a live issue until after the 1967 election. Furthermore, his intentions had just been rendered much more suspect by a number of actions clearly aimed at strengthening his position.

The most ominous of these actions was the appointment in late January of Gershon Collier, the Prime Minister's closest confidante since the PNP days, as Acting Chief Justice in place of C. O. E. Cole, who had been in the Prime Minister's bad graces ever since he had granted an injunction to the APC against the one-party-state committee in June 1966. Mr Justice Cole took over Mr Collier's posts as Ambassador to the United States and United Nations Permanent Representative. Collier's appointment as Acting Chief Justice was greeted with dismay, and members of the Bar Association undertook proceedings to challenge the legality of the appointment. The Prime Minister's response was to appoint Collier to the substantive post of Chief Justice, an action beyond any legal challenge but politically a most unwise act of defiance. His determination to make this appointment made it apparent that the judiciary was to be reshaped into a form more sympathetic to Sir Albert's designs.

At the same time a series of tough new amendments to the Electoral Provisions Act were passed by the House. One provided that instead of a single Supreme Court judge hearing election petitions, a special "election court" consisting of two judges would henceforth sit.[9] One of these judges would almost certainly be the new Chief Justice. A further provision raised the election deposit from Le 200 to Le 500, and raised the proportion of the total vote required for a candidate to save his deposit from one-tenth to one-quarter.[10] This provision could be expected to restrict the number of Independents running against the official SLPP candidates as well as hamper the APC. A third new provision required candidates to "attend or make themselves readily available at the office of the Returning Officer between the hours of nine o'clock in the forenoon and five o'clock in the afternoon of the last day appointed for the receipt of nominations."[11] The effect of this provision was to tie down the APC's key organizers, most of whom were running as candidates, in their own constituencies, instead of leaving them free to

8 / See *Daily Mail*, February 9, 1967.

9 / The Electoral Provisions (Amendment) Act, 1967, Section 1.

10 / *Ibid.*, Section 4. The Leone (Le), the new Sierra Leone currency introduced in 1964, was valued at 10 shillings; thus Le 2 = £1.

11 / *Ibid.*, Section 5.

help candidates elsewhere who were less forceful or less knowledgeable about nomination procedures.

The officials in charge of the election had already been instructed at two secret meetings to do everything possible within legal limits to aid in the return of SLPP candidates. Nomination papers of APC and Independent candidates were to be closely scrutinized for technical errors, and the lists of Presiding Officers at the polls were to be vetted by the SLPP candidates.[12] Some officials apparently went further than this, and supplied extra ballots to SLPP candidates and Paramount Chiefs, although this was not widespread and appears to have been on too small a scale to significantly affect the outcome of any constituency results.[13]

The Elections Commission meanwhile had been "purified" under the guidance of the Chief Elections Officer, a kinsman of Sir Albert's. A number of Creoles whose political loyalty to the SLPP was doubtful were replaced by Mendes.[14] In compiling the voting registers, the Commission's employees were alleged to have omitted some Limbas and other voters who could be assumed to be pro-APC, but an APC spokesman acknowledged that, while this reduced their majority, it did not cost the party any seats. As in the case of the ballot box stuffing, the irregularities in registering voters were not on a large enough scale to alter appreciably the outcome of the election in most constituencies.

The government also undertook a very limited redistribution of seats in the House of Representatives. According to the 1963 Census, all the northern districts should have received additional seats: three in Port Loko, two in Bombali, and one each in Kambia, Koinadugu, and Tonkolili. Several other districts should have lost seats: Bo and Bonthe each should have lost two, as should Freetown, while the Western Rural Area should have been cut back by four. However, the government was more selective in its redistribution. No district lost any seats. The total number of ordinary members' seats was raised from 62 to 66, with one additional seat being awarded to each of Port

12 / See *Report of the Dove-Edwin Commission of Inquiry into the Conduct of the 1967 General Election* [Dove-Edwin Report], p. 7; also testimony of G. L. V. Williams before the Commission, in *Daily Mail*, June 21, 1967, of D. K. Jenkins, *ibid.*, June 22, of Abdul Karim, *ibid.*, June 23, of A. P. Conteh, *ibid.*, July 6.

13 / The largest operation exposed by the Dove-Edwin Commission was in Port Loko South-West, where the Paramount Chief testified he received 1,000 ballot papers two days before the election from the SLPP candidate. See *Daily Mail*, July 15, 1967. The APC candidate won by a majority of 5,915 votes. In other cases, the illicit extra ballots came to light when the persons receiving them turned them over to the APC, which suggests the possibility that some recipients may simply have cast them in the APC boxes. The SLPP candidate in Port Loko South-West said the District Officer told him it was "impossible" to give him 2,000 extra ballots because he [the DO] had other constituencies to take care of.

14 / See testimony of M. G. Foh, Chief Elections Officer, before the Percy Davies Commission. *Daily Mail*, June 28, 1967.

Loko, Koinadugu (the northern district least penetrated by the APC), Kono, and Kenema (which on a population basis had no claim to an additional seat).[15] This redistribution would hardly produce any electoral advantage for the SLPP; the most that could be said for it was that it would serve to dampen northern criticisms that their area was being deprived of its deserved increase in representation.

The APC was already severely handicapped in its attempts to reach the electorate by the Public Order Act of 1965 and a 1966 amendment to it. Under the 1965 Act, each Paramount Chief had absolute discretion to allow or forbid any meeting of twelve or more persons within his chiefdom.[16] An amendment to the act in 1966 gave the Prime Minister power to proclaim for a three-month period the right of police officers to disperse any meeting and arrest without warrant any person refusing to disperse or threatening a breach of the peace.[17] Such provisions could be used to prevent any overt activity by the opposition party.

In January 1967 the government served a sharp warning to the northern Paramount Chiefs, some of whom were becoming apprehensive about their positions if they failed to swing over to the APC. The SLPP member of Koinadugu North, A. H. Kande, held a meeting in the chiefdom of his father-in-law, Paramount Chief Gbwaru Mansaray. As a result of the meeting an argument arose between the two men, the upshot of which was a summons to the chief to attend the District Officer's headquarters. Several hundred of the chief's people accompanied him, and when the District Officer insisted on seeing the chief alone, the people began to stone the office. The government promptly suspended the chief, and a few weeks later deposed and banished him. It was generally believed that the chief had been pro-APC and that his deposition was to be an object lesson for any other chiefs who might be tempted to resist the government in any way.

On February 8, just a few hours after announcing that the one-party-state idea was being dropped for good, the Prime Minister startled the nation with a broadcast claiming a plot had been uncovered to assassinate himself, the Force Commander, Brig. Lansana, and several Ministers and senior civil servants. The plotters, he alleged, were military personnel incited by pronouncements made by Siaka Stevens, Dr Sarif Easmon, and other leaders of opposition to his rule. They had planned to establish an advisory committee including Stevens, Dr Easmon, and Dr Davidson Nicol, the Principal of Fourah Bay College.[18]

15 / See *Gazette*, February 13, 1967, for details of constituencies.
16 / Section 24. In practice, many chiefs already exercised this power, at least against the APC. The new act gave them stronger legal grounds for this action, and as well extended the Chief's authority to cover electoral activity.
17 / The Public Order (Amendment) Act, 1966, Section 2.
18 / See *Daily Mail*, February 9, 1967, for text of PM's broadcast.

The next day it was learned that seven senior army officers, including the Deputy Commander, Col. John Bangura, had been detained. Whether there was actually a plot or not may never be known, but since Bangura was the only northerner among the top half-dozen army officers, his removal served to eliminate a potential source of resistance to the army's being used to keep Sir Albert in power.

With the changes in the Electoral Provisions Act, the pressing of civil servants and the Electoral Commission into the cause of the SLPP, the appointment of a sympathetic Chief Justice, and the various curbs on the APC's freedom of action, the Prime Minister had made considerable progress towards strengthening his position. But he refused to take some further steps which probably would have improved his position still more. Most important of all, he refused to follow the urging of extremists in his Cabinet who tried to induce him to bring in a Preventive Detention Act; he seems to have been motivated here at least as much by a feeling that this was contrary to the "rule of law" as to any calculation that it might backfire against him. He also was careful, in his preparations for the election, to stay strictly within the law; he did not, for example, simply provide for an extra half-million ballots to ensure the SLPP candidates of a "majority." Probably he was restrained by the knowledge that the opposition to him within his own party and within the civil service was formidable enough to sabotage any drastic attempts at rigging. There seems to be a possibility that he was genuinely not willing to go to the limit in search of power. A further factor appears to have been over-confidence engendered by some of his supporters who gave him the impression that, despite the 1966 District Council elections, he and the SLPP were still generally popular.

THE 1967 ELECTION: NOMINATIONS AND CAMPAIGN

On February 16, the Prime Minister announced that the elections for ordinary members would be held on March 17 and for Paramount Chiefs on March 21.[19] In retrospect, holding the Paramount Chiefs' election last appears to have been one more in a series of miscalculations by Sir Albert. While in 1962 the chiefs did not declare their support for the SLPP until after the ordinary members' results were in, there is not much doubt that most could have been forced to do so in 1967, which would have given the SLPP a further cushion of seats in determining who had a majority. But the fact that they were elected later gave the Governor-General an opportunity to exclude them from his calculations in deciding whom to call to form the government. This consideration does not seem to have occurred to Sir Albert; he was apparently confident of winning a popular majority, although his confidence was not shared by all SLPP members.

19 / *Daily Mail*, February 17, 1967.

The SLPP had hoped to win the election at its most easily controlled point, the nominations of candidates, by securing a large number of unopposed returns. The first unfavourable omen for the government appeared at the close of nominations on February 27, when it became apparent that only six SLPP ordinary members and one Paramount Chief were returned unopposed. Only three of these were from constituencies that would probably have gone to the APC.[20] Independents stood in 37 of the 60 contested seats, including 25 of 26 in Mendeland,[21] while the APC surprised all observers by running a total of 52 candidates, including 17 in Mendeland.[22] The APC's feat was little short of astonishing in view of the grounds on which returning officers disqualified them. One was rejected for leaving off the "e" in the name of the "Bonthe South" constituency; two others for signing the nomination papers with their middle names, when these were not in the register; while yet another for *not* including his middle name, which was in the register.[23] The APC used two methods of offsetting this bias among returning officers; they sent a number of lawyers to the various district headquarters on nomination day, and assembled large and menacing crowds outside the headquarters. In at least one constituency, threats by the APC's supporters that they would kill the Returning Officer if he refused to accept their candidate's nomination persuaded that official to allow a nomination to stand. There is also a strong probability that some returning officers were secretly glad to be intimidated into doing their duty fairly. Though the balance of advantage lay with the SLPP, the APC was far from defenceless, since it could muster up overwhelming popular support in the north and Freetown.

The SLPP's allocation of party symbols revealed some deep rifts between pro- and anti-Albert forces. In 1962, all but 2 of the 32 sitting SLPP members were re-nominated as the official party candidates for their constituencies. In 1967, no less than 14 of the 40 sitting SLPP members failed to receive the party nomination. Some of these were dropped by their local selection committees for their failure to work effectively on behalf of the constituency; some, notably Kutubu Kai-Samba and L. A. M. Brewah, did not want the SLPP symbol, whereas several were denied the symbol because the Prime Minister wanted men more closely associated with him. Prince Williams in

20 / These were Dr Hadj Conteh, Tonkolili East; Sahr Kpakima, Kono East; and R. G. O. King, Koya. The others returned unopposed were Sir Albert, his brother Sam Margai, and Maigore Kallon. Conteh and King, it should be added, were returned unopposed only after they had appealed their opponents' nominations to the Electoral Commission.

21 / The Southern Province plus Kailahun and Kenema districts.

22 / It actually had candidates for 61 seats, but 9 of these were unable to get the returning officers to accept their nominations.

23 / See testimony of Dr S. H. Pratt before the Dove-Edwin Commission, *Daily Mail,* July 11, 1967.

Bo town, Mana Kpaka in Pujehun, Y. D. Sesay in Bombali, and S. Mosere in Bo North, as well as Brewah and Kai-Samba, were all opposed by men supposed to be close to Albert Margai. Several of the candidates Albert endorsed were weak men with no local standing. This was particularly noticeable in the north, where no less than five SLPP candidates in Bombali and Tonkolili were Fula and Mandingo "strangers." It appeared that Albert was as anxious to purge his parliamentary party of critics as he was to provide the SLPP with the strongest candidate for every seat.

The APC, for its part, still remained predominantly a "northern man's party," though it did succeed in broadening its selection of candidates. In the Western Area, seven of its eleven candidates were Creoles, including two opportunistic converts to the party, Solomon Pratt and Cyril Rogers-Wright. Pratt had left the post of General Manager of the Sierra Leone Railway a year earlier to pursue his candidacy as an Independent in Mountain constituency against an incumbent Minister. The APC now gave him their party symbol on the grounds that he was a more likely winner than their own long-time party stalwart who had been cultivating the constituency for two years. In Wilberforce, the APC again saw Rogers-Wright as more likely to win than any of their own more loyal but less brilliant possibilities, and on nomination day decided to give him their symbol, despite widespread revulsion in the party.

In Kono, the DPC radicals produced four native-born candidates, though two of them were "young men" of no local standing. Their appeal, as had been true of the party since its inception, was to the poorer, lower-status Konos and to "strangers"; few local "big men" supported them, though it was felt that Chief Mbriwa was secretly on their side. The one area where the APC had trouble finding "sons of the soil" as candidates was in Mendeland. Out of their 17 candidates in this area only 5 were Mende, although 2 others were of other southern tribes.

The APC also tried to win over some of the anti-Albert SLPP supporters. It offered its symbol in Freetown East II to Sanusi Mustapha, but he declined it on the grounds that to accept after all his years with the SLPP would appear too opportunistic.[24] They did reach an "understanding" with Brewah and Frank Anthony that these men would support Stevens in preference to Sir Albert, but were unable to come to terms with Kai-Samba. Beyond this, however, the APC relied largely on its tried and true supporters. All sitting MPs received the party symbol, and the other APC candidates in the north and Freetown were men who had proved themselves in local government. The APC also had far more success in restraining disappointed members from running as Independents than had the SLPP; only four APC members ran against the party's official candidates.

24 / An element of fear may also have entered. One APC man claims Mustapha was afraid Albert would lock him up for life if he sided with the APC.

While the SLPP enjoyed the advantages of being the party in power, including money and police support, the APC's organization and numerous sympathizers within the administration enabled it to compete effectively. The SLPP leaders had ample access to funds, largely extracted from Lebanese and European businessmen, though a large proportion seems to have gone to finance rivalries within the party. Thus Ibrahim Taqi charged that three expatriates – a Lebanese, an Israeli, and an American – were the leading supporters of "an SLPP election fund" and that part of this fund was being used to support Sir Albert's men against two SLPP Ministers.[25] The sums involved were substantial. A Lebanese businessman in Kono claimed that in late 1966 the Lebanese community gave Le 50,000 to Sir Albert,[26] and R. G. O. King claimed he received between Le 24,000 and Le 26,000 in "political gifts" from overseas commercial firms.[27] But again, it is not clear how much of this money was spread beyond the recipients themselves.

The government candidates also enjoyed other advantages, though the usefulness of these was sometimes diluted. In Bonthe North, the SLPP candidate was able to "persuade" launch owners not to take an influential and pro-APC rival, Dr S. H. Pratt, to the District Office in Bonthe on nomination day. This attempt to prevent Dr Pratt's nomination was foiled when an expatriate official of Sherbro Minerals offered Dr Pratt the use of his private launch. The expatriate was deported a few weeks later.[28] In Bo District, the SLPP began using thugs to break up APC meetings. The APC went to the police, whose top man in Bo was an APC sympathizer. The police began to give protection to the APC meetings. Then the government ordered the police to give protection only at meetings authorized by the District Officer, and the District Officer withheld authorization from all APC meetings. Finally, the APC organized its own squad of tough young men for protection, after which there was no more trouble.

More traditional methods of winning support were also employed by both sides. A witness in an election petition against Paramount Chief Dudu Bona of Kono testified that Poro society members of his Tribal Authority were sworn in the Poro bush on the flesh of a cow to vote for the chief against his rival, Chief Tamba Mbriwa.[29] A similar "swearing" ceremony was re-

---

25 / *We Yone*, January 21, 1967. This charge was later confirmed in an interview with one of the parties involved.

26 / Testimony of Ahmed Darwish Fawaz before Forster Commission, *Daily Mail*, September 29, 1967.

27 / Testimony of R. G. O. King before Forster Commission, *Daily Mail*, June 3, 1967.

28 / Testimony of Dr Pratt and Sam Margai before Dove-Edwin Commission, *Daily Mail*, July 11 and August 1, 1967. Dr Pratt's nomination was later rejected because two of his nominators had used their middle names in signing, when these were not on the register.

29 / See *Unity*, July 13, 1968.

ported in Kambia on behalf of Chief Yumkella.[30] An independent candidate in Kenema told the Dove-Edwin Commission that a woman official of the SLPP had called all Bundu society women into the Bundu bush and told them to vote for the SLPP candidate.[31] The APC apparently also made use of "swears" to bring Limbas in some areas solidly behind them, although this hardly seems to have been necessary,[32] in view of the Limbas' strong attachment to the APC.

As the campaign wore on, more dangerous emotions came to the surface. The Prime Minister himself allegedly did his part in stirring up these emotions, charging that a "Temne-Creole axis" which constituted the APC would "cut the Mende man's throat" if it came to power. One Town Chief claimed Sir Albert had told a meeting in Moyamba district that all who wanted to vote for the APC must go to the north, the land of the Temnes.[33] His supporters echoed these sentiments. One SLPP woman in Kenema told a Mende meeting that Independents had taken an oath in the north to support the APC.[34] The APC also used occasional appeals to northern solidarity and against "Mende dominance," but for the most part concentrated its fire on the personal corruption of Sir Albert and his Ministers. However, it did whip up considerable antipathy in Freetown and the north against the Fulas, who leaned heavily toward the SLPP, and whom the APC alleged were mainly Guineans not entitled to vote in Sierra Leone elections. Numerous cases of Fulas being attacked were reported.

In such a tense campaign, with tribal emotions stirred, and the fate of the country's political system so clearly at stake, it was not surprising that violence began to erupt. In Freetown, where the APC was dominant, several SLPP meetings were attacked,[35] while in the south, APC supporters were attacked by mobs, and in one case a truckful of soldiers displaying a red military symbol were fired on by SLPP supporters who thought they were an APC band.[36] On March 3 the government declared a state of emergency in the Western Area, empowering the police to disperse any meeting likely to lead to a breach of the peace. A similar state of emergency had already been proclaimed in Kono two days earlier, and two days before the election the Prime Minister proclaimed it for all other districts except Pujehun.

30 / See *Daily Mail*, July 15, 1968.

31 / Testimony of E. J. Quee Nyagua before Dove-Edwin Commission, *Daily Mail*, July 28, 1967.

32 / I was told this by a Yalunka APC supporter, but was unable to confirm it with any Limbas.

33 / Testimony of Momodu Kamara before Dove-Edwin Commission, *Daily Mail*, July 18, 1967.

34 / Testimony of E. J. Quee Nyagua, *Daily Mail*, July 28, 1967.

35 / See *Unity*, February 27 and 28, 1967.

36 / See *Report of the Dove-Edwin Commission*, pp. 12–13.

Under these controls, March 17 passed without any major outbreaks. There were numerous individual instances of intimidation, notably by southern Paramount Chiefs against suspected APC sympathizers, and by APC supporters against Fulas in Freetown, but there were no mass riots or disturbances. People cast their ballots and then awaited the results in a state of alert watchfulness.

THE 1967 ELECTION: THE PEOPLE SPEAK

As the results of the ordinary members' elections came in it became clear that the SLPP was finally paying the price of Albert Margai's seeking after personal wealth and power, and of its lack of an effectively centralized party organization. Although there were numerous instances of local intimidation and ballot-box stuffing, the SLPP leaders were not able to organize election frauds on a scale sufficient to offset the vastly superior organization and dedication of their opponents.

The most striking feature of the election results was the tremendous upsurge of support for the APC since 1962, and even since the District Council elections of 1966. Table 13: 1 shows the extent of this increase.

TABLE 13:1
Popular vote by party (1962 and 1967)

	1962		1967	
	No. votes	%	No. votes	%
SLPP	230,118	34.7	231,567	35.8
APC[a]	149,172	22.4	286,585	44.3
Inds.	282,724	42.6	129,429	20.0

a/Includes SLPIM in 1962, DPC in 1967.

As long as the Independents could be considered basically SLPP, this result was far from an APC landslide, but in view of the handicaps under which it operated it was a remarkable achievement.

However, these gross figures concealed a sharp regional cleavage in the country. The APC won only 28,033 votes, or less than a tenth of its total, in Mendeland, and captured only 16 per cent of the total vote there.[37] In the Northern Province and Western Area, by contrast, it captured just under three-quarters of the votes officially recorded. The SLPP, for its part, while holding firm in Mende country, could muster barely a quarter of the total votes in the north and the Western Area. In terms of seats, the split was even more pronounced. The SLPP, apart from its unopposed returns, was almost

37 / And this total includes 8,189 votes in Moyamba West, where there were more than enough Temnes present to account for this result.

wiped out outside Mende country; it won one seat out of the 19 it contested in the north, none of 11 in the Western Area, and 2 of the 4 in Kono. In Mende country, on the other hand, its official candidates won 18 of 25, with all but one of the remaining 7 being won by Independents who had been closely associated with the SLPP. The SLPP members elected (including the 6 unopposed) comprised 19 Mendes, 3 from other southern tribes, and only 6 non-southerners, including 3 from Kono.

The APC managed to put together a more broadly based group. It captured, as expected, all the contested seats in the Northern Province except Koinadugu North, and swept all 11 contested Western Area seats. Its DPC affiliates carried 2 of the 4 contested Kono seats, while a prestigious ex-UPP member of Parliament, Valecius Neale-Caulker, won the Moyamba North seat for its only victory in the south. Its 32-man parliamentary group comprised 15 Temnes, 7 from other northern tribes, 7 Creoles, 2 Konos, and one Sherbro, which could be considered representative of all the country except Mendeland. In terms of popular support also, it appeared to be a coalition of all northern tribes plus Creoles and a slight majority of the Kono electorate. In the north, its percentage of the popular vote ranged from a high of 93 per cent in Tonkolili to a low of 53 per cent in Koinadugu. In Freetown it won 73 per cent of the votes, and in the Rural Area 67 per cent; Freetown's population was roughly three-quarters northerners and Creoles, and in the Rural Area these groups comprised about 70 per cent of the population. The distribution of its vote in the south suggested it had very little success in attracting Mende support; only two constituencies, Bo North and Kailahun West, gave the APC more votes than could be readily accounted for by the northerners present.[38]

The people of Sierra Leone, however, were not able to hear these results. The Electoral Commission, working in concert with the Sierra Leone Broadcasting Service and the government-owned *Daily Mail*, let the results out only gradually, taking care to always keep the SLPP in the lead. The election took place on a Friday; by Sunday night the SLBS was announcing party standings as SLPP 31 seats, APC 28, and Independent 2. Five results had not yet been

38 / See page 159, n. 61 for a methodological explanation of the assumptions I have made in calculating relationships between northerners present and APC votes cast. I have suggested that if only members of the five "APC tribes" (Temne, Limba, Loko, Susu, and Mandingo) supported them, APC votes should not exceed 35 per cent of the number of individuals of those tribes recorded by the 1963 Census. In fact, only Bo North with 860 APC votes and 1,477 northerners present (58 per cent), and Kailahun West, with 1,273 APC votes and 2,773 northerners present (46 per cent) were above this proportion. The candidate in Bo North, it should be added, was a Mende. In Kailahun West, there were an additional 2,812 persons of other pro-APC tribes (Yalunka, Koranko, Kono, and Creole) present, and these may account for the APC support. While aggregate figures such as these cannot prove that the APC's support was essentially from northerners and Creoles, they are certainly suggestive.

announced: Kailahun West (which the SLPP was to win), Moyamba West, Port Loko East, Koinadugu Central, and Koinadugu Southeast (all of which fell to the APC). The Paramount Chiefs' elections were to be held on Tuesday, but constitutionally it was uncertain whether they should be considered, since they customarily sided with whoever formed the government, rather than being elected on a commitment to one party or the other.

On Monday the Governor-General proposed, in the light of what he regarded as a tribal pattern of voting which could do serious harm to the country, that the APC and SLPP form a coalition. Stevens, after consulting the APC MPS, rejected this proposal on the grounds that it would be "a betrayal of the electorate and political suicide," and pointed out that the APC had won a clear majority of the *contested* seats, and had received support in nearly all parts of the country.[39] Meanwhile great crowds of APC supporters were chanting "No More Albert, No More Margai, No More Albert Over Me" and "We Want Freedom, Act Now" as they paraded by the State House along the main street.[40] It was probably this massive demonstration that produced a slight note of resignation in the SLPP's party newspaper, *Unity*:

After having been in office for more than a decade during which – never mind what they say – we have provided this country with an example of good government, the SLPP is not afraid to go into opposition because it is confident of setting another better example for history.

But any decision about the future of the party has to be determined on the election results; and unless the results say otherwise, we are not going to be pushed out of office by political hysteria.[41]

The day after the Governor-General proposed a coalition government, four candidates elected as Independents sent a letter to him stating that they were willing to support either party, but that a condition of their supporting the SLPP would be the replacement of Albert Margai as leader.[42] Since two of these candidates had been included in the officially announced totals of SLPP supporters, this showed clearly that Stevens could command the support of 36 ordinary members, whereas Sir Albert could claim the support of only 30.[43] With this evidence at hand, and Stevens' rejection of any coalition, the

39 / See *Think*, Special Election Number, March 21, 1967, for an account of the meeting between the Governor-General, Stevens, and Sir Albert, and for the text of Stevens' letter to the Governor-General.

40 / See *ibid.*; also *Unity*, March 20, 1967.

41 / *Unity*, March 20, 1967.

42 / Letter by Kutubu Kai-Samba, L. A. M. Brewah, Prince Williams, and J. B. Francis to the Governor-General, March 21, 1967. Printed in *Dove-Edwin Report*, Annex E, p. 24. See also testimony of L. A. M. Brewah, *Daily Mail*, June 24, 1967.

43 / One further Independent, Frank Anthony, had written the Electoral Commission denying that he had declared for the SLPP. See testimony before Dove-Edwin Commission, *Daily Mail*, June 24, 1967.

Governor-General took the only correct course and on Tuesday morning summoned Siaka Stevens to the State House and swore him in as Prime Minister.

The Governor-General's action in calling Stevens was subsequently criticized as unconstitutional on the grounds that he was dismissing an incumbent Prime Minister before it was clear that Sir Albert had lost his majority. He should have waited, it was argued, until the results from the Paramount Chiefs' elections were in, since the chiefs were also full members of the House. However, this argument breaks down when we recall that Paramount Chiefs, unlike ordinary members, could be deposed from office by executive action of the Prime Minister; they were in no position to grant or withhold their confidence from an incumbent Prime Minister freely. If the Governor-General were to allow Sir Albert to remain in office until after the Paramount Chief members had been returned, he would be ensuring that an additional twelve members of Parliament would declare their support for Sir Albert. If Stevens were already in office, the chiefs would be obliged to declare their support for him. This position, that the chiefs were "part and parcel of the Government"[44] was one clearly established by custom. In this situation, the only impartial course the Governor-General could follow would be to choose the Prime Minister with no reference to the Paramount Chiefs whatsoever, and given the relative support for the two party leaders among the ordinary members, there can be no doubt that he made the constitutionally correct choice.

While the news that Stevens had been sworn in was spreading by word of mouth and crowds were dancing in the streets, the army abruptly intervened to forestall what would have been the first peaceful transfer of power in West Africa. Troops surrounded State House and informed Stevens that if he tried to leave he would be shot. The Force Commander, Brig. David Lansana, then proclaimed martial law, asserting that no Prime Minister could constitutionally be chosen until all the election results were in.[45] The next day Commissioner of Police William Leigh anounced that the police had "fallen in line" behind the army, but that all orders to the police force would come through him.[46]

The people of Freetown reacted strongly to what they saw as the kidnapping of their Prime Minister. Crowds stoned the police headquarters and set up roadblocks; in trying to clear the streets, riot police and troops killed and wounded a large number of people.[47] The prospect of civil disturbances

44 / Comment of Chief Bai Koblo before Dove-Edwin Commission, *Daily Mail,* July 14, 1967.

45 / *Daily Mail,* March 22, 1967.

46 / See *Unity,* March 23, 1967; also *West Africa,* April 8, 1967, p. 447, which suggests he acquiesced rather reluctantly.

47 / During the period March 21–3, 1967, nine persons were killed by rifle fire, and

involving not only Freetown but also much of the surrounding Northern Province confronted the 1,800 man army and 2,200 man police force, especially if, as appeared to be the case, Lansana was bent on a restoration to office of Sir Albert Margai. Even if the army and police had the ability to cope with widespread uprisings, their willingness to do so was doubtful; while the army officer corps was predominantly Mende, the other ranks, as well as officers and men of the police force, were a mixture of all tribes. Brig. Lansana did try to mollify public opinion by asserting that he had acted as "Custodian of State Security and to maintain law and order,"[48] and by summoning all members of Parliament, including the chiefs,[49] to resolve the crisis.[50]

Who was responsible for this last desperate fling is hard to determine. It appeared that those implicated included Sir Albert and several of the "extremists" in the SLPP, including John Nelson-Williams and Kande Bureh along with some senior civil servants such as John Kallon, S. B. Daramy, Peter Tucker, and Berthan Macauley, who were all present at Brig. Lansana's house during the takeover. Others deeply implicated included the Permanent Secretary of the Ministry of Information, Thomas Decker, who instead of broadcasting the announcement that Stevens had been appointed Prime Minister, went first to the Attorney-General's house and then to Brig. Lansana's house, where Sir Albert and the others were assembled. It is very doubtful if Lansana would have dared proclaim martial law if the SLBS had already broadcast that Stevens was the new Prime Minister. It is possible that Sir Albert himself may not have been as ready as his followers to hang on at all costs; the army officers later claimed that Brig. Lansana was responsible for persuading Sir Albert not to consider a coalition with Stevens – a proposal put forward by the officers. However, the same officers also claimed that Sir Albert had told them, "With you at my back, I will go on the radio and announce myself as Prime Minister."[51] It is probable that Albert himself, with strong encouragement from the "extremists," was responsible for ordering the initial military intervention.

However, events took a new turn on the afternoon of March 23, when a group of officers led by Brig. Lansana's staff officer arrested the Brigadier,

54 treated for gunshot wounds, of whom 42 were admitted to hospital. Reply by Prime Minister Stevens to question in Parliament, July 17, 1968. *Daily Mail,* July 18, 1968.

48 / *Daily Mail,* March 23, 1967.

49 / Ten of whom had just declared for the SLPP. At least three chiefs felt they had declared under duress, and one asserted he was ordered by Sir Albert himself to sign a declaration of support for the SLPP at gunpoint. Chief Bai Koblo before Dove-Edwin Commission, *Daily Mail,* July 18, 1967.

50 / See his statement in the *Daily Mail,* March 23, 1967.

51 / See *West Africa,* April 15, 1967, p. 505, for this account. For accounts of the events leading up to the Brigadier's takeover, see the testimony of various witnesses before the Dove-Edwin Commission, *Daily Mail,* June 28 and 30, July 1 and 3, 1967.

suspended the constitution, and banned all political parties and activities. As "an interim measure" they announced the formation of a National Reformation Council of military and police officers, and a National Advisory Council "of eminent civilians," but pledged that the NRC would "do all in its power to bring about a civilian government in the shortest possible time." However, they accepted Lansana's argument that in "the present tribalistic posture and complete disunity among families and tribes" they had to hold power for the time being.[52]

Reactions to the new regime were mixed. Many up-country people welcomed a return to a situation which resembled the stability of colonial rule, with no divisions caused by party politics. However, offsetting this in the north was the feeling that northerners had been robbed by military intervention of their own long-awaited government, a feeling enhanced by the fact that four of the eight members of the NRC were Mendes. The Creoles, and Freetown people generally, were much more bitterly opposed to the new regime; the intellectual elite, including the Bar Association and the Sierra Leonean staff of Fourah Bay College, were almost unanimous in their demands that civilian rule be restored immediately.[53] The APC leaders declared a boycott of the Civilian Advisory Committee. As a result, the north was represented by a largely discredited collection of SLPP nonentities.

The NRC did take some steps to make itself acceptable. It induced the judges to take an oath of allegiance to the constitution as amended,[54] and it retained senior civil servants in their positions. It hustled Brig. Lansana into diplomatic exile in New York, removed Gershon Collier as Chief Justice, replacing him with the more widely respected Banja Tejan-Sie, and established commissions of enquiry into numerous aspects of corruption under the Margai regime.

Offsetting these popular moves were the drastic curbs it clamped on the press, the austerity budget it introduced, and its failure to make much use of civilian advisers. The press decree was probably the most severe in Africa; it forbade publication of any mention of the SLPP or APC, any defamatory matter concerning the NRC or its individual members, or any statement likely to stir up ill will between different tribes or faiths.[55]

52 / For the text of the broadcast by Major Charles Blake, see *Daily Mail*, March 24, 1967.

53 / For example, see the petition asserting the constitutionality of the Governor-General's action in appointing Stevens, the illegality of Lansana's intervention, and the need for a "speedy return to constitutional and democratic government," submitted by the Sierra Leone Bar Association, April 3, 1967. The Principal of Fourah Bay College, Dr Davidson Nicol, at first consented to serve on the NRC's civilian advisory council, but quickly withdrew as a result of faculty objections.

54 / Viz., giving the NRC full power to issue any decrees it saw fit.

55 / See *Daily Mail*, April 4, 1967; *West Africa*, April 15, 1967, pp. 507–508.

The coming to power of a military regime did not change the basic distribution of forces shaping the Sierra Leone political system. The chiefs still remained the principal channel of government communication to the villages; the bulk of the population still depended on subsistence agriculture for their living. On the other hand, a steadily growing number of socially mobilized individuals continued to load a rising level of demands on the system; school enrolment would grow, roads and transport reach more villages, and more individuals would enter the towns and wage employment. In the immediate future, tribal divisions and a severe financial crisis promised considerable difficulties for the new rulers. It was hard to see the regime's pronouncements that "tribalism is dead" having any real effect in replacing tribal identifications with a national loyalty. The financial crisis meant that in the face of rising expectations, the new regime would have to retrench sharply on its development projects. Such a course would inevitably increase the strain between rulers and people, and lead to increasing repression by a regime which would think it knew what needed to be done, but would encounter increasing resistance in its attempts to obtain the necessary sacrifices.

The military takeover in Sierra Leone was not the inevitable outcome of forces beyond the control of individuals. To a very large extent it was the responsibility of one man, Sir Albert Margai, and the few advisors who encouraged him along the trail towards the one-party state and then to stop his being ousted from office. It need never have happened; even though Sierra Leone might eventually have become more authoritarian as a result of the conflicts between tribes, or between traditionalists and modernizers (and both possibilities, as well as the prospect of a one-party state, would have been increased with an APC government in power), this was by no means a certainty. The lines had not been drawn so firmly that reconciliation between conflicting groups was impossible. The people of Sierra Leone had come very close to operating a democratic political system; it was primarily the manipulations of a few members of the political elite that deprived them of the opportunity to carry it through to the point of removing an unsatisfactory leader.

Conclusions

Conclusions

THE PATTERN OF POLITICS IN SIERRA LEONE

The key features of the Sierra Leone political system from 1951 to 1967 were the continuing dominance of a ruling group which represented a limited stratum of the society, and the reluctance and inability of this ruling group to impose an authoritarian form of rule on the country. Certain evolutionary changes took place during this period, notably the removal of the external constraint of British overrule, the broadening of political participation, and stemming from this, the development of simultaneous class and tribal challenges to the ruling group. However, the ruling group's social composition remained largely unchanged, despite the influx of new social groups into political activity. Throughout the period, the ruling group also remained locally oriented and lacked a strong unifying organization to bind it together or to enforce its values on the rest of society. This helped maintain political competition between differing class, tribal, and local interests, a pattern which we may fairly call pluralist.

These features raise a number of questions. What enabled the ruling group to maintain its dominance as long as it did? How secure was its hold on the society? What factors allowed challenges to the ruling group to persist? How important were the ruling group's own attitudes, and its own organization, in producing this high degree of pluralism? Were the various challenges of a nature that could readily be tolerated?

The individuals who led the SLPP from 1951 until 1967 constituted an elite.[1] Most of them were from, or had close links with, traditional ruling families. This high traditional status was matched by their high status in the

---

1 / In the sense of a group possessing interlocking ties and a common set of norms. See S. F. Nadel, "The Concept of Social Elites," *International Social Science Bulletin,* VIII (1956), 415–17.

"modern" sector of society; most of them had had a fairly high level of schooling, and had worked in occupations of high prestige. The Western-educated men and the Paramount Chiefs formed two occupationally distinct groups within a single elite rather than two separate elites: the Western-educated men maintained such ties to traditional patterns of behaviour as membership in the Poro society, while chiefs elected in the 1950s and 1960s tended to be men who before their election had been employed in the middle or upper levels of the wage economy.[2] The members of the elite developed close personal relations in a variety of ways, particularly in the earlier years when Western education and occupations were sharply restricted; they attended the same schools, met each other in their work, and participated in the same social associations.[3]

Within this elite, a shift in power took place over the years. In 1951, when British officials still held the main instruments of central government control, the electoral process was indirect, and the Western-educated men were few in number, the chiefs as a group were in a stronger position than the Western elite. But in 1954 the power to depose chiefs was gained by African Ministers,[4] and in 1956 direct elections were instituted, enabling the Western elite to bypass the chiefs if they wished and appeal directly to the people. These shifts gave the Western elite control of the central government and with that, the power to force the chiefs to support them and their organization, the SLPP.

But even when the Western-educated men had gained the ascendency, they sought no sweeping changes in Sierra Leone society. The central government was careful not to make any changes in the system of local government which would undermine the chiefs' power. The Western elite as well as the chiefs retained close ties with the land, and with the customs of the people. The competitive electoral system helped ensure that they would not retreat to the capital, and that they would retain their membership in the traditional societies.[5] Furthermore, as individuals who were not complete *parvenus* in the bush, but men of high traditional standing, they had no psychological need to reject the traditional society. They comprised, in short, a highly conservative elite, strongly supporting most of the values of traditional society.

2 / See Little, "Structural Change in the Sierra Leone Protectorate," *Africa*, XXV (1955), for a discussion of this point. A sampling of new chiefs elected from 1962 to 1967 reveals several former traders, two District Council Clerks, and a central government agricultural officer among those elected.

3 / *Ibid.*

4 / The Protectorate (Amendment) Ordinance, 1954.

5 / One MP noted: "We wouldn't elect anyone here who wasn't a member of the Wunde Society." The societies helped reduce the gap between the educated men and their illiterate brothers; one Minister commented, "No matter how many doctorates you have, you are not anybody special when you enter the secret bush."

Two implications of this may be noted. First, while the elite were not likely to encourage social changes, when they did accept the need for a change, they were more likely to be able to persuade the ordinary farmer of its desirability than were the more urbanized Western leaders of other countries. Second, since the chiefs provided a ready-made structure for the organization of the growing electorate, it was fatally easy for the leaders of the SLPP to rely on them for electoral support, rather than build up an autonomous party structure. The chiefs, however, were strongly local in their orientation, and were not interested in encouraging the development of a party organization which might be a rival source of authority.[6] The result was that the party organization at the local level was virtually non-existent. This situation strongly favoured continued domination by the local elite, headed by the chief. With no national organization to back him, a person unacceptable to the dominant local interests would face a difficult and seemingly futile task in contesting for the legislature. But by the same token, an aspiring representative had to cultivate a personal rather than a party appeal to the electorate. Election contests within each constituency were thus largely confined to candidates acceptable to the local elite, appealing to local interests and values.

While the SLPP leaders thus were encouraged to retain reasonably close contacts with the mass of the people, they had no incentive to draw the masses into direct participation in politics, or to try to make sweeping social changes. Even when the franchise was broadened under the encouragement of the British they made no effort to step up party activity, but instead left the chiefs as the principal channel of communication to the grass-roots.

Events in the mid-1950s showed that the chiefs were not especially effective as mediators between the political leaders and the common people. The persistent disturbances in Kono and the Freetown riots of 1955 took place outside the traditional system, and indicated only that the traditional channels for the articulation of demands were irrelevant in such a setting. But the northern riots of 1955–56 showed that even in the predominantly traditional sector of society, the SLPP's channels of communication were dangerously unreceptive to demands contrary to the interests of the traditional rulers. The northern riots marked the first widespread incursion into the political system by persons in the traditional sector but not of the elite. Popular participation became a reality; the question that remained was whether it could be directed into peaceful channels.

The political leaders who made the greatest response to these popular demands, and in the process drew a great number of people from parochial

6 / Such an attitude was not unique to Sierra Leone. Ruth Morgenthau has written of Mali that "the 'chiefs' did not welcome interference from Bamko, not even from PSP agents. They did not want a party structure since locally this could mean sharing power." *Political Parties in French-speaking West Africa*, p. 283.

to participant roles in the political culture, were not the leaders of the SLPP, but those of the opposition parties. Not all the increase in political participation could be attributed to the efforts of political leaders; much of it was a product of the general process of social mobilization, as indicated by the steady growth in the numbers of urban dwellers and wage earners, the spread of communications, and the development of a wide range of associations. But the leaders of opposition parties attempted to draw in these newly available cadres by appealing to both tribal and class antagonisms towards the elite who dominated the SLPP.

Two features marked the succession of challenges to the SLPP ruling elite. The first was the shift in the tribal basis of opposition from the Creoles to the northern tribes. The second was the growing "radicalization" of the opposition as each succeeding opposition group relied less than its predecessor on persons of high traditional status for leadership, and was less concerned with the preservation of traditional institutions. The National Council, the leading opposition group from 1951 to 1955, was an "out" group only on tribal grounds; its leaders were of as high status in Creole society as were the SLPP's within the Protectorate, and it made as little effort to attract mass support. The United Progressive Party, the NC's successor, was still led by Creoles of high status. However, it did try to widen its base of support both among Creoles and up-country by a restrained anti-elite appeal. The Sierra Leone Progressive Independence Movement in Kono, which also arose in 1955 out of tribal dissatisfactions, was led by members of ruling families, but tried to win mass support by attacking the chiefs. In all these cases the basis of dissent was tribal; the leaders shared the high status of the SLPP heads, but the parties sought to compete by drawing in individuals below the level of the elite.

The Peoples National Party which arose in 1958 lacked a tribal basis. Its dissidence was based rather on a desire to speed the pace of social change. Again, its leaders were of high status, but it sought, even more than the previous parties, to gain support from the growing number of mobilized individuals below the level of the elite. In drawing in these individuals the PNP gave them their first taste of political activity, which they were later to put to good use.

The All Peoples Congress, formed in 1960, and its Kono affiliate, the Democratic Peoples Congress, formed in 1965, were "out" groups on both tribal and class grounds. Their leaders had first been drawn into political participation through opposition parties, the PNP and the SLPIM, where most of them had occupied subordinate positions. A definite pattern could be seen here: as the limited gap which separated the PNP and SLPIM leaders from the SLPP was bridged and they were absorbed into the ruling group, the men they had drawn in from lower social strata took up the leadership of opposition movements. These new leaders lacked the connections with the traditional rulers that the old leaders had had; their inclinations were to play up the conflict of interest between the people and their chiefs.

While the "second generation" of opposition parties claimed that class differences were the basis of their conflict with the SLPP, their tribal distinctiveness was a far more crucial factor in their perseverance. Every political party of any significance during the years 1947–67, except the Peoples National Party, had its roots in a tribal cleavage. The earlier cleavage, with the SLPP representing the Protectorate peoples and the National Council and later the UPP founded on Creole support, was too one-sided in terms of numbers to persist once the franchise was widened. But the disaffected Temne and Limba tribesmen who provided the All Peoples Congress with its electoral strength formed as large a voting bloc as the Mendes. They did not control a majority of the seats in Parliament, but they controlled a large enough number to give them a strong bargaining position.

The formal political structure of Sierra Leone encouraged this tribal polarization. In single-member constituencies, the voters (who would normally be tribally homogeneous) could elect the representative who promised to work most strongly for their tribe, or vote for "their" tribal party. A party or candidate would have little to gain by playing down his tribal appeal in any individual constituency. Once the representatives were elected, compromises would have to be made for a government to piece together a parliamentary majority, but these tribal coalitions would not have to be formed until *after* the election. Sierra Leone's weak party leadership and process of bargaining also created a more negative tendency to tribalism. If a dissident region elected members of an opposition party, it would have a less effective voice in the government to press for its share of benefits. If its share of benefits vis-à-vis the other regions declined, its people would probably become more disaffected and even more strongly aligned with the opposition, at least if they formed a large enough group to give hope of gaining power in this way. This process of progressive polarization took place in the north throughout the 1960s and gradually made the APC a more and more tribal and less and less radical party.

The "tribal" discontent which arose among Temnes, Limbas, and other northern tribes was largely a by-product of social mobilization. These areas had been backward long before the APC appeared in 1960.[7] Their discontent arose, strictly speaking, from their becoming aware of their backwardness, an awareness brought about by the spread of information through the migrations of diamond miners, the opening up of new roads and new jobs, and the growth of schooling opportunities and towns. The growth of "tribalism," of

7 / See above, pp. 25–26. Most of the cash crops in Sierra Leone in the colonial period had come from the south and east.

the common identity of all Temnes as against the rest of the world, occurred not in the remote villages but among the transitional individuals who had been drawn part-way into the modern world.[8] That this tribal consciousness appeared at all could be attributed to the fact that some change had occurred in the north; that it took the form of opposition to the ruling group could be said to stem from the belief that the changes taking place seemed to be of lesser magnitude and less beneficial than those in the south. This discontent over the position of northerners, while not fomented as assiduously as popular discontent against the chiefs, was a crucial ingredient in the APC's electoral appeal.

The pattern of opposition, then, was a steady movement from quarrels within a highly restricted political class to attempts by leaders of "commoner" background to draw in all commoners against their traditional rulers, and at the same time a shift from the opposition of a small, highly developed tribal minority to numerically substantial but relatively backward tribal groups. This evolution of opposition movements to the ruling group tremendously increased the extent of popular participation in the political system, both by extending it downward to lower-status groups and by extending it horizontally to major tribes.

Indirectly, the SLPP was responsible for this increase in political participation. One factor in leading opposition parties like the UPP, PNP, and SLPIM to appeal directly to the people was the fact that the SLPP had pre-empted for its own use the traditional structure of chiefly authority. Without the development of a universal franchise, these direct appeals would not of course have been possible; but since the extension of the franchise was an inevitable feature of the decolonization process, we can say that lawful opposition parties had no choice but to go directly to the people and thus to widen political participation. This widening of participation was the major direct contribution of the political system to modernization.

The nature of the SLPP made it easier for its leaders to cope with certain types of challenges than with others. As a loose coalition of leaders primarily interested in preserving the existing social system and bound together basically by the ties of individual self-interest, it was able and willing to reconcile any groups whose demands could be met within the existing political framework. Creole, Kono, and Temne tribal movements, to the extent that they could be satisfied with an increased share of place and pelf within the existing system, were to be accepted as legitimate expressions of grievances, and

8 / Among the earlier manifestations of Temne tribal feeling were the creation of Temne young men's associations and the strengthening of the position of tribal headman in Freetown, both undertaken in the 1940s by Kande Bureh and others because of a feeling that the Temnes in Freetown were being looked down on. See Banton, *West African City*, p. 165.

reconciled rather than suppressed. The particularly gentle handling of the Creoles in the 1950s, including their continued over-representation in the legislature and inclusion in the SLPP, may have been in part a recognition of their capacity to cause trouble by appealing to the British overlords. But, significantly, this gentle treatment of the Creoles continued long after independence and, furthermore, great efforts were also made to reconcile the people of Kono, who did not occupy nearly so strategic a position as the Creoles.[9] Proportionately less effort was made to conciliate the north, at least through the most obvious method of directing development funds there. This suggests the principal limit to reconciliation within the existing framework, the fact that when resources were in short supply, not everyone could receive as much as they felt they deserved. When the whole of the largest province in the country suffered from a lack of schools, roads, and other facilities, it just was not possible to divert enough resources to that area to satisfy its people. Within this limitation, however, the challenge of dissident tribes could be met by a strategy of containment and conciliation.

The class challenge was less easily handled within this particular reconciliation system. The demands of the commoners that their chiefs' abuses be curbed were far from irreconcilable with the continued survival of chieftaincy; in fact the 1955–56 rioters had explicitly declared that they did not wish to destroy that institution.[10] Few of the practices which aroused popular indignation were such an integral part of the traditional chief's role that their suppression would radically alter or undermine the institution: for the most part, the practices which led to complaints were recent innovations brought in by the spread of the money economy. However, many chiefs in the north were not prepared to refrain from these practices, or to recognize the legitimacy of their subjects' protests; they were quite willing to reap the personal benefits of the changes economic development brought, but unwilling to accept any changes in their role which they felt were to their detriment.

The chiefs could have been forced to make some concessions to their peoples' demands by a strong autonomous national authority. But since the SLPP relied on the chiefs for its local support, it could not go strongly against their wishes. It was the firm position of the chiefs within the ruling group, and their unwillingness to compromise, that made class reconciliation difficult.

A third conflict was far less explicit than those between tribes or classes, but still played a part in the Sierra Leone political system. This was the clash

9 / Such as the Mining Area Development Authority grants, and the assignment of a special Kono Development Officer in 1959. It could be argued, of course, that if Kono irritation reached the point of civil disturbance, this would have seriously interfered with the exploitation of Sierra Leone's diamonds.

10 / See above, pp. 81–82.

between "tradition" and "modernity," between the desire to preserve as much as possible of a slowly eroding older way of life and the desire to sweep all aspects of this life away in order to make a fresh start. What made this a particularly difficult conflict to pinpoint was the fact that it was fought as much within individuals as between them. The chief who invested the wealth collected from his people in new cars or Freetown real estate, the senior civil servant who felt obliged to board several of his relatives in his house, and the schoolboy uncertain about how he should regard his illiterate father, all wavered between frequently irreconcilable worlds. This clash could not, therefore, become such a clear line of division between the SLPP and opposition party leaders as class and tribal conflicts. At the most, it can be said that the SLPP leadership leaned more heavily than any opposition party towards a "traditional" viewpoint, while first the UPP and later the APC were particularly prone to support "modern" values. Although seldom articulated, this conflict seems to have lent a sharper edge to the other more apparent conflicts between the SLPP and its opponents. Some chiefs, and Dr Margai, were quite aware that the rapid spread of education and the money economy, and migration to the cities, would render the chiefs' roles irrelevant.[11] The APC leaders, for their part, tended to condemn the traditional system as "Feudalism" and an obstacle in the drive towards a Westernized way of life.

The ruling group was not helpless in the face of continued opposition; if a group could not be reconciled, it could at least be made to suffer significant penalties for its defiance. The SLPP was able to use the chiefs effectively to curtail organized activity by opposition parties at the constituency level, at least in the provinces. While this did not remove the roots of discontent, it did limit the opportunities for parties to fan this discontent or to direct it into electoral channels. We have noted, however, that the SLPP leaders were not prepared to use either patronage or coercion extensively to eliminate opposition. At the national level, they showed a high level of tolerance for opposition leaders, sharing personal patronage freely with them and exempting them from any systematic harassment. In their dealings with constituencies also, they were not wholehearted in their use of patronage. They did not, for example, cut off developments in the northern constituencies which went APC in 1962, or in Freetown after it elected an APC council in 1964.

This sketch of the key features of the Sierra Leone political system still leaves unanswered our opening questions. What permitted the maintenance of this particular pattern of pluralism? If the SLPP was to such a high degree a party of the elite, why had it not been swept away by a more "populist" party? On the other hand, why did this ruling group permit the continuation

11 / One Kono MP charged that the chiefs there deliberately tried to discourage children from attending school.

of so much political competition, even to the extent of maintaining open elections?

THE DETERMINANTS OF THE SYSTEM

The prominent place held by traditional rulers in the Sierra Leone political system becomes more striking when we compare Sierra Leone with other coastal colonies subject to European modernizing influences for the same period of time. Apart from Mauretania, which was hardly penetrated by European influences until recent years, none of the coastal states of West Africa saw the chiefs playing such a prominent role in politics as did Sierra Leone.[12] The obverse of this strong position for the chiefs was the weakness of party organizations; only Senegal and Dahomey even remotely approached Sierra Leone in the looseness and coalitional nature of their ruling parties,[13] and even their electorates had developed a certain degree of attachment to parties rather than individual candidates. In Eastern and Western Nigeria, Ghana, the Ivory Coast, and Guinea, parties led by either a bourgeois or a revolutionary elite penetrated deeply into the social fabric, and largely succeeded in subduing any resistance from the traditional rulers. In Sierra Leone, by contrast, the traditional rulers retained a large share of power, and recruitment to the ruling group depended to a much greater extent upon an individual's connections with the traditional rulers.[14] How did a ruling group

12 / In Western Nigeria the Obas were still influential, but clearly subordinated to the business and professional men who controlled the Action Group. See Sklar, *Nigerian Political Parties*, pp. 235–42. In Senegal, while the Muslim religious leaders were highly influential, the traditional chiefs had faded from the scene under colonial rule. See William Foltz, "Senegal," in Coleman and Rosberg, *Political Parties and National Integration*, p. 47.

13 / For Senegal, see *ibid.* For Dahomey, see Virginia Thompson, "Dahomey," in Gwendolen Carter (ed.), *Five African States: Responses to Diversity* (Ithaca: Cornell University Press, 1963), esp. pp. 210 ff., 244.

14 / In the 1957 House of Representatives, 17 of the 21 non-Creole SLPP members were from ruling families. In the 1962 House, 27 out of 35 were similarly connected. These proportions are far greater than those for any other West African territory except Northern Nigeria. At the time of their independence, these were the proportions of legislators having chiefly connections in various territories: Western Nigeria, 39 out of 120; Northern Nigeria, 83 out of 129; Ghana, 30 out of 108; and the République du Congo, 19 out of 57 (Guy Hunter, *The New Societies of Tropical Africa*, p. 285). The Western Nigerian proportion is particularly interesting in view of the apparent similarity between the Action Group and the SLPP, which were both led by Western-educated men who had begun their parties largely by working through the chiefs. Three factors seem to have been of particular significance in leading the Action Group much further away from reliance on the chiefs than the SLPP. First, the Action Group leaders such as Awolowo, Akintola, and Rotimi Williams were not themselves from

based so largely on an ascriptive elite manage to retain its power? Why was it not swept aside?

The slow pace of modernization in Sierra Leone provides a partial explanation of the survival of the traditional rulers. Many of the social changes which served to draw individuals into a nation-wide interdependent network of social relationships and into participant roles in the political culture were slow in coming to Sierra Leone. Thus in the 25 years from 1931 to 1956 the number of persons in wage employment increased only from 20,000 to 41,087.[15] The number of persons in towns of 10,000 or more increased from about 80,000 in 1931 to 217,000 in 1963, an increase of less than three times in more than three decades.[16] The number of children in school had risen only from 21,000 in 1938 to 29,000 in 1948, and though it accelerated much more rapidly over the next decade and a half, to 102,706 in 1963,[17] children passing through the school system in these later years were only beginning to enter the political system as participants by the end of this period; furthermore, even by 1963, the children in school represented only some 24 per cent of the school-age population.[18] Another important facet of political modernization, direct recruitment into participant roles in the political system by political parties, had been almost totally ignored by the ruling party, and was carried on only under severe handicaps by opposition parties. The weakness of the parties also limited a further modernizing process, the growth of communications between the leaders and the led. The absence of party militants to arouse the population was partly offset by the continuation of competitive elections which forced aspiring representatives to pay some heed to the demands articulated by their constituents. But

ruling families (their titles of "Chief" were honorary); second, there was a far stronger counterweight in Western Nigeria, in the form of the Westernized Yoruba business class, which to a large extent appears to have consisted of self-made men; third and most important, the Action Group developed a very effective party organization, which helped it win elections even without the aid of the chiefs. This meant that Action Group activists without chiefly connections could gain entry to the legislature through their party affiliation.

15 / The figure is taken from the *1931 Census*; the 1956 figure from *Quarterly Statistical Bulletin*, No. 1, 1963, p. 52. This likely understates the rate of increase, since the *1931 Census* probably counted every person in wage employment, whereas the 1956 figure was based on returns from employers of six or more persons. The total number employed was perhaps double this figure. However, a fourfold increase over 25 years is still strikingly low.

16 / Taken from *1931 Census* and *1963 Census*.

17 / See above, Chapter 1, p. 32, for the 1938 and 1948 figures. The 1963 figure is taken from Sierra Leone, *The Development Programme in Education*, p. 4. It should be noted that this figure excludes unassisted schools, and therefore under-represents the rate of increase.

18 / *Ibid.*, p. 5.

demands originating from the grass roots were far less likely to draw people into national alignments than were political communications from the centre outwards. It could also be argued that the weakness of the parties and their lack of any strong ideological inclinations helped to keep the level of demands in the system low. So long as parties were not stirring up the people with new ideas, it was possible for the ruling group to satisfy a fairly large proportion of the demands articulated. Also grass-roots demands generally were not costly. As the society became more modernized, and demands tended to be for paved highways and medical specialists rather than for bush roads and dispensaries, it would become more difficult to maintain the same level of pay-off relative to demand. However, the slow rate of modernization delayed this up-grading of the level of demands.

The proportion of individuals drawn into various processes of social change in Sierra Leone by the late 1950s seems to have been somewhat lower than that in other West African countries, and the rate at which they had been drawn in was slower. According to one survey, the percentage of urban population in Sierra Leone in 1959–60 was 5 per cent; in Guinea, 6 per cent; in the Ivory Coast, 8 per cent; in Dahomey, 10 per cent; in Ghana, 17 per cent; and in Senegal, 19 per cent.[19] Sierra Leone's urban population had expanded relatively slowly over the previous decades: while Sierra Leone's urban population increased by a factor of less than three between 1931 and 1963, the Gold Coast's from 1931 to 1960 had multiplied by a factor of nearly six.[20] In a shorter period, from 1936 to 1956, Senegal's urban population had doubled; Dahomey's increased by a factor of two-and-a-half; Guinea's, by a factor of four; and the Ivory Coast's more than ten times.[21] This more gradual increase in urbanization in Sierra Leone could give traditional institutions more time to adapt to changed conditions,[22] and also involve the uprooting of fewer individuals at any one time. In other indices also Sierra Leone ranked low; in percentage of school-age children in school it ranked above Guinea but below Senegal, the Ivory Coast, and Dahomey,[23] while its percentage of wage earners was less than half that of any other coastal country except Dahomey, which ranked slightly below it.[24]

19 / Calculated from Junod and Resnick, *Handbook of Africa* (New York: New York University Press, 1963).

20 / Austin, *Politics in Ghana*, p. 4.

21 / Ruth Morgenthau, *Political Parties in French-Speaking West Africa*, pp. 412–13.

22 / The institution of Tribal Headman in Freetown, a device developed by the British to aid in the integration of urban immigrants into their new environment, took on many of the functions of chieftaincy, notably the settlement of disputes, even though this was illegal under the Ordinance. See Banton, *West African City*, esp. pp. 146–50.

23 / Junod and Resnick, *Handbook of Africa*. It also ranked far below Ghana, and both the southern regions of Nigeria.

24 / *Ibid.*

While these aggregate rates and amounts of social change suggest that a slightly more promising atmosphere for the survival of chieftaincy existed in Sierra Leone than elsewhere, they were not by themselves sufficiently great to explain why Sierra Leone's evolution was so different from that of its neighbours. The qualitative aspects of the mobilization process were much more significant than its quantitative aspects in accounting for the chiefs' survival. The decisive turning point here had come with the isolation of the Creoles.[25] Aggregate indices of social change in Sierra Leone conceal the fact that of those living in urban areas, working for wages or attending school, a substantial number were Creoles. Since the Creoles by their attitudes over the colonial period and particularly by their final fight in 1948–51 had effectively destroyed their own chances of winning political leadership through a competitive process for at least a generation, political competition had been confined largely to the much smaller group of socially mobilized individuals from the Protectorate.

Within the Protectorate societies, we have noted that opportunities for modernization were much greater for the children of the traditional elite than for commoners. Part of this was due to a deliberate British policy of training the ruling class for new responsibilities. But the fact that the chiefs were in the most advantageous position to tap the flow of money to the Protectorate, and thus to provide education, capital for businesses, and other innovating forces for their children was more important. There were not nearly the same opportunities for commoners, unless they left the chief's control by going to the city; and the only city until the post-war era was Freetown, where they were under considerable pressure to assimilate into the Creole community if they wished to advance.[26] The upshot was that most persons who retained their Protectorate identity and acquired the skills which enabled them to lead a political movement were drawn from the traditional ruling families. As a result the ruling group was fairly homogeneous in social background, at least up to the time when a second generation of mobilized individuals arrived on the political scene.

This ability of ruling families to use their positions to modernize relatively quickly would not by itself have been sufficient to ensure the survival of chieftaincy if that institution had been emasculated by the colonial regime. The limited degree of modernization ensured that chieftaincy would not be irrelevant; but if it were too obviously an instrument of colonial oppression, it could hardly stand against a populist movement. Chieftaincy in Sierra Leone, however, had not been emasculated or subordinated to the

25 / See above, pp. 15–17.

26 / One Protectorate leader claimed a substantial number of prominent "Creoles" were men of up-country origin who had taken Creole names in the 1920s or 1930s to establish themselves in Freetown.

colonial regime as drastically as elsewhere. In contrast with Guinea, for example, chiefs were not treated openly as the lowest rank of the colonial administration; rather, the myth was preserved that each chief was the District Commissioner's "good [and equal] friend."[27] While in practice chiefs in the two territories probably were handled in a rather similar manner, still the psychological difference was important in preserving both their own and their subjects' respect. Also important in preserving their subjects' respect was the fact that the chiefs were not called on to furnish forced labour for the colonial administrators or planters,[28] or to provide tax returns of the level required in, say, Guinea.[29] While it is difficult to obtain accurate information, it seems unlikely that Sierra Leone chiefs exploited their people to a greater extent than the chiefs in Guinea or other French territories,[30] though they probably did not take any less.

The manner in which decolonization was carried out in Sierra Leone also helped spare the chiefs the consequences of subordination to the colonial regime. In territories such as Guinea and the Ivory Coast, where the colonial authorities were reluctant to yield control to a nationalist movement, the chiefs were forced to support the colonial regime against the nationalists. The result was that when the nationalists emerged triumphant, the chiefs were discredited. In Sierra Leone, by contrast, the colonial regime handed over control at least as fast as the only nation-wide political grouping, the SLPP, was ready to receive it. No serious clash ever arose between the colonial regime and the first indigenous group prepared to take power, with the result that the chiefs were not forced to side with the British against their people.

We can conclude that at least up to the mid-1950s the chiefs' continuing strength in the political system could be attributed to this combination of factors: the limited nature of the demands placed on their people through

27 / "My good friend" was the salutation used by both chiefs and District Commissioners in their correspondence with each other. For a description of the French downgrading of the chiefs in Guinea, see Jean Surêt-Canale, "La Fin de la Chefferie en Guinée," *Journal of African History,* VII, 3 (1966), pp. 461–62.

28 / For the political effect of forced labour recruiting in a French territory, see Zolberg, *One-Party Government in the Ivory Coast,* pp. 52–56.

29 / The most drastic levies in Guinea and other French territories came as a result of World War II. In one district of 60,000 (or smaller than any Sierra Leone district), wartime contributions came to some £20,000. The administrative report praised "the zeal of the chiefs" in making this possible, but admitted it was at the cost of "rapid impoverishment of the countryside." Cited in Surêt-Canale, "La Fin de la Chefferie," p. 475. There never was any British levy comparable in weight to this.

30 / In Guinea, chiefs took "customary dues" for the purchase of cars and buildings, and pilgrimages to Mecca. *Ibid.,* p. 479. In Dahomey, the chiefs' exploitation aroused the resentment of the younger educated men, and laid the basis for a conflict between the chiefs and educated men. Thompson, in Carter, *Five African States,* p. 172.

them by the colonial administration; the slow rate of social change through-out the Protectorate; and the fact that there were few potential leaders of political movements who were not connected with chieftaincy.

This situation was gradually changing, however. Not everyone who went to the towns, or found a niche in the wage economy as a trader or lorry driver, or managed to attend school, was of a ruling family. Political parties which had been based on a system of chieftaincy at least as strongly en-trenched as Sierra Leone's had been swept from the field by commoners' parties which had simply out-organized them. The Parti Soudanaise Pro-gressiste in the French Soudan, for example, was during this period losing its electoral support to the Union Soudanaise chiefly because the latter was able to develop a more efficient grass-roots organization.[31] But until the advent of the PNP, there was no party in Sierra Leone which could reasonably hope to establish a mass popular base. By that time the British had largely handed over control of the means of coercion to the SLPP leaders. These leaders were considerably more ready to use the machinery of government to curtail poli-tical rivals than the British regime had been once it accepted African self-government as a legitimate goal. They could make it very difficult for any opposition to organize to the extent that would be necessary to offset their local chiefs' organization. The SLPP leaders were not able to suppress all opposition activity for reasons to be considered below. They were, however, able to handicap opposition parties severely enough that it would take a considerable effort to dislodge them. Particularly when the opposition lacked any strong ideology to sustain them in their battle, the SLPP's control of coercion gave them a considerable advantage in their efforts to retain power.

All of the supports which sustained the position of the chiefs, and of the SLPP as a party of the traditional elite, were gradually being eroded. No matter how little the ruling group did to promote it directly, modernization was advancing. Each road or school built or educational scholarship pro-vided, as a response to some demand, enlarged the number of participants in the political system. Each new immigrant to the towns or entrant into the wage labour force was likely to find that the claims and role of a Paramount Chief had become less relevant to him. All these changes meant that a grow-ing number of individuals would be unlikely to accept the continued rule of the SLPP in its existing form. Either its leaders would have to change their appeal to attract more of the mobilized sections of the population, or they

31 / See Frank Gregory Snyder, *One-Party Government in Mali* (New Haven: Yale University Press, 1965), pp. 79–80. Cf. Thomas Hodgkin and Ruth Morgenthau, "Mali," in Coleman and Rosberg, *Political Parties and National Integration*, pp. 233–38, who cite "the efficiency and democratic character of the ... Union Soudanaise, which showed itself far more capable of managing and mobilizing a mass electorate than the PSP." However, they do stress that an even more important factor in the victory of the Union Soudanaise was that the PSP suffered the liability of being supported by the French, and then in 1956 found this support withdrawn.

would have to restrict the opportunities for these individuals to make their demands heard. Sir Albert Margai's approach indicated that he was trying both of these strategies.

Within the more traditional sector, the SLPP's use of the chiefs to suppress the APC in the north was meanwhile forcing the chiefs into the position they had avoided under the British, alignment with the central government against their own people. To a large extent this was their own fault: their greed in exploiting their subjects had given the APC its opportunity to build a strong base for itself. Once the APC was established, the chiefs were trapped in a dilemma. If they did not suppress it, they risked incurring the displeasure of the SLPP government and of seeing the APC win office as an anti-chief party. But if they tried to suppress it, they would alienate their people still further and become more dependent on support from the central government. Such a situation could not continue indefinitely, particularly if Sierra Leone continued to have free elections. In the traditional, as in the mobilized sector of Sierra Leone, the SLPP's basis of organization drove its leaders into increasingly repressive actions against opposition parties.

Even so the SLPP leaders were clearly not prepared to suppress opposition by any means. Four factors seem to have been particularly important in maintaining a highly pluralist system in Sierra Leone: the entrenchment of a diversity of interests both within the political elite and in the social system as a whole; the personal attitudes and positions of political leaders; the personal links between members of the political elite; and the high status of the ruling group.

The most important factor in entrenching pluralism was the lack of an effective central party organization. Consequently the politicians received no significant help at elections. They neither got funds nor benefited particularly from the party label. As a result, the party leaders were precluded from exercising any effective sanctions against members of the legislature. The lack of party organizations forced politicians to rely more heavily on their own resources. In most cases this meant they would turn to sympathetic chiefs for support; but, even where they established their personal machine, they would inevitably consider the interest of their own constituency ahead of any claims the party leaders might make on them. The SLPP parliamentary group could almost be described as a congress of ambassadors from the various constituencies, held together by their common sympathies as members of ruling families, but not subject to compulsion to do the leaders' bidding. There was no path to top SLPP positions save through Parliament. Neither was there any other effective body, such as a party congress or executive, through which non-parliamentarians could exert leverage.

The weakness of the SLPP as a political party contributed to the entrenchment of pluralism in another way. To the extent that Parliament rather than a party organization provided the focal point for political allegiances, the SLPP legislators were led to see their community of interest with opposition legislators. The relations between government and opposition legislators, as we have noted, were close and cordial.[32] Under such circumstances, the degree of tolerance for the opposition leaders was relatively high. A further result of the supremacy of the legislature was that the SLPP leaders were encouraged to feel somewhat greater respect for governmental institutions, and probably also for constitutional procedures, than was the case in states where the supremacy of the party was openly proclaimed.

Pluralism was also encouraged by the divergences among the elites outside the party system. The composition of the senior civil service and of the Bench was markedly different from that of the political parties; both of these groups were predominantly Creole, and even apart from their commitment to (pluralist) "British" values, they could not be expected to support a concentration of power in the hands of the SLPP leaders. Key elites outside the political system, notably the lawyers and doctors, also were predominantly Creole.

Ordinary members of the society, as well as the elites, supported a pluralist pattern of politics. Many villagers were well aware it was competition for their votes among members of the elite that gave them a chance to have their wishes heeded.[33] The lack of popular enthusiasm for Sir Albert's plans for a one-party state indicated a fairly widespread feeling that the common man's interests were best served by the continuation of a competitive electoral system. This bedrock of popular support, as well as the views of various key elites, also helped to maintain the usefulness of a further bulwark of pluralism, the constitution with its protection of the legislature, certain civil liberties, and the judiciary.

All these supports for pluralism served to reinforce each other. The constitution and the courts put numerous obstacles in the way of a government attempting to crush organized opposition, as the 1965-6 trials for libel and sedition suggested. The SLPP's own backbenchers would resist efforts to change the constitution if they felt the changes would be to their disadvantage, while the Prime Minister could not count on the massive popular support in an election which would have enabled him to change the constitution and the judiciary and to replace the SLPP backbenchers with more amenable followers.

The Sierra Leone political system also demonstrates the importance of

32 / See above, pp. 120-21, 178.

33 / This understanding by illiterate villagers of the leverage given them by political competition was not confined to Sierra Leone. Daniel Lerner has noted that in a Turkish village the older men all felt that, when the parties were competing and needed their votes, they heeded the villagers' wishes. See Daniel Lerner, *The Passing of Traditional Society* (New York: Free Press of Glencoe, 1958), p. 41.

another key factor in determining the nature of a political system in a process of evolution, the attitudes and values of the leaders. While social and environmental factors set constraints to the possible patterns of development of any political system, there is still considerable scope for the personality of an individual leader to make a mark, particularly when rapid evolutionary changes limit the extent to which restraints can be institutionalized. The Ghanaian political system under another leader than Nkrumah, or the Senegalese under someone other than Senghor, could have taken a very different shape within the constraints common to all underdeveloped African countries. The Sierra Leone system too could have been quite different under another leader than Dr Margai. As we have seen, it probably could not have become a revolutionary-centralizing system like Guinea; but it might easily have become a *de facto* one-party state like Senegal, or collapsed into the arms of the military like Dahomey.[34] The importance of Dr Margai's personal attitudes in the operation of the Sierra Leone system is suggested by the rapidity with which it broke down under his successor.

The three key words for describing Dr Margai's attitudes would be caution, certainty, and conciliation. The doctor never acted precipitately; he would try to delay action until he was absolutely satisfied about the course he should take; then would take whatever action would cause the least disturbance. At times, as in the 1955 Freetown riots and the 1955–56 tax riots, this unwillingness to act quickly allowed the situation to deteriorate further; but in most cases, such as the furore over the Cole Report on Ministerial misdeeds in 1963, restraint allowed the problem to dissipate. His restraint was not a sign of weakness; he was quite prepared to jail the APC leaders at the time of independence when this seemed the best way of avoiding disturbances, and to visit any trouble areas personally to try to put down protests. But, by refusing to try to resolve all problems as soon as they arose, he was able to watch many of them dissolve.

His certainty and his conciliatory attitude were closely linked. Dr Margai knew where he was going and what he was trying to do; this was why he could be high-handed with his Cabinet. It also made it easier for him to conciliate opponents; by knowing what he wanted, he could afford to make concessions on other matters that were not so important to him. He did not fear that he was being duped or led astray. His willingness to conciliate was shown on a number of occasions: in 1957, when he offered his brother, Siaka Stevens, and Dr Fitzjohn the portfolios they thought they should have; in 1960, when he brought all opposition leaders along on the constitutional delegation and then into the United Front ministry; and in 1961, when he released the APC leaders from prison a few weeks after Independence Day. In all these instances and others he was able to conciliate from a position of

34 / For a discussion of the divisions in Dahomey which eventually led to paralysis of the party system, see Thompson, in Carter, *Five African States*, pp. 215 ff.

strength; bringing rivals into the Cabinet did not alter his powers as Prime Minister, and the APC men could always be jailed again if necessary. The doctor's strength and his certainty served as supports for pluralism; because he knew what he wanted and was in a position to get his way, he felt no need to destroy his rivals. There could be no gnawing doubt that their ideas might be right, and that they might therefore be entitled to claim his place.

Albert Margai's actions as Prime Minister showed clearly how important his brother's attitudes had been to the maintenance of the Sierra Leone political system. Albert's impetuosity quickly helped land him in difficulties from which his attempts to extricate himself eventually destroyed him. His precipitate decision to dissolve the Freetown city council in 1964 seems to have been born of a considerable overestimation of the degree of popular support he enjoyed; the defeat the SLPP suffered there was the first step in undermining his claim to be the great popular hero, and in leading him to take more repressive measures against the opposition. His attempts to re-organize the SLPP, though not really impetuous, were pursued so energetic-ally that they provoked more resistance than gain. Most serious of all, his attempts to coerce the opposition into accepting the one-party state, rather than to woo them, served simply to consolidate his opponents. It is hard to imagine Sir Milton breathing Sir Albert's fire and slaughter at a public meet-ing: "I will shoot them down bray-bray-bray," "I will pulverize them," "I will demolish them."[35] It is likely that his threats towards the APC stemmed from a lack of certainty and of self-confidence; he was more easily led than his brother.[36] Whatever the cause, his attempt to crush all opposition solidi-fied the north and the Western Area against him, and created grave doubts among even the staunchest supporters of the SLPP. The speed with which tension grew in Sierra Leone politics after 1964 was largely attributable to Albert Margai.

Two further factors supporting pluralism and continued competition in Sierra Leone require mention. The fact that many of the opposition leaders, particularly in the earlier parties, were drawn from the same stratum of society as the SLPP leadership, and that the SLPP and opposition party leaders were linked by family, educational and occupational ties, as well as personal friendship,[37] meant that it was unlikely that the leaders of either side would

35 / In his speeches at Bonthe, March 1965; at Sefadu, May 21, 1965; and at Kambia, December 1965, respectively.

36 / All the Ministers interviewed who had served under both Prime Ministers agreed that Albert was much more ready to be persuaded by others in Cabinet discussions. One added: "Sometimes we think he's too ready to be persuaded."

37 / The close personal relations between Albert Margai and Siaka Stevens developed during their sojourn in England and subsequently in the SLPP and PNP were the most notable example of this; Albert's high regard for Stevens was an important factor in restraining him from taking stronger measures against the leaders of the APC.

wish to destroy the others personally. It also meant that the conflict over values was not a profound one; there was enough similarity of outlook that the government would be unlikely to treat opposition views as dangerous heresies which had to be destroyed. This homogeneity of outlook was diluted somewhat with the advent of the APC and later the DPC; it is noteworthy that these groups, particularly the DPC, were forced to operate in a more clandestine manner than any of their predecessors. Both, however, were founded on too strong a social base to be crushed easily; their strength protected them.

Finally, the high status of the ruling group both in traditional and in modern society served to limit pressures towards authoritarian rule. It helped give the SLPP leaders themselves confidence that they had the right to rule, and thus that they need not be fearful that their legitimacy might be usurped by rival groups. It also served to provide them with legitimacy in the eyes of the people, particularly among the more traditionalist sections of society. With their legitimacy as rulers securely established, the SLPP leaders could afford to be more tolerant towards opposition than the "verandah boys" of Ghana and Guinea, whose right to rule was only validated by their popular support.

Sierra Leone's pluralist system followed a narrow path between authoritarian rule and a collapse into civil strife and chaos. Sufficient cohesion and restraint to avoid a breakdown of order were provided by: the continued hold of the traditional rulers on their people; the conciliatory approach of the SLPP leaders and the moderation of opposition appeals, made possible by the limited extent of the divisions between them; and the fact that the system was able to provide an output of political goods not too far below the input of demands, thanks in part to the fact that the parties had done little to increase the level of demands. Limits on the imposition of authoritarian rule were provided by the entrenched pluralism of the governing party, and the fact that there was no way in which it could be turned into an instrument of a would-be authoritarian ruler; by the strength and key positions of various groups which would oppose any attempt by the SLPP to introduce authoritarian rule; and by widespread popular awareness that the best protection for the interests of the common people was the maintenance of a competitive political system. No one of these safeguards was by itself sufficient, but in conjunction they were adequate to halt the one attempt by a political ruler to make the system a more authoritarian one. A more skilfully managed attempt to bring about a one-party state would probably have succeeded; a major reason for the failure of Albert Margai to eliminate organized opposition was his own ineptitude. However, the various entrenched pluralist features of the system imposed severe obstacles on any leader seeking personal dominance.

But how far was Sierra Leone's pluralism entrenched against the other threat in the system, the prospect that a radical class party would unite the various "have-not" elements of the society and oust the SLPP? To what extent was such a radical movement responsible for the breakdown of the system in 1967? Over the long run – say, two or three decades – I think it was possible that increasing social mobilization would have made the position of the SLPP oligarchy as it existed in 1967 difficult to sustain. Unless the chiefs had learned to moderate their treatment of their people or the SLPP leaders had managed to disengage themselves from the chiefs, growing popular protest would either have led to the eventual triumph of a more broadly based party or else forced the SLPP leaders to impose a much more authoritarian system. Buying off successive sets of leaders, as had been done in Kono, would have postponed such a challenge, but would not have eliminated it. Having said this, I would argue that such a threat to the SLPP was not personified in the APC of 1967. By 1967, the APC leaders were muting such class attitudes as they had previously expressed. They emphasized the need for a regional redistribution of wealth within the framework of the existing system, and condemned Albert Margai for his personal behaviour. Some of the APC's secondary cadres of leaders may have seen their struggle with the SLPP leaders in class terms, but the selection of APC candidates and the tenor of its public pronouncements, as well as its electoral support, suggested that its regional appeals were uppermost in the minds of both leaders and followers.

But since I have already argued that the SLPP *could* handle regional appeals, why did it fail to do so in 1967? One factor I have suggested was that there still was an element of class awareness in the APC's leaders, and that this helped to fortify them against SLPP blandishments. But more important was the failure of Albert Margai as a leader to act effectively. As we have seen, he was within an ace of swallowing the APC at the end of 1965, and if he had succeeded, the drive to the one-party state could hardly have been stopped. His failure to conciliate the APC leaders can be attributed to several factors. First was their suspicion (widely shared) that Albert was essentially tribalist in his vision, and that the one-party state would entrench the Mendes in a dominant position. Second was his continued dependence on the chiefs; even if he had brought in the APC, it appeared likely that the chiefs would remain entrenched, and the APC leaders' "class" attitude was still strong enough to make them doubtful of the desirability of this. Third was his personal greed. While the full extent of Albert's holdings did not become known until he had been ousted from office, it was widely known that he and his close friends were greatly enriching themselves through their government positions. Such actions again were offensive, because of their scale, to many APC supporters and also to the leaders. Finally, it must be said that Albert Margai badly overestimated the strength of his position. He had too many opponents behind him, in the Cabinet, in the civil service, and in the SLPP, to take a very strong line with the APC leaders; yet he did just this. Ultimately, then, the SLPP oligarchy was brought down not by a challenge it was incapable of handling, but because through poor leadership it mishandled a crisis it should have weathered.

How well did the political system developed under Dr Margai serve the needs of Sierra Leoneans? I would postulate three basic needs for such a society. First, the national political leaders must be able to control the society, at least in the negative sense that no other group or individual can induce a substantial part of the population to deny the legitimacy of the constitutional system. Second, there is a need for improvement in the material conditions of life for the populace as a whole, in order to widen the choice of paths to self-fulfilment. Third, the society needs to be mobilized and integrated; the leaders cannot afford to leave the bulk of the populace unaware of the government's existence, or allow the populace to grow into warring nations within the state.

Control of the Sierra Leone polity was facilitated by the continued strength of the chiefs. As long as the chiefs retained their hold over their people, their legitimacy helped legitimatize a central government associated with them. But there was the danger that as the chiefs' position was eroded, so was that of the central government, a situation which was developing by 1967 in both the north and Kono. Their position was likely to be eroded, too, by the fact that the electoral system provided little outlet for class grievances. As the weakness of party organizations led parties to rely on local notables, the ordinary farmer could easily come to feel that he lacked any real voice in the decisions made by the political elite. The competitive electoral system had always given him some leverage, to be sure, but generally his choice was between competing "big men," all of whose interests might well conflict with his. The advent of the APC provided some opening up of this system, giving the ordinary farmer a chance to select a representative who would oppose abuses by his chief. While the severity of the measures used by Albert Margai and the chiefs to crush the APC showed the rather constricted limits under which this choice could be made, still, as long as it was possible for the APC to compete electorally, it was possible for the ordinary farmer to find a peaceful outlet for class as well as other demands.

A frequent charge levelled against the SLPP government was that it failed to follow any grand scheme for economic development, but rather added a bridge here, a marketplace there, student scholarships one day and a modest ploughing service for swamp rice the next. Many of these small-scale incremental expenditures were responses to political pressures lacking any economic justification.[38] This incremental approach could be attributed in large

38 / Kilson has cited a number of examples, notably the Building Materials Scheme, which provided Chiefs and their loyal supporters with several hundred thousand

part to the weakness of the SLPP's organization. A much wider number of voters would be impressed by numerous bulldozed tracks into villages and/or small generators for several towns, than by a single high-quality road in one area, or a dam to generate electricity near a potential industrial site. It was sometimes argued that the need to spread resources widely in a competitive party system was dysfunctional for economic development, and that Sierra Leone would be better off under a more authoritarian system which would be able to concentrate resources on a few key projects having a high rate of return and supporting each other.

However, the arguments regarding economic benefits were by no means all on the side of the authoritarian system. A ruling group unrestrained by an electorate would not inevitably bring about broadly beneficial development projects. Just as often, it appeared, such rulers would concentrate first on benefiting themselves, as the presidential palaces, towering government office buildings, and elaborate housing for Ministers and civil servants all across Africa graphically attested.[39] Sierra Leone's approach to development was far less spectacular than that of several other countries, but it had two major advantages: it avoided any single terribly expensive mistake, and by distributing benefits widely, it helped maintain widespread satisfaction with the system.

The collapse of the SLPP in 1967 has been attributed in large part to its failure to handle the problems of mobilization and tribal divergence. Much of the blame, I have suggested, rests with Albert Margai's personal failings as a leader. But the failure of the SLPP to maintain itself in power did not indicate a breakdown of the "brokerage" system of politics; on the contrary, the APC's success in winning the 1967 election can be taken as confirmation of the success of this system and a commitment by the APC to it.

The electoral system, it is true, did intensify tribal (or at least regional) differences.[40] Once the All Peoples Congress had established a base for itself

pounds in "loans" (generally unrepaid) from central government grants to the District Councils for the construction of houses. See Kilson, *Political Change*, pp. 207–209. The scheme was finally terminated in 1965.

A more spectacular project was the 23-mile, £500,000 paved road running from Pendembu to nowhere in Kailahun District. This road apparently had been secured by the late Resident Minister for the Eastern Province.

39 / For the comments of a sympathetic but perceptive observer, see David Hapgood, *Africa: From Independence to Tomorrow* (New York: Atheneum, 1965), esp. Chapter IV. Also Rene Dumont, *False Start in Africa* (London: Andre Deutsch, 1966), *passim*.

40 / In this discussion I am using the term "tribalism" very loosely to cover both the (generally more visceral) attachment to a linguistic or ethnic group, and the (generally more calculated) attachment to a particular region or section of a country, more properly termed "regionalism." It is, of course, quite possible for a regional population having no distinguishing linguistic or ethnic ties to develop a suprarational attitude, or

in the north, it was bound to be identified as the spokesman for that area. Because the SLPP was a coalition of local interests, the initial disaffection of the Temnes over their apparent exclusion from government was inevitably reinforced. If they could not elect government supporters, they could not make their voice heard, and if they were not listened to by government, they would not elect government supporters.[41] Within the SLPP, as its northern membership fell, the influence of its southern members increased, as did its identification with the Mende tribe. The inevitable result was an increasing polarization along tribal lines, which led ultimately to the high state of tension preceding the 1967 election and coup.

Yet tribalism also played modernizing and stabilizing roles. The growth of tribally based opposition parties, and particularly the APC in the north, served to draw many persons into a wider association than their extended family or village. The APC's identity as "the northern man's party" provided a considerably broader community of identification for many voters than these more familiar groupings. "Tribalism" could hardly fragment the national community, since no such community had ever existed; but it could (and did) knit together in a common sense of identity men who had hitherto owed allegiance only to the much more limited communities of family, village, and chiefdom.

The APC's gradual shift from a class to a regional movement also helped to stabilize the national political structure. Far from threatening to disintegrate the national polity, tribalism in the Sierra Leone situation served to strengthen it. The APC came increasingly to demand that resources be reallocated in a way more equitable to the north, but the satisfaction of this demand required only that the existing organs of government be captured from the Mende-dominated SLPP through an election. In thus being able to

for a "tribal" group to make entirely rational demands (e.g. for equal opportunities for its members in employment) on the national system. What seems to be critical in developing the suprarational attachment is the existence of "structural opposition," the sense of being different from and to some degree in conflict with other sections of the country.

In Sierra Leone, the APC from its inception drew support from at least two major tribes, the Temne and the Limba, with substantial support also developing among several other northern tribes. It is misleading, therefore, to term it a "tribal" movement in the sense that it drew support exclusively from one tribe. However, in that the element of structural opposition existed in the form of "Mende domination" (whether real or imagined is irrelevant), there was the potential for this coalition of northern tribes to develop a strong emotional attachment to "the northern man's party," and this does seem to have occurred to a considerable extent.

41 / In fact the government seemed to lean over backwards to give northerners representation in the Ministry. At the end of 1963, six of the 13 SLPP representatives from the north held Ministerial appointments; only 13 of the 34 SLPP representatives from the Southern and Eastern Provinces (excluding Kono) held appointments.

blame the "tribalism" of the holders of power rather than the political structure itself for their discontent, northerners came to accept the idea of working through that structure, rather than demanding its total overthrow.[42] This willingness to work through the existing framework was not unlimited. If the Mendes had appeared so firmly in control of the political structure that the only way for the north to satisfy its demands would be to overthrow the entire framework, then Sierra Leone's political stability would indeed have been imperilled. But despite Sir Albert Margai's repressive actions against the APC, the situation had not deteriorated to this extent by 1967.

On balance, one would have to say that the Sierra Leone political system from 1951 to 1967 served the interests of Sierra Leoneans reasonably well. The dominance of the SLPP oligarchy, and the tendency of its members to act solely in their own interests, were tempered by the continuance of a competitive electoral system, which eventually passed the critical test of allowing the people to replace an unwanted set of leaders. One could say that the SLPP's failure to arouse the people for the many tasks of nation-building was a shortcoming of the system, but a sceptic could reply that mobilization by itself could not produce a rise in living standards. Without this improvement, in turn, it would be difficult to develop sufficient satisfaction with the system to allow further tasks of nation-building to go forward. The system did allow the people a chance to pass judgment on their leaders; it was only the intervention of a few strategically placed individuals who wished to maintain their power at all costs that prevented this judgment from being implemented.

EPILOGUE

The military officers who had seized power under the banner of the National Reformation Council proved no more popular as rulers than their predecessor. Amid growing suspicions that the NRC would renege on its promise to re-establish civilian rule[43] and talk of deep rifts within its own ranks, the military regime was overthrown on the night of April 17, 1968, by a grassroots revolt. The NCOs and other ranks of both the army and the police force pounced on their officers, and within 24 hours had all of them locked up in Pademba prison. On April 26 Siaka Stevens was once again sworn in as Prime Minister, though as head of a coalition rather than of an APC government. Sir Albert meanwhile reappeared briefly in Freetown to re-assert his

42 / Cf. Immanuel Wallerstein, "Ethnicity and National Integration in West Africa," *Cahiers d'Etudes Africaines*, 3 (October 1960), 137.

43 / A Commission of Inquiry (the Dove-Edwin Commission) had declared that the APC won the 1967 elections, with the implication that the NRC should hand over to this "lawful" government. The NRC thereupon established a Civilian Rule Committee, which reached agreement that there was no need for an election before the restoration of civilian rule.

claims to the leadership of the SLPP, but was bluntly told that the party caucus had already decided to make Salia Jusu-Sheriff the new leader of the SLPP. He then left Sierra Leone and did not return.

Stevens came to power on a tremendous wave of enthusiastic support, not only from the APC's own supporters but also from many SLPP adherents who had become fed up with the military regime. However, the SLPP retained a hard core of support in Mende country, and this hard tribal core gave the new regime serious difficulties in its first months. There were rumours of an impending mercenary invasion to restore Sir Albert, and six months after Stevens took office, tribal rioting forced many Temnes and Mendes to leave each others' territories. A swift crack-down by the government brought the violence under control, but many Mendes remained unreconciled to the change of regime.

Although the APC leaders proclaimed their interest in restoring "normal" civilian rule, the Sierra Leone political system had undergone a significant change. Despite its relatively cautious leadership, the APC rested on a base of support which had hitherto been largely excluded from any share of political power, and could be expected to exert considerable pressure for rapid change. Furthermore, the APC possessed an effective and autonomous party organization, not depending on a scattering of independent local notables. Finally, the SLPP, deprived of the support of the chiefs, lacked any organizational base capable of mounting an effective electoral attack. The only appeal it could make would be to tribal emotions, an appeal which was most likely to lead to its proscription as a danger to the state. The prospect, in short, was for organized opposition to the APC to wither away, and for future conflicts to be fought out within the confines of a single dominant party.

Note on sources

As readers will have noticed, a good deal of the material for this study was obtained through interviews and discussions with the participants in various events. While this technique has the advantage over written documentation of permitting the probing and cross-checking of assertions, it also has its hazards, particularly when it covers a period extending back two decades. Even when there is no overt reason for adjusting one's recollection of events, a considerable amount of (generally self-justifying) selectivity will almost inevitably take place. So far as possible, therefore, I tried to reconstruct accounts of events from at least two independent sources, and where close questioning did not resolve conflicting recollections, relied on the intrinsic plausibility of the accounts and the relative veracity of the participants.

For a general political study of this sort, there are some written sources, although, in the case of Sierra Leone, an interlocking combination of circumstances limited their availability. Three problems common to all tropical African ex-colonies – the physical problem of preserving records against termites, mildew and other hazards, the somewhat covert nature of both anti-colonial and anti-government activities, and the widespread sense of being overwhelmed by problems far more important than the protection of documents for posterity – played their usual roles of reducing the later availability of political parties' materials, newspapers, and even many government documents. Thus from 1959 to 1962, the printing of *Parliamentary Debates* ceased, except for some mimeographed records for the 1961–62 session, while the ritual under the colonial regime of annual reports from the various government departments gradually petered out, with reports lagging further and further behind events.

A specific feature of Sierra Leone compounded the problem of obtaining materials pertaining to party activity. The smallness of the political elite and their close inter-linkage meant that a relatively large proportion of interactions could be oral, while the attenuated nature of party organizations further reduced the likelihood that more than a bare minimum of information would be committed to writing. Party hand-outs, policy statements, and documents of a similar nature were relatively scarce compared to those of, say, Nigerian parties, and were generally mimeographed, as indeed were some newspapers. Their survival rate was accordingly low.

Some materials survived nonetheless. The library at Fourah Bay College, despite the ramshackle nature of its quarters until 1964, managed to preserve a fairly substantial proportion of the newspapers of the 1950s and early 1960s as well as some party materials. (Both the Sierra Leone government and the British Colonial Office appear to have thrown out their holdings of Sierra Leone newspapers for this period.) Some individuals also maintained private collections of documents, although in a few cases visiting researchers seem to have carried off the documents to parts unknown.

In the following bibliography, I have excluded party materials, since these are for the most part unavailable to researchers. I have also provided a greatly abridged list of government documents; there are many others available which contain useful material on political and social events, but generally these are scattered through series of annual reports. The most useful government materials, in addition to those specific items cited below, are (a) *Legislative Council Debates* and *House of Representatives Debates,* and *Protectorate Assembly Proceedings;* (b) *Annual Reports* of the government departments, *Reports of the Director of Audit* on both national and local governments, and *Estimates of Revenue and Expenditure;* (c) in recent years, the growing output of studies and reports from the Central Statistics Office and the Bank of Sierra Leone.

SELECT BIBLIOGRAPHY

Books, articles

Allen, Christopher. "Sierra Leone Politics Since Independence." *African Affairs,* 67 (October 1968), 305–29

Austin, Dennis. "People and Constitution in Sierra Leone." *West Africa,* September 13, 20, 27, October 4, 11, 1952

Bankole-Jones, Sir Samuel. "The Judiciary and the State: The West African Experience." Paper presented at the Second Commonwealth Chief Justices' Conference, Port-of-Spain, Trinidad, April 1968

Banton, Michael. "The Ethnography of the Protectorate." *Sierra Leone Studies,* 4 (1955), 240–49

—— *West African City.* London: Oxford University Press for International African Institute, 1957

Barrows, Walter L. "La Politique de l'armée en Sierra Leone." *Le Mois en Afrique* (December 1968), 54–64

Blyden, Edward W, III. "Sierra Leone: The Pattern of Constitutional Change." Unpublished PHD thesis, Harvard University, 1959

Cartwright, John R. "Shifting Forces in Sierra Leone." *Africa Report,* 13 (December 1968), 26–30

Clarke, John I. *et al. Sierra Leone in Maps.* London: University of London Press, 1966

Cox-George, N. A. *Finance and Development in West Africa: The Sierra Leone Experience.* London: Dobson, 1961

Dalby T. D. P. "Language Distribution in Sierra Leone: 1961–62." *Sierra Leone Language Review,* 1 (1962), 62–67

—— "The Military Takeover in Sierra Leone." *World Today,* 23 (August 1967), 354–60

Dorjahn, V. R. "The Changing Political System of the Temne." *Africa,* xxx, 2 (1960), 110–39

Finnegan, Ruth. *Survey of the Limba People of Northern Sierra Leone.* London: HMSO, 1965

Fyfe, Christopher. *A History of Sierra Leone.* London: Oxford University Press, 1962

—— (ed.). *Sierra Leone Inheritance.* London: Oxford University Press, 1964

Gamble, David P. "Occupational Prestige in an Urban Community (Lunsar) in Sierra Leone." *Sierra Leone Studies,* 19 (July 1966), 98–108

Hair, P. E. H. "Africanism: The Freetown Contribution." *Journal of Modern African Studies,* 5 (December 1967), 521–39

Hargreaves, J. D. "Western Democracy and African Society: Some Reflections from Sierra Leone." *International Affairs,* 3 (July 1955), 327–34

Jellicoe, Margaret. "Women's Groups in Sierra Leone." *African Women,* I, 2 (1955), 35–43

Keith-Lucas, Bryan. "Electoral Reform in Sierra Leone." *Political Studies,* 3 (June 1955), 97–108

Khuri, F. I. "The Influential Men and the Exercise of Influence in Magburaka, Sierra Leone." Unpublished PHD thesis, University of Oregon, 1964

Kilson, Martin. "Sierra Leone Politics: The Approach to Independence." *West Africa,* June 18, 25, July 2, 9, 1960

—— "Grass-Roots Politics in Africa: Local Government in Sierra Leone." *Political Studies,* 12 (February 1964), 47–66

—— *Political Change in a West African State: A Study of the Modernization Process in Sierra Leone.* Cambridge, Mass.: Harvard University Press, 1966

Kirby, Dennis. "Ballots in the Bush: A Case Study on Local Elections in the Bo District of Sierra Leone." *Journal of African Administration,* IX (October 1957), 174–82

Kup, A. P. "An Account of the Tribal Distribution of Sierra Leone." *Man* (August 1960), 116–19

Little, Kenneth. "Mende Political Institutions in Transition." *Africa,* XVII (January 1947), 8–23

—— *The Mende of Sierra Leone.* London: Routledge and Kegan Paul, 1951

—— "Structural Change in the Sierra Leone Protectorate." *Africa,* xxv (July 1955), 217–33

Loveridge, A. J. "The Present Position of the Temne Chiefs in Sierra Leone." *Journal of African Administration* (1957), 115–20

McCulloch, Merran. *The Peoples of the Sierra Leone Protectorate.* London: International African Institute, 1950

Margai, Milton. "Welfare Work in a Secret Society." *African Affairs*
(March 1948), 227–30

Marquand, Hilary A. "The ? Over Sierra Leone." *New Commonwealth,*
39 (April 1961), 216–19

Peterson, John. *Province of Freedom: A History of Sierra Leone, 1787–*
1870. Evanston: Northwestern University Press, 1969

Porter, Arthur T. "The Social Background of Political Decision-makers in
Sierra Leone." *Sierra Leone Studies,* 4 (June 1960), 2–13

—— *Creoledom: A Study of the Development of Freetown Society.* London:
Oxford University Press, 1963

Proudfoot, L. "Toward Muslim Solidarity in Freetown." *Africa,* xxxi,
2 (April 1961), 47–56

Ranson, Brian. *A Sociological Study of Moyamba Town, Sierra Leone.* Zaria:
Amadu Bello University, 1968

Richardson, E. M. and Collins, G. R. "Economic and Social Survey of the
Rural Areas of the Colony of Sierra Leone." London: Unpublished report
of the Research Department, Colonial Office, n.d.

Sankoh, Laminah. *The Two P's, or Politics for the People.* Freetown, n.d.

Scott, D. J. R. "The Sierra Leone Election of May 1957." In *Five Elections In*
Africa, edited by W. J. M. Mackenzie and Kenneth Robinson.
London: Oxford University Press, 1960

Van der Laan, Laurens. *The Sierra Leone Diamonds.* London: Oxford
University Press, 1965

Newspapers
[Dates where given refer to beginning and end of publication. All newspapers
except the *Daily Mail* and *Unity* were suspended in 1967 by the military regime.]

Advance [Bo]. 1960s
African Standard. Early 1950s. Owned by I. T. A. Wallace-Johnson
Daily Guardian. To 1954. Creole
Daily Mail. Subsidiary of *Daily Mirror* (London) to 1965, then sold to
Sierra Leone government
Liberty. 1959. PNP
Observer [Bo]. 1949–57. First official SLPP paper
Salneb Publications (mimeo.). 1963–65. Owned by I. T. A. Wallace-Johnson
Shekpendeh. 1954–67. Owned by Cyril Rogers-Wright
Sierra Leone Weekly News. Creole
Ten Daily News. ca. 1955–60. Owned by Sierra Leone Women's Movement
Think (mimeo.). 1966–67. Creole, pro-APC
Unity. 1965–. Official SLPP paper
Vanguard. ca. 1955–62. Official SLPP paper
We Yone. 1963–67. Official APC paper

Government publications
[Published by Government Printer, Sierra Leone, unless otherwise noted.]

Brooke, N. J. *Report on the Native Court System in Sierra Leone* (1953)
Report of The Commission for Electoral Reform [Keith-Lucas Report] (1954)
Collected Statements on Constitutional Proposals, September 1955 (1955)
Report of the Commission of Inquiry into the Strikes and Riots in Freetown during February 1955 [Shaw Report] (1955)
Statement of the Government of Sierra Leone on the Report, etc. Sessional Paper No. 1 of 1955 (1955)
Report of the Commission of Inquiry into Disturbances in the Provinces (November 1955 to March 1956) [Cox Report] (London: Crown Agents for Overseas Government and Administration on behalf of the Government of Sierra Leone, 1956)
Statement of the Sierra Leone Government on the Report of the Commission, etc. (1956)
Reports of the Commissioners of Enquiry into the Conduct of Certain Chiefs and the Government Statement Thereon (1957)
Further Reports of the Commissioners of Enquiry into the Conduct of Certain Chiefs and the Government Statement Thereon (1957)
Report of the Sierra Leone Constitutional Conference, 1960 (1960)
Ten-Year Plan of Economic and Social Development for Sierra Leone, 1962/63–1971/72 [Carney Report] (1962)
Report of the Commission appointed to enquire into and report on the matters contained in the Director of Audit's Report on the Accounts of Sierra Leone for the Year 1960/61 and the Government Statement thereon [Cole Report] (1963)
1963 Population Census of Sierra Leone. Vol. 1: *Number of Inhabitants;* Vol. 2: *Social Characteristics;* Vol. 3: *Economic Characteristics* (Freetown: Central Statistics Office, 1965)
The Development Programme in Education for Sierra Leone, 1964–1970 [Sleight Report] (1964)
A Progress Report on Economic and Social Development, April 27, 1961–March 31, 1965 (1965)
Report of the Dove-Edwin Commission of Inquiry into the Conduct of the 1967 General Elections in Sierra Leone and the Government Statement Thereon (1967)
Report of the Forster Commission of Inquiry on Assets of Ex-Ministers and Ex-Deputy Ministers (1968)

Index